Commission of the European Communities

XXIst General Report on the Activities of the European Communities

1987

Brussels • Luxembourg • 1988

This publication is also available in the following languages:

ES ISBN 92-825-7778-1
DA ISBN 92-825-7779-1
DE ISBN 92-825-7780-5
GR ISBN 92-825-7781-3
FR ISBN 92-825-7783-X
IT ISBN 92-825-7784-8
NL ISBN 92-825-7785-6
PT ISBN 92-825-7786-4

Cataloguing data can be found at the end of this publication

Luxembourg: Office for Official Publications of the European Communities, 1988

ISBN 92-825-7782-1

Catalogue number: CB-50-87-352-EN-C

The President and the Members of the Commission of the European Communities to the President of the European Parliament

Sir,

We have the honour to present the General Report on the Activities of the Communities, which the Commission is required to publish by Article 18 of the Treaty establishing a Single Council and a Single Commission of the European Communities.

This report, for 1987, is the twenty-first since the merger of the executives.

In accordance with the procedure described in the Declaration on the system for fixing Community farm prices contained in the Accession Documents of 22 January 1972, the Commission has already sent Parliament the 1987 Report on the Agricultural Situation in the Community.

Under Article 122 of the Treaty establishing the European Economic Community, the Commission is also preparing a Report on Social Developments in the Community in 1987.

And, in accordance with an undertaking given to Parliament on 7 June 1971, the Commission is preparing its seventeenth annual Report on Competition Policy.

Please accept, Sir, the expression of our highest consideration.

Brussels, 9 February 1988

Jacques DELORS
Président

Lorenzo NATALI
Vice-président

Karl-Heinz NARJES
Vice-président

Frans ANDRIESSEN
Vice-président

Lord COCKFIELD
Vice-président

Henning CHRISTOPHERSEN
Vice-président

Manuel MARIN

Claude CHEYSSON

Grigoris VARFIS

Willy DE CLERCQ

Nicolas MOSAR

Stanley CLINTON DAVIS

Carlo RIPA di MEANA

Peter SUTHERLAND

Antonio José Baptista
CARDOSO E CUNHA

Abel MATUTES

Peter M. SCHMIDHUBER

The following currency abbreviations are being used in all language versions of the General Report and of the other reports published in conjunction with it.

ECU	=	European currency unit
BFR	=	Belgische frank/franc belge
DKR	=	Dansk krone
DM	=	Deutsche Mark
DR	=	Drachma
ESC	=	Escudo
FF	=	Franc français
HFL	=	Nederlandse gulden (Hollandse florijn)
IRL	=	Irish pound
LFR	=	Franc luxembourgeois
LIT	=	Lira italiana
PTA	=	Peseta
UKL	=	Pound sterling
USD	=	United States dollar

Summary

Contents

The Community in 1987

General survey

The main events and trends of 1987 — the dramatic change in East-West relations, monetary instability, unemployment, the US budget deficit and Third World indebtedness — are all challenges which the Community has to face up to and which raise the question how it can safeguard its prosperity and security and at the same time promote increased cooperation between industrialized and developing countries. For the first time, before the Venice Summit, the Council, at the Commission's request, took a significant step forward by discussing the coordination of economic policies throughout the Community.

Would the Community provide itself with the means to assume its international responsibilities and live up to the new ambitions enshrined in the Single European Act?

Completion of the large internal market by the end of 1992 in line with the decision of the European Council is essential to produce the necessary boost but is not enough in itself to build the Community. Economic convergence and the implementation of flanking policies are the main factors which distinguish a free-trade area from an economic area in which the free movement of workers, goods and capital creates more growth and with it more employment. The large market must therefore lead to the creation of a genuine common economic and social area based on solidarity where the rules of the market and cooperation between the political institutions and the two sides of industry are the order of the day.

The Commission's activities were consequently concentrated on four main objectives:

(i) striving for greater economic cohesion between the regions of the Community through flanking policies capitalizing fully on the interdependence of the Member States' economies in an attempt to obtain higher growth;

(ii) laying the foundations for a European social area geared to progress and an effective fight against unemployment in order to provide economic and social support for completion of the large market;

(iii) *strengthening the European Monetary System by encouraging Member States to cooperate on the regulation of financial and foreign-exchange markets and the liberalization of capital movements;*

(iv) *relaunching Europe's technological offensive using the relevant Community programmes to stimulate the sectors essential to the third industrial revolution and facilitate the necessary changes in the crisis industries.*

Thirty years after the signing of the Treaties of Rome and one year after the accession of Spain and Portugal, the diversity of the Community continued to increase and measures had to be taken to adjust accordingly.

The Single European Act, which entered into force on 1 July after ratification by the parliaments of the Member States in accordance with Article 33,[1] sets new objectives for the Community, including completion of the internal market by 1992 coupled with the strengthening of economic and social cohesion. The Single Act is the expression of a renewed determination to make the improvements essential for decision-making and effective action. It must now be applied forcefully and constructively.

On 15 February, after the President's tour of the Community capitals in the wake of the London European Council in December 1986, the Commission adopted a communication entitled 'The Single Act: A new frontier for Europe', which provides a balanced and coherent blueprint for the Community in the years ahead. The plan it contains not only covers the financing of the Community and the continued reform of the common agricultural policy but also aims to implement the Single Act in its entirety by targeting creation of the common economic area, more vigorous economic growth, greater effectiveness on the part of the institutions, strenthened budgetary discipline, and a common and strong external economic policy.

Presenting the plan to the European Parliament in Strasbourg on 18 February, the President of the Commission made the following statement:

'Europe cannot duck this appointment with itself in 1987. The Single Act puts it under a political obligation to keep this appointment, and what the Commission is proposing is a complete and coherent package setting out the policies and means required in order to implement the Single Act, nothing but the Single Act, but the whole Single Act. What is at issue is indeed the credibility of the construction of Europe...'.

---

[1]   Eleven Member States had deposited instruments of ratification by 31 December 1986. Ireland followed suit on 24 June 1987 after the positive outcome of the referendum held on 26 May.

If it is to succeed in its new responsibilities, the Community must first complete the reforms put in hand, especially since 1984, with a view to adapting its old policies to new conditions: the reform of the common agricultural policy to accommodate the change in production and trade patterns, while safeguarding Community preference, the unified market and financial solidarity and taking into account the preponderance of family-run farms and their role in regional development; the reform of the structural Funds to make of them instruments of economic development, thus illustrating the Community's political resolve to strengthen its economic and social cohesion; and the reform of the financial rules to tighten budgetary discipline. Finally, if it is to be in a position to attain the objectives set out in the Single Act, the Community will have to have the financial resources needed to fulfil the commitments stemming from the Act.

The main priority is to achieve a new balance in the structure of expenditure between now and 1992 by implementing the Commission proposal to double the appropriations of the structural Funds and to contain the upward trend in agricultural expenditure.

The reform of the structural Funds is not the only way to strengthen cohesion: the convergence of economic policies, the beneficial effects of the large internal market, and the positive impact of increased monetary and technological cooperation also have a part to play.

Agricultural expenditure cannot be contained without improving market management, notably by creating a realistic financial framework, introducing stabilizers for the market organizations and reforming the management of EAGGF Guarantee Section expenditure. The cohesion which is a prerequisite for the introduction of stabilizers calls in turn for continuation of a firm external policy.

The Commission proposals for reform of the financial rules to improve budgetary management — strengthening the principle of annuality, increased strictness in the forecasting and utilization of appropriations, improved transparency — are an essential adjunct to budgetary discipline.

The Community needs a budget which is commensurate with the ambitious objectives of the Single Act, which is efficient and which is both a reflection of the solidarity between Member States and regions and a clear indication of what the Community wants for itself and the outside world, in particular as regards development aid policy. On the revenue side the overall objective is to adjust the balance of Member States' contributions to the budget. The Commission has therefore proposed introducing a fourth resource so that contributions reflect relative prosperity more accurately.

Despite the temptation to discuss only short-term problems and defer consideration of the Commission proposals to a later date, the Brussels European Council of 29 and 30 June opted for retaining the Commission package as a whole in its original form.

As regards reform of the common agricultural policy, it confirmed the need for better adjustment of supply to demand through measures enabling the market to play a greater role and agreed that the reforms to be introduced could be accompanied by direct, selective income support. It endorsed the Commission's thinking on the need to rationalize the basic objectives of the structural Funds and to concentrate on specific objectives and stated that it intended to fix a financial objective for allocations to the Funds for 1992 as part of the Community's new financial system and to adopt a multiannual reference framework. The European Council also agreed that the Community must have stable and guaranteed resources enabling it to cope with the consequences of decisions connected with the implementation of its main policies and that the financing system should take greater account of the proportionality of contributions in accordance with the relative prosperity of the Member States; it also insisted that the use of these resources should be subject to effective and binding budgetary discipline.

After the Brussels European Council the Commission accordingly presented the Council and Parliament with formal texts on the four key issues dealt with in its communication on the Single Act:

(i)   new financial resources for the Community;

(ii) strengthened budgetary discipline;

(iii) reform of the structural Funds;

(iv) continued reform of the common agricultural policy.

In November Parliament confirmed its political support for the Commission package by underlining the inseparable link between completion of the large internal market, economic and social cohesion, agricultural policy reform and revision of the financing system.

The European Council ended its Copenhagen meeting of 4 and 5 December without a decision on the programme contained in 'The Single Act: A new frontier for Europe' — which the Commission upholds in full — and decided to meet again in Brussels on 11 and 12 February.

The Community in the world

While the key internal event of 1987 was the entry into force of the Single Act, the dominant feature of the year externally was the continuation or initiation of negotiations with a number of partners. As in 1986, Community action and initiatives in international forums and relations with the developing countries as a whole evolved favourably and were in many cases brought to a satisfactory conclusion. The same was true of relations with virtually all the industrialized countries, though some bilateral differences with the United States and Japan were resolved only after what were at times difficult negotiations.

In accordance with the principles laid down by the European Council, which considers that the strengthening of an open international trading system based on a fair balance between rights and obligations is of prime importance for the prosperity of industrialized and developing countries alike, the Community established its basic position in preparation for the Uruguay Round. The Community also successfully defended these ideas of balance and fairness at the seventh session of the United Nations Conference on Trade and Development, the final act of which largely corresponds to the Community's objectives. This same concept of an open international trading system underlies the Community's approach to its relations with the industrialized countries and is also in line with the declaration issued at the close of the Western Economic Summit in Venice.

In January the Community concluded an agreement with the United States under Article XXIV.6 of the General Agreement on Tariffs and Trade concerning the effects of enlargement. However, it was not long before other problems emerged, including a restrictive US trade bill and the citrus fruit and pasta issue. The latter was resolved after tricky negotiations. The United States also attempted to call in question the structures and operations of the Airbus-Industrie consortium. The Commission and the four Member States concerned responded forcefully, pointing out that the United States civil aircraft industry benefits from aid under military R&D programmes. Implementation of the Directive on hormones is yet another, more recent cause of dispute.

The Community continued its long wait for Japan to translate into action its repeated promises to open up its market. The Council again deplored the worsening of the trade imbalance due to the lack of any real balance of benefits between the two partners and expressed the hope that Japan would take further action to open up its market and implement its trade programme. Meanwhile, action by the Community led to the condemnation by GATT of Japan's discriminatory taxes on imports of Community spirits.

Approving the 10th annual report on cooperation with the countries of the European Free Trade Association, the Council welcomed the considerable progress made in strengthening cooperation, and in particular in establishing, in parallel with the Community's own internal market, the wider European economic area endorsed by the Luxembourg Conference in April 1984. It also adopted decisions concluding two conventions between the Community and the EFTA countries, one on the simplification of trade formalities and the other on common arrangements for goods in transit.

Horizons are widening in relations with the Council for Mutual Economic Assistance and its individual member countries: negotiations are in progress with Czechoslovakia and Hungary; negotiations have also been opened with Romania with a view to an agreement on economic and commercial cooperation.

Community relations with the developing countries evolved positively. The conclusion of post-enlargement protocols and the renewal of the financial protocols with the Maghreb and Mashreq countries provided a fresh boost for the close relations maintained by the Community with all the Mediterranean countries. To allow the Community to respond more effectively to the expectations of certain non-associated developing countries, the Council adopted new guidelines on industrial cooperation between European firms and firms in countries in Latin America, Asia, the Gulf and the Mediterranean at an intermediate stage of development. In the case of Latin America, and notably Central America, the Community also provided support, whenever possible, for regional integration and for moves to restore democracy. But it was in its relations with the ACP States and the poorest countries that the Community was most active. The Council agreed on a common position on the Commission communication calling for a special 100 million ECU Community programme to help certain highly indebted low-income countries of sub-Saharan Africa. In this same spirit of active solidarity, the Council adopted two Regulations establishing a system of compensation for loss of export earnings for least-developed countries not signatory to the Lomé Convention. Finally, it also adopted a Regulation on food-aid policy and management designed to adapt food aid more effectively to current development conditions and requirements and to make it a more efficient instrument in the quest for food security.

These major achievements in Community relations with the developing countries provide a solid basis for continuing the dialogue with the Third World in the run-up to the forthcoming opening of negotiations on a new EEC-ACP agreement to replace the third Lomé Convention, which expires in 1989.

Chapter I

Community institutions and financing

Section 1

Institutions and other bodies

European policy and relations between the institutions

European policy

Single European Act

1. Following a referendum in May,[1] the Irish Constitution was amended, thereby enabling Ireland to ratify the Single European Act.[2] The instruments of ratification were deposited on 24 June.

The Single Act was then able to enter into force on 1 July.[3] The cooperation procedure between Council and Parliament accordingly began to operate in the second half of the year.

'The Single Act: A new frontier for Europe'

2. Under the stimulus of the results of the Fontainebleau European Council in June 1984[4] and bolstered by the initiatives of Parliament and the backing of all sections of society, the European Community has been looking to the future. To begin with, 1985 saw the Heads of State or Government approve

---

[1] Bull. EC 5-1987, point 2.4.4.
[2] Supplement 2/86 — Bull. EC; Twentieth General Report, point 1.
[3] OJ L 169, 29.6.1987; Bull. EC 6-1987, point 2.4.5.
[4] Bull. EC 6-1984, point 1.1.1 *et seq.*

the objective of completing the single market by 1992 (Milan European Council) [1] and then the Single European Act (Luxembourg European Council), which provides the appropriate institutional structure for achieving this objective.

The following year was that of the accession of Spain and Portugal and the launching of the first integrated Mediterranean programmes as a demonstration of the move to promote economic and social cohesion.

By July 1987 the Single European Act had been ratified by all the national parliaments. However, even before this, the Commission had in February sent the Council and Parliament a coherent package of reform proposals to adapt Community policies to the consequences of the Single Act: [2]

(i)   reform of the common agricultural policy, to restore a long-term economic and social future to European farming;

(ii) reform of the Community's structural Funds, to cater for the increase in needs (doubling between 1989 and 1992) and to make the necessary change in the way resources are employed (programme approach);

(iii) reform of the Community budget to instil stricter discipline while at the same time offering greater security in the provision of Community resources, so that the financing arrangements will be consistent with the objectives set for 1992.

This package of reforms was considered twice by the European Council in 1987. First at Brussels in June, [3] the Heads of State or Government expressed their broad agreement with the principles of the three reforms proposed by the Commission. They then returned to the matter at Copenhagen in December [4] after the Council and Parliament had received detailed proposals from the Commission on each of the three areas. [5]

Although some real progress was made at Copenhagen towards finding full agreement on the three reform proposals, including the agricultural issues (stabilizers, direct income support), the European Council failed to produce a total consensus. It preferred to postpone its conclusions until a further meeting at an early date (11 and 12 February 1988) rather than upset the overall balance of the Commission's proposals.

---

1   Bull. EC 6-1985, point 1.2.1 et seq.
2   Bull. EC 2-1987, point 1.1.1 et seq.; Supplement 1/87 — Bull. EC.
3   Bull. EC 6-1987, point 1.1.1 et seq.
4   Bull. EC 12-1987.
5   Bull. EC 7/8-1987, point 1.1.1 et seq.; Bull. EC 9-1987, point 1.5.1.

Implementation of the Single Act

Voting in the Council

3. On 20 July the Council amended [1] its Rules of Procedure, which date from 1979. [2] The amendment concerns the arrangements for calling a vote.

The new version of Article 5 states that in addition to calling a vote on his own initiative, the President of the Council must initiate the voting procedure at the request of a member of the Council or of the Commission, provided that a majority of the Council's members approve. To facilitate this arrangement, Article 2 was also amended to the effect that the provisional agenda for each meeting, to be sent to the other members of the Council and the Commission at least 14 days before the beginning of the meeting, must indicate the items on which the Presidency, delegations or Commission could request a vote.

The Commission adopted the procedural provisions required by these changes in the Council's Rules. It decided, for instance, that for each Council meeting it would systematically indicate that it might request a vote on any agenda item on which the Council was legally capable of deciding by simple or qualified majority.

Implementing powers conferred on the Commission

4. In response to the declaration annexed to the Single Act calling on the Community authorities to set out, before the Act entered into force, the principles and rules on the basis of which the Commission's implementing powers would be defined, the Council, on a proposal from the Commission, [3] adopted a Decision on 13 July laying down the procedures for the exercise of these powers. [4] The Commission will henceforth exercise implementing powers in respect of Council decisions either alone or by one of three committee procedures: advisory committee, management committee or regulatory committee. The Council also inserted a safeguard clause.

The Council added two variants on the regulatory committee and the safeguard clause procedures. On these, however, the Commission made a statement expressing its strongest reservations. On 2 October the President of Parliament

---

[1]   OJ L 291, 15.10.1987; Bull. EC 7/8-1987, point 2.4.12.
[2]   OJ L 268, 25.10.1979; Thirteenth General Report, point 16.
[3]   OJ C 70, 25.3.1986; Twentieth General Report, point 4.
[4]   OJ L 197, 18.7.1987; Bull. EC 6-1987, point 2.4.11.

brought an action before the Court of Justice challenging the Council's Decision. [1]

Composition and functioning of the institutions

Parliament

5. On 20 January Parliament elected Sir Henry (now Lord) Plumb President. [2] Mrs Nicole Pery (S/France), Mr Siegbert Alber (EPP/Germany), Mr Enrique Barón Crespo (S/Spain), Mr Horst Seefeld (S/Germany), Mr Mark Clinton (EPP/Ireland), Mr Mario Didò (S/Italy), Mr Pieter Dankert (S/Netherlands), Mr Guido Fanti (Com/Italy), Mr Georgios Romeos (S/Greece), Mr Thomas Megahy (S/United Kingdom), Mr Roberto Formigoni (EPP/Italy), Mr François Musso (EDA/France), Mr Luis Guillermo Perinat Elio (ED/Spain) and Mr Rui Amaral (LDR/Portugal) were elected Vice-Presidents. Mr Kurt Wawrzik (EPP/Germany), Mr James Provan (ED/United Kingdom), Mr Ernest Glinne (S/Belgium), Mr Hans Nord (LDR/Netherlands) and Mr Angelino Carossino (Com/Italy) were elected Quaestors.

The 518 seats are distributed as follows:

Socialists (S)	165
European People's Party (EPP)	115
European Democratic Group (ED)	66
Communists and Allies (Com)	48
Liberal, Democratic and Reformist Group (LDR)	44
European Democratic Alliance (EDA)	29
Rainbow Group	20
European Right	17
Group for the Technical Coordination and Defence of Independent Groups and Members	12
Non-affiliated	2

6. The main issues debated during the year included the Commission's communication 'The Single Act: A new frontier for Europe', [3] with the new strategy

---

[1] OJ C 321, 1.12.1987.
[2] Bull. EC 1-1987, point 1.1.1 *et seq.*
[3] Supplement 1/87 — Bull. EC; Bull. EC 2-1987, point 1.1.1 *et seq.*

defined by the Commission receiving general approval,[1] the consequences of the Chernobyl nuclear accident,[2] European space policy,[3] the liberalization of public supply contracts,[4] the framework programme of research and technological development (1987-91),[5] the budget problems,[6] the stock market crisis[7] and the results of the Copenhagen European Council.[8]

7.   In the external relations field the main topics of debate were relations with the Council for Mutual Economic Assistance (Comecon) and the Eastern European countries belonging to Comecon,[9] and the agreement between the United States and the Community on the effects of enlargement.[10]

8.   In the field of political cooperation and human rights Parliament passed a number of resolutions, notably on the political dimensions of a European security strategy, the Middle East, human rights in the world in 1985-86 and Community policy in this area, the incompatibility of certain Member States' policies on the right of asylum with human rights, the situation in Chile.

9.   Parliament held 12 part-sessions, during which it adopted 522 resolutions and decisions, including 165 resolutions embodying its opinion (13 on first reading under the cooperation procedure). On second reading, Parliament approved the Council's common position without amendment in five cases and after amendment in four cases.

The new assent procedure (Articles 237 and 238 of the EEC Treaty as amended by the Single European Act) was applied in 20 cases.

Parliament adopted 21 resolutions and decisions under the budget procedure.

It adopted 290 own-initiative resolutions—139 on the basis of reports, 122 by urgent procedure and 29 following an early vote to conclude debates on Commission or Council statements or on oral questions.

Lastly, Parliament took 17 miscellaneous decisions concerning changes in the Rules of Procedure, requests to waive Members' immunity, etc.

---

[1]   OJ C 76, 23.3.1987; Bull. EC 2-1987, point 2.4.7; OJ C 99, 13.4.1987; Bull. EC 3-1987, point 2.4.6; OJ C 156, 15.6.1987; Bull. EC 5-1987, point 2.4.10; OJ C 345, 21.12.1987; Bull. EC 11-1987, point 1.1.1 et seq.
[2]   OJ C 125, 11.5.1987; Bull. EC 4-1987, point 2.4.13.
[3]   OJ C 190, 20.7.1987; Bull. EC 6-1987, point 2.4.17.
[4]   OJ C 246, 14.9.1987; Bull. EC 7/8-1987, point 2.4.14.
[5]   OJ C 281, 19.10.1987; Bull. EC 9-1987, point 2.4.10.
[6]   OJ C 305, 16.11.1987; Bull. EC 10-1987, point 2.4.8.
[7]   OJ C 318, 30.11.1987; Bull. EC 10-1987, point 2.4.15.
[8]   OJ C 13, 18.1.1988; Bull. EC 12-1987.
[9]   OJ C 46, 23.2.1987; Bull. EC 1-1987, point 2.4.6.
[10]   OJ C 76, 23.3.1987; Bull. EC 2-1987, point 2.2.10.

A total of 2 942 written questions were tabled—2 591 to the Commission, 201 to the Council and 150 to the Conference of Ministers for Foreign Affairs (political cooperation). Oral questions numbered 1 109—714 for the Commission, 221 to the Council and 174 to the Conference of Ministers for Foreign Affairs.

10.   At 31 December the establishment plan of the Secretariat comprised 2 946 permanent posts and 382 temporary posts.

Council

11.   Belgium was in the chair for the first half of the year [1] and Denmark for the second half. [2]

12.   At its 78 meetings in 1987 the Council adopted 40 directives, 458 regulations and 125 decisions.

13.   The European Council met in Brussels in June and in Copenhagen in December. [3] The discussion at both meetings centered on the Commission's communication 'The Single Act: A new frontier for Europe'. [4]

14.   Continuing the practice introduced in 1981, Mr Wilfried Martens and Mr Poul Schlüter reported to Parliament on the outcome of the European Council meetings. [5]

15.   There were 1 915 permanent posts and three temporary posts on the Council's establishment plan at the end of the year.

Commission

16.   On 22 September the Representatives of the Governments of the Member States, by common accord, appointed Mr Peter Schmidhuber a Member of the Commission to replace Mr Alois Pfeiffer, who died on 1 August, for the

---

[1] Bull. EC 1-1987, point 3.4.1.; Bull. EC 6-1987, point 3.4.1.
[2] Bull. EC 7/8-1987, point 3.4.1.
[3] Bull. EC 6-1987, point 1.1.1. *et seq.*; Bull. EC 12-1987.
[4] Point 2 of this Report.
[5] Bull. EC 6-1987, point 1.1.10; Bull. EC 12-1987.

remainder of his term of office (until 5 January 1989).[1] Mr Schmidhuber was assigned Mr Pfeiffer's portfolio of economic affairs, regional policy and the Statistical Office.

17.   On 18 September the Commission held a special symposium to mark the retirement of Mr Emile Noël, Secretary-General.[2] The general theme was 'Crisis and progress: the bricks and mortar of Europe'.

18.   The Commission held 45 meetings. It adopted 8 212 instruments (regulations, decisions, directives, recommendations, opinions) and sent the Council 699 proposals, recommendations or drafts for Council instruments and 192 communications, memoranda and reports.

19.   The Commission's establishment plan for 1987 comprised 11 234 permanent posts (including 1 544 LA posts for the language service) and 388 temporary posts (including 20 LA) paid out of administrative appropriations; 2 647 permanent and 406 temporary posts paid out of the research appropriations; 380 permanent posts in the Office for Official Publications; 55 at the European Centre for the Development of Vocational Training and 49 at the European Foundation for the Improvement of Living and Working Conditions.

20.   Under the secondment and exchange arrangements between the Commission and Member States' government departments, 32 Commission officials were seconded to national civil services and 150 national civil servants came to work for Commission departments.

Court of Justice

21.   On 30 September the Court appointed Mr M. Darmon First Advocate-General for one year from 7 October.[3]

22.   Composition of the Chambers:[3]

First Chamber: G. Bosco, President, R. Joliet and F.A. Schockweiler, Judges;

Second Chamber: O. Due, President, K. Bahlmann and T.F. O'Higgins, Judges;

1   OJ L 279, 2.10.1987; Bull. EC 9-1987, point 1.1.1. *et seq.*
2   Bull. EC 9-1987, point 1.2.1. *et seq.*
3   OJ C 307, 17.11.1987; Bull. EC 10-1987, points 2.4.31 and 2.4.32.

Third Chamber: J.C. Moitinho de Almeida, President, U. Everling and Y. Galmot, Judges;

Fourth Chamber: G.C. Rodríguez Iglesias, President, T. Koopmans and C.N. Kakouris, Judges;

Fifth Chamber: G. Bosco, President, J.C. Moitinho de Almeida, U. Everling, Y. Galmot, R. Joliet and F.A. Schockweiler, Judges;

Sixth Chamber: O. Due, President, G.C. Rodríguez Iglesias, T. Koopmans, K. Bahlmann, C.N. Kakouris and T.F. O'Higgins, Judges.

23.   In 1987, 395 cases were brought (144 references for preliminary rulings, 77 staff cases and 174 others). Of the 317 judgments given by the Court, 83 were preliminary rulings, 106 were in staff cases and 128 were in other cases. [1]

24.   There were 606 permanent posts and 40 temporary posts on the Court's establishment plan at 31 December.

Court of Auditors

25.   After consulting Parliament, [2] the Council reappointed Mr Aldo Angioi, Mr Carlos Manuel Botelheiro Moreno, Mr Keld Brixtofte, Mr Richie Ryan and Mr Josep Subirats Piñana and appointed Mr François Hebette to replace Mr Paul Gaudy. Their term of office runs from 18 October 1987 to 17 October 1993. [3]

26.   During the year, in accordance with the Treaties, the Court delivered opinions on Commission proposals concerning the financing of a programme for the disposal of surplus intervention stocks, [4] monitoring the payment of the amounts granted on export of agricultural products [5] and the system of advances in the Guarantee Section of the European Agricultural Guidance and Guarantee Fund. [6]

It also issued special reports on the quality of food aid (the extent to which the products comply with the rules as regards quality, quantity, packaging,

---

1   The Court's judgments are discussed in Chapter IV: Community law.
2   OJ C 305, 16.11.1987; Bull. EC 10-1987, point 2.4.37.
3   OJ L 304, 27.10.1987; Bull. EC 10-1987, point 2.4.37.
4   OJ C 59, 7.3.1987; Bull. EC 2-1987, point 2.4.18.
5   OJ C 147, 5.6.1987; Bull. EC 5-1987, point 2.4.23.
6   Bull. EC 6-1987, point 2.4.27.

time and place),[1] on the management and operation of the system of tobacco premiums,[2] on the system of quotas and additional levies in the milk sector,[3] on Community wine distillation measures[4] and on Community aid to speed up agricultural development in Greece.[5]

27.   There were 310 permanent posts and 56 temporary posts on the Court's establishment plan at the end of the year.

Economic and Social Committee

28.   The sitting of 14 May marked a 'first' for the Economic and Social Committee, when it was attended by the President of the Council, Mr Wilfried Martens.[6] Mr Martens spoke on the two topics on the agenda for the European Council meeting at the end of June: the social dialogue and the Commission's communication 'The Single Act: A new frontier for Europe',[7] which had been presented to the Committee by Mr Delors in February.[8] In November the Committee delivered an opinion and three own-initiative opinions on the various aspects of the Commission's proposals.[9]

29.   The Commission proposals or communications on which the Committee gave opinions during its 10 sessions in 1987 included the action programme for student mobility (Erasmus),[10] the farm price package,[11] the small business action programme,[12] the five-year Community programme of projects illustrating how action on the environment can help to create jobs[13] and speed limits in the Community.[14]

30.   The Committee delivered own-initiative opinions on matters such as a Community rail policy,[15] the impact of economic and political developments in the United States,[16] and the consequences of the Chernobyl nuclear accident.[17]

---

[1]   OJ C 219, 17.8.1987; Bull. EC 6-1987, point 2.4.26.
[2]   OJ C 297, 6.11.1987; Bull. EC 7/8-1987, point 2.4.36.
[3]   OJ C 266, 5.10.1987; Bull. EC 7/8-1987, point 2.4.37.
[4]   OJ C 297, 6.11.1987; Bull. EC 10-1987, point 2.4.35.
[5]   Bull. EC 10-1987, point 2.4.36.
[6]   Bull. EC 5-1987, points 2.4.24 and 2.4.25.
[7]   Bull. EC 2-1987, point 1.1.1. et seq.; Supplement 1/87 — Bull. EC.
[8]   OJ C 105, 21.4.1987; Bull. EC 2-1987, point 2.4.20.
[9]   Bull. EC 11-1987, point 1.1.1. et seq.
[10] OJ C 83, 30.3.1987; Bull. EC 1-1987, point 2.4.37.
[11] OJ C 150, 9.6.1987; Bull. EC 4-1987, point 2.4.47.
[12] OJ C 232, 31.8.1987; Bull. EC 7/8-1987, point 2.4.43.
[13] OJ C 319, 30.11.1987; Bull. EC 9-1987, point 2.4.36.
[14] OJ C 347, 22.12.1987; Bull. EC 10-1987, point 2.4.46.
[15] OJ C 105, 21.4.1987; Bull. EC 2-1987, point 2.4.21.
[16] OJ C 232, 31.8.1987; Bull. EC 7/8-1987, point 2.4.60.
[17] OJ C 232, 31.8.1987; Bull. EC 7/8-1987, point 2.4.59.

31.   The Committee also sent the Community institutions an information report on health. [1]

32.   There were 471 permanent posts on the Committee's establishment plan at 31 December.

ECSC Consultative Committee

33.   The Committee held seven meetings (five ordinary and two extraordinary). It examined the Commission's overall plan for the restructuring of the Community steel industry. [2] It was also consulted on the market for solid fuels [3] and adopted a resolution on the ECSC levy rate. [4]

Administration and management of the institutions

Modernizing the European civil service

34.   Implementation of the modernization policy endorsed by the Commission in 1985 continued. The series of seminars for directors, heads of divisions and specialized departments, assistants to directors-general and staff representatives [5] was completed, and a programme to heighten awareness of the problems of management was distributed to all staff.

A further seminar for directors-general, chaired by Mr Christophersen, one of the Commission Vice-Presidents, was held in October. It highlighted the effort needed in terms of resource management, simplification of procedures, and personnel policy (middle management mobility, training). Relations between the Commission and its departments, horizontal cooperation between directorates-general and the strategy on human relations to be implemented within each department also came under close scrutiny.

Staff Regulations

35.   On 5 October the Council, on a proposal from the Commission, [6] adopted a Regulation introducing special transitional measures for the recruitment of overseas staff of the European Association for Cooperation as officials of

---

[1]   Bull. EC 2-1987, point 2.4.22.
[2]   Bull. EC 5-1987, point 2.4.40; Bull. EC 9-1987, point 2.4.45; Bull. EC 12-1987.
[3]   Bull. EC 3-1987, point 2.4.16; Bull. EC 6-1987, point 2.4.28; Bull. EC 9-1987, point 2.4.46.
[4]   Bull. EC 12-1987.
[5]   Twentieth General Report, point 42.
[6]   OJ C 74, 3.4.1986; Twentieth General Report, point 45.

the European Communities. [1] Their responsibilities as representatives of the Commission have risen to a level that justifies this decision. At the same time it also adopted, on a Commission proposal, [2] a Regulation laying down special and exceptional provisions applicable to officials serving in non-member countries. [1]

36. The two proposals for Council Regulations to bring the conditions of employment of staff at the European Centre for the Development of Vocational Training (Berlin) and the European Foundation for the Improvement of Living and Working Conditions (Dublin) into line with the conditions of employment of other servants [3] were adopted on 23 February. [4]

37. The proposal for a Regulation introducing special measures (similar to those applicable to officials) to terminate the service of temporary staff following the accession of Spain and Portugal was adopted by the Council on 23 July. [5]

Remunerations

38. On 20 October the Council adopted a Regulation adjusting the rate of the special temporary levy provided for in Article 66a of the Staff Regulations. [6] The rate was reduced to 7.62% with effect from 1 July 1987. At the same time it added to its Decision of 15 December 1981 amending the method of adjusting the remuneration of officials and other servants [7] a provision to take account of the improvement in the economic indicators which have been used since 1981 for determining the special levy. [6]

Language services and data processing

Language services

39. The workload of the Joint Interpreting and Conference Service (JICS) has continued to grow, notably as a result of the addition of two further languages following enlargement; 8 600 meetings — equivalent to 105 000 interpreter days — were covered.

---

[1] OJ L 286, 9.10.1987.
[2] OJ C 284, 11.11.1986; Twentieth General Report, point 45.
[3] Twentieth General Report, point 46.
[4] OJ L 72, 14.3.1987.
[5] OJ L 209, 31.7.1987.
[6] OJ L 307, 29.10.1987.
[7] OJ L 386, 31.12.1981.

The JICS intensified its efforts to attract, select and train staff. Seven open competitions for interpreters and assistant interpreters were organized and 24 aptitude tests were held, in particular in Athens, Lisbon and Madrid. The JICS also contributed to training programmes for conference interpreters in Copenhagen, Mons and Paris. Sixteen interpreters from the established staff received study grants to allow them to learn a further working language.

Cooperation with non-member countries in the field of interpreter training also continued, particularly with China, Hong Kong and Yugoslavia.

40.   Despite recruitment difficulties, the translation service stepped up its efforts to consolidate the Spanish and Portuguese units both in Brussels and in Luxembourg, with 35 Portuguese and 25 Spanish candidates being admitted to an intensive training course.

At 31 December the staff complement was 82 Spanish and 63 Portuguese translators (Brussels/Luxembourg), and the aim is to reach figures of 130 and 83 respectively by the end of next year.

41.   The translation workload increased by 5%, partly as a result of the increase in the number of notices of tender. A total of 810 000 pages were translated during the year.

The Sysling project to equip the translation service with computer aids entered the implementation stage after three years of preparation.

The pilot schemes launched to test the Systran machine translation system in the language pairs now available (English-French, French-English, English-Italian, English-German and French-German) were continued, and progress was made in the development of new language pairs (English-Dutch and French-Dutch). Work also began on English-Portuguese, English-Spanish, French-Portuguese and French-Spanish.

The Eurodicautom terminology bank was extended further, especially in the field of new technology. It now contains some 440 000 entries with equivalents in other languages, broken down as follows: French 407 823, English 388 127, German 289 609, Danish 234 712, Dutch 221 968, Italian 199 721, Spanish 139 849, Greek 41 703 and Portuguese 60 101, figures which demonstrate the need to carry on with this work.

On 13 November a cooperation agreement was signed with the Swiss Federal Council laying down the objectives and conditions for pooling available data from both sides under Commission software and jointly developing the base.

Data processing

42.   Implementation of the data-processing strategy defined in 1984[1] for the years 1985-90 continued and notable progress was made in establishing an architecture based on a multi-manufacturer approach. This allows an optimum choice from the products available in order to arrive at the most economical and simplest solutions for the massive expansion of the services offered to end users (e.g. office automation, access to data bases, electronic mail).

Growth in the data-processing field has been sustained: at the end of the year the processing power available on the Computer Centre's machines was 57 mips (million instructions per second) compared with 38 mips in 1986; the number of work stations (terminals, microcomputers, etc.) installed in 1987 was over 500. The total processing power available in Commission departments is now around 140 mips.

43.   This progress in quantitative terms is being accompanied by a training programme designed to provide users with the general and specialist knowledge needed to make best use of the computerized aids available and to enhance the capabilities of the central data-processing departments and of the directorates-general to enable them to exploit their data-processing resources optimally.

44.   Implementation of the Insis programme for collaboration between the institutions, national government departments and industry has made concrete progress in the Commission, for instance with pilot experiments in electronic mail under way in some directorates-general. Cooperation between the institutions and national government departments centres on two main aspects: the adoption of common technical approaches and the establishment of pilot schemes. There is scope for further development, especially in terms of document transfer and the dissemination of information held on national and Community systems.

---

[1]   Eighteenth General Report, point 31.

Section 2

Information for the general public and specific audiences

Information activities

45.   Completion of the internal market by 1992 and a people's Europe were the focal points of Commission information and communication policy this year. Efforts to increase awareness among the general public and to intensify dialogue with the broad sections of public opinion, including women, young people and the working population, were stepped up, though not to the exclusion of the various political groups and the media. The already close cooperation with Parliament's information units was boosted further, thereby making it possible to capitalize fully on the activities of both institutions and to project a common image.

46.   Major events were organized in all the Community countries to mark the 30th anniversary of the signing of the Treaties of Rome, notably in Brussels, where the European festivities drew 350 000 people to the Cinquantenaire Park over a three-day period. The Eurovision Song Contest provided an opportunity to show a 10-minute film sequence on the Community to some 500 million television viewers. In addition, several sporting events, including the European Swimming Championships in Leeds, the European Yacht Race and the European Community Cycle Race, demonstrated the Community's presence in a sector with an exceptionally high media profile.

47.   Following last year's positive experiences in Denmark and Greece,[1] further information campaigns were carried out in other regions of both countries.

48.   The increasingly important role of the audiovisual industry was reflected in the setting-up of the Media programme (measures to encourage the development of the audiovisual industry)[2] and in the preparations for European

---

[1]   Twentieth General Report, point 57.
[2]   Twentieth General Report, point 242.

Cinema and Television Year.[1] The Media programme covers three sectors, namely the production, distribution and funding of audiovisual material. During the year, meetings and consultations were held with experts from the industry (over 1 000 organizations were involved for the three sectors) to set up pilot projects due to be launched in 1988. The Steering Committee for European Cinema and Television Year, under the chairmanship of Mrs Simone Veil, examined some 250 projects submitted by the national committees from the 24 participating countries (the Member States of the Community and the Council of Europe and the other members of the Council for Cultural Cooperation) as well as by the European cinema and television organizations represented on the Committee. The aim of European Cinema and Television Year is to heighten the industry's awareness of the challenge posed by the technological innovations in this area and to enable it to make the most of the opportunities offered by the large market. Finally, the Commission continued to support television and radio coverage of Community news items and to contribute to the production of programmes with a European dimension.

Press, radio and television

49.   The number of journalists accredited to the Commission in Brussels remained high, at over 450 from 50 countries, of whom around 370 were from the press and 80 from radio and television. This total includes some 45 international press agencies.

50.   The Spokesman's Service held 188 meetings with the press on Commission decisions, proposals and reactions, and Commission meetings were covered by 48 press conferences given by the Spokesman. The President and Members of the Commission gave 55 press conferences on key issues, several of which were given jointly with visitors to the Commission.

51.   The Spokesman's Service also conveyed to the press the Commission's position on the occasion of Council and European Council meetings and part-sessions of Parliament. Special arrangements were made for international events, such as the Venice Western Economic Summit, at which the Community was represented.

52.   More than 6 000 information memos and papers were released to the accredited press, while the Information Offices in the Member States and the

---

[1]   OJ C 320, 13.12.1986; Twentieth General Report, points 246 and 772.

Delegations in non-member countries received about 400 telexed memos and commentaries, drafted specially for their own use in keeping their press contacts informed.

Office for Official Publications

53.   The Office for Official Publications prints and distributes the Official Journal and other Community publications on behalf of all the institutions.

The integration of Spanish and Portuguese into the system was completed without difficulty. However, the fact that the Official Journal is now published daily in nine languages led to a further increase in the volume of pages processed and published by the Office; this currently exceeds 400 000 annually for the Official Journal alone. The system for dispatching and distributing the Official Journal was completely reorganized in the interests of speed and economy.

The Commission and the Office for Official Publications continued their efforts to ensure that the content and distribution of the general publications faithfully reflect the main thrust of Community activity.

The Publications Office has started to market some publications in electronic form. Customers can now take out subscriptions for on-line access to the following data bases: TED (Supplement to the Official Journal); Celex (Community law);[1] Pabli (blue pages of *The Courier* listing EDF and Commission development projects); and SCAD (bibliographical information on a selection of publications, documents and articles). Some material is also available on magnetic tape or optical disk.

On the internal organization front, the Office continued its programme to computerize production and management; this will enable it to take on a new role as the sole centre for distributing Community publications.

Statistical Office

54.   The work programme of the Statistical Office, drawn up in close collaboration with the Member States, continued to be geared to the Community's policy priorities.

---

[1]   Points 976 to 979 of this Report.

Detailed discussions were held on the structure of the Community's statistical programmes, in particular on the basis of the suggestions made at the Conference of Directors-General of the national statistical institutes in May. Future programmes should be drawn up in terms of statistical subsystems and contain a reference to the cost of the statistical projects linked to policy initiatives at both national and Community level.

55.   The statistical implications of completion of the internal market were studied in detail, with particular reference to three aspects: first, possible alternatives to replace the source of information on intra-Community trade which will disappear with the ending of administrative formalities at borders; second, improvements to the Community's statistical system with regard to the formulation of statistical standards and the transmission to the Statistical Office of confidential data for use in the production of Community statistics; finally, an inventory of all the statistics which need to be improved to ensure transparency in relation to the internal market — statistics on industry, services, the environment, and technological research and development.

A number of sectoral data bases, such as Trans for transport, TOUR for tourism and Hermes for services, were launched this year, and work is continuing on the Sirene, Acier and MAPR data bases for energy, the steel industry and raw materials respectively.

56.   The Statistical Office continued its efforts to improve the statistics available on employment and unemployment. The annual Community labour force survey, begun in 1983, was carried out in the spring in the 12 Member States.

57.   Forward guidelines for statistics on agriculture were re-examined with reference to the reform of the common agricultural policy. Work continued, albeit slightly behind schedule, on the restructuring of agricultural statistics in Italy, Greece [1] and Portugal. [2]

With regard to statistics on the structure of Community agriculture, the Commission transmitted a draft Regulation to the Council on the 1989/90 census of agricultural holdings and on structural surveys for the period 1992 to 1997. The Eurofarm project, a data base on the structural variables of agricultural holdings, is linked to this programme.

58.   Initial proposals for collecting Community environmental statistics were drawn up and discussed with the Member States. To avoid any duplication of

---

[1]   OJ L 191, 23.7.1986; Nineteenth General Report, point 71.
[2]   Twentieth General Report, point 65.

effort, these proposals are being coordinated with the OECD and integrated into the Corine programme (coordination of information on the environment in Europe). [1]

59.   The Statistical Office produced a new publication on the European Monetary System and the ECU, which contains information on the private use of the ECU and a price index expressed in ECUs. The Office also helped work out the indicators for defining the objectives of the structural Funds.

60.   On the external relations front, the Statistical Office made an active contribution to preparations for the Uruguay Round of multilateral trade negotiations[2] by setting up statistical and tariff data bases for goods and services. The technical cooperation programme was extended to include the training of Portuguese-speaking statisticians in Africa and the application of existing methods, notably in the fields of external trade and national accounts, to new countries and regions.

61.   Finally, the Statistical Office was instrumental in introducing the latest technologies for the collection and dissemination of information as part of the Caddia and Insis programmes, thereby contributing to the establishment of a European information market, which will be of benefit to business and citizens alike.

Historical archives

62.   The Commission released the historical archives of the ECSC High Authority for 1956[3] for consultation. [4]

It published the second volume of an inventory of the historical archives of the European Communities, containing details on the 1953 archive material of the High Authority and the ECSC Consultative Committee. [5]

---

[1]   OJ L 176, 3.7.1984; Eighteenth General Report, point 382.
[2]   Points 746 to 748 of this Report.
[3]   Eighteenth General Report, point 57; Nineteenth General Report, point 73.
[4]   Commission general archives, square de Meeûs 8, B-1040 Brussels.
[5]   Office for Official Publications of the European Communities, L-2985 Luxembourg.

The Commission's relations with workers' and employers' organizations and with the European Youth Forum

63.   The Commission and the workers' and employers' organizations continued the Val Duchesse social dialogue. [1] In November the working party on macroeconomic aspects adopted an opinion on the 1987-88 Annual Economic Report and appealed to the Heads of State or Government to make sure that the Copenhagen European Council was a success. The working party on new technologies and social dialogue adopted an opinion on the training and motivation of workers and on the need to inform and consult them. [2]

The Commission also held many information and consultation meetings at which the workers' and employers' organizations produced opinions and statements on Community policies.

64.   The Youth Forum remained in contact with the Commission, concentrating mainly on youth exchange schemes, the 'YES for Europe' and Erasmus programmes, the training of young people for adult and working life, the Social Fund, and the environment.

---

[1]   Nineteenth General Report, point 74.
[2]   Bull. EC 5-1987, point 1.2.1.

Section 3

Financing Community activities

Main developments

65.   *The Commission prepared a preliminary draft budget for 1988 designed to start the process of giving effect to the Single Act and to be financed under the new own resources arrangements proposed in February.* [1]

At meetings in July, [2] *September* [3] *and October,* [4] *the Council was unable to adopt a draft budget. For the first time, the 5 October deadline set by the Treaty for the adoption of the draft budget was not met. The Commission* [5] *and Parliament* [6] *therefore decided to initiate the procedure provided for in Article 175 of the Treaty to obtain a ruling from the Court of Justice that the Council had failed to satisfy its obligations.*

The Heads of State or Government of the Member States were also unable to find a solution at the Copenhagen European Council on 4 and 5 December. [7] *A further 'extraordinary' meeting of the European Council will therefore be held in Brussels in February. As a result, the provisional-twelfths arrangements will apply at the start of 1988, as they did in the early part of 1987.*

Priority activities and objectives

Future financing of the Community

66.   The own resources available to the Community within the limits set by the Fontainebleau European Council in June 1984 [8] are no longer sufficient to cover Community expenditure. Traditional resources — customs duties and

[1]   Bull. EC 2-1987, point 1.1.1 *et seq.*
[2]   Bull. EC 7/8-1987, point 2.3.3.
[3]   Bull. EC 9-1987, point 2.3.1.
[4]   Bull. EC 10-1987, point 2.3.1.
[5]   Bull. EC 10-1987, point 2.3.2.
[6]   Bull. EC 10-1987, point 2.3.3.
[7]   Bull. EC 12-1987.
[8]   Eighteenth General Report, point 20.

agricultural levies — are tending to stagnate or even fall because of the Community's increasing self-sufficiency in agricultural products and the dismantling of customs tariffs worldwide. The VAT base reflects only the consumption aspect of the Member States' economic capacity and the proportion of GDP accounted for by consumption is also tending to drop. The corrective mechanism introduced at Fontainebleau has reduced available resources, since the VAT ceiling applies only to those Member States financing the correction and not to the Community as a whole. The current system is thus no longer sufficient for financing the policies adopted by the Council, to which the Single Act was meant to give a fresh stimulus. Since 1984, budgets could not have been kept within the 1.4% VAT limit — notably because of the impossibility of writing down the value of stocks of agricultural products — without recourse to repeated makeshifts such as the carryover of appropriations and the time-lag between commitments and payments.

67.   In its communication 'The Single Act: A new frontier for Europe' of 15 February [1] the Commission therefore proposed a new system of sufficient, stable and guaranteed own resources, which would give the Community a period of budgetary security up to 1992. The Commission also proposed tighter budgetary discipline arrangements and new rules for managing the budget.

The main innovation is the introduction of an overall ceiling on Community resources equal to 1.4% of Community GNP. This system has the twin advantage of reflecting more accurately each Member State's ability to pay and eliminating the problem of instability besetting the present own resources. The resources available within this limit of 1.4% of GNP will be as follows: customs duties (including those on products coming under the ECSC Treaty) and agricultural levies — the 10% reimbursement to Member States for collection costs will be discontinued; a levy of 1% on the VAT base; and, as a further innovation, a resource deriving from an additional base corresponding to the difference between GNP and the actual VAT base in each Member State. On the basis of the preliminary draft budget presented by the Commission, [2] the application of the proposed system in 1988 would correspond to a VAT rate of 1.7% under the present system.

68.   The new rules on budgetary discipline proposed by the Commission should promote consensus between the two arms of the budgetary authority. The rules on the containment of agricultural expenditure will have to be applied

---

[1]   Supplement 1/87 — Bull. EC; Bull. EC 2-1987, points 1.1.12 to 1.1.16.
[2]   Points 74 to 76 of this Report.

very strictly so that this expenditure does not increase faster than the own resources base. The multiannual estimates [1] will be the key instrument in enforcing budgetary discipline. The application of the tighter discipline will force each institution to alter its behaviour and to make changes to the rules governing the drafting and the execution of the budget for the purpose of avoiding over-budgetization in certain budget headings, ensuring strict compliance with the principle of budget annuality and the annual ceilings on own resources, and improving the monitoring of budgetary operations.

69.   On 18 November Parliament adopted a resolution on the future financing of the Community. [2]

70.   The Economic and Social Committee adopted an own-initiative opinion on the subject. [3]

71.   On 11 November the Commission sent the Council a proposal for a Decision on the correction of budgetary imbalances. [4]

Budgets

1987 financial year

72.   The 1987 budget was adopted by Parliament by a very large majority on 19 February [5] and declared finally adopted by the President on the same day. [6] Appropriations for commitments totalled 37 414 887 257 ECU and appropriations for payments 36 313 424 475 ECU.

On 14 May the Commission adopted preliminary draft supplementary and amending budget No 1/87 calling in the resources still available in 1987 within the 1.4% VAT limit and providing for a special contribution by the Member States to cover the remaining deficit. [7] As regards the under-budgetization in the EAGGF Guarantee Section, the Commission also proposed replacement of

---

1   Point 79 of this Report.
2   OJ C 345, 21.12.1987; Bull. EC 11-1987, points 1.1.3 to 1.1.5.
3   Bull. EC 11-1987, point 1.1.7.
4   OJ C 346, 22.12.1987; Bull. EC 11-1987, point 2.4.8.
5   OJ C 76, 23.3.1987; Bull. EC 2-1987, point 2.4.11.
6   OJ L 86, 30.3.1987; Bull. EC 2-1987, point 2.3.3.
7   Bull. EC 5-1987, points 1.1.2 to 1.1.4.

the system of advances by a system of reimbursements which should afford better control of the management of appropriations.

The Council departed appreciably from this preliminary draft and in particular revised the statement of revenue in line with the savings to be made. In its draft it reduced some of the appropriations for compulsory expenditure but did not call into question the implementation of Community policies and the non-compulsory expenditure in the budget. [1] On 17 July the President of Parliament declared supplementary and amending budget No 1/87 finally adopted. [2] Although a proposal by its Committee on Budgets to reject it outright did not obtain the special majority required, Parliament passed a resolution in which it 'refuses to associate itself with the procedure for the draft supplementary and amending budget No 1 for the 1987 financial year and does not accept that it can have any binding consequences for the 1988 budget'. [3]

Implementation of the 1986 and 1987 budgets

73.   The rates of utilization of appropriations in 1986 and 1987 are shown in Tables 3a and 3b.

1988 financial year

Preliminary draft budget of the Communities for 1988

74.   On 14 May the Commission established the preliminary draft budget for 1988 [4] and sent it to the Council and Parliament in mid-June. The breakdown of appropriations for commitments and for payments by sector is shown in Tables 3a and 3b.

Political presentation of the budget

75.   The Commission's starting point was that the preliminary draft budget for 1988 must translate into material terms all the Community's political, economic and social objectives. The first steps in the move towards the

---

1   Bull. EC 7/8-1987, point 2.3.2.
2   OJ L 211, 3.8.1987; Bull. EC 7/8-1987, point 2.3.2.
3   OJ C 246, 14.9.1987; Bull. EC 7/8-1987, point 2.4.16.
4   Bull. EC 5-1987, points 1.1.5 to 1.1.11 and 2.3.2.

Community's new frontier will be taken in 1988,[1] which will be the first full year of application of the Single European Act and the proposed new own resources system.[2] The preliminary draft therefore reflected and applied the Commission's proposals concerning new resources, the reform of agricultural policy and the structural Funds and budgetary discipline.[3] The year will also have to see a return to 'budgetary truth' in both revenue and expenditure, which means clearing commitments relating to measures from past years and providing cover for at least some of the potential losses arising from storage of agricultural products. With the new own resources system it was no longer necessary for expenditure forecasts to be artificially contained within the current 1.4% VAT limit. The 1988 preliminary draft must also be seen in the light of the Commission's multiannual forecasts for 1988 to 1992.[4]

The features of these years will be the application of a binding guideline for EAGGF guarantee expenditure and a doubling of structural Fund appropriations. Finally, the preliminary draft complies with the maximum rate of increase for non-compulsory expenditure, which was set at 7.4% for 1988 (as against 8.1% the previous year).

Revenue

76.   The Commission produced its preliminary draft budget on the basis of its proposal to the Council on the own resources system.[4] Under this proposal the total own resources available to the Community in 1988 will be the equivalent of 1.2% of Community GNP, or 46 394.4 million ECU.

Expenditure

77.   The appropriations proposed in the preliminary draft budget for 1988 total 40 933.4 million ECU for commitments and 39 707.9 million ECU for payments, increases of 2.9% and 2.6% over the appropriations for 1987. EAGGF guarantee appropriations total 27 045 million ECU, an increase of slightly less than 5% over the actual requirements for 1987. The amount proposed corresponds to the guideline resulting from application of budgetary discipline.[5]

---

[1]   Supplement 1/87 — Bull. EC; Bull. EC 2-1987, point 1.1.1 *et seq.*
[2]   Point 67 of this Report.
[3]   Bull. EC 5-1987, point 2.3.3.
[4]   Point 79 of this Report.
[5]   Point 68 of this Report.

3-2		6-2			7			
Change		Change			1987 budget[1]			
%	Paym	%	Payments	%	Commitments	%	Payments	%
		+ 3.84	+ 848 800 000	+ 3.84	22 960 800 000	61.31	22 960 800 000	63.48
		+ 3.84	+ 848 800 000	+ 3.84	22 960 800 000	61.31	22 960 800 000	63.48
1.45	+ 33	+ 26.04	+ 204 037 083	+ 27.72	1 017 154 161	2.72	887 125 343	2.45
20.98	− 16	− 14.66	− 10 023 048	− 15.16	59 221 770	0.16	56 074 770	0.16
30.41	− 12	+ 7.24	+ 27 669 024	+ 14.59	243 293 678	0.65	197 293 678	0.55
1.18	− 72	+ 7.87	+ 124 294 757	+ 5.24	3 341 932 192	8.02	2 497 294 757	6.90
23.36	− 64	− 27.01	+ 44 628 703	+ 33.56	189 763 518	0.51	177 628 703	0.40
28.94	− 5	− 5.84	− 8 673 432	− 19.33	30 296 642	0.08	36 203 068	0.10
64.24	− 13	− 82.59	+ 227 574	+ 0.85	13 206 160	0.04	27 067 574	0.07
1.18	− 89	+ 13.65	+ 9 255 649	+ 0.37	2 602 489 678	6.95	2 542 255 649	7.03
5.42	− 4	+ 5.04	+ 5 090 077	+ 8.07	69 874 220	0.19	68 140 540	0.19
31.72	− 24	+ 111.90	+ 40 791 507	+ 111.90	94 979 132	0.25	94 979 132	0.25
39.74	− 11	+ 31.91	+ 10 107 183	+ 46.47	32 252 508	0.09	31 857 508	0.09
3.62	− 282	+ 9.87	+ 447 405 077	+ 7.19	7 694 463 659	20.54	6 615 920 722	18.29
2.36	− 2	24.02	+ 39 727 854	+ 86.52	121 802 644	0.33	85 647 854	0.24
25.62	− 97	+ 56.57	+ 145 326 423	+ 23.12	1 040 216 875	2.78	773 982 673	2.14
26.12	− 6	+ 5.58	+ 1 913 298	+ 10.18	18 515 196	0.05	20 699 548	0.06
39.51	− 23	+ 12.58	+ 11 316 500	+ 17.36	84 490 000	0.23	76 800 000	0.22
100	− 35	+ 100.00	+ 500 000	+ 100.00	2 000 000	0.01	500 000	0.00
28.49	− 164	+ 38.13	+ 198 829 075	+ 26.20	1 267 024 715	3.44	957 630 075	2.66
		+ 5.32	+ 65 940 000	+ 5.32	759 920 000	2.03	759 920 000	2.10
2.59	− 39	− 26.68	− 549 678 572	− 26.68	1 289 161 034	3.44	1 289 161 034	3.56
					819 916 654	2.19	819 916 654	2.27
92.94	− 30	+ 21.50	− 88 964 480	− 1 779.29	− 176 180 158	− 0.48	− 83 961 480	− 0.23
3.60	− 69	− 16.32	− 572 703 052	− 17.33	2 692 817 530	7.19	2 785 033 208	7.70
					p.m.	0	p.m.	0
18.18	− 92	− 26.78	+ 44 322 900	+ 8.01	511 500 000	1.37	572 600 000	1.58
31.81	− 64	− 26.27	+ 60 524 750	+ 27.08	219 555 894	0.59	283 900 000	0.78
19.33	− 27	+ 26.11	+ 34 997 187	+ 39.22	149 732 237	0.40	124 232 237	0.34
32.13	− 7	+ 76.40	− 83 049 122	− 34.89	141 671 667	0.38	54 986 678	0.15
10.07	− 7	+ 8.27	+ 5 580 789	+ 8.27	73 200 789	0.20	73 200 789	0.20
23.22	− 197	− 13.17	+ 62 376 504	+ 5.32	1 097 660 587	2.93	1 108 919 704	3.07
2.93	− 34	+ 8.50	+ 89 114 172	+ 8.50	1 119 307 097	2.99	1 119 307 097	3.09
2.93	+ 17	+ 11.79	+ 65 477 696	+ 11.79	620 744 584	1.66	620 744 584	1.72
0.93	− 16	+ 9.64	+ 154 591 868	+ 9.64	1 740 051 681	4.65	1 740 051 681	4.81
2.89	− 730	+ 3.78	+ 1 139 299 472	+ 3.24	37 452 818 172	100	36 168 355 390	100

| | 2 | | | | 3 | | | |
| | Preliminary draft 1988[2] | | | | Change (2-1) | | | |
%	Commitments	%	Payments	%	Commitments	%	Payments	%
63.48	27 045 000 000	66.07	27 045 000 000	68.11	+ 4 084 200 000	+ 17.79	+ 4 084 200 000	+ 17.79
63.48	27 045 000 000	66.07	27 045 000 000	68.11	+4 084 200 000	+ 17.79	4 084 200 000	+ 17.79
2.45	1 085 000 000	2.65	1 106 900 000	2.79	+ 67 845 839	+ 6.67	+ 219 774 657	+ 24.77
0.16	87 030 000	0.21	66 370 000	0.17	+ 27 808 230	+ 46.96	+ 10 295 230	+ 18.36
0.55	305 390 000	0.75	247 870 000	0.62	+ 62 096 322	+ 25.52	+ 50 576 322	+ 25.64
6.90	3 540 000 000	8.65	2 932 000 000	7.38	+ 198 067 808	+ 5.93	+ 434 705 243	+ 17.41
0.49	144 000 000	0.35	96 000 000	0.24	− 45 763 518	− 24.12	− 81 628 703	− 45.95
0.10	31 270 000	0.08	22 000 000	0.06	+ 973 358	+ 3.21	− 14 203 068	− 39.23
0.07	5 110 000	0.01	60 110 000	0.15	− 8 096 160	− 61.31	+ 33 042 426	+ 122.07
7.03	2 754 640 000	6.73	2 543 000 000	6.40	+ 152 150 322	+ 5.85	+ 744 351	+ 0.03
0.19	92 334 000	0.23	90 434 000	0.23	+ 22 459 780	+ 32.14	+ 22 293 460	+ 32.72
0.25	92 456 000	0.23	92 456 000	0.23	− 2 523 132	− 2.66	− 2 523 132	− 2.66
0.09	42 499 200	0.10	41 849 200	0.11	+ 10 246 692	+ 31.77	+ 9 991 692	+ 31.36
18.29	8 179 729 200	19.98	7 298 989 200	18.38	+ 485 265 541	+ 6.31	+ 683 068 478	+ 10.32
0.24	129 200 000	0.32	110 200 000	0.28	+ 7 397 356	+ 6.07	+ 24 552 146	+ 28.67
2.14	1 050 000 000	2.57	920 000 000	2.32	+ 9 783 125	+ 0.94	+ 146 017 327	+ 18.87
0.06	26 000 000	0.06	25 000 000	0.06	+ 7 484 804	+ 40.43	+ 4 300 452	+ 20.78
0.22	98 940 000	0.24	77 450 000	0.20	+ 14 450 000	+ 17.10	+ 650 000	+ 0.85
0.00	14 000 000	0.03	14 000 000	0.04	+ 12 000 000	+ 600.00	+ 13 500 000	+2 700.00
2.66	1 318 140 000	3.22	1 146 650 000	2.89	+ 51 115 285	+ 4.03	+ 189 019 925	+ 19.74
2.10	p.m.	—	p.m.	—	− 759 920 000	—	− 759 920 000	—
3.56	1 392 290 913	3.40	1 392 290 913	3.51	+ 103 129 879	+ 8.00	+ 103 129 879	+ 8.00
2.27	p.m.	—	p.m.	—	− 819 916 654	—	− 819 916 654	—
−0.23	5 000 000	0.01	5 000 000	0.01	+ 181 180 158	—	+ 88 964 480	—
7.70	1 397 290 913	3.41	1 397 290 913	3.52	−1 295 526 617	− 48.11	−1 387 742 295	− 49.83
—	p.m.	—	p.m.	—	—	—	—	—
1.58	421 800 000	1.03	370 400 000	0.93	− 89 700 000	− 17.54	− 202 200 000	− 35.31
0.80	27 350 000	0.72	245 050 000	0.63	+ 72 794 106	+ 33.16	− 38 850 000	− 13.68
0.34	144 425 000	0.35	140 425 000	0.35	− 5 307 237	− 3.54	+ 16 192 763	+ 13.03
0.15	143 500 000	0.35	73 000 000	0.18	− 171 667	− 0.12	+ 18 013 322	+ 32.76
0.20	82 986 000	0.08	82 986 000	0.08	+ 9 785 211	+ 13.37	+ 9 785 211	+ 13.37
3.07	1 085 061 000	2.53	911 881 000	2.17	− 12 599 587	− 1.15	− 197 058 704	− 17.77
3.09	1 241 471 701	3.16	1 231 474 701	3.25	+ 122 164 604	+ 10.91	+ 122 164 604	+ 10.91
1.72	666 679 683	1.63	666 670 683	1.63	+ 45 935 099	+ 7.40	+ 45 935 099	+ 7.40
4.81	1 908 151 384	4.79	1 908 151 384	4.93	+ 168 099 703	+ 9.66	+ 168 099 703	+ 9.66
100	40 933 372 497	100	39 707 932 497	100	+3 480 554 325	+ 9.29	+3 539 587 107	+ 9.79

78.   The increases in non-compulsory expenditure correspond to the maximum rate of increase for 1988. In absolute terms, the structural Funds account for a substantial proportion of the planned increases.

Five-year financial perspective 1988-92

79.   In its report on the financing of the Community budget [1] the Commission published a five-year financial perspective 1988-92. [2] These forecasts—made at constant prices—may be summed up as follows: the growth in EAGGF guarantee expenditure within the limits of the financial guideline, the doubling of structural Fund appropriations in real terms, the promotion of research and other essential Community policies, the inclusion of the seventh European Development Fund in the budget in 1990-91, the introduction of new policies and the measures for the correction of budgetary imbalances should require an increase in commitment appropriations of around 5.8% a year in real terms. The structure of the budget would consequently change to leave EAGGF guarantee expenditure accounting for slightly more than 50% of total appropriations, with almost 25% for structural operations and 3% for research. The total appropriations for payments required would increase by an average 4.8% a year. The own resources available under the current 1.4% VAT limit would cover only about 75% of the appropriations needed in 1992. However, resources within the new limit of 1.4% of gross national product proposed by the Commission would be sufficient in 1992 and give a safety margin of around 10% of the budget. The actual rate of utilization would increase from around 1.16% of GNP in 1987 to 1.28% in 1992. In letters to the Presidents of the Council and Parliament, the Commission asked the budgetary authority to examine this perspective and establish the contacts needed to reach an interinstitutional agreement on appropriate financial programming for 1988-92. It has already used the perspective as a basis for its preliminary draft budget for 1988. The perspective was examined by the Economic Policy Committee on 25 June [3] and 8 July. [4]

The details of the expenditure and revenue forecasts for the five-year period are contained in Table 4.

[1]   Bull. EC 2-1987, points 1.1.12 *et seq* and 2.3.1.
[2]   Bull. EC 3-1987, point 2.3.1.
[3]   Bull. EC 6-1987, point 2.1.6.
[4]   Bull. EC 7/8-1987, point 2.1.7.

TABLE 4

Expenditure and resources 1987-92

million ECU

	At 1987 prices						Average growth rate (%)
	1987	1988	1989	1990	1991	1992	1992-1987
1. Appropriations for commitments	42 910	44 970	47 420	49 920	53 060	56 740	5.8
2. Appropriations for payments	41 740	43 360	45 370	47 110	49 640	52 710	4.8
3. 1% GNP	36 100	37 060	38 050	39 060	40 100	41 170	2.7
4. Resources within 1.4% GNP	50 550	51 900	53 250	54 700	56 150	57 650	2.7
5. GNP rate in (2: 3)	1.16	1.17	1.19	1.21	1.24	1.28	
6. Margin (4-2)	8 810	8 540	7 880	7 590	6 510	4 940	

Budget procedure

80.   The Council was unable to adopt a draft 1988 budget at its meetings in July [1] and September. [2] A further meeting was arranged for 1 October in the hope of reaching a decision by 5 October. [3] Despite the 10 or so compromises put forward by the Presidency, the Council meeting again ended in deadlock. The Commission upheld and defended its preliminary draft throughout the discussions, which focused mainly on the new own resources system. For the first time, the 5 October deadline laid down in Article 203 of the EEC Treaty for the adoption of the draft budget was not respected. In view of the Council's failure, the Commission [4] and Parliament [5] decided to initiate the preliminary stage of the procedure provided in Article 175 of the EEC Treaty.

81.   The 1988 budget and the future financing of the Community were the main items on the agenda of the European Council meeting in Copenhagen on 4 and 5 December. Not enough common ground was found for decisions to be adopted. The main differences concerned the growth of agricultural expenditure and the new own resources arrangements. Despite an ultimate attempt by the Council on 9 and 10 December, no draft budget was established before the end of the year, and the provisional-twelfths arrangements will operate at the start

[1]   Bull. EC 7/8-1987, point 2.3.3.
[2]   Bull. EC 9-1987, point 2.3.1.
[3]   Bull. EC 10-1987, point 2.3.1.
[4]   Bull. EC 10-1987, points 2.3.2 and 2.4.5.
[5]   OJ C 305, 16.11.1987; Bull. EC 10-1987, points 2.3.3, 2.4.5 and 2.4.12.

of 1988.[1] Parliament and the Commission decided to pursue the procedure against the Council for failure to act and to seek a ruling from the Court of Justice that the Council had failed to fulfil its obligations in the budgetary field.

ECSC budget

82. On 21 July, after taking note of Parliament's opinion[2] and the discussion within the ECSC Consultative Committee, the Commission adopted and published the amending ECSC operating budget for 1987.[3] This budget increases investment interest by 126 million ECU and redeployment aid by 74 million ECU and reduces the amount earmarked for social measures in connection with the restructuring of the steel industry by 90 million ECU.[4]

83. After obtaining Parliament's opinion[5] and informing the ECSC Consultative Committee, the Commission decided on 21 December to maintain the levy rate for 1988 at 0.31% and adopted the ECSC operating budget for 1988 on this basis.[6] Given the ordinary resources expected (levies, net balance from the previous financial year, fines, commitments cancelled, etc.)—estimated at 289 million ECU—and extraordinary resources of 50 million ECU, this should provide full cover for the ECSC's requirements of 339 million ECU for its operating budget. The breakdown of requirements is as follows (in million ECU):

Administrative expenditure	5
Redeployment aid	180
Research subsidies	63
Interest subsidies	47
Measures in connection with the restructuring of the steel industry	44

Implementation of the steel industry restructuring measures depends on the Council agreeing to provide the extraordinary revenue by means of a transfer from the general budget to the ECSC budget.

---

[1] Bull. EC 12-1987.
[2] OJ C 246, 14.9.1987; Bull. EC 7/8-1987, point 2.3.6.
[3] OJ C 207, 4.8.1987; Bull. EC 7/8-1987, point 2.3.6.
[4] Points 278 and 410 of this Report.
[5] OJ C 345, 21.12.1987; Bull. EC 11-1987, points 2.3.7 and 2.4.18.
[6] OJ L 361, 22.12.1987.

Own resources

1987 financial year

84. The VAT rate set in the 1987 budget was 1.3643% for nine Member States, 1.3102% for the Federal Republic of Germany and 0.7982% for the United Kingdom. Portugal is exempted temporarily from applying the common VAT system and therefore paid a financial contribution determined on the basis of the proportion of its GNP to the total GNP of the Member States.

85. The supplementary and amending budget adopted on 17 July [1] made the following changes to the revenue side: the estimate of traditional own resources was reduced by 1 459.9 million ECU because of the decline in the dollar exchange rate; the negative balance of 819.9 million ECU from the 1986 budget was taken into account; the VAT rate was raised to its 1.4% ceiling for nine Member States, 1.3459% for Germany and 0.8339% for the United Kingdom. In addition, 400 million ECU for the cost of collecting own resources in 1987 was deferred to 1988.

86. Actual revenue for the year is shown in Table 5.

TABLE 5

Budget revenue

million ECU

	1987 outturn	1988 estimates
Agricultural levies	1 626.1	1 508.8
Sugar and isoglucose levies	1 471.8	1 753.1
Customs duties	8 936.5	8 993.3
VAT own resources	23 427.4	17 628.6
Own resources from additional base	—	12 260.6
Financial contributions (GNP)	210.6	262.5
Balance of VAT own resources from previous financial years and adjustments to financial contributions	125.2	p.m.
Miscellaneous revenue	403.8	254.2
Total	36 201.4	42 661.1

---

[1]   Point 72 of this Report.

1988 financial year

87.   The Commission's proposal is that 1988 will be the first year of application of the revised financing arrangements for the general budget. The differences compared with the present system are as follows:

 (i) the VAT rate is a fixed 1%, whereas the present system provides for a rate up to a maximum of 1.4%;

 (ii) a new resource will be introduced: the base will be the differences between Member States' gross national product and their VAT bases;

(iii) the maximum own resources available will be the equivalent of 1.2% of Community GNP, or 46 394.4 million ECU.

The revenue estimates in the preliminary draft budget, including the letter of amendment, are shown in Table 5. They are the equivalent of 1.16% of Community GNP.

However, pending the decision on the new own resources system, the present system will continue to apply. The Member States will then have to make a non-repayable advance of 8 495.5 million ECU to finance the preliminary draft.

At all events, until the final adoption of the 1988 budget, the Member States will continue to pay VAT own resources on the basis of supplementary and amending budget No 1/87. [1]

Future financing of the Community budget

88.   In its communication of 15 February 'The Single Act: A new frontier for Europe' the Commission proposed a new own resources system for the Community. [2]

Convergence and correction of budgetary imbalances

89.   The 1987 budget adopted on 19 February [1] and supplementary and amending budget No 1/87 adopted on 17 July [1] included a rebate of 1 633 million ECU to the United Kingdom to correct the imbalance in its budgetary position. This amount was granted and financed by modulation of the VAT

---

[1]   Point 72 of this Report.
[2]   Point 67 of this Report.

rates in accordance with Article 3 of the Council Decision of 7 May 1985 on the system of own resources. [1]

90.   The preliminary draft budget for 1988 provided for a correction of 2 269 million ECU for the United Kingdom for 1987 and a further 244 million ECU for 1986. [2]

91.   The following table shows the percentage of VAT used to correct budgetary imbalances since 1981:

1981	1982	1983	1984	1985	1986[1]	1987	1988
0.117	0.125	0.120	0.082	0.098	0.149	0.127[2]	0.187[3]

[1] Estimate.
[2] Excluding additional payment in 1988 (0.018).
[3] Including 0.018 for 1986.

92.   In its report to the Council and Parliament on the financing of the Community budget, [3] the Commission proposed a reform of the mechanism for the correction of budgetary imbalances. Its proposal is that the United Kingdom's imbalance would in future be corrected by a package of measures involving both revenue and expenditure. On the revenue side, the adoption of the 'fourth resource' (additional payment based on the difference between 1% of GNP and 1% of VAT) would reduce the United Kingdom's deficit, since its share of this resource is lower than its VAT share. As it is intended that this fourth resource should provide a steadily growing proportion of Community finance, this relief element would increase. On the expenditure side, the United Kingdom would benefit from the development of measures for economic and social cohesion, the promotion of new policies and a compensation mechanism based on EAGGF guarantee.

Budgetary discipline

93.   On 15 June the Council determined the 1988 reference framework. [4] The figures required to establish the framework had been sent by the Commission on 13 April [5] in accordance with the Council's conclusions of 4 December 1984 on budgetary discipline. [6]

[1]   OJ L 128, 14.5.1985; Nineteenth General Report, point 99.
[2]   Points 74 to 78 of this Report.
[3]   Points 67 and 68 of this Report.
[4]   Bull. EC 6-1987, point 2.3.6.
[5]   Bull. EC 4-1987, point 2.3.4.
[6]   Eighteenth General Report, point 82.

million ECU

	Commitments	Payments
EAGGF guarantee (maximum expenditure)	22 757	22 757
Other compulsory expenditure	4 030	3 973
Non-compulsory expenditure	11 035	9 910
Total	37 822	36 640

In accordance with these conclusions, the Council had asked for a meeting with Parliament before fixing the reference framework. As in 1987, however, Parliament did not consider such a meeting appropriate in the absence of an agreement on the general objectives of budgetary discipline.

Budgetary powers

Discharge procedure for 1986 and 1987

94. In June the Commission sent the institutions concerned — in an annex to the revenue and expenditure account and balance sheet — its final report [1] on the action taken in response to Parliament's observations in the resolution accompanying the discharge decision in respect of the 1984 budget. [2]

95. On 7 April Parliament adopted two resolutions, [3] one on action taken by the Commission in response to its comments accompanying the decision granting a discharge in respect of the implementation of the 1984 budget, [2] the second informing the Commission of the reasons why it cannot at present be given a discharge in respect of the implementation of the budget for the financial year 1985. On the same day it adopted a number of discharge decisions in respect of the implementation of budgets for 1985; [4] they included discharges to the Management Board of the European Centre for the Development of Vocational Training (Berlin) and the Administrative Board of the European Foundation for the Improvement of Living and Working Conditions (Dublin). Parliament's decision on the discharge in respect of the financial management of the second, third, fourth and fifth European Development Funds during the

---

[1]   Bull. EC 6-1987, point 2.3.7.
[2]   OJ L 150, 4.6.1986; OJ C 120, 20.5.1986; Twentieth General Report, point 104.
[3]   OJ C 125, 11.5.1987; Bull. EC 4-1987, point 2.4.17.
[4]   OJ L 137, 27.5.1987; Bull. EC 4-1987, point 2.3.7.

1985 financial year[1] was accompanied by a resolution[2] containing various comments designed to improve financial management and reiterating its desire to see the EDF entered in the budget by 1990.

96.   On 29 October Parliament adopted a further resolution on action taken by the Commission in response to the comments made in the resolution accompanying the decision granting a discharge in respect of the implementation of the 1984 budget.[3]

On 23 July the Commission sent to the Council and the Court of Auditors for information a communication[4] which it had addressed to Parliament on the action it had taken in response to Parliament's resolution of 7 April deferring the discharge in respect of 1985.[2]

The Commission sent its replies to the Court of Auditors' comments on the 1986 financial year to the Court in October.[5]

Changes to Financial Regulations

97.   On 7 October the Commission sent the Council the third amendment[6] to its proposal of December 1980[7] amending the Financial Regulation of 21 December 1977 applicable to the budget of the Communities.[8] This proposal represents a further adaptation of the proposal of 15 March 1984[9] and supplements the second amendment which the Commission, in accordance with the general guidelines agreed by the Brussels European Council of 29 and 30 June,[10] proposed to the Council on 29 July.[11]

These amendments are the key to action on budgetary reform, discipline and management. They incorporate into the rules the measures proposed by the Commission in 'The Single Act: A new frontier for Europe'[12] and in its report to the Council and to Parliament on the financing of the Community budget.[13]

---

[1]   OJ L 137, 27.5.1987; Bull. EC 4-1987, point 2.3.8.
[2]   OJ L 125, 11.5.1987; Bull. EC 4-1987, point 2.4.17.
[3]   OJ C 318, 30.11.1987; Bull. EC 10-1987, point 2.4.20.
[4]   Bull. EC 7/8-1987, point 2.3.8.
[5]   Bull. EC 10-1987, point 2.3.6.
[6]   OJ C 313, 25.11.1987; Bull. EC 10-1987, point 2.3.8.
[7]   OJ C 119, 21.5.1981.
[8]   OJ L 356, 31.12.1977; Eleventh General Report, points 62 to 64.
[9]   OJ C 97, 9.4.1984; Eighteenth General Report, point 85.
[10]   Bull. EC 6-1987, point 1.1.5.
[11]   OJ C 278, 16.10.1987; Bull. EC 7/8-1987, point 1.1.10.
[12]   Point 67 of this Report.
[13]   Point 79 of this Report.

The main aspects are as follows: more transparent presentation of interinstitutional appropriations; introduction of a specific overall reserve as the corollary to the stricter approach to determining the amount of appropriations; reinforcement of the principle of annuality; amendment of the special provisions for the EAGGF Guarantee Section to permit the application of agricultural stabilizers; application of the principle of annuality and transparency to research programmes; extension of the role of the ECU.

98.   On 23 October the Commission also sent the Council a proposal for a Regulation [1] amending temporarily the Financial Regulation of 21 December 1977 [2] in line with the amendment of the Regulation of 21 April 1970 on the financing of the common agricultural policy [3] which was adopted by the Council on 19 October and which set up until 30 October 1988 a mechanism of 'advances against amounts booked in the accounts'. [4]

Internal financial control

99.   On 18 August the Commission adopted draft decisions on the clearance of the EAGGF guarantee accounts for 1984 and 1985, [5] thus achieving the objective which it had set itself in July 1985 [6] to make up the accumulated backlog in its control activities in two years. On 21 October it amended these decisions to incorporate five cases which had been excluded; [7] the milk quotas for the Federal Republic of Germany, Italy, the Netherlands and Denmark and the consumption aid for olive oil in Italy must still be cleared for 1984 and 1985. Financial Control ensured that the speeding up of these activities did not affect their quality.

100.   Financial Control continued to introduce new methods to improve the systems of control for the structural Funds, research and administrative expenditure. The technological changes in progress will permit the gradual introduction of a computerized approval procedure on the basis of the current experiment at Ispra.

---

[1]   OJ C 298, 7.11.1987; Bull. EC 10-1987, point 2.3.9.
[2]   OJ L 356, 31.12.1977; Eleventh General Report, points 62 to 64.
[3]   OJ L 94, 28.4.1970.
[4]   Point 584 of this Report.
[5]   OJ L 262, 12.9.1987; Bull. EC 7/8-1987, point 2.1.230.
[6]   Nineteenth General Report, point 114.
[7]   OJ L 324, 14.11.1987; Bull. EC 10-1987, point 2.1.171.

101.   In liaison with the Directorates-General which administer the Funds and with the active support of Parliament, Financial Control has also stepped up its training schemes for national controllers by organizing conferences in Greece and Portugal.

102.   In a move to combat fraud affecting the Community budget, the Commission decided on 14 October to set up a central unit under the direct responsibility of the President to coordinate the departmental teams dealing with fraud. [1]

Borrowing and lending operations

103.   Table 6 shows the loans granted each year from 1985 to 1987.

TABLE 6

Loans granted

million ECU

	1985	1986	1987[5]
New Community Instrument[1]	883.7[1]	393.0	447.0[4]
EEC balance-of-payments loans[1]	—	865.0	859.9
ECSC[2]	1 010.5	1 069.2	969.3
Euratom[1]	211.0	443.2	313.7
EIB (from the Bank's own resources)[3]	6 225.0	7 059.9	7 192.3
of which: loans to ACP countries and overseas territories	(167.8)	(150.7)	(161.2)
loans to Mediterranean countries[2]	(416.5)	(231.1)	(27.7)
Total	8 330.2	9 830.3	(9 782.2)

[1] With guarantee from the general budget.
[2] With guarantee from the general budget for 75% of the sums lent, including Spain and Portugal in 1985.
[3] Not covered by the guarantee from the general budget.
[4] See Table 7.
[5] ECU rate at 31 December 1987.

Borrowing operations during the year totalled 3 811.5 million ECU, including 86.1 million ECU from the EIB to refinance earlier operations (as against 541.4 million ECU in 1986).

[1]   Bull. EC 10-1987, point 2.3.10.

Operations concerning the New Community Instrument

New Community Instrument

104.   On 9 March the Council adopted the Decision allowing operations to continue under the New Community Instrument.[1]

105.   On 23 December the Commission sent the Council a proposal[2] for amending this Decision to enable it to provide the additional loans requested by the Greek authorities for the regions hit by the earthquake in September 1986.

106.   NCI loans[3] totalling 447 million ECU were signed in 1987. The loans were granted to promote Community investment, mainly by small and medium-sized firms (86.6%), but also for energy projects (4.9%) and infrastructure (8.5%). Since 1979, loans totalling 5 910.5 million ECU have been made under this instrument (see Table 7).

TABLE 7

NCI loans in 1987 and totals 1979-87

million ECU

	Operations in 1987			Total NCI 1979-87
	Loans without interest subsidy	Loans with interest subsidy[1]	Total	
Denmark	31.8		31.8	502.1
Greece	4.6		4.6	306.1
Spain	113.7		113.7	183.0
France	76.8		76.8	1 143.4
Ireland	—		—	424.0
Italy	174.8	21.4	196.2	2 964.0
Portugal	9.9		9.9	39.8
United Kingdom	14.0		14.0	347.2
Total	425.6	21.4	447.0	5 910.5

[1]   Council Decision 81/19/EEC of 20 January 1981 concerning the earthquake in Italy.

[1]   Point 141 of this Report.
[2]   Bull. EC 12-1987.
[3]   OJ L 112, 28.4.1983; Seventeenth General Report, points 104 and 142.

Interest subsidies on certain NCI and EIB loans for the reconstruction of regions struck by earthquake in Italy and Greece [1]

107.   Subsidized loans totalling 48.2 million ECU were granted to Italy in 1987 in accordance with the Council Decision of January 1981. Loans of this type granted since 1981 now total 975.5 million ECU (See Table 8).

The interest subsidies on outstanding loans continued to be paid on the annual due dates. They amounted to 26.6 million ECU for Italy and 2 million ECU for Greece.

TABLE 8

Loans with interest subsidies to Italy for the reconstruction of regions affected by earthquakes — 1987

	Loans signed					Subsidies paid[1]	
	Situation at 1.1.1987 (million ECU)	Operations in 1987	Situation at 31.12.1987			Amount (million ECU)	%
			Number	Amount (million ECU)	%		
NCI	611.5	21.4	15	632.9	64.9	17.8	66.9
EIB	315.8	26.8	28	342.6	35.1	8.8	33.1
Total	927.3	48.2	43	975.5	100.0	26.6	100.0

[1]   Interest subsidies of 3% per year for up to 12 years. These amounts cover all loans signed since 1981.

EEC balance-of-payments loans

108.   Following the Council Decision of 9 December 1985 [2] to grant a Community loan of 1 750 million ECU to Greece in two instalments under the Regulation of 16 March 1981 concerning the Community loan mechanism

[1]   OJ L 37, 10.2.1981; OJ L 367, 23.12.1981. For the application of interest subsidies, see the annual reports from the Commission to the Council and Parliament on borrowing and lending activities. Latest report: 1986 (Bull. EC 9-1987, point 2.1.3).
[2]   OJ L 341, 19.12.1985; Nineteenth General Report, point 158.

designed to support the balances of payments of Member States,[1] the Commission decided to pay the second instalment of the loan and raised the corresponding equivalent of 859.9 million ECU on the capital markets in January[2] and February.[3]

Financing ECSC activities

109. In 1987 the Community continued to support coal and steel industry investment through ECSC financial loans totalling 412.8 million ECU.

ECSC loans paid out in 1987 totalled 969.3 million ECU, 99.9 million ECU less than the 1 069.2 million ECU in 1986.

Loans for the steel industry fell from 663 million ECU in 1986 to 129.6 million ECU in 1987. Funds for the coal industry totalled 283.2 million ECU and loans to promote consumption of Community steel under the second paragraph of Article 54 of the ECSC Treaty,[4] totalled 60.7 million ECU.

Low-interest loans were provided for conversion investments consistent with the priority objective of job creation conversion in areas affected by the restructuring of the steel industry and for promotion of coal utilization. Loans for workers' housing were given at the extremely favourable rate of 1% per year.

Loans granted in 1987 totalled 969.3 million ECU. They break down as follows: 639.7 million ECU for industrial projects (799.5 million ECU in 1986), 304.3 million ECU for conversion programmes (243.5 million ECU in 1986) and 25.3 million ECU for workers' housing (26.2 million ECU in 1986).

110. The ECSC continued to look to the capital market for funds, raising a total of 1 487 million ECU, including 348.6 million ECU to refinance earlier operations (compared with 1 517.4 million ECU in 1986, including 710.2 million ECU to refinance earlier operations).

---

[1]   OJ L 73, 19.3.1981; Fifteenth General Report, point 125.
[2]   Bull. EC 1-1987, 2.3.11.
[3]   Bull. EC 2-1987, 2.3.11.
[4]   OJ C 121, 17.5.1985.

Financing Euratom activities

111. The Commission continued its lending operations on behalf of Euratom under the Council Decision of December 1985 [1] which increased to 3 000 million ECU the total amount which the Commission is authorized to raise to finance investment in nuclear power stations and the enrichment of fissile materials.

112. At 31 December loans made during the year (at rates obtaining at end of year) totalled 313.7 million ECU (compared with 443.2 million ECU in 1986). This year's loans went to five firms.

The grand total since such operations began in 1977 is now 2 753.1 million ECU (at the rates obtaining when contracts were signed).

Euratom raised a total of 853.4 million ECU in 1987, including 307.8 million ECU to refinance earlier operations (compared with 488.2 million ECU in 1986, including 292 million ECU to refinance earlier operations).

European Investment Bank

113. Since the activities of the European Investment Bank — an autonomous Community institution — in 1987 are described in its annual report, only the main figures are set out here. [2]

Financing operations by the Bank both inside and outside the Community amounted to 7 192.2 million ECU from its own resources and 650.3 million ECU from resources supplied by the Community, a total of 7 842.5 million ECU in 1987 compared with 7 544.8 million ECU in 1986.

---

[1]   OJ L 334, 12.12.1985; Nineteenth General Report, point 123.
[2]   Copies of the report and of other publications relating to the Bank's work and its operations can be obtained from the main office (110 boulevard Konrad Adenauer, L-2950 Luxembourg, tel. 43791) or from its offices in Belgium (rue de la Loi 277, B-1040 Brussels, tel. 230 98 90), Italy (Via Sardegna 38, I-00187 Rome, tel. 47191), the United Kingdom (68 Pall Mall, London SW1Y 5ES, tel. 839 3351), Greece (Ypsilantou Odos 13-15, Kolonaki, 10675 Athens, tel. 724 98 11/12/13) and Portugal (144-156 Avenida de Liberdade, 8°, P-1200 Lisbon, tel. 32 89 89).

TABLE 9

EIB loans in the Community in 1987

	From own resources (million ECU)	From NCI resources (million ECU)	Total	
			million ECU	%
Belgium	37.1	—	37.1	0.5
Denmark	283.5	31.8	315.3	4.2
Germany (FR)	276.5	—	276.5	3.7
Spain	593.7	113.7	707.4	9.5
Greece	160.2	4.6	164.8	2.2
France	929.8	76.8	1 006.5	13.5
Ireland	178.6	—	178.6	2.4
Italy	2 916.0	196.2	3 112.2	41.8
Luxembourg	1.6	—	1.6	—
Netherlands	18.0	—	18.0	0.2
Portugal	380.0	9.9	389.9	5.2
United Kingdom	1 119.8	14.0	1 133.7	15.2
Miscellaneous (Article 18)	108.7		108.7	1.5
Community	7 003.4	447.0	7 450.4	100.0

The loans granted for projects in the Community totalled 7 450.4 million ECU (95% of all financing operations): 7 003.4 million ECU came from the Bank's own resources and 447 million ECU from NCI resources. [1] The total in 1986 was 7 071.1 million ECU. The breakdown by country is shown in Table 9.

Loans for regional development projects account for 58% of all loans in the Community and for 62% of the aid from the Bank's own resources, illustrating the priority given by the Bank to this objective and confirmed in the Single Act. Operations designed to serve the Community's energy objectives (2 226.8 million ECU) dropped somewhat, but loans for infrastructure projects of Community interest [2] (680.8 million ECU) again increased, while loans for environmental protection rose from 701.7 million ECU to 1 572.9 million ECU.

Aid to industry also increased appreciably: individual loans totalled 937 million ECU, including 474.1 million ECU for projects introducing or developing advanced technologies. A further 1 619 million ECU was granted in the form

---

[1] Point 106 of this Report.
[2] The credit agreement for the Channel Tunnel (FF 10 000 million or UKL 1 000 million) did not give rise to any loans in 1987 and is not included in this figure.

of global loans to intermediaries, including 387 million from NCI resources; some 2 869 credits totalling around 1 014 million ECU were onlent to small and medium-sized businesses from global loans.

114. Operations outside the Community totalled 392.1 million ECU, as against 473.7 million ECU in 1986, of which 188.8 million ECU was from the Bank's own resources. Because of delays in the negotiation and application of new protocols with Mediterranean countries, loans of only 42.8 million ECU could be granted from the amounts still available under the existing protocols. In the ACP countries, by contrast, with the gradual implementation of the third Lomé Convention, 161.2 million ECU was lent from the Bank's own resources and 188.2 million ECU in risk capital from budget funds.

115. The Bank obtained the funds it required for lending operations from its own resources by raising a total of 5 592.7 million ECU on the international capital markets or on the national markets of certain member and non-member countries. Most of this amount was collected in the form of public issues and private placings at fixed rates.

General budget guarantee for borrowing and lending operations

116. The guarantee by the Community budget can cover both borrowings and lendings. [1] For borrowings the Community provides the budget guarantee to its own lenders when floating an issue under one of its financial instruments — balance-of-payments facility, Euratom loans, New Community Instrument. For loans granted, the guarantee is given to the European Investment Bank for the loans it makes from its own resources under the Mediterranean protocols.

In 1987 authorized borrowing and lending operations guaranteed by the general budget totalled 20 130 million ECU; at 31 December the guarantee was in operation for 9 977 million ECU of Community borrowings and for loans of 2 218.9 million ECU granted out of the EIB's own resources.

At 31 December the commitments in interest and capital covered by the budget guarantee for 1987 totalled 2 248 million ECU (including 1 030 million ECU in interest).

---

[1]   The role of the Community's budget guarantee and the—very slight—risk involved are described in the Nineteenth General Report, point 131.

Aid to Portugal

117.   On 30 October the Commission signed contracts with seven Portuguese financial institutions for providing interest subsidies on bank loans to small and medium-sized businesses in order to promote employment.[1] This pilot scheme, for which a specific heading has been set aside in the Community budget[2] at Parliament's request, is a precursor to the co-financing of the regional aid scheme for Portugal.

---

[1]   Bull. EC 10-1987, point 2.3.20.
[2]   Bull. EC 6-1987, point 2.1.16.

Chapter II

Building the Community

Section 1

Economic and monetary policy

Main developments

118.   *The main features of the international economy in 1987 were persistent current account imbalances between the major industrialized countries and growing indebtedness in the developing countries. Closer international cooperation after the Louvre agreement in February led to some success in stabilizing dollar exchange rates, but from mid-October the dollar began to depreciate once more and financial and capital markets were affected by serious disturbances.*

Growth in the Community remained weak, at all events inadequate to bring down the level of unemployment, which is the Community's worst problem. To attain its objective of reinforcing internal growth, the Commission has been pressing for determined application of the cooperative Community strategy for more employment-creating growth [1] through improved coordination of budgetary and monetary policies, the speeding up of completion of the large internal market and the strengthening of economic and social cohesion in the Community.

On several occasions the two sides of industry, expressing their views in the context of the social dialogue conducted at Community level at the Commission's invitation,[2] reaffirmed their support for this strategy.

---

[1]   OJ L 377, 31.12.1985; Nineteenth General Report, points 133 and 134.
[2]   Point 63 of this Report.

Priority activities and objectives

Strengthening the EMS

119.   As requested by the Community's Finance Ministers on 12 January, [1] the Monetary Committee and the Committee of Central Bank Governors made useful suggestions for strengthening the operating mechanisms of the European Monetary System, which were subsequently endorsed by the Ministers for Economic and Financial Affairs at their informal meeting in Nyborg on 12 September. [2]

120.   To ensure better coherence and compatibility not only between the various economic policy tools used by the Member States but also between actual performances, the medium-term surveillance procedure has been reinforced. The procedure is based on a set of macroeconomic indicators which have been defined for the particular needs of managing the EMS, but are complementary to those which it has been agreed to use at international level.

121.   With the increased mobility of capital, any strains developing in the EMS must be dealt with rapidly. Thus, while the basis for cooperation will still be a broad consensus on the thrust of monetary policy, the main focus will henceforth be on very short-term management of exchange rates, where a close surveillance procedure has also been introduced.

This pragmatic approach, which does not require any institutional changes to the system, is accompanied by some adjustments to the EMS mechanisms, especially those relating to very short-term financing, acceptance of the ECU and intramarginal intervention.

The economic situation

122.   In a world economic environment where imbalances continue to give cause for concern, economic growth in the Community in 1987 was lower than forecast in the latest annual economic report. [3] For the Community as a whole, GDP growth is unlikely to exceed 2% in real terms, compared with 2.6% in 1986. The main causes of this output trend are the weakness of exports (external

---

[1]   Bull. EC 1-1987, point 2.1.1.
[2]   Bull. EC 9-1987, point 1.3.1 *et seq.*
[3]   OJ L 385, 31.12.1986; Twentieth General Report, points 129 and 130.

demand having slowed down more than expected) and the downward revision of firms' investment plans (exchange-rate movements having damaged the price competitiveness of European manufacturers). Moreover, private consumption did not perform quite as well as expected.

123.   Inflation continued to slow down, in particular in the countries where it was still high, bringing greater convergence in this field; the increase in consumer prices was only marginally above 3% in 1987, compared with 3.7% in 1986.

124.   In 1987 the rise in unemployment was checked for the first time thanks to the employment growth recorded since 1985. But unemployment is still about 12% and remains the Community's most serious problem.

125.   In 1987 money supply growth accelerated, probably to over 10% by the end of the year, compared with 8% in 1986.

126.   EMS central rates were realigned on 12 January. [1]

Coordination of economic and monetary policies

127.   In accordance with the Council Decision of 18 February 1974 on the attainment of a high degree of economic policy convergence, [2] the Council examined the economic situation in the Community on three occasions. At the first examination, on 9 March, [3] it concluded that there was no need to adjust the economic policy guidelines for 1987 on the cooperative strategy for full employment, adopted at its meeting in December 1986 in the annual economic report. [4]

At the second examination, on 13 July, [5] the Council again concluded that it was not necessary at that stage to adjust the economic policy guidelines for 1987. [4] It backed the idea of quickly introducing measures to boost internal demand should growth slow down further.

[1]   Bull. EC 1-1987, point 2.1.1.
[2]   OJ L 63, 5.3.1974.
[3]   Bull. EC 3-1987, point 2.1.2.
[4]   OJ L 385, 31.12.1986; Twentieth General Report, point 129.
[5]   Bull. EC 7/8-1987, point 2.1.2.

128.   Following the turmoil on financial and foreign-exchange markets in late October, the Council affirmed on 16 November that the Member States were determined to improve the conditions for further internally generated non-inflationary growth and to contribute to the reduction of external imbalances. [1]

At the third examination, on 7 December, [2] the Council, acting on a proposal from the Commission, [3] after receiving the opinions of Parliament [4] and the Economic and Social Committee, [5] adopted the annual report on the economic situation in the Community and approved economic policy guidelines for the Member States for 1988. In the preamble to the report the Commission stressed the need for the economic forecasts to be revised because of the fall in share prices on the stock markets of the industrialized countries and because of the sharp fall in the dollar.

129.   In 1987 the European Council met in Brussels and Copenhagen. At its meeting in Brussels, [6] which was entirely devoted to examining the Commission's communication 'The Single Act: A new frontier for Europe', [7] it unanimously adopted conclusions for the short term on the system of monetary compensatory amounts, the 1987 budget and the research appropriations in that budget. The conclusions for the medium term were approved by only 11 Member States.

At its Copenhagen meeting, the European Council discussed these matters further. [2] The Heads of State or Government decided to hold a special European Council meeting in Brussels in February 1988.

130.   At the close of the Western Economic Summit held in Venice from 8 to 10 June, [8] the Heads of State or Government of the seven industrialized countries taking part and the representatives of the Community issued a major economic declaration confirming the commitments entered into in Paris on

---

[1]   Bull. EC 11-1987, point 2.1.2.
[2]   Bull. EC 12-1987.
[3]   Bull. EC 10-1987, point 1.4.1 et seq.
[4]   OJ C 345, 21.12.1987; Bull. EC 11-1987, point 2.1.3.
[5]   Bull. EC 11-1987, point 2.4.35.
[6]   Bull. EC 6-1987, point 1.1.2 et seq.
[7]   Supplement 1/87 — Bull. EC; Bull. EC 2-1987, point 1.1.1 et seq.
[8]   Bull. EC 6-1987, points 1.2.6 and 3.7.1 et seq.

23 February ('Louvre agreement')[1] and Washington[2] and stressed in particular the usefulness of coordinating economic policies.[3]

Medium-term economic development in the Community

131.   At the end of April a report prepared at the Commission's request by a group of independent experts chaired by Mr Padoa-Schioppa was presented to the press.[4] The report, entitled 'Efficiency, stability and equity: A strategy for the evolution of the economic system of the European Community', examines the implications of two decisions taken in 1985 — one on enlarging the Community to include Spain and Portugal and the other on creating, by 1992, a market without internal frontiers. The report makes several recommendations arguing for simplified methods of preparing Community legislation; closer monetary policy coordination; stronger redistributive functions for the budget and the Community's lending instruments; more open markets; and a cooperative growth strategy[5] to achieve a higher growth rate and ensure successful enlargement and completion of the internal market.

European Monetary System

Operation of the EMS

132.   The year 1987 began with a further realignment of central rates within the EMS, on 12 January.[6] It was agreed in response to the sliding dollar and capital movements, but the background was more favourable than on the occasion of earlier realignments, given increased convergence of economic fundamentals. The adjustments of at most 3%, together with the Louvre agreement,[7] have since enabled parities to be kept stable in the EMS.

---

[1] At the Louvre, the Finance Ministers and the Central Bank Governors of the Group of Seven agreed that the substantial exchange-rate changes since the Plaza agreement (September 1985) had now brought their currencies within ranges broadly consistent with underlying economic fundamentals and that they would cooperate closely to foster stability of exchange rates around the levels obtaining at the time.
[2] The Louvre agreement was confirmed at the meeting of the IMF Interim Committee held in Washington in April (Bull. EC 4-1987, point 2.1.3).
[3] Point 752 of this Report.
[4] Bull. EC 4-1987, point 1.1.1 et seq.
[5] OJ L 377, 31.12.1985; Nineteenth General Report, point 133; OJ L 385, 31.12.1986; Twentieth General Report, points 129 and 130.
[6] Bull. EC 1-1987, point 2.1.1.
[7] Point 130 (footnote 2) of this Report.

During the course of the year, the EMS operated efficiently against the backcloth of major changes in the degree of liberalization of capital movements and increasingly sophisticated financial markets which created wider scope for speculative capital movements.

After the realignment of central rates on 12 January,[1] better coordinated interest-rate management was more effective in stabilizing exchange rates inside the system.

Strengthening the EMS and the role of the ECU

133.   At their informal meeting in Nyborg on 12 September,[2] the Community's Ministers for Economic and Financial Affairs agreed to a number of measures to strengthen the EMS.

134.   On 13 May the Bank of Spain[3] and on 10 November the Bank of Portugal[4] put their signatures to the Agreement of 13 March 1979 between the Central Banks of the Member States laying down the operating procedures for the European Monetary System.[5] Thus formally members of the system, Spain and Portugal now hold positions in the EMS similar to those of the United Kingdom and Greece.

135.   On 16 June the Central Council of the Deutsche Bundesbank decided to change the way it applies the rules of currency law to transactions subject to its authorization and to permit the private use of the ECU on the same terms as the use of foreign currencies.[6] Portugal having permitted the ECU to be quoted on the Lisbon stock exchange since 15 September 1985, the ECU is now recognized on either a *de facto* or a *de jure* basis by all Member States.

136.   At the beginning of July the Commission decided to step up its drive to promote the ECU and to use it more widely in implementing the Community budget.[7]

---

[1]   Bull. EC 1-1987, point 2.1.1.
[2]   Points 119 to 121 of this Report.
[3]   Bull. EC 5-1987, point 2.1.3.
[4]   Bull. EC 11-1987, point 2.1.6.
[5]   OJ L 379, 30.12.1979; Thirteenth General Report, point 84.
[6]   Bull. EC 6-1987, point 2.1.4.
[7]   Bull. EC 7/8-1987, point 2.1.4.

The Community and the international monetary system

137.   The annual meeting of the International Monetary Fund, held in Washington in early October, [1] was preceded by two preparatory meetings of the IMF Interim Committee. The Community was represented by Mr Palle Simonsen, President of the Council, and Mr Abel Matutes, Member of the Commission.

138.   On 9 and 10 April the Interim Committee of the IMF held its 28th meeting, at which discussion focused mainly on the world economic situation, the development of international trade and especially the problems of indebtedness of certain developing countries. [2]

139.   At its 29th meeting, held in Washington from 29 September to 1 October, [1] the Interim Committee recognized that the problem of the developing countries' debt would take longer than expected to solve; it favoured the idea of reducing the debt burden of the poorest countries by applying lower interest rates. At the preliminary meetings of the Groups of Five and of Seven, [1] the industrialized countries members of those Groups reaffirmed all aspects of the Louvre agreement and stressed the need for a new strategy to deal with international debt, in particular the debt of the poorest countries.

Initiatives and measures taken by the Community

Financial engineering

140.   Opinions were adopted on 16 September by Parliament [3] and on 22 October by the Economic and Social Committee [4] on the proposal for a Decision on financing major Community infrastructure projects, [5] on which the Council had held an initial exchange of views on 5 May, [6] in the light of the ideas set out in a more general communication on financial engineering. [7]

---

1   Bull. EC 9-1987, point 2.1.6.
2   Bull. EC 4-1987, point 2.1.3.
3   OJ C 281, 19.10.1987; Bull. EC 9-1987, point 2.1.4.
4   Bull. EC 10-1987, point 2.4.47.
5   OJ C 80, 27.3.1987; Twentieth General Report, point 152.
6   Bull. EC 5-1987, point 2.1.5.
7   Twentieth General Report, point 152.

Extension of the New Community Instrument (NCI IV)

141. On 9 March, following the common position agreed on 8 December 1986, [1] the Council adopted the Decision extending the activities of the New Community Instrument (NCI IV). [2]

The European Investment Bank Informed the Council that it was willing to play a part in implementing the measures envisaged on 8 December 1986. [3]

Borrowing and lending

142. Under the balance-of-payments support mechanism, the Commission made borrowings on capital markets to fund the second instalment of the Community loan to Greece. [4]

143. On 18 September the Commission transmitted to the Council and to Parliament its seventh annual report on the Community's borrowing and lending activities, dealing with 1986. [5] The report gives a comprehensive picture of the use made of the Community's structural lending instruments and brings out the continuing concentration on the productive sector, with strong growth of individual loans to small and medium-sized businesses. There was also a significant increase in loans for infrastructure projects and a sharp rise in those to the energy sector.

---

[1] Twentieth General Report, point 153.
[2] OJ L 71, 14.3.1987; Bull. EC 3-1987, point 2.1.3.
[3] Bull. EC 3-1987, point 2.1.3.
[4] Point 108 of this Report.
[5] Bull. EC 9-1987, point 2.1.3.

Section 2

Completing the internal market

Main developments

144.   This is the third year of the programme to remove physical, technical and tax barriers by 1992, as set out by the Commission in its White Paper on completing the internal market and approved at the Milan meeting of the European Council in June 1985.[1] Above all, however, 1987 is the year in which the Single European Act, which is of supreme importance to the attainment of the internal market goal, came into force.[2] The fact that its entry into force was delayed from 1 January to 1 July is bound to affect the timetable contained in the White Paper, as it will undoubtedly take some months to smooth out minor hitches in applying the new decision-making mechanisms. This is particularly true of the cooperation procedure between Council and Parliament. However, these important events should not eclipse the significant progress made on individual proposals in the White Paper.

There can be no question but that most headway has been made by the Commission, which has adopted a large number of proposals that make it clearer what the internal market will look like in 1992; these proposals cover such cornerstones as public procurement, standardization, indirect taxation and the free movement of capital.

By the end of the year the Commission had put forward proposals[3] concerning two thirds of the measures listed in its June 1985 White Paper as being necessary to the completion of the internal market; it has set itself the objective of completing its programme of proposals (with the exception of veterinary and plant-health legislation) before the end of 1988. The Council had adopted 67 internal market instruments by 31 December 1987, and 126 proposals are still being discussed in the Council or Parliament.[4] Although the timetable set out in the White Paper has not been totally adhered to, considerable progress has thus been made, particularly if account is taken of the size of the programme

---

[1]   Nineteenth General Report, points 162 to 166.
[2]   Point 1 of this Report.
[3]   Annex to this section (at end of Report).
[4]   Annex to this section (at end of Report).

for the first three years and the fact that the qualified majority option was not available before 1 July 1987.

The Commission also notes growing interest on the part of the business community in the undertaking, and above all a highly positive attitude towards the ultimate objective. The Council still has five years to reach a decision on all the necessary measures. This may seem long, but in the circumstances it is very little. The important thing is that the process has been set in train and is virtually irreversible.

145.   *The political impetus given by the European Council meeting at The Hague* [1] *to a people's Europe, i.e. the efforts to give the people of Europe the feeling of belonging to one political entity, is producing practical results. The Council's decision to set up the Erasmus programme on student mobility is a compelling token of this political resolve, as is the decision of the European Council to bring about a general system of recognition of diplomas in 1988. These achievements are a measure of the will to advance in the direction indicated in 1985 in the two reports by the* ad hoc *People's Europe Committee chaired by Mr Adoninno,* [2] *even if in areas such as the free movement of individuals no practical results have yet been achieved.*

This new approach is also reflected in the launch of a Community cooperation scheme concerning mutual aid in emergencies. The Council and the Representatives of the Governments of the Member States, meeting within the Council, showed their determination to act together in civil protection matters by adopting a resolution on 25 June on the setting-up of a permanent network of liaison officers, the adoption of a civil protection guide and the exchange of personnel responsible for civil protection, and in particular for simulation exercises.

Priority activities and objectives

Liberalization of government procurement

146.   Liberalization of government procurement continued [3] to be one of the Commission's priorities in the drive to dismantle the barriers still dividing the common market. On 18 March the Commission pursued its strategy for opening

---

[1]   Twentieth General Report, point 284.
[2]   Nineteenth General Report, point 278; Supplement 7/85 — Bull. EC.
[3]   Twentieth General Report, point 160.

up this sector to genuine Community-wide competition by adopting a proposal for a Council Directive which would require Member States to provide suppliers and contractors with means of quick relief against irregularities in tendering and award procedures for procurement and construction contracts and would enable the Commission to intervene to suspend award procedures in appropriate cases.[1] As well as tightening up enforcement by increasing the availability of legal redress and the Commission's powers to obtain information and to monitor and intervene in proceedings, the strategy calls for action on a number of other fronts: it aims to bring public utilities (telecommunications, energy, water and transport), which are now excluded, within the scope of the legislation, and to ensure that greater attention is paid to compliance with the competitive tendering rules in projects supported by the structural Funds or with low-interest finance from the European Investment Bank. The action programme also seeks to reconcile the rules on open procurement with Community regional policy and to take account of the industrial policy implications of the liberalization.

147.   As part of the action programme, the Commission decided on 26 May to set up an Advisory Committee on the Opening-up of Public Procurement to serve as a sounding board for the views of business interests involved in government contracts for supplies, construction works and services.[2] The advice from the Committee will be especially valuable for the liberalization of procurement in the sectors at present excluded.

The proposal for a Council Directive coordinating the laws, regulations and administrative provisions relating to the application of Community rules on procedures for the award of public supply and public works contracts,[3] so as to require Member States to provide means of redress against breaches of the competitive tendering rules and to enable the Commission to intervene to order a suspension of award procedures was sent to the Council on 1 July, the first day of the operation of the new procedures introduced by the Single European Act.[4] In October the Economic and Social Committee gave its opinion[5] on the proposal, in which it supported the principle but felt that the Directive should go further in the direction of harmonizing national provisions, particularly as regards time limits and penalties and the Commission's power to order suspension.

---

[1]   Bull. EC 3-1987, point 1.2.1 et seq.
[2]   OJ L 152, 12.6.1987; OJ L 338, 28.11.1987; Bull. EC 5-1987, point 2.1.23; OJ C 317, 28.11.1987; Bull. EC 11-1987, point 2.1.32.
[3]   OJ C 230, 28.8.1987; Bull. EC 7/8-1987, point 2.1.21.
[4]   Point 1 of this Report.
[5]   Bull. EC 10-1987, point 2.4.40.

To take account of the results of the renegotiation [1] of the GATT Agreement on Government Procurement, [2] the Commission on 1 June amended [3] its proposal of 19 June 1986 [4] for a Council Directive amending the Council Directive of 21 December 1976 on coordination of provisions for the award of public supply contracts [5] and deleting certain provisions of the Directive of 22 July 1980. [6] On 2 October it further amended [7] its proposal in order to incorporate the majority of the amendments which had been proposed by Parliament [7] under the cooperation procedure instituted by the Single European Act.

148.   On 4 November the Commission approved for publication a Users' Guide to the Community rules on Open Government Procurement, which is intended to raise the level of compliance by increasing public awareness of the rules. [8]

149.   In November the Council decided, [9] on a proposal from the Commission, to approve the Protocol amending the GATT Agreement on Government Procurement [1] and to authorize its signature on the Community's behalf. The Commission duly signed the Protocol for the Community on 16 November. The Protocol, which will enter into force on 16 February 1988, makes several amendments to the original Agreement of April 1979. [10] It extends the Code to new types of contract, lowers the value threshold from which contracts are covered from 150 000 to 130 000 SDR, and requires further items of information in tender notices.

Technical harmonization and standards

150.   Under the new approach to technical harmonization [11] the Council, acting on a proposal from the Commission, [12] adopted a Directive in June on the approximation of the laws of the Member States on simple pressure vessels [13]

1   Point 889 of this Report.
2   Twentieth General Report, point 978.
3   OJ C 161, 19.6.1987; Bull. EC 6-1987, point 2.1.18.
4   OJ C 173, 11.7.1986; Twentieth General Report, point 160.
5   OJ L 13, 15.1.1977; Tenth General Report, point 132.
6   OJ L 215, 18.8.1980; Fourteenth General Report, point 137.
7   OJ C 303, 13.11.1987; Bull. EC 10-1987, point 2.1.18.
8   Bull. EC 11-1987, point 2.1.31.
9   OJ L 345, 9.12.1987; Bull. EC 11-1987, point 2.2.71.
10   Thirteenth General Report, point 494.
11   OJ C 136, 4.6.1985; Nineteenth General Report, point 210.
12   OJ C 89, 15.4.1986; Twentieth General Report, point 215.
13   OJ L 220, 8.8.1987; Bull. EC 6-1987, point 2.2.14.

and reached a common position on 18 December concerning a proposal for a Directive on toy safety. [1] The new approach was also reflected in the proposal for a Directive on safety in the design and construction of a wide range of machinery transmitted by the Commission to the Council on 22 October. [2]

151.   On 20 February the Commission sent the Council two proposals for Directives relating to the procedure for the provision of information in the field of technical standards and regulations, [3] one extending the scope of the Directive of 28 March 1983 [4] to all industrially-manufactured products other than agricultural products, the other establishing a procedure for the provision of information in the field of technical standards and regulations applying to agricultural products, making the latter subject to the amended provisions of the 1983 Directive. [4]

Both these proposals honour commitments made by the Commission in its June 1985 White Paper on completing the internal market. [5] Taken together with the Directive of 22 December 1986 relating to high-technology medicinal products, [6] Article 5 of which refers to the Directive of 28 March 1983, [4] this represents the establishment of a general procedure for the provision of information on the drafting of technical regulations for all products. This machinery will constitute an essential means of preventing new technical barriers to trade and thereby help to bring about a genuine single market. It will also play a major part in the creation of a technical environment common to all businesses.

Creation of a European financial area

152.   On 4 November the Commission transmitted to the Council a communication together with three proposals for legal instruments (two directives and a regulation) [7] designed to give effect to the principle of complete liberalization of capital movements set out in Article 67 of the Treaty; [8] this is an essential aspect of the creation of an integrated financial area which must accompany

---

1   Point 523 of this Report.
2   Bull. EC 11-1987, point 2.1.21.
3   OJ C 71, 19.3.1987; Bull. EC 2-1987, point 2.1.8.
4   OJ L 109, 26.4.1983; Seventeenth General Report, point 150.
5   Nineteenth General Report, points 162 to 166.
6   OJ L 15, 17.1.1987; Twentieth General Report, point 210.
7   Bull. EC 10-1987, point 1.1.1 et seq.
8   OJ L 332, 26.11.1986; Twentieth General Report, point 161.

completion of the large internal market by 1992,[1] an objective laid down by the Single Act.[2]

The first proposal is for a new Council Directive, based on Article 69 of the Treaty, which would extend liberalization to all capital movements (financial loans and credits, current and deposit account operations, investments in short-term securities). Provision has been made for a specific safeguard clause for counteracting disruptive short-term capital movements, and Spain, Ireland, Portugal and Greece would be granted additional time for implementing the Directive. The second proposal is for a Directive amending the Directive of 21 March 1972 on regulating international capital flows[3] with a view to placing at Member States' disposal the necessary instruments for applying the specific safeguard clause where appropriate. The third proposal is for a Regulation providing for the introduction of a single medium-term financial support instrument combining the existing medium-term financial assistance[4] and Community loan[5] mechanisms; the conditions under which such support can be granted would be broadened to cover the needs arising both from liberalization of capital movements and from balance-of-payments difficulties.

Removal of intra-Community tax frontiers

153.   On 7 August the Commission sent to the Council a communication containing a package of proposals for Directives relating to VAT and excise duties[6] which are designed to do away with tax controls at the Community's internal frontiers as part of the drive to complete the single Community market by 1992.[6] In the case of VAT, the Commission has proposed that rates should be brought closer together and that their number should be limited to two — a reduced rate for items of basic necessity and a standard rate for other goods — with a maximum permitted difference of 5 or 6 percentage points (a band of between 4% and 9% for reduced rates and between 14% and 20% for the standard rate) so as not to cause deflections of trade. VAT would in future be paid by the purchaser of the goods at the rate applicable in the country where the sale takes place, with the Treasury in the country of the seller collecting this tax; a clearing mechanism would be introduced to enable the revenue collected to be distributed at regular intervals by member country of consump-

---

1   Nineteenth General Report, points 162 to 166.
2   Twentieth General Report, point 2; Supplement 2/86 — Bull. EC.
3   OJ L 91, 18.4.1972.
4   OJ L 73, 27.3.1971.
5   OJ L 73, 19.3.1981; Fifteenth General Report, point 125.
6   OJ C 250, 18.9.1987; OJ C 251, 19.9.1987; OJ C 252, 22.9.1987; Bull. EC 7/8-1987, point 1.2.1 *et seq.*

tion. In the case of excise duties, the Commission has proposed that there should be complete harmonization of duties for those products which continue to be subject to this type of tax: mineral oils, alcoholic beverages and tobacco.

Civil protection

154.   On 25 June the Council and the Representatives of the Member States meeting within the Council adopted the resolution on the introduction of Community cooperation on civil protection [1] which they had approved on 25 May. [2] The resolution incorporates most of the Commission's proposals [3] and constitutes an important first step towards coordinated action in areas of direct and immediate concern to the people of Europe.

The Commission has taken a number of measures within the framework which the resolution lays down. It has organized a study of civil protection data banks so that all the Member States can make available to each other full information on the structures and resources available to deal with disasters. Ultimately, this will lead to installation of a warning system. As part of its work on intensifying and consolidating cooperation between the Community and the Council of Europe, [4] the Commission acceded in September to the open partial Agreement on the prevention of, protection against, and organization of relief in major natural and technological disasters, [5] which opens the way to cooperation, particularly with non-member countries in the Mediterranean area.

BUSINESS ENVIRONMENT

Removal of physical frontiers

Checks on goods

Customs union: the external dimension

155.   Harmonization of customs legislation being a prerequisite for completion of the internal market and for the Community's effective participation in the international economic order, the Commission pursued the work of codifying

1   OJ C 176, 4.7.1987; Bull. EC 6-1987, point 2.1.10.
2   Bull. EC 5-1987, point 2.1.8.
3   Bull. EC 4-1987, point 2.1.5.
4   Point 905 of this Report.
5   Bull. EC 9-1987, point 2.2.46.

customs rules. Externally, it continued to prove a dependable partner of other countries and groups of countries through its participation in the activities of various international bodies, in particular the Customs Cooperation Council (CCC). With a view to strengthening mutual cooperation, special attention was devoted to relations with the European Free Trade Association, collaboration with which proved fruitful in such areas as the movement of goods and rules of origin. [1]

Harmonization of customs rules on trade with non-member countries

Common Customs Tariff

156.   Active preparations continued for the introduction on 1 January 1988 of the Harmonized Commodity Description and Coding System (HS) and of the integrated Community tariff (Taric). [2] As the Common Customs Tariff (CCT) has undergone no significant change since its introduction in 1968 [3] and since the changes will affect not only the customs authorities but also all those concerned with the import and export of goods, the Commission has made sure that the new rules to be applied from 1988 will be fully operational; it has accordingly helped with the training of national officials and future users of the new arrangements.

157.   In April the Council adopted a Decision concerning the conclusion of the International Convention on the Harmonized Commodity Description and Coding System. [4] This Decision, based on a Commission proposal, [5] will affect all the Commission's activities in the tariff field. The instrument of acceptance of the convention was deposited on 22 September on behalf of the Community. [6] The Harmonized System, which was drafted in the Customs Cooperation Council, is intended to replace universally the CCC nomenclature as the basis for the tariff and statistical nomenclatures used by the Community, and also the other tariff nomenclatures used by the Community's trading partners. On 23 July the Council accordingly adopted, on a proposal from the Commission, [7] a Regulation on the tariff and statistical nomenclature and on the CCT. [8] This Regulation is of great importance not only because it introduces the combined

---

[1]   Points 169 and 170 of this Report.
[2]   Twentieth General Report, point 165.
[3]   OJ L 165, 21.9.1966; OJ L 172, 22.7.1968; Second General Report, point 1.
[4]   OJ L 198, 20.7.1987; Bull. EC 4-1987, point 2.1.49.
[5]   OJ C 120, 5.4.1984; Eighteenth General Report, point 160; Bull. EC 2-1987, point 2.1.47.
[6]   Bull. EC 9-1987, point 2.1.63.
[7]   OJ C 154, 12.6.1987; Bull. EC 5-1987, point 2.1.58.
[8]   OJ L 256, 7.9.1987; Bull. EC 7/8-1987, point 2.1.20.

tariff and statistical nomenclature (CN) and the Taric but also because it sets out in clear terms the concept of the CCT laid down in Article 9 of the EEC Treaty and defines fully and organically the powers of the Council and the Commission in this area. It entrusts to the Commission the task of amending the Community legislation based on the former CCT and Nimexe nomenclatures so as to adapt it to the CN and, for routine administrative matters, provides that the Commission shall be assisted by a management committee to replace the former regulatory committee and make it possible to operate more effectively, in particular by shortening the time taken over decisions. In order to satisfy the need to inform business and trade, the Office for Official Publications published in June the full version of the CN and a concordance table designed to facilitate the classification of goods under the new nomenclature.

158.   Further to the Agreement concluded with the United States in January on the consequences of enlargement,[1] the Council adopted on 16 March, on a proposal from the Commission,[2] a Regulation[3] amending the Regulation of 24 November 1986 on the CCT for 1987.[4] This Regulation introduces reductions in customs duties for a range of products and certain tariff heading amendments.

159.   The adjustment of the bilateral central rates in the European Monetary System in January[5] resulted in the adoption of new rates for converting the ECU into national currencies for the purposes of determining the tariff classification of goods and specific CCT duties.[6]

Economic tariff matters

160.   Normal application of the CCT is waived in many instances by tariff measures generally adopted by Council Regulation. Such measures, whether required under agreements or introduced unilaterally, involve reductions in customs duties or zero-rating in respect of some or all imports of the products concerned. They take the form of Community tariff quotas, tariff ceilings or total or partial suspension of duties.

161.   In 1987 215 tariff quotas or ceilings were opened pursuant to commitments entered into by the Community during the GATT multilateral trade

---

[1]   Point 754 of this Report.
[2]   Bull. EC 2-1987, point 2.1.46.
[3]   OJ L 76, 18.3.1987; Bull. EC 3-1987, point 2.1.64.
[4]   OJ L 345, 8.12.1986; Twentieth General Report, point 163.
[5]   Point 132 of this Report.
[6]   OJ C 14, 20.1.1987; Bull. EC 1-1987, point 2.1.38.

negotiations, under bilateral agreements with non-member countries or on a unilateral basis in order to secure the Community supply situation for certain products.

162.   For the same reason, and also in many cases with the aim of encouraging Community industry to use or introduce new technology, the Council temporarily suspended duties on 1 073 products or groups of products, mainly chemicals and products of the electronics or aircraft industries. Tariffs were also suspended on a number of agricultural and fishery products, to improve the supply of certain types of food and honour commitments entered into with certain preferential non-member countries.

163.   The Regulations giving effect to generalized tariff preferences on imports from developing countries were renewed as part of the Community's development aid policy. The main changes made involve the updating of the quotas opened and a wider differential of preferential treatment to the advantage of less competitive countries.[1] In addition, quotas for specific products were replaced by fixed amounts in order to ensure equal access for all importers to the whole Community market and greater certainty in the use of preferential amounts.

Customs valuation

164.   In order to monitor the pattern of trade in perishable goods imported into the Community, the Commission amended, by Regulation adopted on 16 December,[2] the list of goods covered by the simplified valuation procedures[3] and the list of marketing centres used under this system. At the same time, it · adapted the classification of such goods to the new CN.[4]

165.   The entry into force of the Harmonized System had repercussions on residual customs duties applicable to trade between Spain and Portugal and the other Member States. On 21 December the Council redefined on the basis of the CN the basic duties to be applied in the Community of Ten with a view to the calculation of successive tariff reductions.[4] The tariff nomenclatures contained in the preferential agreements with non-member countries were also amended to take account of the entry into force of the Harmonized System.[4]

---

[1]   Points 832 to 835 of this Report.
[2]   OJ L 355, 17.12.1987; Bull. EC 12-1987.
[3]   OJ L 154, 13.6.1981; Fifteenth General Report, point 191.
[4]   Bull. EC 12-1987.

Customs procedures with economic impact

166.   The Council formally adopted on 13 July, on a proposal from the Commission, [1] a Regulation on the temporary importation free of import duties of containers from non-member countries. [2]

167.   On 31 July the Commission adopted three Regulations. [3] The first [4] concerns customs arrangements in general and amends certain provisions of the existing implementing Regulations [5] so as to enable the single administrative document to be used from 1 January 1988. The second Regulation [6] concerns certain provisions implementing the Regulation of 24 July 1986 on outward processing relief arrangements and the standard exchange system. [7] These provisions concern the general conditions for authorizing use of the arrangements and their operation and the question of administrative cooperation. The third Regulation [4] amends the implementing Regulation of 24 November 1986 on inward processing relief arrangements, [8] introducing certain simplifications and adjusting the administrative cooperation procedures.

168.   The Commission also adopted, on 7 August, a Regulation [9] amending the Regulation of 24 November 1986 [8] by laying down special rules for the inward processing arrangements in respect of durum wheat and, in September, three Regulations[10] concerning the rules for the use of inward processing arrangements and equivalent compensation for durum wheat where pasta products resulting from the processing of such wheat are intended to be exported to the United States and released for consumption there.[11]

Origin

169.   As part of the follow-up to the Luxembourg Joint Declaration of 9 April 1984,[12] the Commission continued its efforts to bring about a further substantial simplification of the documents used to certify the origin of goods.[13] The

---

1   OJ C 4, 7.1.1984; Seventeenth General Report, point 209.
2   OJ L 196, 17.7.1987; Bull. EC 7/8-1987, point 2.1.75.
3   Bull. EC 7/8-1987, points 2.1.74, 2.1.76 and 2.1.77.
4   OJ L 215, 5.8.1987.
5   OJ L 171, 29.6.1984; OJ L 331, 19.12.1984; Eighteenth General Report, point 168; OJ L 351, 12.12.1986; Twentieth General Report, point 174.
6   OJ L 230, 17.8.1987.
7   OJ L 212, 2.8.1986; Twentieth General Report, point 173.
8   OJ L 351, 12.12.1986; Twentieth General Report, point 174.
9   OJ L 219, 8.8.1987; Bull. EC 7/8-1987, point 2.1.78.
10   OJ L 251, 2.9.1987; Bull. EC 9-1987, point 2.1.60; OJ L 278, 1.10.1987; Bull. EC 9-1987, point 2.1.61.
11   Point 755 of this Report.
12   Eighteenth General Report, point 652.
13   Twentieth General Report, point 176.

simplified procedure, which is scheduled to have effect from 1 January 1988 under the Decisions of the EEC-EFTA joint committees, [1] will allow approved exporters to make declarations on invoices irrespective of the value of the goods.

170. In connection with the introduction of the Harmonized System (HS) on 1 January 1988, the Council adopted, on 19 October, on the basis of proposals from the Commission, the draft Decisions [2] of the EEC-EFTA joint committees under which the rules relating to Protocol 3 [3] concerning the definition of the concept of 'originating products' and methods of administrative cooperation will be recast and, in addition, a single list of processing criteria will be introduced, with all the rules applying to a given product being presented alongside the HS nomenclature code for the product concerned. On 13 and 26 October the Commission also proposed that the Council adopt rules of origin based on the same principles in the context of preferential agreements, notably under the Lomé Convention and the Mediterranean agreements. [4] The Commission is continuing to draw up similar rules for the other preferential arrangements.

171. To take account of the introduction of the HS on 1 January 1988, proposals [5] were sent to the Council for amending unilateral acts concerning the rules of origin, [6] which it had adopted. [7] At the same time the Commission adopted two Regulations relating to rules of origin under unilateral preferential arrangements. [8]

General legislation

172. On 30 March the Council adopted an amendment, [9] acting on a proposal from the Commission,[10] to the Regulation of 19 May 1981, the general aim of which was to expand and strengthen the scope for action by the Commission and the Member States in controlling fraud in trade with non-Community

---

[1] Point 770 of this Report.
[2] Bull. EC 10-1987, point 2.1.56.
[3] OJ L 323, 11.12.1984; Eighteenth General Report, point 171.
[4] Bull. EC 10-1987, point 2.1.57.
[5] Bull. EC 12-1987.
[6] Twentieth General Report, point 177.
[7] Ceuta, Melilla, Canary Islands; the Faroes; accession of Spain and Portugal.
[8] Generalized system of preferences; non-preferential rules adopted pursuant to the Regulations of 23 and 29 December.
[9] OJ L 90, 2.4.1987; Bull. EC 3-1987, point 2.1.62.
[10] OJ C 181, 19.7.1986; Twentieth General Report, point 182.

countries. [1] The Regulation has two new features. First, the information which the Member States must supply to the Commission now covers not only general matters but also those of specific Community interest. In addition, the Commission is authorized to organize missions to non-member countries, carried out at its own expense by Commission officials or officials designated by the Member State or States concerned.

173.   On 13 July the Council adopted, on a proposal from the Commission, [2] a Regulation on customs debt. [3] From 1 January 1988 this Regulation will replace the Directive of 25 June 1979, [4] the principles of which it takes over and improves by means of a more uniform application of the relevant rules, which are of vital importance for administering the customs union and giving the public greater certainty in the law.

174.   On 30 November the Council adopted a common position [5] on the proposal for a Regulation determining the persons liable for payment of a customs debt. [6]

175.   On 14 October the Commission adopted a Regulation [7] establishing provisions for the implementation of the Council Regulation of 1 December 1986 laying down measures to prohibit the release for free circulation of counterfeit goods. [8]

Intra-Community trade: the internal dimension

Simplification of customs checks and formalities

Single administrative document

176.   In preparation for the introduction on 1 January 1988 of the single administrative document within the Community, [9] the Commission continued its efforts to widen the area of application of this document. [10]

---

1   OJ L 144, 2.6.1981; Fifteenth General Report, point 203.
2   OJ C 261, 29.9.1984; Eighteenth General Report, point 175.
3   OJ L 201, 22.7.1987; Bull. EC 7/8-1987, point 2.1.73.
4   OJ L 179, 17.7.1979; Thirteenth General Report, point 149.
5   Bull. EC 11-1987, point 2.1.78.
6   OJ C 340, 28.12.1982; Sixteenth General Report, point 207; OJ C 189, 17.7.1984; Eighteenth General Report, point 174.
7   OJ L 291, 15.10.1987; Bull. EC 10-1987, point 2.1.51.
8   OJ L 357, 19.12.1986; Twentieth General Report, point 178.
9   OJ L 79, 21.3.1985; Nineteenth General Report, point 189.
10 Twentieth General Report, point 183.

177.   As part of the implementation of the Luxembourg Joint Declaration of 9 April 1984 [1] and the process of completing the internal market, the Commission negotiated two Conventions with the EFTA countries, [2] on the basis of authorization given by the Council on 3 March 1986 [3] and 9 February this year. [4] The first extends the use of the single document to trade between the Community and the EFTA countries and also to trade between the EFTA countries themselves, while the second institutes a common transit procedure in such trade. On 28 April [5] and 15 June [6] respectively the Council adopted the Decisions concerning the conclusion of the two Conventions, which were signed in Interlaken on 20 May [7] and will take effect from 1 January 1988. [8]

Simplification of transit procedures

178.   On 11 June the Council adopted a Regulation [9] amending the Regulation of 13 December 1976 on Community transit. [10] It will enter into force on 1 July 1988 and is one of the measures mentioned in the White Paper as an intermediate measure on the way to completion of the internal market. It removes, subject to certain conditions, the requirement for a guarantee in intra-Community transit operations.

179.   On 27 March the Commission adopted [11] a Regulation consolidating and adjusting the provisions for the implementation of the Community transit procedure and introducing certain simplifications of that procedure. [12] On 18 September it adopted a Regulation on the documents to be used for the purpose of implementing Community measures entailing verification of the use and/or destination of goods. [13]

---

[1]   Eighteenth General Report, point 652.
[2]   Bull. EC 3-1987, points 2.1.59 and 2.1.60.
[3]   Twentieth General Report, point 189.
[4]   Bull. EC 2-1987, point 2.1.44.
[5]   OJ L 134, 22.5.1987; Bull. EC 4-1987, point 2.1.47.
[6]   OJ L 226, 13.8.1987; Bull. EC 6-1987, point 2.1.59.
[7]   Bull. EC 5-1987, points 2.1.53 and 2.1.54.
[8]   Bull. EC 11-1987, point 2.1.76.
[9]   OJ L 157, 17.6.1987; Bull. EC 6-1987, point 2.1.58.
[10]   OJ L 38, 9.2.1977; Eleventh General Report, point 167.
[11]   OJ L 107, 22.4.1987; Bull. EC 3-1987, point 2.1.61.
[12]   OJ L 38, 9.2.1977; Eleventh General Report, point 167; OJ L 179, 11.7.1985; Nineteenth General Report, point 190.
[13]   OJ L 270, 23.9.1987; Bull. EC 9-1987, point 2.1.59.

Common frontier posts

180.   On 3 June the Commission adopted a Regulation [1] laying down detailed rules for the application of the Regulation of 1 December 1986 [2] concerning the abolition within the framework of the TIR Convention [3] of customs formalities on exit from a Member State at a frontier between two Member States.

Coordinated development of computerized administrative procedures

181.   The project for the coordinated development of computerized administrative procedures (CD project), [4] under the Caddia programme, [5] was a valuable aid in activities requiring coordination at Community level in order to be more effective.

The development of a system for the computerized administration of the integrated tariff and statistics nomenclature (Taric) marks a notable step forward. [6] A number of pilot projects were launched to promote the standardization of electronic transmission and communication between the Commission and the Member States.

Agriculture and health protection

*Legislation on plant health, seeds and
propagating material, and feedingstuffs*

182.   The Council adopted amendments to the Community's legislation on plant health in order to integrate Spain and Portugal fully into the regime from 1 March 1987. [7] On 2 March the Council, acting on a Commission proposal, [8] standardized the models for the phytosanitary certificates to be used in intra-Community trade in plants and plant products. [9] On 13 March the Commission sent a communication to the Council setting out its new plant health strategy for the final stage of the programme set out in the White Paper on completing

---

[1]   OJ L 144, 4.6.1987; Bull. EC 6-1987, point 2.1.60.
[2]   OJ L 341, 4.12.1986; Twentieth General Report, point 185.
[3]   OJ L 252, 14.9.1978.
[4]   OJ L 33, 8.2.1986; Twentieth General Report, point 190.
[5]   OJ L 96, 3.4.1985; Nineteenth General Report, point 70.
[6]   Twentieth General Report, point 190.
[7]   OJ L 382, 31.12.1986.
[8]   OJ C 186, 13.7.1984; Eighteenth General Report, point 439.
[9]   OJ L 151, 11.6.1987; Bull. EC 3-1987, point 2.1.177.

the internal market.[1] The communication gives a more comprehensive account of the individual measures contemplated and the ways they will affect each other.

183.   On 9 March the Council amended[2] the annex to an earlier Directive[3] to ban the marketing and use of products containing nitrofen, EDB (1,2-dibromoethane) and EDC (1,2-dichloroethane) because of the risks they present for human health and, in some cases, the environment.

184.   In the course of the year the Commission adopted three Directives updating certain detailed technical provisions of the Community seed arrangements relating to beet, fodder crops, cereals, oil and fibre plants, and vegetables.[4] In addition, through the mechanism of the Common Catalogue of Agricultural Plant Species,[5] the Commission accelerated, with effect from 1 January 1987, the procedure for admitting to freedom of movement in the rest of the Community most of the varieties unrestricted in Spain, and vice versa.

185.   On 19 October the Council, acting on a proposal from the Commission,[6] adopted two Decisions[7] amending those of 27 June 1985 on the equivalence of seed multiplied and produced in certain non-member countries,[8] extending their validity in respect of seven countries.

186.   On 16 February the Council adopted guidelines for the assessment of additives in feedingstuffs within the framework of the Community authorization procedure.[9] The guidelines list the studies to be carried out by applicants to ensure safety and efficacy. For its part the Commission adopted several Directives in the course of the year to adapt the Community provisions on additives, undesirable substances and products, and straight and compound feedingstuffs to the latest developments in scientific and technical knowledge.[10]

---

[1]   Bull. EC 3-1987, point 2.1.179.
[2]   OJ L 71, 14.3.1987; Bull. EC 3-1987, point 2.1.178.
[3]   OJ L 33, 8.2.1979; Twelfth General Report, point 304.
[4]   OJ L 49, 18.2.1987; OJ L 273, 26.9.1987.
[5]   OJ C 336A, 31.12.1986.
[6]   Bull. EC 7/8-1987, point 2.1.224.
[7]   OJ L 304, 27.10.1987; Bull. EC 10-1987, point 2.1.163.
[8]   OJ L 195, 26.7.1985; Nineteenth General Report, point 199.
[9]   OJ L 64, 7.3.1987.
[10]   OJ L 110, 25.4.1987; OJ L 102, 14.4.1987.

187.   On 19 October the Council finally adopted provisions fixing maximum permitted levels for pesticide residues in feedingstuffs, [1] first proposed by the Commission in 1977. [2]

Veterinary and livestock husbandry legislation

188.   On 13 February the Commission sent a proposal to the Council for a Directive to remove all health barriers to trade in egg products and thereby contribute to the establishment of the internal market for these products. [3]

189.   On 25 May the Commission sent a proposal to the Council for a Decision on a system of frontier controls for livestock and livestock products imported from non-member countries, the purpose being to simplify the controls while continuing to ensure adequate health safeguards. [4]

190.   On 19 August the Commission sent a proposal [5] to the Council for a Directive setting out the guarantees required for application of the derogation provided for in the Council Directive of 31 December 1985 banning the use of certain substances with a hormonal or thyrostatic effect. [6] On 18 November the Council adopted transitional measures to maintain present trade arrangements until 31 December 1988, [7] while confirming that the use of hormonal substances for fattening purposes would be prohibited from 1 January 1988. [8]

191.   After receiving the opinion of Parliament, [9] the Commission on 22 October sent the Council an amendment[10] to its proposal for a Directive on fresh meat and the minimum fees to be charged for the health inspection of such meat.[11]

On 21 December the Commission sent the Council a proposed Directive on health problems affecting the production, placing on the Community market and importation from non-member countries of minced meat and meat in pieces of less than 100 grams.[12]

---

1   OJ L 304, 27.10.1987; Bull. EC 10-1987, point 2.1.162.
2   OJ C 197, 18.8.1987; Eleventh General Report, point 323.
3   OJ C 67, 14.3.1987; Bull. EC 2-1987, point 2.1.136.
4   OJ C 153, 11.6.1987; Bull. EC 5-1987, point 2.1.172.
5   Bull. EC 7/8-1987, point 2.1.220.
6   OJ L 382, 31.12.1985; Nineteenth General Report, point 203; Twentieth General Report, point 195.
7   OJ L 339, 1.12.1987; Bull. EC 11-1987, point 2.1.209.
8   Twentieth General Report, point 195.
9   OJ C 281, 19.10.1987; Bull. EC 9-1987, point 2.1.155.
10   OJ C 298, 7.11.1987; Bull. EC 10-1987, point 2.1.160.
11   OJ C 302, 27.11.1986; Twentieth General Report, point 199.
12   Bull. EC 12-1987.

192.   The eradication of the principal diseases prevailing on Community territory facilitates the achievement of the internal market. The Community therefore decided to make a financial contribution towards the eradication of African swine fever in Spain and Portugal.[1] The duration of the measures to combat classical swine fever was extended.[2] This ongoing campaign is accompanied by measures to reinforce controls[3] and to extend until 31 December 1991 the rules applying to trade in pigmeat and live pigs.[2] In the context of swine fever eradication, the Council recognized[4] certain parts of France,[5] Greece[5] and the Netherlands[6] as officially swine-fever-free.

193.   Significant progress was made in the control of brucellosis, tuberculosis and bovine leucosis. The Council decided to institute a further three-year measure in the Community to ensure complete eradiction of these diseases.[7]

194.   On the question of protection, the Commission took measures in response to the improvement in the foot-and-mouth disease situation in Italy[6] and problems concerning classical swine fever in Belgium.[8]

195.   The Council approved new arrangements for the preparation of pigmeat products in Member States in which African swine fever is prevalent[9] and completed the introduction of harmonized rules for pure-bred breeding cattle.[10]

Implementation of Article 115

196.   In the run-up to the creation of the single internal market and with a view to completing gradually the establishment of a common commercial policy, the Commission adopted on 22 July a Decision,[11] superseding the Decision of 20 December 1979,[12] which consolidates and specifies the procedures for authorizing the protective measures taken pursuant to Article 115 of the EEC Treaty.

---

[1]   OJ L 382, 31.12.1986; Twentieth General Report, point 198.
[2]   OJ L 34, 5.2.1987; Bull. EC 1-1987, point 2.1.101; OJ L 99, 11.4.1987; Bull. EC 4-1987, point 2.1.118; Bull. EC 6-1987, point 2.1.181; OJ L 286, 3.10.1987; Bull. EC 9-1987, point 2.1.153.
[3]   OJ L 280, 3.10.1987; Bull. EC 9-1987, point 2.1.153.
[4]   OJ L 353, 16.12.1987; Bull. EC 12-1987.
[5]   OJ L 194, 15.7.1987; Bull. EC 6-1987, point 2.1.183.
[6]   OJ L 283, 6.10.1987.
[7]   OJ L 24, 27.1.1987; Twentieth General Report, point 198.
[8]   OJ L 238, 21.8.1987.
[9]   OJ L 279, 2.10.1987; Bull. EC 9-1987, point 2.1.154.
[10]   OJ L 167, 26.6.1987.
[11]   OJ L 238, 21.8.1987; Bull. EC 7/8-1987, point 2.1.14.
[12]   OJ L 16, 22.1.1980.

Checks on individuals

197.   Commission proposals and Council decisions that are of direct concern to individuals (tax exemptions, easing of intra-Community controls) are reported in the second part of this section ('A people's Europe'). [1]

Removal of technical and legal frontiers

Free movement of goods

Prevention of further barriers

198.   Council Directive 83/189/EEC of 28 March 1983 laying down a procedure for the provision of information in the field of technical standards and regulations [2] is an essential tool for preventing the emergence of any new barriers to trade as a result of the adoption of draft national standards or technical regulations; it also provides special opportunities for creating a technical environment common to all firms, enabling them to develop, maintain or strengthen their competitiveness on the internal market or on markets outside the Community.

The number of draft technical regulations notified by Member States is increasing yearly. In 1987 there were 34.2% more received than in 1986; from the date the Directive entered into force to the end of the year, the Commission received a total of 458 notifications. During the process of examining the drafts, there was closer dialogue both between the Member States themselves and with the Commission, notably in the standing committee set up under the Directive; this reflects a move towards greater transparency in national standards programmes and draft standards.

The Commission prepared a comprehensive report on the implementation of the Directive for transmission to the Council early in 1988.

Removal of existing technical barriers

199.   In 1987 the Council adopted technical harmonization directives for the following industrial products: simple pressure vessels, [3] in accordance with the new approach to harmonization; distinctive numbers and letters indicating the

---

[1]   Points 260, 261 and 271 to 273 of this Report.
[2]   OJ L 109, 26.4.1983; Seventeenth General Report, point 156; Eighteenth General Report, point 139; Nineteenth General Report, points 211 and 212.
[3]   Points 150 and 151 of this Report.

Member States;[1] nominal quantities and nominal capacities permitted for certain prepacked products;[1] and front-mounted roll-over protection structures on agricultural and forestry tractors;[2] and two amendments to the framework Directive of 6 February 1970 relating to the EEC type approval of motor vehicles,[3] one concerning a definition of off-road vehicles[2] and the other a simplification of administrative procedures.[4]

This brings the number of directives of this kind adopted by the Council to 189.

On 18 December the Council adopted a common position[5] on the proposal for a Directive[6] amending the Directive of 19 December 1974 on the making-up by volume of certain prepackaged liquids.[7]

The Commission also adopted directives in certain areas adapting existing directives to technical progress. These concerned *inter alia* radio interference caused by electrical household appliances[8] and the suppression of radio interference on fluorescent lighting luminaires.[8]

The number of such directives adopted by the Commission is now 85.

200. A number of proposals were transmitted during the year. They concerned safety in the design and construction of a wide range of machinery,[9] electromagnetic compatibility,[10] spray-suppression and lateral-protection devices on commercial vehicles,[11] amendments to the framework Directive on agricultural and forestry tractors,[12] and the final aspects to be regulated to complete legislation on the EEC type approval of tractors.[13]

On 3 December the Council meeting on the environment adopted, in pursuance of Article 100a of the EEC Treaty as amended by the Single European Act, a common position on two proposals for Directives, one relating to emissions of gaseous pollutants from private cars and the other to emissions of gaseous pollutants from heavy goods vehicles.[14]

---

[1]   OJ L 192, 11.7.1987; Bull. EC 7/8-1987, point 2.1.13.
[2]   OJ L 220, 8.8.1987; Bull. EC 6-1987, point 2.1.12.
[3]   OJ L 42, 23.1.1970.
[4]   OJ L 192, 11.7.1987; Bull. EC 6-1987, point 2.1.12.
[5]   Bull. EC 11-1987.
[6]   OJ C 317, 10.12.1986; Twentieth General Report, point 208.
[7]   OJ L 42, 15.2.1975.
[8]   OJ L 155, 16.6.1987; Bull. EC 6-1987, point 2.1.15.
[9]   Bull. EC 11-1987, point 2.1.21.
[10]   OJ C 322, 2.12.1987; Bull. EC 11-1987, point 2.1.22.
[11]   OJ C 265, 5.10.1987; Bull. EC 7/8-1987, point 2.1.15.
[12]   OJ C 88, 3.4.1987; Bull. EC 1-1987, point 2.1.9.
[13]   OJ C 218, 17.8.1987; Bull. EC 4-1987, point 2.1.9.
[14]   Point 504 of this Report.

201.   On 10 March Parliament delivered an opinion [1] on the Commission's communication of 18 November 1985 concerning Community foodstuffs legislation [2] and on its subsequent four proposals for Directives relating to food additives, [3] materials and articles intended to come into contact with foodstuffs, [4] foodstuffs intended for particular nutritional uses [4] and labelling. [4] To take account of Parliament's views the Commission amended its four proposals on 26 May and 1 June. [5]

On 5 October, acting under the cooperation procedure set out in Article 149 of the Treaty (as amended by the Single European Act), the Council adopted a common position [6] on the proposal for a Directive relating to extraction solvents used in the production of foodstuffs and food ingredients [7] —on which it had reached agreement in June [8] —and the proposal for a Directive relating to flavourings and source materials for their production. [9]

The Commission also adopted Directives on some aspects of foodstuffs: on 4 April a Directive on the indication of alcoholic strength by volume in the labelling of alcoholic beverages,[10] made mandatory by the Council Directive of 26 May 1986;[11] and on 6 October an initial Directive laying down Community methods of sampling for chemical analysis for the monitoring of preserved milk products.[12]

The Commission sent the Council new proposals relating to indication of the manufacturing lot.[13] In carrying out its task of administering Community legislation, it sent the Council two proposals for further[14] amendments[15] to the Directives relating to fruit juices and certain similar products[16] and fruit jams, jellies and marmalades.[17] On 8 December the Commission transmitted a

[1]   OJ C 99, 13.4.1987; Bull. EC 3-1987, points 2.1.10 to 2.1.14.
[2]   Nineteenth General Report, point 215.
[3]   OJ C 116, 16.5.1986; Twentieth General Report, point 209.
[4]   OJ C 124, 23.5.1986; Twentieth General Report, point 209.
[5]   OJ C 154, 12.6.1987; OJ C 161, 19.6.1987; Bull. EC 5-1987, point 2.1.14.
[6]   Bull. EC 10-1987, point 2.1.11.
[7]   OJ C 312, 17.11.1983; Seventeenth General Report, point 157; OJ C 77, 23.3.1985; Nineteenth General Report, point 215.
[8]   Bull. EC 6-1987, point 2.1.186.
[9]   OJ C 144, 13.6.1980; Fourteenth General Report, point 126; OJ C 103, 24.4.1982; Sixteenth General Report, point 154.
[10]   OJ L 113, 30.4.1987; Bull. EC 4-1987, point 2.1.13.
[11]   OJ L 144, 29.5.1986; Twentieth General Report, point 583.
[12]   OJ L 306, 28.10.1987; Bull. EC 10-1987, point 2.1.13.
[13]   OJ C 310, 20.11.1987; Bull. EC 11-1987, point 2.1.24.
[14]   OJ C 24, 31.1.1987; OJ C 25, 3.2.1987; Twentieth General Report, point 209.
[15]   Bull. EC 12-1987.
[16]   OJ L 311, 1.12.1975; Ninth General Report, point 242.
[17]   OJ L 205, 13.8.1979; Thirteenth General Report, point 104.

proposal[1] to amend for the ninth time the Directive of 24 July 1973 relating to cocoa and chocolate products for human consumption.[2]

Lastly, on 14 October the Commission sent the Council and Parliament a communication[3]—as envisaged when it put forward its proposal for a Directive on the official inspection of foodstuffs[4]—on the current situation regarding the monitoring of foodstuffs in the Member States and an action programme for cooperation at Community level in this area.

202.   On 15 December the Commission adopted for transmittal to the Council a set of four proposals for Directives aimed at extending the scope of Directives on proprietary medicinal products to cover other such products currently excluded.[1]

On 9 February the Council adopted a recommendation concerning tests relating to the placing on the market of proprietary medicinal products,[5] thus completing its work on the Commission's package of five proposals relating to high-technology medicinal products.[6]

The Economic and Social Committee delivered its opinion, on 23 September,[7] on the proposal for a Directive relating to the transparency of measures regulating the pricing of medicinal products for human use and their inclusion within the scope of the national health insurance system.[8]

203.   As regards chemical products, the Council adopted on 18 December a common position[1] on the proposal for a Directive relating to the classification, packaging and labelling of dangerous preparations.[9]

On 30 November the Council adopted a common position[10] on the proposal for an amendment[11] to the Directive of 18 December 1975 on the approximation of the laws of the Member States relating to fertilizers[12] so as to extend the

---

[1]   Bull. EC 12-1987.
[2]   OJ L 228, 16.8.1973.
[3]   Bull. EC 10-1987, point 2.1.12.
[4]   OJ C 20, 27.1.1987; Twentieth General Report, point 209.
[5]   OJ L 73, 16.3.1987; Bull. EC 2-1987, point 2.1.12.
[6]   OJ L 15, 17.1.1987; OJ C 122, 22.5.1986; Twentieth General Report, point 210; OJ C 293, 5.11.1984; Eighteenth General Report, point 145.
[7]   OJ C 319, 30.11.1987; Bull. EC 9-1987, point 2.4.26.
[8]   OJ C 17, 23.1.1987; Twentieth General Report, point 210.
[9]   OJ C 211, 22.8.1985; Nineteenth General Report, point 214; OJ C 353, 30.12.1987; Bull. EC 11-1987, point 2.1.160.
[10] Bull. EC 11-1987, point 2.1.11.
[11] OJ C 12, 16.1.1987; Twentieth General Report, point 211.
[12] OJ L 24, 30.1.1976; Ninth General Report, point 91.

rules laid down for solid fertilizers to cover liquid fertilizers. The Directive of 22 June 1977 on methods of sampling and analysis for fertilizers,[1] also applies to liquid fertilizers.

On 24 November the Commission adopted an amendment[2] to that Directive, and on 21 December sent the Council a proposal[3] to amend the Directive of 18 December 1975[4] in respect of calcium, magnesium, sodium and sulphur in fertilizers.

The Commission continued its preparatory work, in accordance with the guidelines for a new approach to technical harmonization and standards,[5] on a Directive on personal protective equipment, which has the dual purpose of ensuring free movement of such equipment and maximum possible user safety.

204.　In the building sector, the Commission continued working on the rational use of energy and on fire safety. As regards the former, the study on a preliminary draft Eurocode was circulated with a view to holding information meetings in January 1988. A seminar on fire safety was organized in Luxembourg in September.

On 15 January the Commission sent the Council a proposal for a general Directive[6] which applies to construction products the new approach to technical harmonization and standards. It continued its work on essential requirements.

The Commission also continued drafting Eurocodes, five of which have been published and circulated in the Member States. Two new Eurocodes are being published; work on drafting a code for structural work is continuing.

Implementation of the new approach to technical harmonization and standards

205.　In line with the resolution of 7 May 1985 on a new approach to technical harmonization and standards,[5] in June the Council adopted a Directive on the approximation of the laws of the Member States regarding simple pressure vessels.[7]

---

[1]　OJ L 213, 22.8.1977; Eleventh General Report, point 160.
[2]　OJ L 342, 4.12.1987; Bull. EC 11-1987, point 2.1.27.
[3]　Bull. EC 12-1987.
[4]　OJ L 24, 30.1.1976; Ninth General Report, point 91.
[5]　OJ C 136, 4.6.1985; Nineteenth General Report, point 210.
[6]　OJ C 93, 6.4.1987.
[7]　Point 150 of this Report.

Commission proposals

206.   On 20 February the Commission sent the Council two proposals for Directives on the procedure for the provision of information in the field of technical standards and regulations; the first aims to extend the field of application of the Directive of 28 March 1983 to all industrially manufactured products, and the second to introduce a similar information procedure for agricultural products. [1] In September the Economic and Social Committee endorsed these proposals. [2] After receiving Parliament's opinion [3] the Commission sent the Council on 25 November an amendment [4] to its initial proposal incorporating the changes it was able to accept. Parliament delivered a favourable opinion [5] on the second proposal and on 30 November the Council adopted a common position [6] on these proposals.

Increasing European standardization

207.   On 18 December the Council adopted a resolution calling on the Commission to pursue its work with a view to transmitting new proposals to extend Community harmonization to new quantity ranges concerning household products. [7]

208.   On 14 December the Commission sent the Council a communication on consumer involvement in standardization, especially in national and European standards organizations. [8]

209.   Pursuing the Community's harmonization and standardization policy, the Commission gave CEN (the European Committee for Standardization) and Cenelec (the European Committee for Electrotechnical Standardization) a number of remits to draft standards concerning, in particular, gas appliances, toys, payment cards, advanced production technology and other areas of information technology. There are more standardization programmes in preparation, in the building products and machinery sectors. On the basis of these

---

[1]   Point 151 of this Report.
[2]   OJ C 319, 30.11.1987; Bull. EC 9-1987, point 2.4.24.
[3]   OJ C 345, 21.12.1987; Bull. EC 11-1987, point 2.1.17.
[4]   OJ C 3, 7.1.1988; Bull. EC 11-1987, point 2.1.18.
[5]   OJ C 345, 21.12.1987; Bull. EC 11-1987, point 2.1.19.
[6]   Bull. EC 11-1987, point 2.1.20.
[7]   Point 535 of this Report.
[8]   Bull. EC 12-1987.

remits, CEN and Cenelec have already drawn up several European standards and pre-standards concerning unleaded petrol and information technology.

Recognition of tests and certificates

210. Continuing its efforts to implement the provisions of the Council resolution of 7 May 1985,[1] the Commission started to frame general principles for a Community policy for the recognition of evidence of conformity and to work on the technical instruments essential to such a policy.

The technical work carried out in 1987 made it possible to produce a first draft of general criteria for the evaluation of certification bodies and testing laboratories, based on existing international documentation (ISO/IEC guides and ILAC documents). There should be general European consensus on these documents, leading to their approval by CEN and Cenelec in accordance with the remits given to them by the Commission. In addition, the Commission is continuing to promote development of the Promolog database, which is to contain all the relevant information on certification bodies, procedures and systems in the Community and EFTA countries.

Progress on policy has necessarily been slower, dependent as it is on the exploitation of technical results. A few priority areas have been identified, however — notably the establishment of machinery for laboratory accreditation and the promotion of systems for the supervision of manufacture which will eventually make it possible to have recourse to simplified certification procedures based more upon the manufacturer's 'declaration of conformity'.

211. On 18 December the Council reached a common position[2] on the proposal for a Directive on the inspection and verification of the organizational processes and conditions under which laboratory studies are planned, performed, recorded and reported for the non-clinical testing of chemicals (good laboratory practice).[3]

Government procurement

211a. Commission proposals and Council decisions relating to government procurement are reported elsewhere in this section, under 'Priority activities and objectives'.[4]

---

1   OJ C 136, 4.6.1985; Nineteenth General Report, point 210.
2   Bull. EC 12-1987.
3   OJ C 13, 17.1.1987; Twentieth General Report, points 211 and 561.
4   Points 146 to 149 of this Report.

Free movement of workers

212. Commission proposals and Council decisions that are of direct concern to individuals (removal of restrictions, mutual recognition of qualifications, access to occupations, special rights, passport union, and tourism) are reported in the second part of this section ('A people's Europe'). [1]

Common market in services

Financial services

213. Considerable headway was made in 1987 in completing the internal market in financial services, in line with the White Paper on completing the internal market. [2] Further substantial progress in this field is envisaged in the Commission's communication concerning the complete liberalization of capital movements. [3]

A new impetus was provided by the judgments delivered by the Court of Justice on 4 December 1986 in the insurance field, [4] which reinforced the principle of mutual recognition and defined in general terms the harmonization work still necessary for its application.

At international level, the first exploratory talks on internal market matters (banking legislation, insider trading) were held on 9 October with experts from EFTA countries. [5] In the context of the Uruguay Round of GATT talks [6] too, aspects specific to financial services were identified as a key area in the negotiations on trade in services; [7] they were also discussed in the OECD. [8]

---

[1] Points 262 to 269 of this Report.
[2] Nineteenth General Report, points 162 to 166.
[3] Point 152 of this Report.
[4] Cases 220/83 *Commission v France*, 252/83 *Commission v Denmark*, 205/84 *Commission v Federal Republic of Germany* and 206/84 *Commission v Ireland;* Twentieth General Report, points 221 and 1036.
[5] Point 770 of this Report.
[6] Twentieth General Report, point 810.
[7] Points 746 and 748 of this Report.
[8] Point 894 of this Report.

Banks

214.   In order to take account of the changes suggested by Parliament, the Commission amended, on 27 May,[1] its proposal for a Directive on freedom of establishment and freedom to provide services in the field of mortgage credit.[2]

215.   The Commission began drafting a proposal for a second Directive on the coordination of banking legislation, which will extend the scope of the first Directive (77/780/EEC)[3] with a view to completing the harmonization required for ensuring mutual recognition of supervisory systems and so establishing the principle of supervision by the Member State in which the head office is located, together with the procedure of the issue of a single banking licence recognized throughout the Community.

216.   At the same time, the Commission started work on a proposal for a Directive on the solvency ratio applicable to credit institutions, which will lay down rules for the calculation of the ratio to be observed between own funds and risk assets.

217.   The Banking Advisory Committee, chaired by Mr T. O'Grady-Walshe, General Manager of the Central Bank of Ireland, devoted much of its three meetings this year to an examination of these two proposals, which are the last remaining banking measures scheduled in the White Paper on completing the internal market.

218.   As required by the first Directive on the taking up and pursuit of the business of credit institutions,[3] the Commission published the list of credit institutions authorized to do business in the Member States, reflecting the situation at 31 December 1986.[4]

Insurance

219.   Following the judgments delivered by the Court of Justice on 4 December 1986 clarifying the scope of Articles 59 and 60 of the Treaty with regard to freedom to provide insurance services,[5] the Council resumed its work with a

---

[1]   OJ C 161, 29.6.1987; Bull. EC 5-1987, point 2.1.87.
[2]   OJ C 42, 14.2.1985; Eighteenth General Report, point 243; Nineteenth General Report, point 224.
[3]   OJ L 322, 17.12.1977; Eleventh General Report, point 211.
[4]   OJ C 61, 9.3.1987; OJ C 151, 9.6.1987; OJ C 233, 31.8.1987.
[5]   Cases 220/83 *Commission v France*, 252/83 *Commission v Denmark*, 205/84 *Commission v Federal Republic of Germany* and 206/84 *Commission v Ireland;* Twentieth General Report, points 221 and 1036.

view to the rapid adoption of the proposal for a second Directive on the coordination of legislation relating to insurance [1] and reached a common position on 18 December. [2]

220. On 22 June the Council adopted, [3] on a proposal from the Commission, [4] a Directive on credit and suretyship insurance. On the same day it adopted, [5] on a proposal from the Commission, [6] a Directive on legal expenses insurance. These two Directives supplement and clarify the provisions of the first coordinating Directive on the taking up and pursuit of the business of direct insurance other than life assurance (73/239/EEC). [7]

221. On 20 May the Commission transmitted to the Council a report [8] on the second phase of negotiations with Switzerland [9] on the conclusion of an agreement on the taking up and pursuit of the business of direct insurance other than life assurance. [10]

*Stock exchanges and other institutions
in the securities field*

222. On 21 May the Commission transmitted to the Council a proposal for a Directive on insider trading, [11] which aims to establish a uniform basis within the Community for combating the fraudulent use of privileged stockmarket information which certain individuals can obtain, enabling them to make substantial gains at the expense of other investors.

223. On 22 June the Council adopted, [12] on a proposal from the Commission, [13] a Directive amending Directive 80/390/EEC of 17 March 1980 coordinating

---

1   OJ C 32, 12.2.1976; Tenth General Report, point 229.
2   Bull. EC 12-1987.
3   OJ L 185, 4.7.1987; Bull. EC 6-1987, point 2.1.83.
4   OJ C 245, 29.9.1979; Thirteenth General Report, point 177; OJ C 5, 7.1.1983; Sixteenth General Report, point 247.
5   OJ L 185, 4.7.1987; Bull. EC 6-1987, point 2.1.84.
6   OJ C 198, 7.8.1979; Thirteenth General Report, point 177; OJ C 78, 30.3.1982; Sixteenth General Report, point 245.
7   OJ L 228, 16.8.1973.
8   Bull. EC 5-1987, point 2.1.90.
9   Twentieth General Report, point 231.
10 OJ C 154, 13.6.1983; Seventeenth General Report, point 255, Eighteenth General Report, point 239; Nineteenth General Report, point 232.
11 OJ C 153, 11.6.1987; Bull. EC 4-1987, point 2.1.65.
12 OJ L 185, 4.7.1987; Bull. EC 6-1987, point 2.1.85.
13 OJ C 110, 24.4.1987; Bull. EC 3-1987, point 2.1.88; OJ C 148, 6.6.1987;Bull. EC 5-1987, point 2.1.91.

the requirements for the drawing-up, scrutiny and distribution of the listing particulars to be published for the admission of securities to official stock exchange listing. [1] The Directive provides for the mutual recognition of listing particulars where applications for admission to official listing are made simultaneously or within a short interval in at least two Member States.

224. On 4 September the Commission transmitted to the Council an amendment [2] to its proposal for a Directive on information to be published when major holdings in the capital of a listed company are acquired or disposed of. [3]

225. On 16 November the Council arrived at a common position [4] on the proposal for a Directive [5] amending, as regards the investment policies of certain undertakings for investment in transferable securities (Ucits), the limits set in Article 22 of Directive 85/611/EEC on Ucits, which was adopted on 20 December 1985. [6]

226. On 15 October the Commission made known its intention of withdrawing its proposal for a Directive [7] amending Council Directive 85/611/ EEC [6] as regards jurisdiction in disputes arising from the marketing of units of Ucits; a solution will have to be found to this problem under the Brussels Convention of 27 September 1968. [8]

227. The Commission continued its cooperation with the Committee of Stock Exchanges in the EEC [9] over the implementation of the IDIS project (Interbourse Data Information System), designed to link the various stock exchanges in the Community.

228. The Commission completed its examination of ways of establishing or reinforcing links between national systems for the settlement of securities transactions (security clearing). It is currently considering what further action it should take in this matter. [10]

---

[1] OJ L 100, 17.4.1980; Fourteenth General Report, point 207.
[2] OJ C 255, 25.9.1987; Bull. EC 9-1987, point 2.1.73.
[3] OJ C 351, 31.12.1985; Nineteenth General Report, point 236; Twentieth General Report, point 236.
[4] Bull. EC 11-1987, point 2.1.108.
[5] OJ C 155, 21.6.1986; Twentieth General Report, point 235.
[6] OJ L 375, 31.12.1985; Nineteenth General Report, point 234.
[7] OJ C 129, 28.5.1986; Twentieth General Report, point 235.
[8] OJ L 299, 31.12.1972; Sixth General Report, point 133; OJ L 304, 30.10.1978; Twelfth General Report, point 115; OJ L 388, 31.12.1982; Sixteenth General Report, point 162.
[9] Eighteenth General Report, point 248; Nineteenth General Report, point 235; Twentieth General Report, point 237.
[10] Twentieth General Report, point 238.

New technologies and related services

Audiovisual services

Cinema

229.   Under the Treaty rules on State aid, the Commission carried out a joint examination with five Member States of their national laws on aid to the film industry. One of the conditions governing the granting of such aid is that certain functions in the film-making process are carried out by nationals. It also examined coproduction agreements between Member States.

Broadcasting

230.   On 1 July the Economic and Social Committee issued its opinion [1] on the proposal for a Directive on the coordination of certain provisions in the Member States relating to broadcasting. [2]

231.   The Commission pursued [3] or initiated 13 actions against Member States (six infringement proceedings and seven complaints), with a view to ending discriminatory practices which restrict the freedom of broadcasting within the Community.

New means of payment

232.   On 19 January the Commission sent the Council and Parliament a communication on new payment cards, [4] an initiative which will make it possible for the European citizen to use his payment card anywhere in the Community.

233.   Of the measures envisaged in the communication, the recommendation on a European code of conduct has been adopted, [5] the standardization remits are being carried out [6] and the consumer protection measures are being prepared. [7]

---

[1]   OJ C 232, 31.8.1987; Bull. EC 7/8-1987, point 2.4.20.
[2]   Twentieth General Report, point 241; Supplement 5/86 — Bull. EC.
[3]   Twentieth General Report, point 243.
[4]   Bull. EC 1-1987, point 1.3.1 *et seq.*
[5]   Point 533 of this Report.
[6]   Point 360 of this Report.
[7]   Point 534 of this Report.

Transport services

234.   On 30 June the Council decided, acting on a proposal from the Commission, to increase by 40% the Community authorizations for the carriage of goods by road for 1987.[1] This Decision constitutes the first step of a flexible transition towards the elimination in 1992/93 of the quantitative restrictions on access to the international road haulage market.[2]

235.   In March the Commission sent to the Council a proposal for a Regulation laying down the conditions under which non-resident carriers may operate national road passenger transport services within a Member State;[3] the purpose of this proposal is to bring about freedom to provide services in this sector, so it is in keeping with the White Paper on completing the internal market.[4]

236.   The Council adopted two Decisions implementing the sea transport measures introduced in December 1986[5] — one relating to transport with West African and Central African States, the other authorizing Italy to ratify an agreement with Algeria which did not include the conditions the Commission had considered necessary in its proposal.[6]

237.   On 7 December the Council reached agreement on a package of measures concerning air transport,[7] which constitutes an important first step towards the introduction of a common civil aviation policy.

Capital movements

Liberalization of capital movements and removal of exchange controls

238.   On 4 November the Commission transmitted to the Council a communication together with a set of proposals designed to establish the principle of complete liberalization of capital movements in the Community with a view to the creation of a European financial area.[8]

---

1   Point 625 of this Report.
2   OJ L 221, 7.8.1986; Twentieth General Report, point 239.
3   OJ C 77, 24.3.1987; Bull. EC 2-1987, point 2.1.169.
4   Nineteenth General Report, points 162 to 166.
5   OJ L 378, 31.12.1986; Twentieth General Report, point 711.
6   Point 641 of this Report.
7   Points 622 and 644 of this Report.
8   Point 152 of this Report.

239. On 31 July the Commission, acting under Article 108(3) of the EEC Treaty, repealed [1] the Decision authorizing Italy to maintain in force certain protective measures relating to capital movements. [2] This was in response to the measures to relax exchange controls taken by the Italian authorities on 15 May. [2] On 16 December, again under Article 108(3), the Commission renewed [3] until the end of 1988 the Decision authorizing Ireland to continue to apply protective measures in respect of outward portfolio investment. [4]

Tax measures to promote the development of a common market in financial services

Taxation of transactions in securities

240. With a view to removing obstacles to the free movement of capital, the Commission transmitted to the Council on 14 April an amended proposal [5] for a Directive relating to indirect taxes on transactions in securities, [6] which provides for the elimination of such taxes by 1 January 1990.

A propitious legal and tax environment for businesses

Company law

241. Following adoption of Council Regulation (EEC) No 2137/85 of 25 July 1985 on the European Economic Interest Grouping (EEIG), [7] Member States continued [8] to prepare for the legislative changes necessary to enable such groupings to be registered and to operate effectively throughout the Community from 1 July 1989. The Contact Committee set up by the Regulation held its second meeting in October to review progress.

---

1   OJ L 224, 12.8.1987; Bull. EC 7/8-1987, point 2.1.5.
2   Bull. EC 5-1987, point 2.1.4.
3   OJ L 5, 8.1.1988; Bull. EC 12-1987.
4   OJ L 8, 10.1.1985.
5   OJ C 115, 30.4.1987; Bull. EC 4-1987, point 2.1.70.
6   OJ C 133, 14.6.1976; Tenth General Report, point 189.
7   OJ L 199, 31.7.1985; Nineteenth General Report, point 243.
8   Twentieth General Report, point 255.

Economic and commercial law [1]

242.   On 25 May the Council and the Ministers for Justice meeting within the Council adopted a resolution expressing their wish that application of the Brussels Convention of 27 September 1968 on Jurisdiction and the Enforcement of Judgments in Civil and Commercial Matters should be extended rapidly to the whole of the Community. [1]

Intellectual and industrial property [2]

Trade marks

243.   At its meeting on internal market matters on 30 November [3] the Council held an initial discussion on unsettled problems concerning the proposal for a first Directive harmonizing the Member States' trade-mark legislation. [4]

Patents

244.   Portugal passed new patents legislation [5] in order to meet its obligations under the Act of Accession. [6]

245.   On 26 October the Council adopted a Commission proposal on the extension of legal protection of topographies of semiconductor products in respect of persons from certain non-Community countries and territories. [7]

Company taxation

246.   On 4 November the Commission sent to the Council a communication, together with three proposals for legal instruments, aimed at establishing the principle of complete liberalization of capital movements. [8]

---

[1]   Commission proposals and Council Decisions that are of direct concern to companies in the area of economic and commercial law are reported in Section 4 of this chapter, 'Businesses': point 297 of this Report.
[2]   Commission proposals and Council decisions that are of direct concern to companies in the area of intellectual and industrial property are reported in Section 4 of this chapter, 'Businesses': points 295 and 296 of this Report.
[3]   Bull. EC 11-1987, point 2.1.29.
[4]   OJ C 351, 31.12.1985; Nineteenth General Report, point 247.
[5]   Decree-Law No 40/1987, 27.1.1987.
[6]   Nineteenth General Report, point 249.
[7]   Point 295 of this Report.
[8]   Point 152 of this Report.

Application of Community law

247.   Removing barriers to the free movement of goods and services within the Community is one of the Commission's priority objectives in establishing the internal market.[1] It is reflected in the infringement procedures initiated by the Commission and in the efforts undertaken to make the principles governing the free movement of goods and services more transparent.

Infringements

248.   The procedure laid down in Article 169 of the EEC Treaty in response to failure by a Member State to fulfil its obligations is the primary instrument for safeguarding the free movement of goods within the Community, guaranteed by Articles 30 and 36 of the Treaty. The Commission initiates the procedure whenever it establishes that the Treaty provisions have been infringed by a particular agency in a Member State. A variety of circumstances may cause it to reach such a conclusion.

In most cases, a complaint is lodged with the Commission by a firm, an individual, an association or even another Member State in respect of draft standards or technical regulations notified by Member States pursuant to Directive 83/189/EEC of 28 March 1983;[2] if a Member State adopts standards or regulations without due regard to any comments made by the Commission in a detailed opinion, its opinion will be deemed to constitute formal notice of institution of proceedings. Such standards and regulations are examined as a matter of course to ascertain their compatibility with Articles 30 to 36 of the EEC Treaty.

The cases examined include some that are referred to by Members of the European Parliament in written or oral questions and some that are opened by the Commission acting on its own initiative in response to information appearing in the press or in Member States' official gazettes. Lastly, the Commission sees to it that Member States take the necessary measures to comply with the judgments of the Court of Justice. Failure to comply leads to proceedings being instituted under Article 171 of the Treaty.

The *Beer* judgment[3] given by the Court of Justice on 12 March was one of the major developments in this field during the year. It broadly endorses the

[1]   Nineteenth General Report, points 162 to 166.
[2]   OJ L 109, 26.4.1983; Seventeenth General Report, point 156.
[3]   Case 178/84 *Commission v Federal Republic of Germany:* point 933 of this Report.

guidelines adopted by the Commission on the basis of the Court's decision in *Cassis de Dijon* and provides some interesting clarification of the limits to Member States' powers in regulating the use of additives. The Commission will set out in a notice the conclusions it has drawn from the Court's most recent judgments concerning the free movement of foodstuffs. [1]

On a number of occasions during the year, the Commission acted against national rules establishing compulsory certification procedures for verifying a model's conformity to the relevant national technical specifications in force and for checking the conformity of series-produced vehicles with the approved model. Such procedures oblige manufacturers in other Member States to adapt production to those technical specifications and prevent the importation of vehicles legally manufactured there in accordance with technical specifications different from those in force in the Member State of destination. The Commission contested some of these procedures, emphasizing that they must be genuinely necessary for safeguarding the objective in view and that, in any event, their purpose must not be to verify compliance solely with national technical specifications when compliance with other rules permits attainment of the objective in equivalent manner. In this connection, the Commission also stressed the need to implement the principle that checks, analyses and tests carried out in Member States should not be repeated.

The telecommunications market is expanding rapidly and experiencing far-reaching changes. Alongside the harmonization drive in this sector, notably with regard to networks, the Commission took issue with national rules whereby imports of telecommunications equipment have to comply to the letter with national technical specifications and to undergo a lengthy and costly type-approval procedure to ensure that those specifications are met.

Transparency

249. The principles underlying the free movement of goods will remain a dead letter as long as individuals and firms in the Community remain unaware of the rights they enjoy by virtue of the Community legal order and do not exercise those rights, if need be by availing themselves of the means of redress open to them. To that end, the Commission has, for a number of years, been striving to make individuals and firms more aware of those principles as they apply in particular sectors and of the cases in which it has intervened to put an end to any violations.

---

[1]   Point 249 of this Report.

The Commission is also striving for greater transparency of its infringement procedures. In this connection, it now publishes an annual report to Parliament on the monitoring of the application of Community law. [1] It also decided to disseminate more widely the reasoned opinions it adopts when it finds that a Member State has failed to fulfil its Treaty obligations.

Lastly, the Commission put in hand a study on the conditions under which the harmful effects stemming from an infringement of the rules governing the free movement of goods are remedied in each Member State. Firms or individuals that have been harmed by a barrier to intra-Community trade must receive proper compensation.

Removal of tax frontiers

Indirect taxation

250. On 7 August the Commission sent to the Council and to Parliament a communication to which were attached eight proposals for Directives designed to eliminate, with a view to completion of the internal market, [2] tax frontiers within the Community. [3]

Turnover tax (VAT)

251. On 9 February the Commission transmitted to the Council a proposal [4] for a Directive amending for the third time the Directive of 28 March 1983 [5] determining the scope of Article 14(1)(d) of the sixth Directive [6] as regards exemption from value-added tax on the final importation of certain goods. The proposal contains a number of amendments, some incorporated at Parliament's request, intended to facilitate the importation into one Member State from another of goods of negligible value, printed matter and publications of various

1 The fourth annual report, covering 1986, was published in OJ C 338, 16.12.1987.
2 Nineteenth General Report, points 162 to 166 and 257.
3 Point 153 of this Report.
4 OJ C 53, 28.2.1987; Bull. EC 1-1987, point 2.1.40.
5 OJ L 105, 23.4.1983; Seventeenth General Report, point 280.
6 OJ L 145, 13.6.1977; Eleventh General Report, point 219.

types. The Economic and Social Committee gave its opinion on the proposal on 13 May. [1]

252.   On 11 April the Council authorized a derogation measure [2] requested by the United Kingdom pursuant to Article 27 of the sixth Directive. This was intended, as part of anti-avoidance measures, to prevent taxable persons artificially reducing the price of supplies or imports of goods or of supplies of services to totally or partially exempt persons with whom they have certain family, legal or business ties. On 23 July the Council adopted a Decision [3] authorizing the United Kingdom to apply a measure derogating from Article 17 of the sixth Directive, allowing businesses with an annual turnover of less than 340 000 ECU to postpone until 30 September 1990, as part of an optional scheme, the right of deduction of tax until it has been paid to the supplier.

253.   On 6 April Parliament gave its opinion [4] on the Commission's proposals for an 18th and a 19th Council Directive on the harmonization of the laws of the Member States relating to turnover taxes. [5] In response to Parliament's wishes, the Commission on 25 June amended [6] its proposal for an 18th Directive. [7] It also transmitted to the Council in December an amendment [8] to its proposal for a 19th Directive [9] that takes account of the opinions of the Economic and Social Committee and Parliament.

254.   After Parliament had delivered its opinion, [10] the Commission sent to the Council on 4 November amendments [11] to its proposal of 9 October 1986 for a Directive relating to turnover taxes in respect of the scheme applicable to small and medium-sized businesses. [12]

255.   In November the Commission withdrew [13] its proposal for a seventh Council Directive on the harmonization of the laws of the Member States relating to turnover taxes—common system of value-added tax—to be applied to works of art, collectors' items, antiques and used goods. [14]

---

[1]   OJ C 180, 8.7.1987; Bull. EC 5-1987, point 2.4.28.
[2]   OJ L 132, 21.5.1987; Bull. EC 4-1987, point 2.1.54.
[3]   OJ L 213, 4.8.1987; Bull. EC 7/8-1987, point 2.1.88.
[4]   OJ C 125, 11.5.1987; Bull. EC 4-1987, point 2.1.55.
[5]   OJ C 347, 29.12.1984; Eighteenth General Report, points 254 and 255.
[6]   OJ C 183, 11.7.1987; Bull. EC 6-1987, point 2.1.68.
[7]   OJ C 347, 29.12.1984; Eighteenth General Report, point 254.
[8]   Bull. EC 12-1987.
[9]   OJ C 347, 29.12.1984; Eighteenth General Report, point 255.
[10]   OJ C 190, 20.7.1987; Bull. EC 6-1987, point 2.1.71.
[11]   OJ C 310, 30.11.1987; Bull. EC 11-1987, point 2.1.90.
[12]   OJ C 272, 28.10.1986; Twentieth General Report, point 267.
[13]   Bull. EC 11-1987, point 2.1.91.
[14]   OJ C 26, 1.2.1978, and OJ C 136, 31.5.1979.

Supervision of the application of Community provisions

256.   In 1987 the Court of Justice delivered four judgments in actions brought by the Commission for infringement of Article 95 of the EEC Treaty or of the sixth VAT Directive.[1] In the VAT Directive case it ruled that notaries and sheriffs' officers in the Netherlands engage in an economic activity within the meaning of the Directive and that services supplied by them must therefore be taxed.[2] In the Article 95 cases it found against the tax arrangements for bananas applicable in Italy on the ground that they infringed the second paragraph of the Article,[3] but declared that the differential taxation of wine and beer in Belgium[4] and the taxation of natural sweet wines and liqueur wines in France[5] were in keeping with that provision.

257.   Six proceedings were terminated by the Commission, since the Member States in question had amended their legislation in line with Community law. The first concerned Belgium and the Netherlands in connection with the rights of option provided in Annex G to the sixth VAT Directive;[1] the second Ireland in connection with a reduction in the taxable amount; the third Italy in connection with the refunding of VAT to foreign taxable persons; and the others Belgium and France in connection with the form for obtaining tax exemption. In addition, the Commission discontinued Court proceedings against Germany in respect of the inclusion of foreign-based companies in the single-taxable-entity concept *(Organschaft)*, and against Italy for failure to apply the Court's judgment in Case 278/83 concerning a discriminatory charge to duty on sparkling wines, as both Member States had brought their legislation into line.

258.   Examination of cases of failure to comply with the *Gaston Schul* judgment[6] concerning arrangements for taxing imported second-hand goods was continued;[7] the Commission sent reasoned opinions to the United Kingdom, Luxembourg, Italy, Ireland, France, Germany, Denmark, Spain and Greece.

---

[1]   OJ L 145, 13.6.1977; Eleventh General Report, point 219.
[2]   Case 235/85 *Commission v Netherlands*.
[3]   Case 184/85 *Commission v Italy*.
[4]   Case 356/85 *Commission v Belgium*.
[5]   Case 196/85 *Commission v France*.
[6]   Case 15/81 *Gaston Schul v Inspecteur der Invoerrechten en Accijnzen* [1982] ECR 1409; OJ C 13, 21.1.1986.
[7]   Twentieth General Report, point 276.

259.   The procedures initiated or continued by the Commission pursuant to Article 95 of the EEC Treaty are reviewed in the annual report to Parliament on the monitoring of the application of Community law.[1]

A PEOPLE'S EUROPE

Removal of physical frontiers

Elimination of intra-Community controls

260.   The Council continued its examination[2] of the proposal for a Directive on the easing of controls and formalities for nationals of the Member States when crossing intra-Community borders.[3]

Legislation on weapons

261.   On 6 August the Commission transmitted to the Council a proposal for a Directive on the control of the acquisition and possession of weapons.[4]

Free movement of persons

Right of entry and residence

Right of residence

262.   The Commission continued its efforts to speed up the process of adopting the proposal for a Directive on a right of residence for nationals of Member States in the territory of another Member State.[5]

---

[1]   OJ C 338, 16.12.1987.
[2]   Twentieth General Report, point 288.
[3]   OJ C 131, 30.5.1985; Nineteenth General Report, point 295.
[4]   OJ C 235, 1.9.1987.
[5]   OJ C 207, 17.8.1979; Thirteenth General Report, point 123; OJ C 188, 25.7.1980; Fourteenth General Report, point 140; OJ C 171, 10.7.1985; Nineteenth General Report, point 282.

Right of establishment

Freedom to take up and pursue activities as self-employed persons

263.   Freedom of movement for architects and pharmacists within the Community is becoming a reality. National provisions to give effect to the Directives on freedom of movement and mutual recognition of diplomas for these occupations had to be introduced by 6 August in the case of architects [1] and by 1 October in the case of pharmacists. [2] For architects, however, freedom to provide services will not become effective until 6 August 1988.

Mutual recognition of diplomas

Operation of existing arrangements

264.   The Commission continued to operate existing arrangements for the mutual recognition of diplomas, bringing them into line with the changes which have occurred. On 2 December it sent the Council a proposal for a Directive [3] making essentially technical amendments to the Directives on doctors, [4] nurses responsible for general care, [5] dental practitioners, [6] veterinary surgeons [7] and midwives. [8] On 29 December the Commission put up a proposal for a Directive [9] amending the Directives on nurses responsible for general care, [5] the main aim of which is to introduce into their training weightings relating to the theoretical and clinical components.

265.   Under the Community's action programme against cancer, [10] the Commission continued its work on preparing proposals aimed at stepping up the training of doctors, nurses and dentists in this field.

---

[1]   OJ L 223, 21.8.1985; OJ L 376, 31.12.1985; Nineteenth General Report, points 285 and 286; OJ L 27, 1.2.1986; OJ L 87, 2.4.1986; Twentieth General Report, point 293.
[2]   OJ L 253, 24.9.1985; OJ L 372, 31.12.1985; Nineteenth General Report, points 285 and 286.
[3]   OJ C 353, 30.12.1987; Bull. EC 11-1987, point 2.1.15.
[4]   OJ L 167, 30.6.1975; Eighth General Report, point 336; OJ L 43, 15.2.1982; Sixteenth General Report, point 167.
[5]   OJ L 176, 15.7.1977; Eleventh General Report, point 142.
[6]   OJ L 233, 24.8.1978; Twelfth General Report, point 116.
[7]   OJ L 362, 23.12.1978; Twelfth General Report, point 116.
[8]   OJ L 33, 11.2.1980; OJ L 375, 31.12.1980; Fourteenth General Report, point 139.
[9]   Bull. EC 12-1987.
[10]   OJ C 336, 28.12.1985; Nineteenth General Report, points 298 and 449.

With the cooperation of the Advisory Committee on Training in Nursing, the Commission held a symposium on 20 and 21 October on the subject of changes in health care and training of nurses in the twenty-first century.[1] The Commission also contributed to the progressive implementation of the Directive on specific training in general medical practice[2] by supporting a seminar on this topic organized by the European Union of General Practitioners in Luxembourg on 7 and 8 December.[3]

General system for the recognition of higher education diplomas

266.   In spite of great efforts at all levels to respect the original deadline (1987), it proved impossible to adopt the proposal for a Directive on a general system for the recognition of higher education diplomas.[4] Work on the proposal is proceeding at a steady rate, the objective being that expressly stated by the European Council in Brussels in June,[5] namely that it should be adopted 'with all possible speed and in any event before the end of 1988'.

Tourism

267.   Following the Decision establishing a consultation and coordination procedure in the field of tourism,[6] an Advisory Committee on Tourism was set up and met twice during the year.

268.   On 23 and 24 November the Commission held a conference on tourism and the completion of the internal market by 1992,[7] which focused on promoting the Community as a destination for tourists (from both Community and other countries), improving working conditions in the tourist industry and improving the seasonal and geographical distribution of tourism in the Community.

269.   In April a public hearing on tourism was held in Parliament with representatives of the national authorities and tourist bodies in the Member States with the aim of reviewing Community activities in the field.

---

1   Bull. EC 10-1987, point 2.1.9.
2   OJ L 267, 19.9.1986; Twentieth General Report, point 295.
3   Bull. EC 12-1987.
4   OJ C 217, 28.8.1985; Supplement 8/85 — Bull. EC; Nineteenth General Report, point 286; OJ C 143, 10.6.1986; Twentieth General Report, point 294.
5   Bull. EC 6-1987, point 1.1.4.
6   OJ L 384, 31.12.1986; Twentieth General Report, point 304; Supplement 4/86 — Bull. EC.
7   Bull. EC 11-1987, point 2.1.14.

Taxation

Tax exemption

270.   On 4 February the Commission transmitted to the Council a proposal [1] to amend the Directive of 28 March 1983 on tax exemptions within the Community for certain means of transport temporarily imported into one Member State from another. [2] This would help to bring about a 'people's Europe' by facilitating the temporary importation of vehicles by nationals of Member States. On 13 May the Economic and Social Committee adopted an opinion on the proposal. [3]

271.   On 16 March the Council adopted, on a proposal from the Commission, a Directive [4] amending the Directive of 28 May 1969 [5] as regards a derogation granted to Denmark relating to the rules governing turnover tax and excise duty on imports in international travel.

272.   On 14 April the Economic and Social Committee adopted an opinion [6] on a proposal [7] to amend the Council Directive of 28 March 1983 on tax exemptions applicable to permanent imports from a Member State of the personal property of individuals. [2]

273.   In order to take account of changes in consumer prices, the Commission sent to the Council on 22 December a proposal for a Directive [8] amending for the ninth time the Directive of 28 May 1969 on tax exemptions for travellers [9] and a proposal for a Directive amending for the fifth time the Directive of 19 December 1974 on the tax reliefs to be allowed on the importation of goods in small consignments of a non-commercial character within the Community. [10] These proposals contain increases in the exemption ceilings.

Civil protection

274.   On 25 June the Council and the Representatives of the Governments of the Member States meeting within the Council adopted a resolution on the introduction of Community cooperation on civil protection which they had approved on 25 May. [11]

---

[1]   OJ C 40, 18.2.1987; Bull. EC 1-1987, point 2.1.40.
[2]   OJ L 105, 23.4.1983; Seventeenth General Report, point 280.
[3]   OJ C 180, 8.7.1987; Bull. EC 5-1987, point 2.4.29.
[4]   OJ L 78, 20.3.1987; Bull. EC 3-1987, point 2.1.69.
[5]   OJ L 133, 4.6.1969; OJ L 183, 16.7.1985.
[6]   OJ C 150, 9.6.1987; Bull. EC 4-1987, point 2.4.45.
[7]   OJ C 5, 9.1.1987; Twentieth General Report, point 311.
[8]   Bull. EC 12-1987.
[9]   OJ L 133, 4.6.1969.
[10]   OJ L 354, 31.12.1974; Eighth General Report, point 172.
[11]   Point 154 of this Report.

Section 3

Industrial strategy

Main developments

275. Community industry became increasingly competitive in 1987, in spite of the economic and financial turbulence towards the end of the year. This improvement was made possible by a more favourable international climate together with the Commission's continued efforts to rationalize the Community's industrial structures—chiefly in the traditional industries—and to modernize the industrial base in the high-technology sectors.[1] Changes in the macroeconomic parameters, in particular the considerable fluctuations on the financial and foreign exchange markets at the end of the year, cast a shadow over the prospects for Community industry in 1988, in terms both of the domestic market and of exports. This change in market conditions makes it all the more essential to complete the internal market, an objective which seems to offer the surest guarantee that Community industry will remain competitive.

With this in view, the Commission has started to draw up a progress report on the situation and on the prospects for industries producing goods and providing services within the Community. This report will provide all political, economic, industrial and social decision-makers with an overall view of the state of industry in the Community and thus enable them to define more clearly the strategies to be adopted in preparing for the advent of the single internal market in 1992.

Steel

276. The steel industry had a fairly good year in 1987,[2] with the significant drop in production in 1986 resulting from the worsening of the general economic situation after the middle of the year, which had given rise to fears, at the beginning of 1987, of a renewed recession in steelmaking activities. Although the deterioration in the trade balance caused by the fall in the dollar in 1986

---

[1] Policies on information technology, telecommunications and industrial technologies are reported in Section 6 of this chapter 'Telecommunications, information technology and innovation'.
[2] Bull. EC 3-1987, point 2.1.27; Bull. EC 6-1987, point 2.1.20; Bull. EC 9-1987, point 2.1.22.

led to a slowing-down of capital goods investments, economic activity was scarcely affected thanks in particular to sustained private consumption. Following a slow start at the beginning of the year, the steel industry benefited in the second quarter from a slight recovery in steel demand due primarily to the continuing high level of activity in sectors producing consumer durables, including the motor industry, and the buoyancy of the construction industry. As a result, it was possible to consolidate and even, in some cases, to increase prices slightly during the last quarter. At the national level, however, the trends were highly divergent, the British and Spanish markets exhibiting greater dynamism than the rest of the Community. Nevertheless, the net result in 1987 will be a slight decline (of the order of 1%) in consumption. The balance of trade in steel showed signs of recovery, [1] following a deterioration in 1986 due mainly to currency adjustments, with steel orders from non-member countries having picked up since the end of 1986; in addition, the increase in imports observed in 1986 came to a halt in the last few months of that year. Consequently, Community steel production remained virtually constant (125 million tonnes) as a result of the improvement in the balance of trade in this sector. The Commission's survey of ECSC investment in 1987 indicates that steel industry investment is on the decline but is nevertheless higher than estimated and is focused to an increasing extent on rolling and downstream operations while expenditure on the liquid stage is dropping off.

277.   The Commission continued the process of adapting supply to demand by establishing quarterly quotas for production and deliveries within the Community with the aid of abatement rates [2] based on the analysis of the steel market published in the forward programmes. [3] The Commission endeavoured to ensure that its estimates did not depress prices, by revising them where necessary in order to balance supply and demand. For instance, it raised the quotas for some product categories in mid-quarter. [4]

The production and delivery quotas applied this year covered the same products as in 1986, with the exception of galvanized sheet, which was deregulated with effect from 1 January 1987. [5] Apart from deletion of Article 15B relating to

---

[1]   Bull. EC 9-1987, point 2.1.21.
[2]   OJ L 54, 24.2.1987; Bull. EC 2-1987, point 2.1.15; OJ L 136, 26.5.1987; Bull. EC 5-1987; point 2.1.30; OJ L 269, 22.9.1987; Bull. EC 9-1987; point 2.1.9.
[3]   OJ C 47, 24.2.1987; Bull. EC 2-1987, point 2.1.24; OJ C 101, 14.4.1987; Bull. EC 3-1987, point 2.1.27; OJ C 208, 5.8.1987; Bull. EC 7/8-1987; point 2.1.31; OJ C 296, 6.11.1987; Bull. EC 9-1987, point 2.1.122; Bull. EC 12-1987.
[4]   OJ L 33, 4.2.1987; Bull. EC 2-1987, point 2.1.14; OJ L 118, 6.5.1987; Bull. EC 5-1987, point 2.1.29; OJ L 206, 28.7.1987; Bull. EC 7/8-1987, point 2.1.26; OJ L 313, 4.11.1987; Bull. EC 11-1987, point 2.1.38.
[5]   OJ L 348, 10.12.1986; Twentieth General Report, point 329.

traditional deliveries,[1] the Decision on the quota system was modified in two further important respects during the year: on 20 May the Commission decided to allow a proportion of the production quotas to be converted into quotas for delivery within the Community,[2] subject to certain conditions, in order to take account of adverse trends in exports to non-Community countries, which were particularly marked for some Community steel undertakings. It also decided, as a precautionary measure, to repeal[3] the Decision it had taken in November 1986[4] in an attempt to avoid the transfer of references for products in category Ic (galvanized sheet), when liberalized, leading to the artificial swelling of the references for products remaining under the quota system. In addition, the Commission continued monitoring the measures taken under the crisis arrangements. It adopted several Decisions under Article 58 of the ECSC Treaty imposing penalties for exceeding quotas[5] and under Article 61 for transactions failing to observe the minimum prices in force.[6]

278.   The expectations aroused by the announcement by the European Confederation of the Iron and Steel Industry (Eurofer) at the end of 1986 of a concerted plan to cut the remaining surplus production capacities[7]—estimated by the Commission at about 30 million tonnes of hot-rolled products, all categories included—undoubtedly called in question the liberalization timetable envisaged in 1985,[8] as the Council approved only the deregulation of galvanized sheet[9] with effect from 1 January 1987, and not of the majority of long products as proposed by the Commission.[1] However, at a meeting in March[10] the Council accepted the Commission's analysis that the closures firmly proposed by Eurofer[11] would be insufficient for flat products and heavy sections; at a meeting in June it asked the Commission to put forward Community measures which might prompt the undertakings to reduce existing surplus capacity.[12] On the basis of the communication concerning a new crisis plan for the European steel industry for the period 1988-90 transmitted to it by the Commission on 18 September,[13] the Council reaffirmed[14] its support for the rules

---

1   Twentieth General Report, point 329.
2   OJ L 136, 26.5.1987; Bull. EC 5-1987, point 2.1.31.
3   OJ L 136, 26.5.1987; Bull. EC 5-1987, point 2.1.32.
4   OJ L 325, 20.11.1986; Twentieth General Report, point 329.
5   OJ C 123, 9.5.1987; Bull. EC 4-1987, point 2.1.21; Bull. EC 11-1987, point 2.1.39.
6   OJ C 18, 24.1.1987; Bull. EC 1-1987, point 2.1.15; OJ C 94, 7.4.1987; Bull. EC 3-1987, point 2.1.25.
7   Twentieth General Report, point 327.
8   Nineteenth General Report, point 300.
9   OJ L 348, 10.12.1986; Twentieth General Report, point 329.
10 Bull. EC 3-1987, points 2.1.20 to 2.1.26.
11 Bull. EC 1-1987, point 2.1.16; Bull. EC 3-1987, point 2.1.20a; Bull. EC 5-1987, point 2.1.26.
12 Bull. EC 6-1987, point 2.1.19.
13 OJ C 272, 10.10.1987; Bull. EC 7/8-1987, point 2.1.25.
14 Bull. EC 9-1987, point 2.1.7.

set out in the Aid Code currently in force, [1] and approved the Commission's idea of linking the new quota system, which is planned to run for three years from 1 January 1988, to the commitments the steel industry must give in respect of adequate restructuring.

The Three Wise Men appointed by the Commission [2] at the Council's request [3] presented their report on 13 November. [4] It shows that steel firms are not prepared to commit themselves to cutting capacity by the equivalent of an over-capacity of more than 16 million tonnes of hot-rolled wide strip, heavy plate and heavy sections. On the other hand, these firms are asking for production quotas to be maintained for those three product categories, while recognizing that these quotas can no longer be based on what is obviously a crisis situation as regards hot-rolled wide strip. The authors of the report take the view that, in the absence of firm commitments by the companies concerned to reduce capacity, transitional measures should be introduced leading to the abolition of all production quotas. They agree that, if the market is to be stabilized, capacity must be cut by a substantial amount similar to that estimated by the Commission and that the Aid Code should not be altered. Accordingly, they are asking the Council to give priority attention to the Commission's proposals regarding the social and regional measures to be adopted. [5]

After examining this report, the Commission transmitted to the Council on 26 November a communication [6] amending the communication of 29 July concerning a new crisis plan for the steel industry for the period 1988-90. [7] As a result of the Council's conclusions regarding this communication, [8] the Commission decided [9] that the quota system extended to 30 June 1988 for categories I, II and III should exclude wire rod and merchant bars; in the case of hot-rolled sheet (category II) and heavy sections (category III), the system could be extended to 1990 if the Commission receives undertakings relating to a reduction of at least 75% of the excess capacity; in the case of categories Ia and Ib the Commission considers that with present market conditions deregulation is necessary after 30 June 1988. The Commission will, at the same time, continue with its social and regional policies[10] in the light of the Council's decisions.

[1]   OJ L 340, 18.12.1987; Nineteenth General Report, points 374 and 375.
[2]   Bull. EC 10-1987, point 2.1.21.
[3]   Bull. EC 9-1987, point 2.1.7.
[4]   Bull. EC 11-1987, point 2.1.34.
[5]   Points 410 and 453 of this Report.
[6]   OJ C 9, 14.1.1988; Bull. EC 11-1987, point 2.1.35.
[7]   OJ C 272, 10.10.1987; Bull. EC 7/8-1987, point 2.1.25.
[8]   Bull. EC 12-1987.
[9]   OJ C 350, 29.12.1987; Bull. EC 12-1987.
[10] Points 410 and 453 of this Report; Bull. EC 12-1987.

279.   The specific measures decided upon in 1986 for the transition period [1] continued to be applied to the Spanish and Portuguese steel companies. These measures basically consist of restrictions on the level of deliveries of Spanish and Portuguese steel products to the rest of the Community market [2] and an extension of the restructuring period during which provisions similar to those of the former Aid Code are applied to these companies. The Commission verified that Spain was taking steps to fulfil its commitment to reduce its steel industry's production capacity to a level not exceeding 18 million tonnes by 31 December 1988.

Although the Spanish and Portuguese steel industries are not subject to quotas, the Commission decided on 7 April to amend for these countries the question-naires annexed to the Decisions regarding the system of monitoring and production quotas and their obligation to declare their deliveries of certain steel products, in order to have a full record of the production and deliveries of their steel companies. [3] On 9 November, having received the assent of the Council, the Commission decided to fix the level of deliveries of steel products of Spanish origin onto the rest of the Community market, excluding Portugal, at 935 000 tonnes and deliveries of steel products of Portuguese origin onto the rest of the Community market, excluding Spain, at 100 000 tonnes during 1987. [2] The safeguard clause granted to Spain was extended by two months in 1988 to enable the Commission to examine the new application. [4]

280.   In the context of the external measures, [5] which complement the meas-ures taken within the Community and are designed to stabilize the market as a whole during the restructuring phase, the Commission extended the bilateral arrangements [6] with 11 of the 13 countries with which it concluded such arrangements in 1986. The arrangement with South Africa was not extended owing to the embargo Decision, [7] nor were the arrangements with Australia, whose exports to the Community are very limited, and Japan, with which the Community has a system based on a simple exchange of letters. By contrast, the Community concluded an arrangement with Venezuela for the first time, at the latter's request. The Council confirmed the policy pursued this year by the Commission as regards negotiating arrangements for 1988 and authorized

---

[1]   Twentieth General Report, point 332.
[2]   OJ L 324, 14.11.1987; Bull. EC 11-1987, point 2.1.40.
[3]   OJ L 101, 11.4.1987; Bull. EC 4-1987, point 2.1.22.
[4]   OJ C 350, 29.12.1987; Bull. EC 12-1987.
[5]   Points 736 to 738 of this Report.
[6]   Bull. EC 1-1987, point 2.1.22; Bull. EC 2-1987, point 2.1.26; Bull. EC 3-1987, point 2.1.35.
[7]   OJ L 268, 19.9.1986; Twentieth General Report, point 336.

it to conclude agreements with the 12 countries currently subject to the arrangement. [1]

Om 18 November the Commission extended for another year [2] its recommendation on surveillance of imports, [3] and added further provisions so as to take account of the new nomenclature. [4]

The Commission continued monitoring steel trade with non-Community countries in general and took various autonomous measures (surveillance and safeguard measures, anti-dumping duties). On 5 May the Commission published a communication amending the basic import prices for certain ordinary-steel products to bring them into line with changes in the rates of exchange. [5] On 27 April it adopted a recommendation on advance Community surveillance of imports of certain products originating in non-member countries, [3] and confirmed it on 18 November, [2] with the result that the number of products subject to an import licence now corresponds exactly to the list in the arrangements, thus facilitating administration. Finally, on 24 June the Commission authorized the Member States to institute intra-Community surveillance of the importation of certain iron and steel products originating in non-member countries which are in free circulation in another Member State. [6]

Motor industry

281.   Provisional figures show that car production in the Community increased by 6% in 1987 (giving a total of 11 million vehicles), while demand was up 10% (at 10.8 million units). This is attributable to the fact that the Japanese share of the Community market has risen from 9% to 10%, and Community exports have dropped by 6% (giving a total of 1.8 million vehicles).

The European manufacturers of mass-produced cars substantially improved their financial situation compared with 1986, a year in which they had already made overall profits in excess of 1 000 million ECU following five loss years. The fall in the dollar did halt the expansion of receipts for manufacturers of top-of-the range vehicles, but their financial position is basically very sound. European carmakers have now shed most of their surplus production capacity.

---

[1]   Bull. EC 12-1987.
[2]   OJ L 328, 19.11.1987; Bull. EC 11-1987, point 2.1.51.
[3]   OJ L 112, 29.4.1987; Bull. EC 4-1987, point 2.1.31.
[4]   Point 157 of this Report.
[5]   Bull. EC 4-1987, point 2.1.29.
[6]   OJ L 201, 22.7.1987; Bull. EC 6-1987, point 2.1.36.

The Community market for light commercial vehicles (under six tonnes) continued to expand at the same pace in 1987 as in 1986 (by 11%, to reach 1.08 million units), but the market share of Japanese manufacturers increased from 13.7% to 14.3%. In the heavy commercial vehicle sector (over six tonnes), European production began to increase again in 1987 (by about 4%) to reach 300 000 units (compared with 420 000 in 1980, before the collapse of the export markets). The situation has therefore improved considerably, both financially and from the point of view of capacity utilization.

Shipbuilding

282.   On 27 January the Council adopted the sixth Directive on aid to the shipbuilding industry. [1] On 31 July the Commission sent to the Council a second communication [2] expanding on the guidelines set out in its communication of 16 October 1986 on the industrial, social and regional aspects of this sensitive sector. [3] In it the Commission sets out the measures it considers desirable with regard to future reductions in production capacity, the revival of the internal market, research and development, and cooperation in the marine equipment subsector. It stresses the efforts made by Community shipbuilders over the last 10 years to reduce production capacity by more than 45%, and to put an end to the over-capacity in merchant fleets, the need to increase Community resources and measures in the social and regional sectors in order to smooth the way for further capacity reductions and the value of international consultation with all shipbuilding countries in order to bring about more rigorous restructuring.

Textiles

283.   The improvement in the Community's textiles and clothing industry between 1984 and 1986 petered out in 1987. As in 1986, the (moderate) increase in consumption in the Community chiefly benefited non-Community producers, whose exports to the Community market increased considerably without this being offset by a corresponding growth in exports from the Community.

The conditions governing international trade have a major influence on the outlook for the industry: the fall in the dollar and the more restrictive United

---

[1]   Point 382 of this Report.
[2]   Bull. EC 7/8-1987, point 2.1.19.
[3]   Twentieth General Report, point 339.

States policy on imports have increased external pressure on the Community market. Moreover, the ultimate fate of the American bill designed to limit imports to the United States of textiles and clothing irrespective of their origin [1] will have a major effect on the practical scope of the GATT Multifibre Arrangement, which has been extended until the end of 1991, [2] and of the bilateral agreements under the MFA. [3]

This climate of growing international competition underlines the importance of the policy to promote innovation which is being conducted under the Community's Brite programme [4] with a view to improving competitiveness, in particular in the clothing sector. The initial results of this programme have been encouraging.

Services

284.   As services are increasingly important in terms of economic and industrial development, the Commission has set up an administrative unit to coordinate the various Community initiatives in this rapidly expanding sector. Analyses have been carried out to take stock of the latest studies of the service industries. These analyses confirm that business services will have a major role to play in the adaptation of production structures. Studies have been made of 15 sectors of business services, and contacts have been established with the professional bodies concerned.

285.   In implementation of the 1987 action plan referred to in its communication to the Council on the new payment cards, [5] the Commission adopted and published a European Code of Conduct relating to Electronic Payment [6] in the form of a recommendation, which governs relations between financial institutions, traders and service establishments, and consumers. The Committee on Commerce and Distribution (CCD) had issued an opinion on this subject. [7] The Commission continued its consultations within the CCD and the *ad hoc* Working Party of Government Experts [8] with a view to defining, on the basis of greater knowledge of the socio-economic and cultural role of itinerant

---

[1]   Point 754 of this Report.
[2]   Twentieth General Report, points 815 to 817.
[3]   Twentieth General Report, points 804 and 805.
[4]   Point 323 of this Report.
[5]   Point 533 of this Report.
[6]   Point 232 of this Report.
[7]   Bull. EC 5-1987, point 2.1.19.
[8]   Bull. EC 5-1987, point 2.1.20.

trading, the provisions that should be taken to supplement the national and Community regulations in force regarding this occupation with the aim of accelerating the process of European integration.

The CCD also took part, as a consultative body of the Commission, in the Uruguay Round, in determining the practical implications of the liberalization of trade in goods and its possible extension to certain transnational service transactions. [1]

Aerospace

286. Following the two bilateral meetings in 1986 between representatives of the European Airbus consortium and the United States, and following repeated representations in the GATT Committee on Trade in Civil Aircraft, [2] in February the United States called for an extraordinary meeting of the Committee in order to arrive at a common interpretation of Articles 4 (incentives) and 6 (subsidies) of the Agreement on Trade in Civil Aircraft. The discussions which took place this year between the United States and the Community, and the papers submitted informally by the Community, resulted in a reconciliation of views regarding Article 4 of the Agreement, but profound differences remain regarding Article 6. [3]

Other industries

287. The Commission's Advisory Committee on Forestry and Forestry-based Industries met twice in plenary session during the year. It also set up a number of specialist working parties to facilitate more detailed discussions. The Committee's work centred on the outlook for the supply of wood in the Community, standardization problems, obstacles to the completion of the internal market, seed and seedling resources and forestry research.

288. The Commission received requests for safeguard measures from the footwear industry as a result of the increasingly rapid market penetration of footwear imported from non-Community countries, especially from the Far East; the normal procedures have been triggered.

---

[1] Points 746 and 748 of this Report.
[2] Points 756 and 757 of this Report.
[3] Bull. EC 7/8-1987, point 2.2.66.

Section 4

Businesses

Main developments

289.   On 20 May the Commission adopted its first report [1] on the implementation of the small business action programme approved by the Council on
3 November 1986. [2] This document describes the marked progress made in
improving the business environment and the supply of services to help firms
become more adaptable in the context of the internal market.

Priority activities and objectives

Establishment and development of assistance, innovation and cooperation networks

290.   Under the small business action programme [2] and the Community's
information policy in general, the Commission launched [3] in September the
first phase of the pilot scheme for Euro info centres [4] with the opening of 39
information centres throughout the Community, integrated into the existing
structures and competent to advise and assist firms. These centres are to answer
questions from SMEs regarding such matters as the internal market (the legal,
regulatory, technical and social factors governing intra-Community trade) and
their entitlement to aid under Community policies. This network is being set
up as part of the overall strategy of improving communications with SMEs, so
that their needs can be assessed quickly.

291.   As envisaged in the small business action programme, [2] the Commission
sent a proposal to the Council on 23 January for a four-year Community
programme, allocated 17.5 million ECU, for setting up business and innovation
centres. [5] The programme would establish a European Business and Innovation

---

[1]   Bull. EC 5-1987, point 2.1.21.
[2]   OJ C 287, 14.11.1986; Twentieth General Report, points 349 and 350.
[3]   Bull. EC 7/8-1987, point 2.1.23.
[4]   Bull. EC 4-1987, point 2.1.18.
[5]   OJ C 33, 11.2.1987; Bull. EC 1-1987, point 2.1.13.

Centre Network (EBN), and alter the geographical targeting of Community aid in this sector.

292.   Also, the Commission sent the Council, Parliament and the Economic and Social Committee a communication[1] on 3 August on the new instrument to be used by the Business Cooperation Centre (BCC) to improve cooperation between European firms: the Business Cooperation Network (BC-Net).[2] This network, provided for in the action programme[3] will provide a link between business advisers and enable them to respond very quickly to offers of and requests for cooperation. A call for cooperation addressed to business advisers was issued on 21 August with the aim of linking up some 250 advisers during the initial phase of the project.[4] For subcontracting purposes, the BCC prepared a glossary of electronics terminology and a practical guide to the legal aspects of contracts.

293.   Finally, in December the Commission launched 'Europartnership 1988', a pilot project designed to promote the development of small firms in Ireland by encouraging cooperation agreements between them and firms from other Community regions.[5]

Improving the business environment

294.   Generalizing the system of impact statements,[6] which now accompany any proposal likely to have an effect on business competitiveness and employment, has improved internal coordination between Commission departments and given the Council and Parliament an additional information tool. The Committee of Heads of Industrial Policy Departments made a first assessment of the new system[7] and reviewed and examined measures taken to improve the business environment,[7] notably those introduced by the Member States to reduce administrative burdens in the spirit of the Council's statement of 20 October 1986.[8] The overall impact of Community legislation relating to SMEs was also the subject of a study that should lead to further simplification measures.

---

[1]   Bull. EC 7/8-1987, point 2.1.24.
[2]   Twentieth General Report, point 356.
[3]   OJ C 287, 14.11.1986; Twentieth General Report, points 349 and 350.
[4]   OJ C 224, 21.8.1987; Bull. EC 7/8-1987, point 2.1.24.
[5]   Bull. EC 12-1987.
[6]   Twentieth General Report, point 352.
[7]   Bull. EC 2-1987, point 2.1.13; Bull. EC 4-1987, point 2.1.16.
[8]   Twentieth General Report, point 351.

Industrial property [1]

295.   On 26 October the Council adopted [2] a Commission proposal on the temporary extension of legal protection of original topographies of semiconductor products in respect of persons from certain non-member countries and territories [3] so that unlimited reciprocal protection can be ensured during the period preceding effective implementation of the Directive of 16 December 1986. [4]

After the adoption of this Directive, the Community asked to be represented as such at the forthcoming Diplomatic Conference on Integrated Circuits, to be held in 1988-89 under the auspices of the World Intellectual Property Organization (WIPO). The Commission has already presented the Community's standpoint at the third meeting of the WIPO Committee of Experts on Intellectual Property in this field. [5]

296.   Portugal adopted new legislation on patents, thereby fulfilling its obligations under the Treaty of Accession. [6]

Economic and commercial law

297.   On 25 May the Council and the Ministers for Justice meeting within the Council adopted a resolution [7] expressing the wish that the Brussels Convention of 27 September 1968 on Jurisdiction and the Enforcement of Judgments in Civil and Commercial Matters [8] be extended rapidly to the whole of the Community. They noted that this would necessitate opening negotiations with Spain and Portugal at the earliest opportunity.

Public procurement

298.   The Commission's proposals and the Council's decisions concerning public procurement are covered under 'Priority activities and objectives' in Section 2 ('Completing the internal market') of Chapter II of this Report. [9]

1   For matters not directly related to businesses, see points 243 and 244 of this Report.
2   Bull. EC 6-1987, point 2.1.17.
3   OJ L 313, 4.11.1987; Bull. EC 10-1987, point 2.1.17.
4   OJ L 24, 27.1.1987; Twentieth General Report, point 258.
5   Bull. EC 4-1987, point 2.1.17.
6   Point 244 of this Report.
7   OJ C 175, 3.7.1987; Bull. EC 5-1987, points 2.1.22 and 2.4.3.
8   OJ L 304, 30.10.1978; Twelfth General Report, point 115; Sixteenth General Report, point 162.
9   Point 141 of this Report.

Supply of business services; improving the adaptability of firms to the internal market

299.   On 9 March the Council adopted the Decision that had been the subject of a common position approved on 8 December 1986 extending activities under the New Community Instrument (NCI IV). [1]

300.   As was contemplated in the small business action programme, [2] the Commission transmitted to the Council a proposal for a programme and two communications concerning, respectively, the creation of business and innovation centres, the pilot phase of the project for Euro info centres (centres for European business information) and the implementation of the BC-Net project. [3] In October, the Venture Consort pilot project, which was launched in 1985 with the cooperation of the European Venture Capital Association (EVCA) to encourage venture capital activities throughout the Community, [4] was extended and allocated 1.9 million ECU for 1987.

301.   In November the Commission inaugurated the BACH (business accounts harmonized data bank). [5]

---

1   Points 146 to 149 of this Report.
2   OJ C 287, 14.11.1986; Twentieth General Report, points 349 and 350.
3   Points 290 to 293 of this Report.
4   Seventeenth General Report, point 610; Nineteenth General Report, point 691.
5   Bull. EC 11-1987, point 2.1.33.

Section 5

Research and technology

Main developments

302.   For research and technological development 1987 will be seen as a milestone. The most important event of the year was the adoption and launching of the framework programme (1987-91), the first framework programme for research and technological development based on the Single Act and a medium-term planning tool enabling the Community to prepare its R&TD work for the next five years.

Although formally adopted only in September, regrettably behind schedule and with a budget that is the bare minimum acceptable, the framework programme was nevertheless set in hand extremely swiftly: by the end of the year, the Commission had put forward proposals for specific programmes representing some 75% of its total budget.

Five of the proposed programmes have already been formally adopted by the Council: the programme coordinating medical research, with its two major sections on cancer and AIDS, the fisheries research programme, the RACE programme relating to telecommunications, the second programme on science and technology for development, and the revised research programme on radiation protection, which includes a number of activities prompted by the Chernobyl accident.

A new factor introduced by the Single Act, the procedure for cooperation with the European Parliament, whereby the latter takes a greater part in the decision-making process and proposals are examined in two readings, applies to non-nuclear R&TD programmes: the first reading of the proposals for the second phase of the Esprit programme and for the revision of the Brite programme was concluded in December with the adoption by the Council of common positions on both proposals.

Another important development was the preparation and transmission of a communication on a new outlook for the Joint Research Centre, which sets out proposals for a major reshaping of the JRC in order to adapt it to changes in the Community and give it a new impetus, thus securing it an undisputed position in the European research and technological development system.

The year also saw confirmation of the increasing role played by the Community in international scientific and technical cooperation. The framework agreements for scientific and technical cooperation between the Community and five EFTA countries were given final approval by the Council, and specific agreements were prepared. In the field of controlled thermonuclear fusion, in which it is a world leader, the Community entered into negotiations with the United States, the Soviet Union and Japan with a view to concluding an agreement on building an experimental reactor, known as ITER.

Priority activities and objectives

New JRC research programme

303. The entry into force of the Single European Act,[1] the adoption of the new framework programme (1987-91)[2] and the renewal of the JRC's current (1984-87) multiannual programme[3] provide a unique opportunity to reshape the Joint Research Centre. On 29 October the Commission, intent on taking up this challenge, sent the Council a proposal for a new programme (1988-91)[4] which follows on from the discussions that have been taking place since March 1986[5] and is based in particular on the report drawn up at the Commission's request by the panel of high-level industrial experts.

304. The aim is to achieve a fundamental reorganization which will enable the JRC to adapt to changes in the Community and will give it a new impetus, thus securing it an undisputed position in the European R&D system.

In its proposal, the Commission takes the view that the new JRC should remain firmly established in the Community system, in which it forms an integral part of Europe's R&D strategy; it should therefore continue to play its institutional role of providing scientific and technical support for the common policies, while opening itself more widely to the outside world.

Although the Commission must remain the JRC's main customer — which does not mean that the JRC has a monopoly on Community work — it is proposed that the Joint Research Centre look for other clients; with that end

---

1   Point 1 of this Report.
2   Point 307 of this Report.
3   OJ L 3, 5.1.1984; Seventeenth General Report, point 568.
4   Bull. EC 10-1987, point 1.3.1 *et seq.*
5   Bull. EC 3-1987, point 2.1.37.

in view, it would be encouraged to make available to national bodies or the industries of the Member States a range of specialized, neutral and independent scientific facilities such as research or service contracts, cooperative projects or industrial clubs. Preparatory research would be developed in order to promote the pursuit of scientific excellence in a world that is undergoing constant scientific and technological change and support the Community's technological strategy.

305. The JRC's financial resources would derive only partly from the execution of specific research programmes, i.e. appropriations under the framework programme. The remainder of the JRC's funding would come chiefly from clients, either within the Commission for scientific and technical support activities or through contracts concluded with Member States, national bodies or the private sector.

306. It is in the operation and management of the JRC that the Commission proposes to make the most immediate and far-reaching changes. Such changes should constitute a clean break with past policies; they are intended to grant the JRC as a whole a greater degree of independence and managerial flexibility.

The Commission wishes in future to establish a clearer distinction between programme management and resource management. As far as the latter is concerned, operational scientific teams would be given the greatest possible independence and made fully responsible for all the scientific, administrative and financial aspects of their work.

To that end, the JRC would be redivided into nine scientific institutes: one for each of the Establishments at Geel, Karlsruhe and Petten, five for the Ispra Establishment (where the matrix structure of departments for projects and disciplines would be abandoned) and a ninth at a site to be determined.

These internal structural changes should be backed up by substantial reform of the present consultation structure. This would essentially mean strengthening the powers of the JRC's Board of Governors, abolishing the Scientific Council for the whole of the JRC and streamlining the specialized advisory structures, which would be limited to one committee per scientific institute.

Community R&TD policy

The framework programme (1987-91)

307. On 28 September the Council formally adopted [1] the framework programme of Community activities in the field of research and technological development (1987-91) [2] following a meeting with a delegation from Parliament on the common position it had adopted in July. [3]

The framework programme comprises eight activities, and the total amount deemed necessary is broken down between them as follows:

million ECU

Activities/research areas		Amounts deemed necessary
Quality of life		375
Health	80	
Radiation protection	34	
Environment	261	
Towards a large market and an information and communications society		2 275
Information technology	1 600	
Telecommunications	550	
New services of common interest (including transport)	125	
Modernization of industrial sectors		845
Science and technology for manufacturing industry	400	
Science and technlogy of advanced materials	220	
Raw materials and recycling	45	
Technical standards, measurement methods and reference materials	180	
Exploitation and optimum use of biological resources		280
Biotechnology	120	
Agro-industrial technologies	105	
Competitiveness of agriculture and management of agricultural resources	55	
Energy		1 173
Fission: nuclear safety	440	
Controlled thermonuclear fusion	611	
Non-nuclear energies and rational use of energy	122	
Science and technology for development	80	80

---

[1] OJ L 302, 24.10.1987; Bull. EC 9-1987, point 2.1.32.
[2] OJ C 275, 31.10.1986; Twentieth General Report, point 358.
[3] Bull. EC 7/8-1987, point 2.1.49.

million ECU

Activities/research areas	Amounts deemed necessary
Exploitation of the sea bed and use of marine resources	80
Marine science and technology	50
Fisheries	30
Emprovement of European S/T cooperation	288
Stimulation, enhancement and use of human resources	180
Use of major installations	30
Forecasting and assessment and other back-up measures (including statistics)	23
Dissemination and utilization of S/T research results	55
Total	5 396

Apart from the 1 084 million ECU deemed necessary for research programmes already adopted or being implemented, the total amount deemed necessary for the framework programme was set at 5 396 million ECU, of which not more than 4 533 million ECU is to be committed from the budget for the implementation of specific programmes up to the end of 1991.

Out of this total of 5 396 million ECU, the amount deemed necessary for specific programmes to be adopted between 1987 and 1991 was provisionally set at 4 979 million ECU on 28 September. The Council, acting unanimously, will decide at a later date on whether to add the remaining 417 million ECU.

The JRC research programme

308. On 29 October the Commission sent the Council a communication on a new outlook for the Joint Research Centre. [1]

International cooperation

309. European cooperation on scientific and technical research (COST) continued with the entry into force of memoranda of understanding in respect of the following COST projects: COST 220 'Communication protocols for terminals intended for telecommunication use by disabled people', COST 221 'Telephone amplification for the hearing-impaired', COST 309 'Road and weather conditions', COST 311 'Simulation of ship movements', COST 74 'Use of UHF/

---

[1] Points 303 to 306 of this Report.

VHF radar wind profiles for improving weather forecasting, COST B2 'Software in nuclear medicine' and COST 90 bis and 91 bis 'Food technology'.[1] A number of memoranda of understanding relating to transport and materials, due to expire in 1987, were extended for between one and three years.

310. The framework agreements for scientific and technical cooperation between the Communities and Austria, Finland, Norway, Sweden and Switzerland, which were signed in 1985 and 1986,[2] were finally concluded by the Council on behalf of the European Economic Community[3] and by the Commission on behalf of Euratom.[4] These agreements have already entered into force and the relevant joint committees have been set up. In this connection two draft specific agreements with Switzerland concerning research on wood[5] and advanced materials (Euram subprogramme)[6] were transmitted to the Council. Other draft specific agreements in fields covered by Community R&D programmes dealing with stimulation, the environment and materials are being negotiated with several EFTA countries.

311. Scientific and technical cooperation with the developing countries which have agreements with the Community increased significantly in the course of the year. Existing relations with a number of countries (China, Israel, Yugoslavia, members of Asean, Mexico and Brazil) were intensified; a genuine scientific dialogue was initiated with countries in Asia and Latin America (India, Bangladesh, Pakistan, Uruguay, Andean Pact and Central American countries).

312. International cooperation with industrialized countries was stepped up, notably with the signing of two cooperation agreements with Canada in the fields of radiation protection and raw materials[7] and the opening of negotiations for an agreement on thermonuclear fusion.[8]

---

1   All 12 Member States and three other countries (Sweden, Switzerland, Finland) take part in these two projects. The success of the COST 90, 91, 90 bis and 91 bis projects has led the Commission to contemplate extending Community/COST cooperation in food science and technology under a draft 'Umbrella' programme.
2   OJ L 313, 22.11.1985; Nineteenth General Report, point 330; OJ L 78, 24.3.1986; OJ L 216, 5.8.1986; Twentieth General Report, point 365.
3   OJ L 71, 14.3.1987; Bull. EC 2-1987, point 2.1.32.
4   OJ L 71, 14.3.1987; Bull. EC 3-1987, point 2.1.42.
5   OJ C 282, 20.10.1987; Bull. EC 9-1987, point 2.1.37.
6   OJ C 325, 4.12.1987; Bull. EC 11-1987, point 2.1.55.
7   Bull. EC 7/8-1987, point 2.1.52.
8   Point 336 of this Report.

Space

313. The Commission adopted, at the end of December, a memorandum from Mr Narjes, Member of the Commission responsible for research and science, on the Community's role in the space sector,[1] requesting the Commission departments concerned to prepare a communication on this subject for transmission to the Council and Parliament in the course of 1988.

Main areas of action in Community R&TD

Quality of life

Health

314. On 17 November the Council formally adopted a new Community R&D coordination programme in the field of medical and health research (1987-91).[2] On 28 September it had adopted a common position[3] on the Commission proposal,[4] which was an amended version of the original proposal sent to the Council and Parliament in October 1986.[5] The programme was allocated a budget of 65 million ECU over a period of five years, 49% of which will be devoted to research on cancer and AIDS. The programme also covers medical technology, health problems related to ageing and the development of health services.

315. The Commission decided, under Article 55 of the ECSC Treaty, to grant 11 million ECU of financial aid to 68 social research projects.[6]

Radiation protection

316. On 30 July the Commission sent the Council a proposal[7] revising the multiannual research and training programme in the field of radiation protection (1985-89),[8] increasing the programme allocation by 10 million ECU for

---

[1]   Bull. EC. 12-1987.
[2]   OJ L 334, 24.11.1987; Bull. EC 11-1987, point 2.1.62.
[3]   Bull. EC 9-1987, point 2.1.45.
[4]   OJ C 340, 18.12.1987; Bull. EC 9-1987, point 2.1.47.
[5]   OJ C 50, 26.2.1987; Twentieth General Report, point 393.
[6]   Bull. EC 3-1987, point 2.1.34; Bull. EC 6-1987, points 2.1.27, 2.1.28 and 2.1.50; Bull. EC 9-1987, point 2.1.28.
[7]   OJ C 302, 12.11.1987; Bull. 7/8-1987, point 2.1.61.
[8]   OJ L 83, 25.3.1985; Nineteenth General Report, point 367.

research into the short and long-term effects of nuclear accidents like the one which occurred at the Chernobyl nuclear power station in 1986.[1] The Council adopted this proposal in 21 December.[2] Work has also continued in the other fields covered by the programme, including age-related factors in radionuclide metabolism, exposure to radon in homes and exposure criteria for patients undergoing X-ray examination for purposes of medical diagnosis.

317. Following the nuclear accident at Chernobyl, the JRC developed a data bank (REM) on measurements of environmental radioactivity levels which allows access to all the information needed to develop models of the transfer of radionuclides in land and water ecosystems and in the food chain.

318. On 9 October the Community signed a memorandum of understanding with Canada on cooperative projects in the various areas covered by the radiation protection programme.[3]

Environment

319. Some 200 projects were selected for financing under the fourth multiannual research programme in the field of the environment (1986-91)[4] following various calls for research proposals.[5] These projects fall within a number of the research sectors covered by the programme, including the environmental protection sector (effects of acid deposition on historic buildings and monuments, water and soil quality, noise pollution, etc.) and climatology (effects of the accumulation of CO_2 in the atmosphere).

In May, in Grenoble, the Commission held an important symposium on the effects of air pollution on land and water ecosystems.[6]

320. Environmental research also continued at the JRC. Further progress was made on the Ecdin data bank on dangerous chemical substances, and the European inventory of existing chemical substances (Einecs), which lists 100 116 different substances, was published. In the field of industrial hazards, the Ispra risk management support system (Irims) continued to develop and a start was made on the construction of an explosion-resistant building for a project

---

[1] Twentieth General Report, point 392.
[2] Bull. EC 12-1987.
[3] Point 312 of this Report.
[4] OJ L 159, 14.6.1986; Twentieth General Report, point 396.
[5] OJ S 116, 19.6.1986; OJ S 157, 16.8.1986; Twentieth General Report, point 396.
[6] Bull. EC 5-1987, point 2.1.45.

studying chemical accidents (Fires). Under the programme on the applications of remote sensing, a new project providing support for the gathering of agricultural statistics was started and the study of upwelling currents off the north-west African coast was continued.

Information technology and telecommunications

321.   In December the Council adopted a common position on the proposal for a Regulation adopting the second phase of the Esprit programme. [1]

322.   On 14 December the Council adopted the main phase of the research programme on advanced technologies in the field of telecommunications (RACE) (1987-91). [2]

Industrial technologies

Brite

323.   The Brite [3] research programme (1985-88) [4] entered its final phase. The second call for research proposals [5] attracted 471 proposals involving 2 230 organizations; 112 projects were selected involving 573 organizations (60% of which were industrial firms — 41% of these being small businesses — 24% research centres and 16% universities). Forty-six contracts have already been signed on the basis of the available appropriations. [6]

In July the Commission sent the Council a proposal concerning the revision of the Brite programme, whereby its allocation would be increased by 60 million ECU to finance the other high-quality proposals selected. [7] The Council adopted a common position on this proposal on 21 December. [8]

324.   Ten working seminars, bringing together partners in projects from the same technical field, were held under the programme. The Brite symposium in

---

[1]   Point 356 of this Report.
[2]   Point 354 of this Report.
[3]   Basic research in industrial technologies for Europe.
[4]   OJ L 83, 25.3.1985; Nineteenth General Report, point 351.
[5]   OJ C 22, 29.1.1987; Bull. EC 1-1987, point 2.1.27.
[6]   Bull. EC 9-1987, point 2.1.41.
[7]   OJ C 238, 4.9.1987; Bull. EC 7/8-1987, point 2.1.59.
[8]   Bull. EC 12-1987.

December was attended by some 1 000 people for the purpose of interchange and discussion. [1]

Materials

325.   The multiannual research programme on raw materials and advanced materials (1986-89) [2] got fully under way in 1987. Under the Euram subprogramme (European research on advanced materials), 896 proposals representing 308 research projects were submitted in response to the call for proposals; [3] 91 projects were selected. Under the subprogrammes on primary raw material and the recycling of non-ferrous metals, 360 and 76 proposals were received, of which 59 and 19 respectively were selected. Projects were also selected under the subprogramme on wood as a renewable raw material. In April the Commission held a seminar [4] in Munich to disseminate the results of this subprogramme of the 1982-85 raw materials research programme. [5]

326.   The work at the JRC Establishment at Petten on high-temperature materials continued, including the development of models for predicting the behaviour of steel tubes subjected to severe mechanical stresses and the effects of high-temperature corrosion and the development of the HTM data bank on high-temperature materials based on results obtained under the COST project on gas turbines.

In July, in Genoa, the Commission held the first European workshop on high-temperature superconductor materials and their applications. [6] This workshop, which was attended by more than 500 scientists, took stock of recent results in this field, that is to say, the spectacular increases in temperature which confer on certain materials the property of superconductivity (zero resistance to the passage of an electric current).

Technical steel research

327.   Steel research and pilot demonstration projects were continued under Article 55 of the ECSC Treaty. A total of 37 million ECU was allocated to these projects. Under the research programme based on the medium-term

---

[1]   Bull. EC 12-1987.
[2]   OJ L 159, 14.6.1986; Twentieth General Report, point 379.
[3]   Bull. EC 2-1987, point 2.1.36.
[4]   Bull. EC 4-1987, point 2.1.38.
[5]   OJ L 174, 21.6.1982; Sixteenth General Report, point 571.
[6]   Bull. EC 7/8-1987, point 2.1.60; Bull. EC 9-1987, point 2.1.42.

guidelines for technical steel research (1986-90),[1] 100 projects costing some 26 million ECU were selected from about 180 proposals. Under the fifth annual programme of pilot and demonstration projects,[2] 16 projects costing 11 million ECU were selected from 19 proposals.

Technical coal research

328.   The Commission decided, under Article 55 of the ECSC Treaty, to grant 25 268 400 ECU in financial aid to 68 projects on technical coal research.[3]

Scientific standards; reference materials and methods

329.   Implementation of the research programme in the field of applied metrology and reference materials (1985-87)[4] by the Community Bureau of Reference (BCR) continued: some 200 reference materials were certified and distributed on request to Community laboratories.

The Commission also transmitted to the Council in September a proposal for a new BCR programme in the field of applied metrology and chemical analysis (1988-92) aimed at providing technical support for Community harmonization activities, in particular those which are necessary for the completion of the internal market.[5] It is to cover five areas: foodstuffs and agricultural products; the environment; health; metals; and physical measurements for trade and industry.

330.   At the JRC Establishment at Geel, in the context of the work on fusion technology, new standard neutron data were acquired on the linear and Van de Graaff accelerators, in particular data relating to tritium. In the nuclear reference materials sector, the Regular European Interlaboratory Measurements Evaluation Programme (Reimep) was launched, involving the characterization of the reference materials uranium hexafluoride and plutonium oxide. At the same time the Geel Establishment continued and developed its support for the BCR programme.

---

[1]   OJ C 294, 16.11.1985; Nineteenth General Report, point 586.
[2]   OJ C 81, 24.3.1983; Seventeenth General Report, point 586.
[3]   Bull. EC 3-1987, point 2.1.50; Bull. EC 11-1987, point 2.1.60.
[4]   OJ L 26, 28.1.1983; Sixteenth General Report, point 577.
[5]   OJ C 304, 14.11.1987; Bull. EC 9-1987, point 2.1.43.

Biological resources

Biotechnology

331. The 1985-89 biotechnology action programme(BAP) [1] continued during the year. The last contracts for the first phase were signed, bringing the total number of contracts to 262 representing 93 transnational joint research projects involving between two and six partners from the various Member States. Sixteen industrial firms have committed themselves to these projects; 169 others have expressed a specific interest in one or other of the projects and are attending meetings of contact groups held as part of the various programme events. Of the 262 contractors, 181 have submitted their first activity report this year, and the first annual programme report was published in December. In addition, 81 training contracts were negotiated, corresponding to 73.8 man/years.

332. On 29 October the Commission transmitted to the Council a proposal [2] concerning a revision of the BAP, increasing its allocation by 20 million ECU in order to step up Community action in the fields of biotic material collection and risk assessment and to secure the participation of Spain and Portugal in the programme.

'Concertation' activities in the biotechnology field also continued: the Sobela conference, bringing together in Brussels biotechnology experts from the Latin American countries and representatives of the Member States, laid the foundation for closer collaboration between the laboratories of two continents.

Agro-industrial technologies

333. In the field of agro-industrial technologies, 856 replies were received in response to a call for expressions of interest [3] and were analysed by the Commission. They highlight an interest in Community action in four areas, namely whole-crop harvesting and bio-refineries, production of animal feedingstuffs, production of agricultural feedstocks for industry and the use of biotechnology for pest control. On 22 December the Commission sent the Council a

---

[1]   OJ L 83, 25.3.1985; Nineteenth General Report, point 354.
[2]   Bull. EC 10-1987, point 2.1.39.
[3]   OJ S 137, 18.7.1986; Twentieth General Report, point 374.

proposal[1] for a multiannual (1988-93) programme in these various sectors (Eclair). [2]

Agriculture

334.   In the field of agricultural research, on 19 March the Council decided, [3] on a proposal from the Commission, [4] to amend the Decision of 12 December 1983 adopting joint research programmes and programmes for coordinating agricultural research (1984-88). [5] The aim of this new decision is to strengthen these research programmes by increasing the original appropriation from 30 million to 50 million ECU, in order to bring about a reorientation of the common agricultural policy.

In September the Commission drew up a list of 12 research contracts, involving 3 160 000 ECU of Community funding, to be concluded with research centres and institutes in the fields of energy in agriculture, Mediterranean agriculture and plant productivity.

Energy

Nuclear fusion energy

335.   Under the research and training programme in the field of controlled nuclear fusion (1985-89), [6] significant results were obtained on the Joint European Torus (JET): plasma currents in excess of 5 million amperes were maintained for five seconds and temperatures of 140 million °C were attained in the 'hot ion mode'. The second neutral particle injection line and the last of the high-frequency heating units, which will enable the additional plasma heating power to be raised to 40 million watts in the near future, were installed. Progress was also made with the building of medium-sized tokamaks in associated laboratories, particularly the Tore-Supra superconductor tokamak at Cadarache in France. Design work on the Next European Torus (NET) continued and the main performance specifications were selected.

---

1   Bull. EC 12-1987.
2   European collaborative linkage of agriculture and industry through research.
3   OJ L 85, 28.3.1987; Bull. EC 3-1987, point 2.1.51.
4   OJ C 273, 29.10.1986; Twentieth General Report, point 391.
5   OJ L 358, 22.12.1983; Seventeeth General Report, point 592.
6   OJ L 83, 25.3.1985; Nineteenth General Report, point 332.

In August the Commission sent the Council a proposal for a Regulation adopting a new research and training programme (1987-91) in the field of controlled thermonuclear fusion, [1] a proposal for a Decision amending the Statutes of the JET Joint Undertaking so that the duration of the project could be extended until 1992 [2] and a communication on the environmental impact and economic prospects of fusion. [2]

336.   Under its multiannual fusion programme (1984-87) the JRC continued its work in the field of technology and safety studies. It also participated in the design of NET, constructing a physical model of the reference configuration and initiating studies on the resistance of the first wall to thermal fatigue.

In June the Council authorized the Commission to negotiate an agreement with Japan on cooperation between fusion laboratories; [3] the negotiations have now entered a decisive phase. Following statements at the highest level on the subject of international collaboration in the field of fusion, representatives of the world's four major programmes (Euratom, United States, Japan and the Soviet Union) met at the invitation of the International Atomic Energy Agency in Vienna in March [4] to explore the scope for coordinating their efforts in order to produce by 1990 a preliminary design for the International Thermonuclear Experimental Reactor (ITER), with the four collaborating parties providing contributions commensurate with their status, and to coordinate their research support activities. On 5 October the Council adopted a Decision laying down the guidelines for the Commission to follow in the negotiations on ITER. [5] A technical working group was set up which recommended that research workers from the four programmes should work together for periods of a month or more on a site chosen by those in charge of the programmes. The representatives of the four parties met again in Vienna on 18 and 19 October. [5] Garching, in the Federal Republic of Germany, has been chosen as the technical site for 1988, and a formal four-party agreement is to be concluded in the early months of the year.

Nuclear fission energy

337.   JRC research on reactor safety continued under the multiannual programme (1984-87) [6] and the shared-cost part of the action programme allocated to the JRC following the Council Decision of late 1984. [7] As regards structural

---

1   OJ C 247, 15.9.1987; Bull. EC 7/8-1987, point 2.1.55.
2   Bull. EC 7/8-1987, point 2.1.55.
3   Bull. EC 6-1987, point 2.1.45.
4   Bull. EC 3-1987, point 2.1.47.
5   Bull. EC 10-1987, point 2.1.34.
6   OJ L 3, 5.1.1984; Seventeenth General Report, point 568.
7   Eighteenth General Report, point 566.

reliability, the results of the PISC II project highlighted the need to amend Section XI of the ASME Code. With regard to the safety of pressurized water reactors, experiments on the LOBI facility (pressurized water test loop) with different validation codes (including the German Drufan and the French Cathare) continued. [1] In the field of fast breeder reactor (LMFBR) safety, the development of the European accident code (EAC-1) was completed; work on the EAC-2 code and in-pile testing (Scarabee and Mol-7c) continued.

338.   Under the third programme of research and development in the field of radioactive waste management and storage (1985-89), [2] studies continued on the forms of waste most suited to final storage and on storage in deep geological formations, in particular in the experimental installations in rock salt at Asse, Germany, and in a clay stratum at Mol, Belgium. The evaluation of the suitability of various geological environments for final storage was completed (Phase 2 of the Pagis project). Various coordinated programmes (Chemval, COCO, etc.) were launched to increase knowledge of the physico-chemical phenomena related to the migration of radionuclides in the geosphere (Mirage project).

Preparations continued at the JRC Ispra Establishment for the construciton of technical facilities to study alternative methods of radioactive waste processing (Petra). In July the Commission transmitted to the Council, Parliament and the Economic and Social Committee a communication on the present situation and prospects in the field of radioactive waste management, [3] accompanied by a report updating the 1983 status report on radioactive waste management. [4]

339.   In the field of research on nuclear fuels and actinides being conducted at the JRC Establishment at Karlsruhe (Institute for Transuranic Elements), apart from basic research on actinides, work on the characterization of nuclear aerosols and the development of a uranium-plutonium mixed fuel continued, and methods for recovering actinides from waste and fuel liquors were improved. At the same time, as a contribution to reactor safety research, fuel debris from the damaged Three Mile Island reactor in the United States was analysed in the hot cells at Karlsruhe.

340.   Work undertaken in the field of safeguards and inspection of fissile materials included the holding of a first training course for IAEA and Euratom

---

1   Eighteenth General Report, point 566; Nineteenth General Report, point 334.
2   OJ L 83, 25.3.1985; Nineteenth General Report, point 336.
3   Bull. EC 7/8-1987, point 2.1.56.
4   Seventeenth General Report, point 581.

inspectors in the new plutonium handling laboratory (Preperla), [1] the design and development of prototype systems for reviewing surveillance data recorded on video tape, the development of software for evaluating plutonium isotope composition and the installation of an expert system for the analysis of data on the transfer of nuclear materials between installations.

341. As regards the decommissioning of nuclear installations, the shared-cost research programme (1984-88) [2] became fully operational, with a total of 69 contracts. A number of results have already been obtained not only in the laboratory but also from full-scale demonstrations of the decommissioning of five nuclear reactors and other installations in the fuel cycle. These have shown that large radioactive components can be decontaminated and cut up with a minimum of secondary waste and with low operator doses.

Non-nuclear energy

342. The implementation of the third R&D programme in the field of non-nuclear energy (1985-88) [3] continued, with some 575 research projects started in 1985 and 1986 being successfully concluded. More than 150 new contracts were signed in 1987 in the various areas covered by the programme, in particular a geothermal energy project using hot dry rocks on the Greek island of Milos involving partners from four different countries, and on the Soultz site in Alsace. [4]

342a. Three calls for research proposals were published for the subprogrammes on solar energy (Building 2000), [5] energy conservation (fuel cells) and new energy vectors (direct liquefaction of coal). [6] Out of the 71, 15 and 24 proposals received, 26, five and eight projects respectively were selected.

343. Several meetings of contractors were held, as well as major international conferences on solar architecture (6 to 10 April in Munich), fuel cells (4 and 5 June in Taormina) and biomass (15 to 22 May in Orléans). [7]

344. The JRC continued to implement its 1984-87 non-nuclear energy programme. [8] Its activities, particularly in the field of cell testing systems and

---

1   Twentieth General Report, point 386.
2   OJ L 36, 8.2.1984; Eighteenth General Report, point 564.
3   OJ L 83, 25.3.1985; Nineteenth General Report, point 340.
4   Bull. EC 7/8-1987, point 2.1.57.
5   OJ C 59, 7.3.1987, OJ S 47, 7.3.1987; Bull. EC 3-1987, point 2.1.48.
6   OJ C 205, 1.8.1987; Bull. EC 7/8-1987, point 2.1.58.
7   Bull. EC 5-1987, point 2.1.44.
8   OJ L 3, 5.1.1984; Seventeenth General Report, point 568.

photovoltaic equipment, included the development of an infrared laser and scanner for qualification testing and the development of a new solar simulator design (with appropriate calibration techniques); activities related to thermal systems included the development of a new methodology for the monitoring of buildings with passive solar architecture and the use of a three-dimensional computer model for improving energy conservation in buildings.

Science and technology for development

345.   On 14 December the Council formally adopted [1] the second programme on science and technology for development (1987-91) proposed by the Commission, [2] on which it had adopted a common position in September. [3] This new programme, with an estimated budget of 80 million ECU, is intended to strengthen scientific cooperation with Third World countries, on which the Community has been working since 1982, in the fields of agriculture, medicine, health and nutrition. The specific research projects cover a large number of topics, including the improvement of tropical food crops, integrated pest control techniques, new fishing methods, management of tropical forest ecosystems, evaluation and utilization of water resources, the combating of parasitic diseases (malaria, sleeping sickness, bilharziasis, etc.), bacterial diseases (leprosy, tuberculosis, etc.) and viral diseases (haemorrhagic fever, viral hepatitis, AIDS, etc.) and environmental health.

Marine resources

346.   On 19 October the Council adopted [4] a Regulation on the coordination and promotion of research in the fisheries sector [5] and a Decision adopting Community research and coordination programmes in this sector. [6] These programmes, estimated at 30 million ECU for the period 1988-92, cover fisheries management, fishing methods, aquaculture and the utilization of fishery products.

---

[1]   OJ L 355, 17.12.1987; Bull. EC 12-1987.
[2]   OJ C 24, 31.1.1987; Twentieth General Report, point 398; OJ C 340, 18.12.1987; Bull. EC 9-1987, point 2.1.50; Bull. EC 11-1987, point 2.1.65.
[3]   Bull. EC 9-1987, point 2.1.48.
[4]   OJ L 314, 4.11.1987; Bull. EC 10-1987, point 2.1.40.
[5]   OJ C 243, 22.9.1980; Fourteenth General Report, point 405; OJ C 312, 3.12.1985; Nineteenth General Report, point 361.
[6]   OJ C 111, 25.4.1987; Bull. EC 4-1987, point 2.1.39.

European scientific and technological cooperation

Stimulation plan

347. Implementation of the plan to stimulate European scientific and technical cooperation and interchange (1985-88) [1] continued in 1987. By the end of the year it included 364 joint research projects involving the equivalent of 2 550 full-time scientists from 950 different teams. The Brain research project [2] on neurocomputing (the study of computing systems based on a model of the human brain) was officially launched in November.

348. On 23 July the Commission sent the Council a communication accompanied by a proposal for a Decision on a Community support plan to facilitate access to large-scale scientific facilities of European interest (1988-92). [3] The aim of this plan is to ensure optimum utilization of the large-scale scientific facilities available in the Community (particle accelerators, astronomic observatories, oceanographic vessels) by providing Community support for measures designed to render them more highly specialized—and hence more complementary—than at present, and by facilitating access by research workers from all over the Community.

349. In October the Commission sent the Council a proposal for a plan to stimulate the international cooperation and interchange necessary for European researchers (1988-92) known as Science. [4] This plan, which should enable the equivalent of 7 000 to 8 000 full-time researchers to be involved by 1992, is an extension of the 1985-88 stimulation plan. [5]

Evaluation activities

350. The Commission continued its evaluations of research programmes in keeping with its proposal for a new research evaluation programme. [6] Evaluations of the programmes on solar, wind and biomass energy and on the Community Bureau of Reference were published in 1987. The FAST programmes and three COST projects were also evaluated; evaluations of the

---

1   OJ L 83, 25.3.1985; Nineteenth General Report, point 327.
2   Basic research in adaptive intelligence and neurocomputing.
3   Bull. EC 7/8-1987, point 2.1.62.
4   OJ C 14,19.1.1988; Bull. 9-1987, point 2.1.51.
5   Point 347 of this Report.
6   OJ C 14, 20.1.1987; Twentieth General Report, point 363.

programmes on science and technology for development, Brite, biotechnology and non-nuclear energy are in progress.

The Commission also drew up a proposal for a programme of evaluation support activities. A start has already been made on this work, including the setting up of a data bank on research evaluation and meetings of national experts, to serve as a basis for the establishment of the '12 + 1 network' which will connect the Commission's evaluation service with its counterparts in the Member States.

Work started under the second research programme on forecasting and assessment in science and technology (FAST II) [1] continued, and the programme is now close to completion. In all, 38 research activities will have been undertaken—26 carried out under contract by 96 centres and research groups in the Community, and the remaining 12 via European networks involving 116 research institutes. Over 150 FAST occasional papers have been published on the results of these activities.

On 29 October the Commission sent the Council a proposal for a FAST III programme (1988-92). [2]

Dissemination and utilization of research results [3]

351.   The Commission made a start on drawing up appropriate measures for implementing the dissemination and utilization section of the new framework programme (1987-91). [4]

---

[1]   OJ L 293, 25.10.1987; Seventeenth General Report, point 572.
[2]   Bull. EC 10-1987, point 2.1.33.
[3]   Point 361 of this Report.
[4]   Point 307 of this Report.

Section 6

Telecommunications, information technology and innovation

Strategic objectives and main developments

352.   *The efforts carried out in the R&TD field since 1984 produced concrete and highly satisfactory results in 1987. Studies and initiatives to promote a powerful common market for telecommunications and information technology equipment and services were intensified and broadened; they focused on four main areas:*

(i) *Strengthening of the technological base of the electronics, information and telecommunications industries. Phase one of the Esprit programme has now reached the stage where the 227 projects launched over the past three years are beginning to deliver a substantial number of usable results, as shown by the demonstrations given at the fourth Esprit conference, which was attended by over 4 000 people. In December the Council adopted a common position on phase two of Esprit (doubling of the effort under phase one, with a target of 5 000 to 6 000 research workers involved in R&D projects) and adopted the main phase of RACE. At the same time, the framework programme of Community R&TD activities adopted in September[1] assigns a major role to telecommunications and information technology (IT): 45% of the amounts deemed necessary should be allocated to those fields over the period 1987-91.*

(ii) *General thinking on the future of telecommunications in the Community. By publishing a Green Paper on the development of the market for telecommunications services and equipment, the Commission opened the debate with all the parties concerned (Member States, network operators, industries, users and trade unions) to help define common policies for the future shape of the telecommunications industry in view of the radical technological and legislative changes that can be expected.*

(iii) *Organization of a large European market for information equipment and services. Standardization work is developing satisfactorily. Several dozen draft IT standards and European telecommunications standards are in*

---

[1]   Point 307 of this Report.

preparation and new conformity testing services are to be set up in the Community, which will pave the way for a unified and transparent market and the opening-up of public procurement.

Among measures to stimulate the supply of and demand for new services, the Council adopted a programme on trade electronic data interchange systems (Tedis) and a Directive and a recommendation on mobile communications; the Commission sent the Council a proposal on the development of an information services market and three proposals for programmes on the use of information, telecommunications and broadcasting technologies in services such as education and training (Delta), the biomedical sector (AIM) and road safety (Drive).

(iv) *Contribution to economic and social cohesion in the Community. The introductory phase of the STAR programme on the development of telecommunications infrastructures and services in the less-favoured areas of the Community began in 1987. In addition, an integrated Mediterranean programme was set up in the field of IT with the aim of encouraging the introduction of human and material infrastructures and technological and industrial capacities in IT services in Greece.* [1]

Telecommunications

353.   Following the example of the United States, Japan and the United Kingdom, most Member States have begun in-depth discussions on the national regulatory structures affecting telecommunications with a view to preparing them for increased competition within the European economic area. As it considers that it should be involved in the process at an early stage so as to ensure a consistent approach at Community level and to open the necessary debate with all concerned, in June the Commission transmitted to the Council, Parliament and the Economic and Social Committee a Green Paper on the development of the common market for telecommunications services and equipment. [2]

New initiatives were also taken in pursuance of the five main lines of the Community telecommunications policy: [3]

(i) *Framing of a common strategy for the development of telecommunications networks and services. On 25 June the Council adopted two instruments* [4]

---

[1]   Point 475 of this Report.
[2]   Bull. EC 6-1987, point 1.4.1 *et seq.*
[3]   Twentieth General Report, point 401.
[4]   OJ L 196, 25.6.1987; Bull. EC 6-1987, point 2.1.53.

proposed by the Commission, [1] — a recommendation on the coordinated introduction of mobile communications and a Directive on the frequency bands to be reserved for the coordinated introduction of mobile communications in the Community.

(ii) *Creation of a Community-wide market for telecommunications equipment.* Cooperation between the European Conference of Postal and Telecommunications Administrations (CEPT) and the European Committees for Standardization (CEN) and Electrotechnical Standardization (Cenelec) continued with a view to preparing the common technical specifications of the European telecommunications standards to be used in the context of the Council Directive of 24 July 1986 on the initial stage of the mutual recognition of type-approvals for telecommunications terminal equipment. [2] Following the publication of the Green Paper, the CEPT undertook to set up a European standards institute. This is currently at the study stage.

(iii) *Implementation of a programme of research and development in advanced communications technologies for Europe (RACE) (1987-91).* [3] On 14 December the Council adopted [4] the Decision on the implementation of the main phase of the programme. [5] This aims to ensure that European industry, network operators and information providers will be prepared for the introduction of a European broadband integrated telecommunications system in 1995. On 17 September Parliament adopted a legislative resolution embodying its opinion in first reading on this proposal. [6]

(iv) *Implementation of a Community programme to promote the development of less-favoured regions by giving them improved access to advanced telecommunications services (STAR programme).* [7] The first half of the year was devoted to identifying with the Member States the projects to be included in the programme. Implementation was commenced during the latter half of the year.

(v) *Coordination of negotiating positions within international organizations dealing with telecommunications.* The Commission's activity related principally to the coordination of Community policy on trade in telecommunications.

---

[1] OJ C 69, 17.3.1987; Bull. EC 2-1987, point 2.1.38.
[2] OJ L 217, 5.8.1986; Twentieth General Report, point 401.
[3] Research and development in advanced communications technologies for Europe.
[4] Point 354 of this Report.
[5] OJ C 304, 28.11.1986; Twentieth General Report, point 401; Bull. EC 11-1987, point 2.1.68.
[6] OJ C 281, 19.10.1987; Bull. EC 9-1987, point 2.1.53.
[7] Point 463 of this Report.

RACE

354.   On 14 December the Council adopted [1] the Commission's proposal for the implementation of the main phase of the RACE programme, [2] on which it reached a common position in September. [3] The amount deemed necessary for implementation is 1 100 million ECU, 50% of which is to be provided from the Community budget. The programme follows the RACE definition phase, completed late in 1986, and covers the period 1987-92. It is a step towards the planned introduction on a Community scale by 1995 of integrated broadband communications, taking account of the development of integrated services digital networks. RACE aims to boost and speed up the development of broadband integrated communications technology in Europe thanks to cooperation in the fields of pre-competitive R&D and the drafting of common functional specifications, in preparation for the drafting of standards. It also aims to help complete the internal market in telecommunications equipment and services and to improve the capacities of Community industry in this area so that it can remain competitive on the world market. The programme will thus make a contribution to the general provision of a wide range of advanced telecommunications services in the Community at low cost. The work carried out in the context of RACE will have to complement other measures pursuing the same objective; synergy will be ensured with other activities at European level — including Esprit — and at national level. In anticipation of this, the Commission published a call for tenders on 1 July. [4]

Information technology

Esprit [5]

355.   The Esprit programme, now in its fourth year, has reached the stage where the 227 projects begun in the period 1984-86 — involving almost 3 000 scientists and engineers — are producing a substantial quantity of usable results.

356.   On 21 December the Council adopted a common position [1] on the Commission's proposal for the second phase of Esprit; this was presented to

[1]   Bull. EC 12-1987.
[2]   OJ C 304, 28.11.1986; Twentieth General Report, point 401; Bull. EC 11-1987, point 2.1.68.
[3]   Bull. EC 9-1987, point 2.1.52.
[4]   OJ C 173, 1.7.1987; Bull. EC 7/8-1987, point 2.1.63.
[5]   European strategic programme for research and development in information technologies.

the Council on 29 July in the form of a specific programme within the framework programme for research and technological development 1987-91. [1] The proposal takes account of the Council resolution of April 1986 [2] and is based on the technical results available from phase one, which were described in the communication the Commission sent to the Council in December 1986. [3] The proposal notes the growing costs of research and development resulting from the extreme vitality of the IT sector and the severe constraints that this places on the industry. Fierce international competition and the increase in resources being allocated to research and development worldwide have necessitated a coordinated approach in Europe.

On the basis of the results obtained under phase one of Esprit, [4] three fields of pre-competitive research and development are covered by the second phase (Esprit II): microelectronics, information processing systems and IT application technologies. Application-specific integrated circuits (ASICs), the design of complex and highly reliable information-processing systems and computer-aided design are receiving special attention. Phase two also includes selected fields of basic research such as molecular electronics and artificial intelligence, which aim to stimulate activity in certain IT areas of strategic importance.

It is expected that some 5 500 research scientists will be working together on Esprit projects by 1990, i.e. double the number employed under phase one.

The fourth Esprit conference, which was held in Brussels from 28 to 30 September, was an impressive demonstration of the commitment of Europe's IT industry to the Esprit programme: 4 000 delegates took part and 130 technical reports were presented; there were over 50 technical demonstrations of Esprit projects. [5]

Combined use of IT and telecommunications in general applications

357.   On 1 June the Council adopted [6] the Commission's proposal [7] for the extension until the end of 1992 of the period of validity of the Council Decisions of March 1985 and February 1986 on, respectively, cooperation in the

1   OJ C 283, 21.10.1987; Bull. EC 7/8-1987, point 2.1.65.
2   OJ C 102, 29.4.1986; Twentieth General Report, point 403.
3   Twentieth General Report, point 403.
4   OJ L 67, 9.3.1984; OJ L 81, 24.3.1984; Eighteenth General Report, point 195.
5   Bull. EC 9-1987, point 2.1.54.
6   OJ L 145, 5.6.1987; Bull. EC 6-1987, point 2.1.55.
7   OJ C 55, 3.3.1987; Bull. EC 2-1987, point 2.1.40.

automation of data and documentation for imports/exports and agriculture (Caddia) and the coordinated development of computerized administrative procedures (the CD projects). [1] Fully automated procedures for the management and financial control of the agricultural markets are now operational.

358.   On 5 October the Council adopted, on a proposal from the Commission, [2] a communications network Community programme on trade electronic data interchange systems (Tedis). [3].

359.   Future developments in IT, telecommunications and broadcasting offer a wide range of possible applications in areas of general interest such as education, health and road-traffic management. In order to make the most of these possibilities, the Commission considers that urgent Community action is needed to define the functional specifications and minimum common standards to enable the technologies concerned to be combined to best effect while adapting them to users' specific needs. In this connection, in July the Commission sent the Council a proposal for the implementation of the Delta [4] programme on learning technology, [5], the AIM [6] programme on biomedical computing [7] and the Drive [8] programme on road transport information infrastructures. [9]

Standardization in IT and telecommunications

360.   The Council Decision of 22 December 1986 on standardization in the field of information technology and telecommunications[10] strengthened the procedures for scheduling standardization work and laid down methods for application of the principle of reference of standards in public procurement.

Standardization work given to the competent European bodies, CEN and Cenelec, with the cooperation of the CEPT, has grown substantially and demonstrates the vitality of European standardization in new-technology areas. There are currently 64 standardization remits in hand. Several of the tasks

1   OJ L 96, 3.4.1985; OJ L 33, 8.2.1986.
2   OJ C 2, 8.10.1987; Twentieth General Report, point 405.
3   OJ L 285, 8.10.1987; Bull. EC 10-1987, point 2.1.45.
4   Developing European learning through technological advance.
5   OJ C 265, 5.10.1987; Bull. EC 7/8-1987, point 2.1.67.
6   Advanced informatics in medicine in Europe.
7   JO C 335, 31.12.1987; Bull. EC 7/8-1987, point 2.1.69.
8   Dedicated road and intelligent vehicles in Europe.
9   OJ C 335, 31.12.1987; Bull. EC 7/8-1987, point 2.1.68.
10   OJ L 36, 7.2.1987; Twentieth General Report, point 408.

entrusted to those bodies are a direct contribution to fulfilment in the IT field of the integration objectives set for 1992 in the context of completion of the internal market (the compatibility of new electronic payment systems and electronic exchange of trade or customs data necessary for the introduction of the single administrative document).

The work given to the CEPT in order to prepare the common technical specifications, known as European telecommunications standards (NETs), needed for the implementation of the Council Directive of 24 July 1986 concerning the first phase of the establishment of mutual recognition of type approval for telecommunications terminal equipment[1] has been speeded up, and some 10 NETs are in preparation.

The very positive results obtained from the conformance testing services (CTS) programme to promote the launching of harmonized services for checking the conformity of products to standards have led the Commission to make a second call for proposals covering the field of IT and telecommunications.[2] The numerous proposals received (about 60) will allow several trial services essential to the application of the standards in these sectors to be set up.

Dissemination and follow-through of R&TD results obtained under Community and national programmes

361. Efforts to protect, follow through and disseminate Community R&TD results in 1987 resulted in over 2 000 new publications being entered in the Euro-abstracts (EABS) data base[3] and published in the monthly magazine *Euro-abstracts,* 150 patent applications, the opening of some 15 follow-through dossiers, the signature of two licence agreements and the announcement of the placing on the market of 10 innovations.

The Commission took part in four specialist exhibitions and at each one presented several different inventions developed under Community R&TD programmes and recently placed on the market.

Under a subsidy contract signed with an Italian firm in December 1985[3] the construction of a pilot plant for the desulphurization of flue gases from power plants, based on the Ispra Mark XIII A process invented at the JRC,[4] has

[1]   OJ L 217, 5.8.1986; Twentieth General Report, point 401.
[2]   OJ C 135, 20.5.1987; OJ S 97, 20.5.1987.
[3]   Nineteenth General Report, point 692.
[4]   OJ C 317, 28.11.1984; Eighteenth General Report, point 587.

begun and should be completed early in 1988. Tests on this plant will last two years.

Removal of barriers to and promotion of innovation

362.   In order to extend the plan for the transnational development of the supporting infrastructure for innovation and technology transfer,[1] on 9 June the Council adopted the strategic programme for innovation and technology transfer (Sprint).[2] It has a budget of 8.6 million ECU and covers the period 25 November 1986 to 31 December 1988. Several projects launched under the transational plan went on to produce significant results:

(i) support for transnational cooperation between advisory bodies led to over 50 technological cooperation agreements between firms, notably small and medium-sized firms;

(ii) the setting up of 16 networks for joint sectoral research centres enabled 75 technical centres or similar bodies of the 12 Member States to form groupings in areas such as wood, footwear, welding and plastics;

(iii) the 'Europeanization' of over 20 technology conferences;

(iv) concertation between Member States and the Community in the field of design, patents and the modernization of traditional industries enabled the first European design prize to be launched.[3]

In order to continue the implementation of the priority lines of action, a call for proposals was made;[4] some 500 application dossiers were received.

Two pilot projects on innovation funding were launched: the European Venture Capital Institute, which aims to train venture capitalists, and the preparation of investment forums.

---

[1]   OJ L 353, 15.12.1983; Seventeenth General Report, point 609.
[2]   OJ L 153, 13.6.1983; Bull. EC 6-1987, point 2.1.56.
[3]   Bull. EC 2-1987, point 2.1.42; Bull. 6-1987, point 2.1.57.
[4]   OJ C 196, 25.7.1987; Bull. EC 7/8-1987, point 2.1.71.

Removal of barriers to and promotion of the development of information services

Specialized information

363. The implementation of the five-year programme for the development of the specialized information market (1984-88) [1] continued, principally with the launching of a demonstration programme involving 11 materials data bases, the development of an information network on the production and use of enzymes and the creation of videotex information services for farming and small businesses in peripheral areas. Projects implemented this year cost 3.9 million ECU. An evaluation report was drawn up on the results of the third plan of action 1981-83, [2], on the initial (two-year) period of the five-year programme and on the results and consequences of the Docdel [3] programme.

Information services

364. After consulting representatives of information users and providers and the senior officials advisory group for the information market (ISUG, ISPG and SOAG), on 4 August the Commission presented to the Council a proposal on the implementation at Community level of a policy and a plan of priority action for the development of an information services market. [4]. Four main aims were defined: to set up an internal market for information services by the end of 1992; to stimulate and strengthen the competitive capability of European suppliers of information services; to promote the use of advanced information services in the Community; and to reinforce joint efforts to achieve the internal and external cohesion of the Community with respect to information services.

The priority action plan is to be implemented in two phases, the first of which will be a two-year introductory phase. A call for declarations of interest was published. [5] Other projects were also proposed and work is in progress, notably for achieving closer cooperation between libraries and improving and extending access to these resources using new information technology.

---

[1] OJ L 314, 4.12.1984; Eighteenth General Report, point 588.
[2] OJ L 220, 6.8.1981; Fifteenth General Report, point 598.
[3] Document delivery programme; Eighteenth General Report, point 591.
[4] OJ C 249, 17.9.1987; Bull. EC 7/8-1987, point 2.1.71.
[5] OJ C 188, 17.7.1987.

Removal of language barriers

365.   As part of its fourth action plan for the improvement of information transfer between languages (1986-90), [1] the Commission continued to develop the Systran machine translation system for nine language pairs. The pilot project for the transfer to Europe of scientific and technical information from Japan was extended until 1988.

The Eurotra programme to create an advanced machine translation system was extended to include Spanish and Portuguese. [2] It was evaluated by a group of independent experts which recommended moving on to the next phase of the programme (1988-90).

---

[1]   Nineteenth General Report, point 701.
[2]   OJ L 341, 4.12.1986, Twentieth General Report, point 420.

Section 7

Competition [1]

Main developments

366. The Commission continued its work on several pieces of legislation, including two block exemption Regulations under Article 85(3) for franchising and know-how licensing agreements, drafts for which were published in August. The Council in December adopted a package of liberalization measures in air transport and on 30 November cleared the way for the final stages of work on a European merger control Regulation.

367. In the State aid field, the Commission clarified the criteria for applying Article 92(3)(a), which allows exceptionally high rates of aid to be granted in areas with an abnormally low standard of living or severe underemployment. The poorest areas now classified in this category hold about 20% of the Community's population.

Priority activities and objectives

Know-how licensing and franchising

368. In August the Commission published two draft Regulations granting a block exemption from Article 85(1) of the EEC Treaty for know-how licences [2] and franchising agreements. [3] The know-how licensing Regulation, which lists the restrictive clauses covered by the exemption or considered to be unobjectionable from the point of view of competition, seeks — like the block exemption Regulation for patent licences which the Commission issued in 1984 [4] — to foster a more dynamic climate for innovation and the dissemination of new technology in European industry by facilitating technology transfer. Another purpose of the proposed block exemption, besides providing greater

---

[1]   For further details see the *Seventeenth Report on Competition Policy,* to be published in April.
[2]   OJ C 214, 12.8.1987; Bull. EC 5-1987, point 2.1.68.
[3]   OJ C 229, 27.8.1987; Bull. EC 6-1987, point 2.1.72.
[4]   OJ L 219, 19.8.1984; Eighteenth General Report, point 210.

certainty as to the law for licensors and licensees, is to prevent abuse of know-how licensing for anti-competitive ends, such as dividing up markets and other restrictions of competition.

The draft block exemption for franchising applies to franchises for distribution or services, but not 'franchises' for manufacturing, which are quite different and usually involve the licensing of patents, know-how and/or trade marks. It lists the restrictions exempted, other common clauses that are generally not restrictive of competition, clauses that will prevent the exemption applying (the 'black list'), and a number of other conditions for the exemption. An 'opposition' procedure is also provided for the rapid clearance of agreements containing clauses of types not specifically exempted but not containing any of the blacklisted clauses.

Air transport

369.   In June the Council reached agreement in principle on a package of liberalization measures in the civil aviation industry [1] covering capacity, market access, fares [2] and application of the competition rules. The competition part of the package [3] includes a procedural Regulation under Article 87 of the Treaty giving the Commission wider powers of investigation and enforcement and a Regulation enabling it to issue block exemptions from Article 85(1) for agreements and concerted practices concerning in particular capacity sharing, revenue pooling, fares, computer reservation systems, in-flight catering and slot allocation at airports. The block exemptions will be subject to very strict conditions and will be limited to an initial period of three years. In December the Council formally adopted the package. [4]

General rules applying to undertakings

370.   On 30 November the Council gave its broad approval [5] to the Commission's proposals for a Community merger control system. [6]

---

[1]   Bull. EC 6-1987, point 2.1.227.
[2]   Points 622 and 644 of this Report.
[3]   OJ C 182, 9.7.1984; Eighteenth General Report, point 245; Twentieth General Report, points 428 and 715.
[4]   Bull. EC 12-1987.
[5]   Bull. EC 11-1987, point 2.1.92.
[6]   OJ C 92, 31.10.1973; Seventh General Report, point 153; OJ C 36, 12.2.1982; Fourteenth General Report, point 207; OJ C 51, 23.2.1984; Eighteenth General Report, point 214; Twentieth General Report, point 425.

371.   On 17 November the Court of Justice upheld[1] the Commission's decision of March 1984 under Article 85 on the shareholding links between the tobacco multinationals Philip Morris Inc. and Rembrandt Group Ltd.[2]

372.   The Commission published draft block exemption Regulations for know-how licences and franchising agreements.[3]

Rules of competition applied to undertakings

373.   In 1987 the Commission adopted 15 decisions applying Articles 85 and 86 of the EEC Treaty and one decision rejecting a complaint. There were 11 decisions applying Article 86 of the ECSC Treaty. A further 57 cases were settled by dispatch of administrative letters, and 334 cases were settled without a decision being taken. At 31 December there were 3 427 cases pending, of which 2 919 were applications or notifications (190 of them received in 1987), 344 complaints by firms (93 registered in 1987) and 166 proceedings on the Commission's own initiative (30 commenced in 1987).

374.   In relation to distribution arrangements, the Commission continued to act against firms that take measures contrary to Article 85(1) to prevent parallel trading. In a decision concerning Tipp-Ex Vertrieb GmbH & Co. KG and four of its exclusive distributors, it ordered the firms to discontinue agreements and concerted practices aimed at preventing dealers exporting Tipp-Ex products to other Member States.[4] In another decision, Sandoz Prodotti Farmaceutici SpA was ordered to remove the words 'export prohibited' from its invoices.[5] Fines were imposed in both cases. Decisions were also taken imposing fines on Fisher-Price[6] and Konica[6] for attempting to protect national markets for toys and colour film.

The Commission also took a number of decisions granting exemption under Article 85(3). In two cases, De Laval-Stork[7] and Olivetti-Canon,[7] agreements setting up joint ventures were exempted. Exemptions were also granted for marketing cooperation between British Leyland and Unipart,[7] for arrange-

---

1   Bull. EC 11-1987, point 2.1.93.
2   Eighteenth General Report, point 222.
3   Point 368 of this Report.
4   Decision of 10.7.1987: OJ L 222, 10.8.1987; Bull. EC 7/8-1987, point 2.1.92.
5   Decision of 13.7.1987: OJ L 222, 10.8.1987; Bull. EC 7/8-1987, point 2.1.93.
6   Decision of 28.12.1987; Bull. EC 12-1987.
7   Decision of 22.12.1987; Bull. EC 12-1987.

ments on the French early potato market, [1] and for the rules for admission to an international dental equipment exhibition. [2] In each case the Commission considered that although the arrangements fell within Article 85(1) they satisfied the tests of Article 85(3).

375.   In another decision on franchising, the Commission granted exemption under Article 85(3) for the standard-form franchise agreement of Computerland Europe SA, [3] judging that the restrictions imposed by the agreement were necessary for the system's satisfactory operation. It also confirmed its policy on commodity terminal markets [4] by granting negative clearance from Article 85(1) for the Rules and Regulations of the Baltic International Freight Futures Exchange Ltd (Biffex). [5] A know-how licensing agreement in the baking industry between the US company Rich Products and the British firm Jus-Rol was also exempted. [6]

376.   In a decision under Article 86, the Commission found the specialist nail gun manufacturer Hilti AG guilty of abusing its dominant position and fined the company 6 million ECU. [6]

The rules of competition applied to forms of State intervention

General aid schemes

377.   The Commission completed the first stages of its work on the inventory of aid schemes in operation in the Member States, [7] which includes estimates of the volume of expenditure on the schemes. The importance of this transparency exercise is heightened by the drive to dismantle the remaining internal barriers in the Community by 1992. After bilateral consultations with each Member State, the Commission was able to finalize figures for aid expenditure in most of them. The parallel operation of drawing up an inventory of aid schemes in operation in the Member States was almost completed. [7] The exercise has

---

[1]   Decision of 18.12.1987; Bull. EC 12-1987.
[2]   Decision of 18.9.1987: OJ L 293, 16.10.1987.
[3]   OJ L 222, 10.8.1987: Bull. EC 7/8-1987, point 2.1.91.
[4]   OJ L 369, 31.12.1985; Nineteenth General Report, point 384; OJ L 3, 6.1.1987; OJ L 19, 21.1.1987; Twentieth General Report, point 440.
[5]   OJ L 222, 10.8.1987; Bull. EC 7/8-1987, point 2.1.97.
[6]   Decision of 22.12.1987; Bull. EC 12-1987.
[7]   Nineteenth General Report, point 376; Twentieth General Report, point 442.

demonstrated the need for such data to be supplied by Member States on a regular basis, both when schemes are notified and in annual reports on the operation of each scheme.

378.   The Commission took steps to obtain strict compliance with its policy on notification of all elements of aid packages[1] and rigorously implemented its policy on the recovery of aid granted illegally.

379.   The Commission reviewed its policy on the discretionary exceptions from the State aid rules contained in Article 92(3) of the EEC Treaty, in the light of enlargement and the provisions in the Single European Act for increasing economic and social cohesion. After a careful examination it decided[2] that in future the exception provided for in subparagraph (a) — for aid that promotes the economic development of areas where the standard of living is abnormally low or where there is severe underemployment — would be applied to areas in which GDP was at least 25% below the Community average, namely Greece, Ireland, Northern Ireland, Portugal, the French overseas departments, and parts of Italy (the Mezzogiorno) and Spain. It considered that this would allow greater flexibility in the types of aid that could be permitted for developing these regions. In the remainder of the Community, regional aid would continue to be assessed on the basis of subparagraph (c), under which aid facilitating development in certain economic areas may be permitted provided it does not affect trading conditions to an extent contrary to the common interest.

Industry aid schemes

380.   Continuing its strict monitoring of aid to specific industries to ensure that government funds are not used to confer an unfair competitive advantage on some firms at the expense of others, the Commission maintained a particularly close watch on sensitive sectors such as steel, shipbuilding, man-made fibres, textiles and the motor industry. It also continued its policy of ordering the recovery of aid granted illegally by Member States and found to be incompatible with the common market.

381.   In the textile and clothing industry, the Commission extended for a further two years[3] until 19 July 1989[4] the system of control of aid to man-made fibre and yarn manufacturers introduced in 1977.

---

1   Twentieth General Report, point 443.
2   Bull. EC 4-1987, point 2.1.61.
3   OJ C 171, 10.7.1985; Nineteenth General Report, point 392.
4   OJ C 183, 11.7.1987; Bull. EC 4-1987, point 2.1.63.

382.   Under the sixth Directive on aid to shipbuilding, which took effect at the beginning of the year, [1] the Commission scrutinized and took decisions on the schemes in force in all the shipbuilding Member States except Italy, Greece, Belgium and the Netherlands. It also disposed of a number of cases outstanding from the fifth Directive, [2] notably concerning the United Kingdom, [3] Denmark [4] and Italy, [5] and dealt with about 20 cases raised by Member States under Article 4(5) of the sixth Directive where there was competition between different Community yards for a contract. [1] After consulting the Member States, the Commission left the ceiling on total production aid of all types (direct and indirect) for new building in 1988 at the 1987 level of 28%. [6]

383.   The Commission continued to apply its Decision on aid to the steel industry. [7] In the Spanish [8] and Portuguese [6] industry, it authorized aid for rationalization in accordance with the terms of the Act of Accession. Finally, in two decisions concerning aid for steel businesses coming under the EEC Treaty it called on the Belgian and French Governments to recover aid granted unlawfully from Tubemeuse [9] and the Usinor/Sacilor group.[10]

384.   The Commission applied its rules for aid for research and development[11] to a first batch of cases involving Germany,[12] the Netherlands,[13] Italy,[14] and Denmark,[15] as a result of which it ordered the Member States to notify not only their schemes and programmes for supporting R&D but also any individual award of aid to projects, national or multinational, whose total cost in any one Member State exceeds 20 million ECU.

---

[1]   OJ L 69, 12.3.1987; Bull. EC 1-1987, point 2.1.49; Twentieth General Report, point 446.
[2]   OJ L 137, 23.5.1981; Fifteenth General Report, point 218; OJ L 371, 30.12.1982; Sixteenth General Report, point 230; OJ L 2, 3.1.1985; Eighteenth General Report, point 226.
[3]   Bull. EC 2-1987, point 2.1.58.
[4]   Bull. EC 2-1987, point 2.1.59.
[5]   Bull. EC 11-1987, point 2.1.99.
[6]   Bull. EC 12-1987.
[7]   OJ L 340, 18.12.1985; Nineteenth General Report, point 374.
[8]   Bull. EC 3-1987, point 2.1.82; Bull. EC 7/8-1987, point 2.1.112.
[9]   OJ L 227, 14.8.1987; Bull. EC 2-1987, point 2.1.61.
[10]   OJ L 290, 14.10.1987; Bull. EC 3-1987, point 2.1.83.
[11]   OJ C 83, 11.4.1986; Twentieth General Report, point 444.
[12]   Bull. EC 2-1987, point 2.1.55.
[13]   Bull. EC 5-1987, point 2.1.72.
[14]   Bull. EC 4-1987, point 2.1.60; Bull. EC 7/8-1987, point 2.1.100.
[15]   Bull. EC 9-1987, point 2.1.69.

Regional aid schemes

385.   Apart from the fundamental reappraisal of how the Treaty should be applied to regional aid,[1] the Commission continued its ongoing work of assessing the Member States' regional schemes. It approved schemes in Spain[2] and Portugal.[3]

386.   The Commission completed its scrutiny of the 14th,[4] 15th[5] and 16th[6] general plans of the German joint federal/*Land* regional aid programme, terminating the Article 93(2) proceedings against the first two and authorizing the third without proceedings.[6] These decisions were taken only after the Commission had received assurances from the Federal Government that the assisted areas and ceilings would be significantly reduced. From 1 January 1988, only 38% (rather than 45%) of Germany's population would live in assisted areas and the regional aid ceilings would be cut. Further cuts would be made on 1 January 1990 (ceilings) and 1 January 1991 (percentage of population).

387.   The Commission terminated the Article 93(2) proceedings against regional aid schemes in Belgium after the government had made substantial changes[7] and issued a decision ordering further scaling-down of the Danish scheme.[8]

State monopolies

388.   The Commission continued the Article 169 (infringement) proceedings instituted against Greece for failing to adequately reform its oil monopoly[9] with service of a second reasoned opinion on the Greek Government.[10]

389.   The legislation altering the Spanish oil monopoly[11] was judged inadequate to meet the requirements imposed by Article 48 of the Act of Accession

---

1   Point 379 of this Report.
2   Bull. EC 5-1987, point 2.1.77.
3   Bull. EC 3-1987, point 2.1.76; Bull. EC 5-1987, point 2.1.78.
4   OJ C 170, 9.7.1986.
5   OJ C 213, 11.8.1987; Bull. EC 3-1987, point 2.1.74.
6   Bull. EC 12-1987.
7   Bull. EC 7/8-1987, points 2.1.105 and 2.1.106.
8   Bull. EC 7/8-1987, point 2.1.107.
9   Twentieth General Report, point 452.
10 Bull. EC 5-1987, point 2.1.86. First opinion: Nineteenth General Report, point 401.
11 Boletín oficial del Estado No 10, 12.1.1987.

and the Commission accordingly commenced Article 169 proceedings against the Spanish Government in this case. With regard to the tobacco monopoly, the Spanish Government sent the Commission draft regulations supplementing the Royal Decree of 12 December 1986 on the import and wholesale and retail distribution of tobacco products.

390.   The Commission made recommendations [1] to the Portuguese Government under Article 208 of the Act of Accession on reforming its alcohol and oil monopolies to remove discrimination against other Member States. [2]

391.   Recommendations were also made to the French Government under Articles 48 and 208 of the Act of Accession to liberalize access to the French market for Spanish and Portuguese matches, tobacco products and potash fertilizers. [3]

391a.   The Commission decided to commence Article 169 proceedings against Belgium in respect of the Government's exclusive rights to import and supply low-speed modems and first telex terminals. [4]

Public enterprises

392.   Finding that Greece had still not complied with its Decision of 24 April 1985 [5] under Article 90(3) on legislation which unfairly favoured State-owned insurance companies in the insurance of public property and in insurance taken out in connection with loans from State banks, the Commission decided to continue the Article 169 proceedings. [6]

393.   On 24 July the Commission ordered the Spanish Government under Article 90(3) to discontinue arrangements for subsidizing the air and ferry fares of Spanish residents of the Canary and Balearic Islands travelling to the mainland. [7] The lower fares were not available to nationals of other Member States.

---

[1] OJ L 306, 28.10.1987; Bull. EC 10-1987, point 2.1.70; Bull. EC 12-1987.
[2] Twentieth General Report, point 454.
[3] OJ L 203, 24.7.1987; Bull. EC 7/8-1987, point 2.1.122.
[4] Bull. EC 12-1987.
[5] OJ L 152, 11.6.1985; Nineteenth General Report, point 403.
[6] Twentieth General Report, point 455.
[7] OJ L 194, 15.7.1987; Bull. EC 7/8-1987, point 2.1.121.

Section 8

Employment, education and social policy

Main developments

394. *As part of the implementation of the Single European Act, the Commission adopted a work programme in the field of safety, hygiene and health at the workplace. This programme is intended to step up measures taken to improve the working and living conditions of workers and reduce accidents at work and occupational diseases.*

With close to 16 million persons out of work, unemployment — particularly long-term unemployment — notably among young people, remains one of the Community's main concerns. The Commission has therefore implemented two education cooperation programmes (Comett and Erasmus) and continued its endeavours relating to the vocational training of young people and their integration in working life.

Priority activities and objectives

Implementation of the action programme on employment growth

395. Under the action programme on employment growth set out by the Council in its resolution of 22 December 1986, [1] the Commission drew up a list of policies implemented and proposed new initiatives in a memorandum on action to combat long-term unemployment [2] and in a communication to the Council on local employment initiatives adopted in particular since 1984. [3] The Commission also stepped up a number of ongoing activities in areas such as the promotion of youth employment, [4] the extension of the mutual information system on employment (Misep), [5] the survey of innovatory prac-

---

[1]   OJ C 340, 31.12.1986; Twentieth General Report, point 460.
[2]   Bull. EC 5-1987, point 2.1.94.
[3]   OJ C 161, 21.6.1984; Eighteenth General Report, point 278.
[4]   OJ C 193, 20.7.1983; Seventeenth General Report, point 296.
[5]   Nineteenth General Report, point 411.

tices in firms [1] and the problem of frontier workers and improvement of the Community system for the international clearing of vacancies and applications for employment (Sedoc). [2]

Finally, the Commission intensified its action to improve the environment for small businesses, [3] notably by transmitting to the Council a communication on internal and external adaptation of firms in relation to employment [4] and on the development of continuing in-firm vocational training for adult employees, on which the Council adopted conclusions. [5] It also expressed its intention to develop still further the 'Val-Duchesse' social dialogue at Community level. [6]

The Erasmus programme

396.   On 15 June, acting on a proposal from the Commission, [7] the Council took a Decision adopting the European Community action scheme for the mobility of university students (Erasmus), [8] which it had approved in May. [9] A total of 85 million ECU was set aside for the scheme for the first three academic years (1987/88 to 1989/90): 10 million ECU from the 1987 budget, 30 million ECU for the 1988 budget and 45 million ECU for the 1989 budget.

Of the 85 million ECU, 31 million is to be allocated to the European Network for University Cooperation, the academic recognition of diplomas and periods of study and complementary measures, and 54 million to student grants. During the first three years, such grants are to be awarded to some 25 000 students and 3 000 financial aids granted to universities to enable them to establish programmes for the exchange of students and teachers.

In the first year, 398 of the 900 proposals for exchange programmes submitted to the Commission for the 1987/88 academic year received Community assistance;[10] these programmes will form the basis of the European University Network. Similarly, 1 142 exchanges were approved from among the 2 500 applications received by the Commission from university staff wishing to go to universities in other Member States. Finally, as another aim of Erasmus is

---

[1]   Bull. EC 5-1987, point 2.1.96.
[2]   Nineteenth General Report, point 413; Twentieth General Report, point 463.
[3]   Points 290 and 294 of this Report; Bull. EC 5-1987, point 2.1.95.
[4]   Bull. EC 5-1987, point 2.1.98.
[5]   OJ C 178, 7.7.1987; Bull. EC 6-1987, point 2.1.96.
[6]   Point 438 of this Report.
[7]   OJ C 73, 2.4.1986; Twentieth General Report, point 475.
[8]   OJ L 166, 25.6.1987; Bull. EC 6-1987, point 2.1.93.
[9]   Bull. EC 5-1987, points 1.3.1 and 1.3.2.
[10]   Bull. EC 10-1987, point 2.1.79.

to improve provisions on the recognition of diplomas and periods of study, measures were taken to launch a pilot project in the 1988/89 academic year on the automatic transfer of course credits between the universities taking part so as to develop in the long term the Community network of information centres in this sector.

Employment

Employment and the labour market

397. The improvement in the employment situation went hand in hand with a stabilization of unemployment at a high level (around 12% of the working population). The least-favoured areas and social groups are those most affected by unemployment in terms of duration and intensity. At the same time, forms of employment are changing under the dual pressure of unemployment and competition. In these circumstances, the Commission concentrated its efforts on implementing the policy guidelines — notably on long-term unemployment, local job creation schemes and employment of young people — set out in the Council resolution of 22 December 1986. [1]

398. On 14 April the Commission sent to the Council a proposal for a Regulation on the organization of a labour force sample survey in the spring of 1988. [2]

399. The working party on the underground economy, set up following the discussion at the Hague meeting of the European Council in June 1986 of the problems caused by illicit work, [3] met on two occasions to draw up a report on the causes, nature and extent of this phenomenon and on its implications in policy terms. [4]

Freedom of movement of workers

400. The Commission continued the action contemplated in its guidelines for a Community migration policy, which the Council confirmed in its resolution of 16 July 1985, [5] in particular by preparing the revision of a number of

---

[1] Point 395 of this Report.
[2] Bull. EC 4-1987, point 2.1.72.
[3] Twentieth General Report, point 19.
[4] Bull. EC 1-1987, point 2.1.53; Bull. EC 3-1987, point 2.1.91.
[5] OJ C 186, 26.7.1985.

provisions relating to freedom of movement for workers, so as to take account of the ruling given by the Court of Justice and of the circumstances currently prevailing.

European Social Fund and structural operations

Measures in favour of certain Member States

401. On 10 September the Greek Government asked the Commission for a three-year extension of the Council Regulation of 26 March 1984 providing exceptional support of 120 million ECU for Greece in the social field.[1] On 22 December, acting under this Regulation, the Commission approved applications from the Greek Government for assistance for 1987 totalling approximately 12 million ECU.[2]

European Social Fund

402. In 1987 available commitment appropriations totalled 3 150.41 million ECU; the amounts committed are shown in Table 10.[3]

TABLE 10

Appropriations committed

million ECU

Operations to assist young people under 25:	
Less-favoured regions	1 063.45
Other regions	1 297.65
Operations to assist people aged 25 or over:	
Less-favoured regions	308.00
Other regions	383.50
Specific operations	97.46
Total	3 150.06

---

[1] OJ L 88, 31.3.1984; Eighteenth General Report, point 283.
[2] Bull. EC 12-1987.
[3] Full information on the Social Fund's activities will be given in its annual report, to be published in July.

403.   The breakdown by Member State shows that around 20.60% of the assistance approved went to Italy, 18.81% to the United Kingdom, 14.39% to Spain, 12.28% to France, 11.22% to Portugal, 6.63% to Ireland and 5.80% to Greece.

404.   Applications were submitted for a total of 5 971.89 million ECU. The overall volume of eligible applications corresponded to a sum of 5 147.20 million ECU, exceeding the appropriations available by 63.38%.

405.   Of the total of 3 836.37 million ECU for applications given priority classification, the reduction was applied to 704.57 million ECU; 99.99% of commitment appropriations were utilized.

406.   Payment appropriations for 1987 amounted to 2 843.79 million ECU, of which 2 542.25 million ECU was entered in the budget for the same year, while the remaining 301.54 million ECU consisted of appropriations carried over from 1986.

Measures for ECSC workers

407.   The Commission assisted 11 602 workers affected by the restructuring of the coal and steel industries.[1] A sum of 82 391 750 ECU of conventional redeployment aid was granted under Article 56(2)(b) of the ECSC Treaty, in the form of income support allowances in the event of early retirement, unemployment or re-employment and in the form of contributions towards reintegration in new jobs. Table 11 gives a breakdown by country and by industry of redeployment aid, both conventional and under the interim programme, granted to ECSC workers in 1987.

408.   The Commission signed bilateral agreements with Spain and Portugal, backdated to 1 January 1986, setting out the details of redeployment aid granted to workers affected by the restructuring programmes for the steel industry.[2]

409.   The conventional assistance provided in 1987 was backed up by an interim programme of accompanying social measures amounting to 34 million ECU for steelworkers.[3] Aid given under this programme is designed to facilitate

---

[1]   Bull. EC 7/8-1987, point 2.1.131; Bull. EC 9-1987, point 2.1.27.
[2]   Bull. EC 7/8-1987, point 2.1.33; Bull. EC 9-1987, point 2.1.27.
[3]   Point 278 of this Report.

early retirement or the re-employment of younger workers. In this way the ECSC continues, as far as its own resources allow, to implement social measures that were interrupted in 1984 by the Council's refusal [1] to authorize the transfer of resources made available in the general budget. In 1988 the Commission will take a decision — within the limits of funds not utilized in 1987 (141 608 250 ECU) — on outstanding applications for assistance made in 1987.

TABLE 11

Redeployment aid

(conventional aid plus additional programme)
Appropriations committed in 1987

	Coal industry		Steel industry and iron ore mining	
	Workers	Aid (ECU)	Workers	Aid (ECU)
Belgium	—	—	1 716	2 882 750[1]
Germany (FR)	5 143	17 461 000[1]	1 459	3 520 000
France	—	10 118 750[1]	—	—
Italie	—	—	187	—
Netherlands	—	—	936	1 132 500
United Kingdom	—	38 784 750	2 161	8 492 000[2]
Total	5 143	66 364 500	6 459	16 027 250

[1]   Applications made in 1986.
[2]   Partly applications made in 1986.

410.   The Commission's proposals[2] to provide 50 million ECU in 1988-90 to assist workers who will be affected by restructuring in the steel industry were not accepted by the Council.[3]

411.   The Commission laid down new procedures and conditions for the granting of conversion loans under Article 56(2)(a) of the ECSC Treaty for

---

[1]   Twentieth General Report, point 331.
[2]   OJ C 272, 10.10.1987; Bull. EC 7/8-1987, point 2.1.34.
[3]   Point 278 of this Report.

investments which create alternative employment opportunities for redundant workers in the coal and steel industries. [1]

Measures for shipbuilding workers

412.   On 31 July the Commission transmitted to the Council a proposal for a Regulation instituting a specific Community programme (with a budget of 71.5 million ECU) of accompanying social measures to assist workers in the shipbuilding industry who are made redundant or threatened with redundancy, [2] which would supplement measures already available under the European Social Fund.

Education and vocational training

Cooperation in education

413.   On 15 June the Council adopted the Community action programme on student mobility (Erasmus). [3] On 7 August the Commission brought an action against the Council to have the Court declare null and void the addition of Article 235 to the legal basis of the Decision and the last recital in the preamble to the Decision stating the reasons for the said legal basis. [4]

414.   Under the Community action programme for cooperation between universities and industry in education and training for technology (Comett), [5] the Commission accepted more than 160 projects representing some 5.8 million ECU in financial support in July [6] and some 437 projects representing 8.5 million ECU in December. [7]

415.   On 14 May the Council and the Ministers of Education meeting within the Council adopted conclusions on in-service teacher training, [8] the fight

1   OJ C 173, 1.7.1987; Bull. EC 7/8-1987, point 2.1.32.
2   OJ C 291, 31.10.1987; Bull. EC 7/8-1987, point 2.1.132.
3   Point 396 of this Report.
4   Case 242/87 *Commission v Council*: OJ C 242, 9.9.1987; Bull. EC 7/8-1987, point 2.4.34.
5   OJ L 222, 8.8.1986; Twentieth General Report, point 473.
6   Bull. EC 7/8-1987, point 2.1.136.
7   Bull. EC 12-1987.
8   OJ C 221, 8.8.1987; Bull. EC 5-1987, point 2.1.107.

against illiteracy[1] — confirming the commitment of 4 June 1986[2] — and failure at school in the Community.[3]

416.   From 5 to 7 May the Commission took part in the 15th session of the Standing Conference of European Ministers for Education in Helsinki.[4]

Youth exchanges

417.   On 26 February the Commission amended[5] its proposal for a Council Decision setting up a 'Yes for Europe' action programme to promote youth exchanges in the Community.[6] Some 2 000 grants will be made, totalling 2.3 million ECU.

European University Institute

418.   The Commission contributed the sum of 1 690 000 ECU to the academic and research activities of the European University Institute in Florence[7] (research projects, library, publications, language department, Jean Monnet scholarships for qualified researchers, Jean Monnet chair, summer schools, Centre for Documentation and Research on European Integration).[8]

419.   On 5 June Spain acceded to the convention setting up the European University Institute. On 19 October the Spanish Prime Minister, Mr Felipe González, gave the annual Jean Monnet lecture on the subject of 'The Community of Twelve on the way to European Union: target 1992'.

---

[1]   Bull. EC 5-1987, point 2.1.93.
[2]   Eighteenth General Report, point 294.
[3]   Bull. EC 5-1987, point 2.1.105.
[4]   Bull. EC 5-1987, point 2.1.102.
[5]   OJ C 77, 24.3.1987; Bull. EC 2-1987, point 2.1.70.
[6]   OJ C 72, 27.3.1986; Twentieth General Report, point 477.
[7]   The activities of the European University Institute are described in its annual report and in an information leaflet, both obtainable from the Institute itself (Badia Fiesolana, 5 via dei Roccettini, San Domenico di Fiesole, I-50016 Firenze).
[8]   Point 62 of this Report.

Specific measures relating to vocational training

420.   On 15 June, after Parliament [1] and the Economic and Social Committee [2] had delivered their opinions, the Council adopted conclusions on the communication sent by the Commission on 23 January on continuing vocational training for employees in undertakings. [3]

421.   Parliament adopted a resolution on 16 October on paid educational leave. [4]

422.   On 18 March the Commission presented to the Council a proposal for a Decision on an action programme for the training and preparation of young people for adult and working life, [5] on which Parliament and the Economic and Social Committee gave their opinions on 20 November [6] and 14 May [7] respectively. In the light of these opinions the Commission sent an amended proposal to the Council on 25 November. [8]

423.   As part of the process of implementing [9] the Council Decision of 16 July 1985 on the comparability of vocational training qualifications between the Member States, [10] the Commission published the agreed comparable qualifications in the hotel and catering, motor vehicle repair and construction industries in November.

European Centre for the Development of Vocational Training

424.   On 15 and 16 September the Centre's information network held its annual meeting in Berlin, at which the following questions were examined: computerization of the Centre's catalogues, the development of its thesaurus and circulation in the Member States of information on the Community's vocational training activities. [11]

[1]   OJ C 156, 15.6.1987; Bull. EC 5-1987, point 2.1.110.
[2]   OJ C 180, 8.7.1987; Bull. EC 5-1987, point 2.1.111.
[3]   Point 395 of this Report.
[4]   OJ C 305, 16.11.1987; Bull. EC 10-1987, point 2.4.119.
[5]   OJ C 90, 4.4.1987; point 2.1.96.
[6]   OJ C 345, 21.12.1987; Bull. EC 11-1987, point 2.1.121.
[7]   OJ C 180, 8.7.1987; Bull. EC 5-1987, point 2.4.32.
[8]   OJ C 4, 8.1.1988; Bull. EC 11-1987, point 2.1.122.
[9]   Twentieth General Report, point 479.
[10]   OJ L 199, 31.7.1985; Nineteenth General Report, point 427.
[11]   Bull. EC 9-1987, point 2.1.84.

Social security and living and working conditions

Social security and other schemes

425.   On 27 October the Commission transmitted to the Council a proposal for a Directive [1] completing implementation of the principle — as defined in the Directive of 19 December 1978 [2] — of equal treatment for men and women in statutory and occupational social security schemes. [3]

426.   The Commission selected 16 research projects for Spain and 10 for Portugal under the Council Decision of 22 December 1986 [4] expanding the specific Community action to combat poverty [5] to those countries.

427.   During the 1986/87 academic year the Executive Committee of the Paul Finet Foundation examined 948 applications and awarded 822 scholarships for a total of BFR 15 600 465.

Social security for migrant workers

428.   The Administrative Commission on Social Security for Migrant Workers examined a number of questions relating to the application of Regulations Nos 1408/71 [6] and 574/72 [7] on the application of social security schemes to employed persons and members of their families moving within the Community (consolidated on 2 June 1983 [8] and amended on 13 June 1985 [9]) and adopted five decisions addressed to national institutions and authorities.

429.   The Court of Justice delivered eight judgments in cases referred by national courts for preliminary rulings on the interpretation of these Regulations.[10] Eighteen cases are still before the Court.[11]

---

1   OJ C 309, 19.11.1987; Bull. EC 10-1987, point 2.1.85.
2   OJ L 6, 10.1.1979; Twelfth General Report, point 213.
3   OJ L 225, 12.8.1986; Twentieth General Report, point 493.
4   OJ L 382, 31.12.1986; Twentieth General Report, point 483.
5   OJ L 2, 3.1.1985; Eighteenth General Report, point 302.
6   OJ L 149, 5.7.1971.
7   OJ L 74, 27.3.1972.
8   OJ L 230, 22.8.1983; Seventeenth General Report, point 326.
9   OJ L 160, 24.6.1985; Nineteenth General Report, point 434.
10 Joined Cases 379/85, 380/85, 381/85 and 93/86; Case 375/85; Case 377/85; Joined Cases 82/86 and 103/86; Case 22/86; Case 37/86; Case 43/86.
11 Cases 20/85, 79/85, 197/85, 93/86, 313/86, 323/86, 21/87, 58/87, 83/87, 143/87, 147/87, 151/87, 154/87, 155/87, 159/87, 192/87, 236/87 and 269/87.

430.   The programme of exchanges of officials enabled 17 officials responsible for dealing with migrant workers to familiarize themselves with the procedures applied in another Member State.

Equal treatment for women and men

431.   The Commission continued to implement its medium-term programme (1986-90) [1] approved by the Council in its July 1986 resolution. [2] On 27 October the Commission transmitted to the Council a proposal for a Directive completing the implementation of the principale of equal treatment between men and women in statutory and occupational social security schemes. [3] It also set up the contact networks and operations provided for by the programme, arranged seminars with a variety of partners and developed its policy of support for positive action with a view to the setting up of businesses and local employment initiatives by women.

432.   On 26 May the Council adopted conclusions, on the basis of two communications from the Commission, [4] on legislation to protect women [5] and vocational training for women. [6] On 24 November the Commission likewise adopted a recommendation on the latter area, [7] which it sent on 4 December for information purposes to the Council, the Member States, Parliament and the Economic and Social Committee.

433.   On 14 October Parliament adopted four resolutions dealing with the reintegration of women into working life, women in sport, the depiction and position of women in the media and discrimination against immigrant women and female migrant workers in legislation and regulations in the Community. [8]

434.   The court of Justice delivered a number of preliminary rulings relating to the application of Community Directives on equal treatment of men and women. [9]

---

1   OJ C 356, 31.12.1985; Nineteenth General Report, point 437; Supplement 3/86 — Bull. EC.
2   OJ C 203, 12.8.1986; Twentieth General Report, point 492.
3   Point 425 of this Report.
4   Bull. EC 3-1987, points 2.1.101 and 2.1.102.
5   OJ C 178, 7.7.1987; Bull. EC 5-1987, point 2.1.113.
6   OJ C 178, 7.7.1987; Bull. EC 5-1987, point 2.1.112.
7   OJ C 342, 4.12.1987; Bull. EC 11-1987, point 2.1.127.
8   OJ C 305, 16.11.1987; Bull. EC 10-1987, point 2.4.11.
9   Points 960 and 961 of this Report.

Social integration of handicapped persons

435.   On 24 July the Commission sent to the Council two proposals for Decisions constituting a second Community action programme for disabled persons. [1] The proposals relate to the vocational rehabilitation and economic integration of people with disabilities and to their social integration and independent living. This programme, covering the years 1988-91, will tie in with the programme adopted by the Council and the Ministers of Education meeting within the Council on 14 May to promote the integration of handicapped children in ordinary schools. [2] On 16 October Parliament adopted an opinion on these proposals [3] and the Economic and Social Committee endorsed them on 21 October. [4]

Labour law and living and working conditions

436.   The final phase of the second instalment [5] of aid under the 10th ECSC subsidized housing scheme [6] began in 1987. Some 2 000 dwellings were constructed, purchased or modernized, which brings to 194 000 the total number of dwellings financed by ECSC funds by the end of 1987.

European Foundation for the Improvement of Living and Working Conditions

437.   The Dublin-based European Foundation for the Improvement of Living and Working Conditions continued to implement its four-year programme (1985-88). [7] This year it launched a survey of opinions on the role of the parties affected by the introduction of new technologies in firms and organized two seminars, the first on changes in labour law and social security in matters of working time and non-typical forms of employment and the second on the social aspects of biotechnology.

---

[1]   OJ C 257, 28.9.1987; Bull. EC 7/8-1987, point 2.1.141.
[2]   OJ C 211, 8.8.1987; Bull. EC 5-1987, point 2.1.106.
[3]   OJ C 305, 16.11.1987; Bull. EC 10-1987, point 2.1.89.
[4]   Bull. EC 10-1987, point 2.4.44.
[5]   Twentieth General Report, point 499.
[6]   OJ C 119, 14.5.1985; Nineteenth General Report, point 444.
[7]   Nineteenth General Report, point 445.

Social dialogue and industrial relations

438. The social dialogue between the two sides of industry, initiated and developed under Article 118b of the Treaty and established on the basis of conclusions reached at the meeting at Val Duchesse Château (on the outskirts of Brussels) on 12 November 1985,[1] was actively pursued in 1987 with the encouragement of the Commission. The meeting between the Commission and top-level representatives of employers' and workers' organizations in the Member States which was held in Brussels on 7 May on the joint initiative of the Commission and the Presidency of the Council, confirmed the readiness of the two sides of industry to proceed together along the path taken and gradually step up the social dialogue at Community level.[2]

The Working Party on Macroeconomics, which met on 24 March and 26 June[3] with a Member of the Commission in the chair, discussed the topic of profitability and the social aspect of both private and public investment.

At its meeting on 26 November it adopted a joint opinion on the 1987-88 annual economic report.[4] The Working Party on New Technologies and the Social Dialogue, which met on 6 March,[5] 21 May[6] and 10 November[7] with a Commission Vice-President in the chair, adopted a joint opinion on the training and motivation of the workforce and on providing workers with information and consulting them and/or their representatives when new technologies are introduced in firms. It held preliminary discussions on the consequences of the new technologies in terms of adaptability and flexibility, particularly with regard to improving the competitiveness of European firms and working conditions and terms of employment.

439. The social dialogue at industry level continued to develop as in 1986, in line with the intention expressed by the Commission in its 1987 programme.[8]

The existing Joint Committees (agricultural workers,[9] road transport,[10] sea fishing[11]) were renewed, and a Joint Committee on Maritime Transport was set up.[12]

---

1   Nineteenth General Report, point 74; Twentieth General Report, point 458.
2   Bull. EC 5-1987, point 1.2.1.
3   Bull. EC 6-1987, point 2.1.91.
4   Point 63 of this Report.
5   Bull. EC 3-1987, point 2.1.93.
6   Bull. EC 5-1987, point 2.1.100.
7   Bull. EC 11-1987, point 2.1.115.
8   Supplement 1/87 — Bull. EC; Bull. EC 2-1987, point 2.4.6.
9   Bull. EC 6-1987, point 2.1.90; OJ L 240, 22.8.1987; Bull. EC 7/8-1987, point 2.1.126.
10   Bull. EC 6-1987, point 2.1.89; Bull. EC 7/8-1987, point 2.1.127.
11   Bull. EC 5-1987, point 2.1.99; OJ L 240, 22.8.1987; Bull. EC 7/8-1987, point 2.1.126.
12   OJ L 253, 4.9.1987; Bull. EC 7/8-1987, point 2.1.128.

A series of meetings and contacts was organized with management and workers in industries for which there are no Joint Committees (banking, shipbuilding and construction).

Health and safety

Public health

440.   On 15 May the Council and the Ministers for Health meeting within the Council reaffirmed [1] the broad lines of Community public health activities laid down in May 1986, [2] adopting conclusions concerning AIDS [3] which included the convening of an *ad hoc* working party of public health officials to establish a common strategy and the introduction of arrangements for systematically informing international travellers about AIDS. They also approved [4] the Commission's proposal for an action plan against cancer (1987-89) [5] and noted [6] the communication from the Commission on the control of drug abuse. [7]

441.   In accordance with the decisions taken by the Council on 26 January [8] the Community — represented by a Member of the Commission — took part in the International Conference on Drug Abuse and Illicit Trafficking [9] held in Vienna from 17 to 26 June.[10] The Conference approved a policy declaration laying down guidelines for national, regional and international action to be taken to limit the scourge of drug abuse. The Community's policy, as outlined at the Conference, focused initially on North-South cooperation (which was allocated a budget of 5.5 million ECU for 1987) but could be extended to other areas of cooperation (customs, health, etc.) in the future.

During the Conference an agreement was signed between the Community and the UN Fund for Drug Abuse Control, under which the Community is to contribute 500 000 ECU.[10]

---

1   Bull. EC 5-1987, point 2.1.118 *et seq.*
2   Twentieth General Report, point 503.
3   OJ C 178, 7.7.1987; Bull. EC 5-1987, point 2.1.119.
4   Bull. EC 5-1987, point 2.1.121.
5   OJ C 50, 26.2.1987; Twentieth General Report, points 317 and 504.
6   Bull. EC 5-1987, point 2.1.118.
7   Twentieth General Report, points 318 and 505.
8   Bull. EC 1-1987, point 2.1.65.
9   Twentieth General Report, point 506.
10 Bull. EC 6-1987, point 2.1.105.

442.   The Commission continued its efforts [1] to make it easier for the Member States to adopt and introduce a European emergency health card. [2].

Health and safety at work

443.   On 18 September Parliament delivered an opinion [3] on the proposal for a Directive on the protection of workers from the risks related to exposure to benzene at work. [4]

444.   On 23 September the Economic and Social Committee delivered an opinion [5] on the proposal [6] to amend the Council Directive of 27 November 1980 on the protection of workers from the risks related to exposure to chemical, physical and biological agents at work. [7]

444a.   Consequently, on 12 November [8] the Commission sent to the Council amendments to the two above proposals as well as an amendment [9] to its proposal for a Directive on the protection of workers by prohibiting certain agents and/or work practices. [10]

445.   With the reinforcement of the Community's powers in the health field resulting from the Single Act, [11] the Commission adopted a new programme on safety, hygiene and health at work, [12] to build on the measures already taken in this sector. After consulting the Advisory Committee on Safety, Hygiene and Health Protection at Work, the Commission drew up proposals for a Council Directive on carcinogenic products [13] and the use of machines. [14]

Health and safety (ECSC)

446.   The Mines Safety and Health Commission held plenary meetings at which it examined means of reducing the risk of explosion and fire in mine workings with auxiliary ventilation and of improving the protection of workers

1   Bull. EC 12-1987.
2   OJ C 184, 23.7.1986; Twentieth General Report, point 503.
3   OJ C 281, 19.10.1987; Bull. EC 9-1987, point 2.1.92.
4   OJ C 349, 31.12.1985; Nineteenth General Report, point 453.
5   OJ C 319, 30.11.1987; Bull. EC 9-1987, point 2.4.34.
6   OJ C 164, 2.7.1986; Twentieth General Report, point 508.
7   OJ L 327, 3.12.1980; Fourteenth General Report, point 269.
8   Bull. EC 11-1987, point 2.1.136
9   OJ C 3, 7.1.1988; Bull. EC 11-1987, point 2.1.136.
10   OJ C 270, 10.10.1984; Eighteenth General Report, point 323.
11   Twentieth General Report, points 1 to 5; Supplement 2/86 — Bull. EC.
12   Bull. EC 9-1987, 2.1.91.
13   Bull. EC 1-1987, point 2.1.69; Bull. EC 2-1987, point 2.1.75.
14   Bull. EC 3-1987, point 2.1.110; Bull. EC 6-1987, point 2.1.106.

in the event of such accidents, as well as ways of reducing the health risks associated with exposure to dust in mines and quarries. [1]

447.   The Commission decided, under Article 55 of the ECSC Treaty, to grant 11 million ECU of financial aid to 68 projects relating to health, ergonomics, safety and hygiene in mines and the steel industry (ECSC social research).

Health and safety (Euratom)

448.   The Commission delivered opinions, under Article 33 of the Euratom Treaty, on two draft radiation protection measures [2] and, under Article 37, on four plans for the discharge of radioactive effluent from nuclear installations. [3]

449.   On 27 January the Commission sent the Council a proposal for a Regulation on a permanent system laying down maximum permitted radio-activity levels for foodstuffs, feedingstuffs and drinking water in the case of a nuclear accident. [4]

450.   On 7 April the Commission sent the Council a proposal [5] for a Decision to extend the responsibilities of the Advisory Committee on Safety, Hygiene and Health Protection at Work [6] to include health protection against the dangers arising from ionizing radiations on which the Economic and Social Committee delivered an opinion. [7]

451.   On 5 May the Commission transmitted to the Council a proposal for a Decision on a Community system of rapid exchange of information in cases of abnormal levels of radioactivity or of a nuclear accident. [8]

---

[1] Bull. EC 2-1987, point 2.1.77.
[2] Bull. EC 1-1987, point 2.1.71; Bull. EC 11-1987, point 2.1.138.
[3] Point 700 of this Report.
[4] Point 694 of this Report.
[5] OJ C 111, 25.4.1987; Bull. EC 3-1987, point 2.1.111.
[6] OJ L 185, 9.7.1984; Eighth General Report, point 243.
[7] OJ C 319, 30.11.1987; Bull. EC 9-1987, point 2.4.35.
[8] Point 696 of this Report.

Section 9

Regional policy

Main developments

452.   *The entry into force of the Single European Act,* [1] *which makes regional policy an integral part of the EEC Treaty, was a major feature of 1987. The reduction of regional disparities — notably the development of the least-favoured regions and the conversion of declining industrial regions — is fundamental to the strengthening of economic and social cohesion (the new Articles 130a and c). The Commission must now seek to achieve this goal not only by granting assistance from the ERDF and the other financial instruments, but also by taking the cohesion objective into account when it prepares and implements the common policies and the measures for completion of the internal market (Article 130b).*

It was with this in mind that the Commission presented to the Council, pursuant to Article 130d of the Treaty as amended by the Single Act, a comprehensive proposal aimed at clarifying and rationalizing the tasks, increasing the efficiency and coordinating the activities of the structural Funds. [2]

Priority activities and objectives

Community programmes

453.   This year saw a major expansion in regional operations in the form of programmes. Two Community programmes, STAR (advanced telecommunications services) and Valoren (utilization of endogenous energy potential), have now started to be implemented following the Commission Decision of 22 October. [3] And, as a means of tackling the regional consequences of the difficulties facing the shipbuilding and steel industries, the Commission pro-

---

[1]   Point 1 of this Report.
[2]   Point 482 of this Report.
[3]   Point 463 of this Report.

posed to the Council two new Community programmes to assist the regions affected by restructuring — Renaval for shipbuilding [1] and Resider for steel. [2] The programmes are to be part-financed by the ERDF pursuant to the Fund Regulation, [3] at a cost over the next three years of 200 million ECU and 300 million ECU respectively.

Together with social measures, the proposed regional conversion programmes are to support restructuring in the shipbuilding and steel industries by helping to develop new economic activities in the worst-hit areas. This will make a direct contribution to attainment of the objective of converting declining industrial regions through Community structural policies. [4]

454.   At the same time, a large number of programmes were launched under the ERDF's former non-quota section or in the form of national programmes of Community interest (NPCIs), an option which most Member States have taken up.

Decentralization and overseas regions

455.   In view of the difficulties that the peripheral regions and islands in the Community might experience in adjusting to the requirements associated with completion of the internal market by 1992, [5] the Commission proposed the establishment of structures and mechanisms that would make it easier to anticipate and resolve their problems. [6] For instance, it announced the setting up of a task force to monitor the problems of the French overseas departments and those of the Canary Islands, Ceuta-Melilla, the Azores and Madeira. [7]

456.   In conjunction with the leading European organizations of regional and local authorities, the Commission examined ways and means of involving them in the formulation and implementation of the Community's regional policy. This should lead to a Consultative Council of Local and Regional Authorities being set up to advise the Commission.

---

[1]   OJ C 291, 31.10.1987; Bull. EC 7/8-1987, point 2.1.146.
[2]   OJ C 272, 10.10.1987; Bull. EC 7/8-1987, point 2.1.146.
[3]   OJ L 169, 28.6.1984; Eighteenth General Report, points 344 to 347.
[4]   Points 477 and 478 of this Report.
[5]   Nineteenth General Report, points 162 to 166.
[6]   Point 482 of this Report.
[7]   Bull. 6-1987, point 2.1.118.

Regional policy coordination

Regional impact assessment of Community policies

457.   The Commission made an analysis of the regional consequences of the further restructuring needed to return the steel industry to lasting competitiveness. [1] The analysis shows that the areas that will be affected include not only the major steel-producing areas, which have been beset by serious difficulties for many years, but also a number of other areas which have so far remained unscathed by virtue of locational advantages which are now being eroded. The problems of conversion in these latter areas are especially acute because their economic and social structures are overdependent on one large firm and because they are too remote to be able to exploit the economic opportunities open to them. The principal regional policy measure designed to compensate for some of the 80 000 jobs expected to be lost in the steel industry is the Resider programme. [2]

458.   In continuing its analysis of the regional effects of the common agricultural policy (CAP), [3] the Commission found that most of the outlying regions in the south of the Community together with Ireland were receiving a lower level of spending per person employed than the other regions because of the low productivity of labour on their farms. It also noted that the new Community guidelines for agriculture would require major structural adjustments in the rural areas. Accordingly, in its proposals on the reform of the structural Funds, [4] it envisages that the ERDF will also contribute to the development of alternative economic activities in the rural areas most affected by the reform of the CAP.

Regional development programmes and Regional Policy Committee

459.   The regional development programmes provide a frame of reference for Regional Fund assistance and are a key instrument for coordinating Member States' regional policies. This year the Commission examined the third-

---

[1]   Point 278 of this Report.
[2]   Point 479 of this Report.
[3]   Points 540 to 544 of this Report.
[4]   Point 482 of this Report.

generation programmes for Berlin, France, Luxembourg, Italy, the Netherlands and the United Kingdom.

460.   The Regional Policy Committee held two meetings during the year, chaired by Mr Sallois. [1] The Committee was informed [2] of the progress made by the Commission with regard to implementation of Article 130d of the EEC Treaty, as amended by the Single European Act, [3] and delivered an opinion [4] on the third periodic report on the social and economic situation and development of the regions of the Community. [5] It also adopted an opinion on the third-generation regional development programmes (1986-90) for the Netherlands and the United Kingdom. [2]

Periodic report on the regions

461.   After consulting the Regional Policy Committee, [4] the Commission on 5 June transmitted [6] to the Council the third periodic report on the social and economic situation and development of the regions of the Community. [7] The report covers the situation of the regions in the early 1980s and developments since the 1960s. In the context of enlargement of the Community to 12 Member States and implementation of the Single European Act, the report gives an up-to-date and detailed analysis of regional disparities in production, employment, productivity, population trends and other factors. It also makes a number of forward-looking assessments.

Financial operations

European Regional Development Fund

462.   The ERDF was allocated commitment appropriations totalling 3 341.9 million ECU, equivalent to 9% of the Community budget, of which 124.5

---

[1]   Bull. EC 3-1987, point 2.1.115; Bull. EC 4-1987, point 2.1.86.
[2]   Bull. EC 3-1987, point 2.1.115.
[3]   Twentieth General Report, points 1 to 5; Supplement 2/86 — Bull. EC.
[4]   Bull. EC 4-1987, point 2.1.86.
[5]   Point 461 of this Report.
[6]   Bull. EC 5-1987, point 2.1.127.
[7]   Eighteenth General Report, point 336.

million ECU was intended to finance specific Community operations under Article 45 of the Fund Regulation. [1] In nominal terms, this is 7.87 % higher than in 1986; given the slowdown in inflation since then, this meant an appreciable real increase in resources that was not, however, commensurate with the widening of regional disparities consequent upon the accession of Spain and Portugal.

Community programmes

463.   Under the first two Community programmes (STAR — advanced tele-communications services — and Valoren — exploitation of endogenous energy potential), [2] the Commission in October approved, [3] after consulting the Fund Committee [4] and on the basis of the proposals submitted in April by the Member States concerned (France, Greece, Ireland, Italy, Portugal, Spain and the United Kingdom), a series of assistance programmes amounting to 777 million ECU in the case of STAR and 393 million ECU in the case of Valoren.

464.   On 31 July and 18 September the Commission sent to the Council two proposals for Regulations concerning two Community programmes to be part-financed by the ERDF: the Renaval programme to assist the conversion of shipbuilding areas, and the Resider programme to assist the conversion of steel areas. [5]

465.   The Commission also continued its preparations for new Community programmes designed to establish a better link between regional development or conversion operations and the objectives of Community policy on research and technological development and environmental policy.

Other programmes

466.   After consulting the Fund Committee, [6] the Commission approved [7] 25 new special programmes costing 159 million ECU in connection with the specific Community regional development measures [8] instituted under the

---

[1]   OJ L 169, 28.6.1984; Eighteenth General Report, points 344 to 347.
[2]   OJ L 305, 31.10.1986; Twentieth General Report, point 519.
[3]   Bull. EC 10-1987, point 2.1.100.
[4]   Bull. EC 9-1987, point 2.1.95.
[5]   Point 453 of this Report.
[6]   Bull. EC 5-1987, point 2.1.130; Bull. EC 9-1987, point 2.1.95.
[7]   Bull. EC 6-1987, point 2.1.113; Bull. EC 10-1987, point 2.1.101.
[8]   OJ L 350, 27.12.1985; Nineteenth General Report, point 479.

Fund's former non-quota section with a view to assisting areas adversely affected by industrial difficulties (steel, shipbuilding, textiles, fisheries and energy).

467.   In additon, 27 national programmes of Community interest (NPCIs) were approved this year, some of them receiving assistance from other Community financial instruments as well, either as integrated measures [1] or as integrated Mediterranean programmes. [2] Eleven of the programmes approved are to receive a total contribution from the ERDF of 721.5 million ECU.

The ERDF contribution approved for the other NPCIs totals 1 156 million ECU and involves the following individual programmes: Limburg [3] and West Flanders [3] in Belgium; Start Lolland [4] in Denmark; Asturias [3] in Spain; Nord/Pas-de-Calais, [5]   Auvergne, [5]   Central   Brittany, [4]   Charente-Maritime, [3] Réunion, [3] Lozère [3] and Limousin [5] in France; a road development programme in Ireland; Birmingham [4] and West Lothian-Bathgate [4] in the United Kingdom; and an aid scheme for productive investment [4] in Portugal.

Projects

468.   The Commission adopted 10 series of grant decisions in March, [6] June, [7] July, [8] October, [9] November[10] and December. [4] Altogether, 3 702 investment projects (4 352 in 1986) costing a total of 9 368 million ECU (10 286 million ECU in 1986) received grants totalling 299.16 million ECU. Infrastructure projects accounted for 91% and industrial, craft industry and service sector projects for 9% of grants. Taking industrial projects alone, the expected number of permanent new jobs is put at 28 450, of which 5 233 in Italy, 1 142 in France, 5 847 in Germany, 9 387 in the United Kingdom, 4 547 in Ireland, 106 in Belgium, 1 698 in Denmark and 490 in Greece. In many cases, Commission grants provide the remaining finance needed and speed up project implementation, especially where it is a question of improving the infrastructure

---

[1]   Point 477 of this Report.
[2]   Point 475 of this Report.
[3]   Bull. EC 10-1987, point 2.1.102.
[4]   Bull. EC 12-1987.
[5]   Bull. EC 6-1987, point 2.1.112.
[6]   Bull. EC 3-1987, points 2.1.117 and 2.1.118.
[7]   Bull. EC 6-1987, points 2.1.110 and 2.1.111.
[8]   Bull. EC 7/8-1987, point 2.1.147.
[9]   Bull. EC 10-1987, point 2.1.103.
[10]   Bull. EC 11-1987, point 2.1.142.

of regions faced with problems of underdevelopment or of carrying out major investment projects regarded as having an interregional impact. In certain other cases, grant decisions were tied to conditions for the reallocation of assistance to projects that, for lack of financing resources, would have been postponed.

Indigenous development potential

469.   Pursuant to the Fund Regulation,[1] which provides for Community financing in respect of 'consistent sets of measures' aimed at improving the service and technological environment for small businesses and creating new activities in industry, craft industry and tourism, the Commission, having consulted the ERDF Committee, approved 18 sets of measures for 1987, of which 10 were in France, four in Belgium, two in Ireland, one in the United Kingdom and one in the Netherlands.

Financing of studies

470.   Acting under Article 24 of the Fund Regulation,[1] the Commission decided to grant 6.73 million ECU to finance 26 studies closely connected with Fund operations or promoting more efficient use of Fund resources: three concerned Denmark,[2] 13 the United Kingdom,[3] one Ireland,[4] two Portugal,[5] one Italy,[6] three France[7] and three the Community as a whole.[7]

---

[1]   OJ L 169, 28.6.1984; Eighteenth General Report, points 344 to 347.
[2]   Bull. EC 4-1987, point 2.1.87; Bull. EC 5-1987, point 2.1.129.
[3]   Bull. EC 4-1987, point 2.1.87; Bull. EC 5-1987, point 2.1.129; Bull. EC 6-1987, point 2.1.114; Bull. EC 10-1987, point 2.1.104.
[4]   Bull. EC 5-1987, point 2.1.129.
[5]   Bull. EC 6-1987, point 2.1.114; Bull. EC 10-1987, point 2.1.104.
[6]   Bull. EC 10-1987, point 2.1.104.
[7]   Bull. EC 12-1987.

TABLE 12

ERDF operations in 1987
(provisional)

million ECU

	Commitments						Payments
	Programmes	Projects		Indigenous potential	Studies	Total	
		Industry	Infrastructure				
Belgium	13.7	1.3	7.6	1.0		23.6	23.0
Denmark	3.1	5.1	4.2	—	0.1	12.5	15.6
Germany (FR of)	—	63.0	51.3	—		114.3	60.9
Greece	107.6	1.5	192.7	—		301.8	287.4
Spain	27.3	—	633.4	—		660.7	345.4
France	125.7	3.4	133.3	8.8	5.4	276.6	263.7
Ireland	66.9	24.7	69.5	0.9	0.1	162.1	133.9
Italy	30.9	122.2	787.5		0.1	940.7	550.8
Luxembourg	1.0	—	2.3			3.3	2.3
Netherlands	5.3		15.1			20.4	19.4
Portugal	29.0		359.7		0.2	388.9	222.8
United Kingdom	131.2	43.6	450.7	1.8	0.9	628.2	519.3
Community	541.7	264.8	2 707.3	12.5	6.8	3 533.1	2 444.0

Conversion loans

471.   The sustained rate of ECSC conversion loan applications[1] noted in 1985[2] and 1986[3] slackened: total lending amounted to 238 million ECU and 17 800 jobs were created. Of the 40 million ECU or so made available to finance interest-rate subsidies on conversion loans under the 1987 ECSC budget, 75 % was used to increase the amounts allocated previously for earlier loans.

---

[1]   The revised operating principles (Twentieth General Report, point 535) were published in OJ C 173, 1.7.1987.
[2]   Nineteenth General Report, point 482.
[3]   Twentieth General Report, point 535.

TABLE 13

	1975-86		1987		1975-87	
	1	2	1	2	1	2
Belgium	143.8	7 437	23.022	1 726	166.822	9 163
Denmark	11.7	854	—	—	11.700	854
Germany (FR of)	1 028.8	69 708	53.040	3 974	1 081.840	73 682
France	268.5	17 827	51.298	3 846	319.798	21 673
Ireland	4.4	420	—	—	4.400	420
Italy	380.6	22 110	33.636	2 521	414.236	24 631
Luxembourg	25.8	2 100	—	—	25.800	2 100
Netherlands	18.6	1 255	14.921	1 117	33.521	2 372
United Kingdom	1 132.7	60 627	9.200	672	1 141.900	61 299
Greece	5.0	375	—	—	5.000	375
Spain			32.725	2 454	32.725	2 454
Portugal			20.000	1 500	20.000	1 500
Saar/Lorr./Lux. transfrontier operation	100.0	5 000	—	—	100.000	5 000
Community	3 119.9	187 713	237.842	17 810	3 357.742	205 523

[1] Amount of loans granted (in million ECU).
[2] Number of jobs created/to be created.

Business and innovation centres

472.   Further action to promote the establishment of a European network of business and innovation centres (BICs) was taken on three fronts: 12 new BICs, the financing for which had been decided in 1986, [1] were set up to encourage the establishment of new and innovative small firms and to help existing ones to diversify; 10 new measures were taken to prepare for BICs in industrial development areas covered by Community regional policy; [2] continuing support was provided for the European Business and Innovation Centre Network (EBN), an international association promoted by the Commission and set up in November 1984 by a number of BICs and technology parks. [3]

473.   The Commission also sent to the Council a proposal for a Decision concerning a programme to create and develop BICs and their network. [4]

[1]   Twentieth General Report, point 536.
[2]   Bull. EC 4-1987, point 2.1.88; Bull. EC 7/8-1987, point 2.1.149; Bull. EC 12-1987.
[3]   Eighteenth General Report, point 355.
[4]   Point 291 of this Report.

Section 10

Coordination of structural instruments

Main developments

474. *Shortly after the entry into force of the Single European Act[1] and in accordance with Article 130d of the EEC Treaty, the Commission presented to the Council a comprehensive proposal for clarifying and rationalizing the tasks of the structural Funds and for increasing their efficiency and coordinating their activities with the aim of improving the Community's economic and social cohesion.[2]*

At the same time, the Commission continued to implement the reforms already set in train concerning assistance to the Mediterranean regions (IMPs) and use of integrated development operations (IDOs); it also presented proposals for two programmes for converting areas affected by restructuring of the steel and shipbuilding industries.

Priority activities and objectives

Implementation of IMPs

475. The Commission formally approved 13 IMPs: the seven French IMPs, covering Aquitaine,[3] Corsica,[4], Languedoc-Roussillon,[5] Provence-Alpes-Côte d'Azur,[4] Midi-Pyrénées,[5] Ardèche and Drôme,[4] and six Greek IMPs, covering information technology,[6] western Greece and the Peloponnese,[7] northern Greece,[7] Attica,[8] the Aegean islands,[8] and eastern and central Greece.[8] This means that, with the IMP for Crete in progress since 1986,[9] all the Greek and

---

[1]   Point 1 of this Report.
[2]   Twentieth General Report, point 548.
[3]   OJ L 14, 19.1.1988; Bull. EC 7/8-1987, point 2.1.153.
[4]   Bull. EC 7/8-1987, point 2.1.153.
[5]   OJ L 12, 16.1.1988; Bull. EC 7/8-1987, point 2.1.153.
[6]   Bull. EC 7/8-1987, point 2.1.154.
[7]   Bull. EC 7/8-1987, point 2.1.155.
[8]   Bull. EC 10-1987, point 2.1.109.
[9]   Twentieth General Report, point 542.

French IMPs have been launched; they can now be implemented since the seven programme contracts covering all the IMPs for France under the first allocation for 1986-88 were signed by the Commission and France on 17 July[1] and the contracts for the six remaining IMPs by the Commission and Greece in October[2] and December.[3] Examination of the 17 Italian programmes[4] is at a fairly advanced stage; they should start to be implemented in the first half of 1988. The launching of the IMP for Molise is planned for the beginning of 1988,[5] the Commission having formally adopted it in December.[3]

476.　Finally, the Commission examined the first reports assessing the measures in preparation for implementation of the IMPs, almost all of which have been set in train.

Integrated operations

477.　On 16 March, on the basis of the principles set out in its July 1986 communication[6] on the content of the integrated approach[7] and the procedures for implementing it, the Commission approved an integrated action programme for the Oost-Groningen/Oost-Drenthe region of the Netherlands.[8] And on 15 December it approved a number of integrated development operations concerning Ariège, Auvergne, central Brittany, the island of Réunion, Limousin and east Tarn/south Aveyron (France).[3] The examination of other applications is well under way.

478.　In addition, a number of preparatory studies for such operations were continued. It should soon be possible for integrated operations to be launched on the basis of their findings, in particular those of the seven studies in progress in Spain and Portugal.[9] A further seven feasibility studies were part-financed by the Community during the year.[3] On 14 October the Commission finalized[10] the Community support programme for the modernization of Portuguese

1　Bull. EC 7/8-1987, point 2.1.153.
2　Bull. EC 10-1987, point 2.1.111.
3　Bull. EC 12-1987.
4　Twentieth General Report, point 542.
5　Bull. EC 10-1987, point 2.1.110.
6　Twentieth General Report, point 544.
7　OJ L 197, 27.7.1985; Nineteenth General Report, points 465 to 468.
8　OJ L 94, 8.4.1987; Bull. EC 3-1987, point 2.1.121.
9　Twentieth General Report, point 547.
10　Bull. EC 10-1987, point 2.1.112.

industry, drawn up at Portugal's request,[1] which will also have the integrated approach procedures applied to it.

479. Acting on the basis of the new Single Act provisions regarding economic and social cohesion,[2] the Commission adopted on 16 July[3] and 17 September[4] proposals for Regulations concerning two Community programmes designed to deal with the social[5] and regional[6] aspects of restructuring of the shipbuilding[7] and steel[8] industries.

Structural assistance in regions affected by natural disasters

480. In the course of the year, the stricken area of Kalamata in Greece was assisted under the special measure adopted at the end of 1986. Community grants were provided, and the Council was asked to approve Community loans with interest-rate subsidies, totalling 100 million ECU on 22 December.[9]

481. On 15 December the Commission decided to introduce a special measure involving deployment of various structural instruments in the parts of northern Italy (notably the Valtellina) seriously affected by the bad weather in the summer.[9] The operation is to focus on reconstructing infrastructures and revitalizing agriculture and the economy in general.

Attainment of the economic and social cohesion objectives set by the Single Act

Reform of the structural Funds

482. In accordance with the guidelines[10] adopted by the European Council on 29 and 30 June for implementing the Commission communication entitled 'The Single Act: A new frontier for Europe'[11] and in line with the agreement

---

1   Twentieth General Report, point 547.
2   Supplement 2/86 — Bull. EC; Nineteenth General Report, point 9.
3   Bull. EC 7/8-1987, points 2.1.132, 2.1.146 and 2.1.156.
4   OJ C 272, 10.10.1987; Bull. EC 7/8-1986, points 2.1.146 and 2.1.156.
5   Points 410 and 412 of this Report.
6   Point 453 of this Report.
7   Twentieth General Report, point 546.
8   Nineteenth General Report, point 484.
9   Bull. EC 12-1987.
10   Bull. EC 6-1987, point 1.1.4.
11   Supplement 1/87 — Bull. EC; Bull. EC 2-1987, point 1.1.1 *et seq.*

reached between the Commission and the Council, the Commission presented [1] to the Council on 4 August — pursuant to Article 130d of the Treaty (as amended by the Single European Act) and following its preliminary draft in April [2] — a comprehensive proposal for reforming the structure and functioning of the structural Funds on which Parliament and the Economic and Social Committee delivered their opinions on 19 November. [3] This is a proposal for a framework Regulation, on which, pursuant to the Single Act, the Council is to act unanimously within one year; the Commission will then put forward implementing Regulations for each Fund, which the Council will adopt by a qualified majority, and a Regulation laying down arrangements for the coordination of the structural instruments; a communication on the role of the EIB and the other financial instruments will also be prepared.

The reforms proposed seek to improve the effectiveness of Community structural measures by means of better overall coordination and multiannual programming. The Commission proposal revolves around four guiding principles that are indissolubly linked to one another:

(a) concentration of resources on five priority objectives: (i) promoting the development and structural adjustment of the less-developed regions; (ii) converting the regions affected by industrial decline; (iii) combating long-term unemployment; (iv) helping to place young people in jobs; (v) speeding up the adjustment of agricultural structures and promoting the development of rural areas;

(b) increase in the financial resources available (doubling the commitment appropriations for the structural Funds in real terms between now and 1992);

(c) rationalization of operating methods, with a three-stage process for the Community's structural operations based on the three principles of complementarity with national operations, partnership between the Commission and the Member States, and planning: (i) Member States to submit plans setting out their requirements, notably as regards utilization of Community structural instruments; (ii) Community support frameworks defining priorities and identifying the structural operations needed to be drawn up in

---

1   OJ C 245, 12.9.1987; Bull. EC 7/8-1987, points 1.1.1 and 1.1.2.
2   Bull. EC 4-1987, point 2.1.90.
3   OJ C 345, 21.12.1987; Bull. EC 11-1987, points 1.1.8 and 1.1.9.

consultation; (iii) at the operational stage, programmes to be the preferred policy instrument;

(d) simplification and harmonization of the rules for managing the Funds (programming, multiannual budget management, monitoring and assessment of operations, etc.).

These arrangements are scheduled to have effect from 1 January 1989.

Section 11

Environment

Main developments

483.   Since 1987 had been designated 'European Year of the Environment' the Commission redoubled its efforts to enhance public awareness in Europe of the importance of protecting the environment and to promote the application of the principles set out in the fourth action programme[1] — especially its new approach of making environment policy an integral part of all the other policies, whether national or Community.

In specific aspects of this programme, the Council adopted Directives on the lead content of petrol and on emissions of gases from private cars and heavy goods vehicles.

As well as being a 'European' year, 1987 proved very successful where international cooperation too was concerned. The Community and 24 countries concluded the Montreal Protocol, and the Community particularly commended the report by the World Commission on Environment and Development. The Community also continued to participate in work under the various international conventions on water protection.

Priority activities and objectives

Protecting the ozone layer

484.   The Protocol on chlorofluorocarbons (CFCs)[2] to the Vienna Convention for the Protection of the Ozone Layer[3] was signed in Montreal on 16 September by 24 countries, including most of the Member States of the Community, and by the Council and the Commission on behalf of the Community.[4] In accordance with the Council mandate of 25 November 1986,[2] the Commission had

---

[1]   OJ C 63, 18.3.1986; Twentieth General Report, point 549.
[2]   Twentieth General Report, point 565.
[3]   Nineteenth General Report, point 509.
[4]   Bull. EC 9-1987, point 2.1.114.

taken part in the negotiations on the Protocol, [1] which provides for a freeze in the consumption and production of CFCs at 1986 levels. Production will later be cut to 80% and then (in July 1998) to 50% of those levels. The Protocol also provides for a freeze in the consumption and production of halogens at 1986 levels. The measures provided for by the Protocol — which includes a special clause on regional economic organizations and takes into account the special situation in developing countries — will be subject to constant review as well as complete four-yearly scientific assessments of the foreseeable degree of depletion of the ozone layer.

The signing of the Protocol represents a major success in the field of international cooperation in environmental matters: this is the first time that so many countries have reached agreement on environmental protection measures and that a measure of this type has been adopted with the aim of preventing future damage to the environment rather than repairing existing damage. This undertaking is particularly significant in that it was given before a complete range of substitute products was available.

General measures

Fourth programme on the environment; financial contributions

485.   On 19 October the Council and the Representatives of the Governments of the Member States adopted a resolution [2] based on a communication from the Commission [3] on the continuation and implementation of a Community policy and action programme on the environment. [4]

486.   On 23 July, acting on a proposal from the Commission, [5] the Council formally adopted a Regulation [6] extending the Regulation of 28 June 1984 on the financing of certain environmental projects. [7]

[1]   Bull. EC 2-1987, point 2.1.93; Bull. EC 5-1987, point 2.1.145.
[2]   OJ C 289, 29.10.1987; Bull. EC 10-1987, point 2.1.116.
[3]   OJ C 70, 18.3.1987; Twentieth General Report, point 550.
[4]   OJ C 3, 7.1.1987; Twentieth General Report, point 550.
[5]   OJ C 18, 24.1.1987; Twentieth General Report, point 574.
[6]   OJ L 207, 2.7.1987; Bull. EC 7/8-1987, point 2.1.164.
[7]   OJ L 176, 3.7.1984; Eighteenth General Report, point 382.

Legal aspects

487.   Enforcement of Community law in the Member States has been tightened up even further, as shown by the increase in the number of complaints registered and examined, the number of proceedings under Article 169 and the number of Court judgments in this field. The Commission provided more information for the general public on Community law relating to the environment;[1] in particular, it organized two meetings of civil servants from the Member States to discuss problems arising from the application of the Community Directives on water and waste.

488.   Nevertheless, the number of notifications from the Member States under the standstill agreement of 5 March 1973[2] remains insignificant, mainly because proposed national legislation tends to be notified under the Directive of 28 March 1983[3] even when it is mainly concerned with environmental protection. This has led to the Commission taking administrative measures to ensure complete consistency between the objectives aimed at by Articles 8a and 100a (completion of the internal market) and Articles 130r and 130t (conservation, protection and enhancement of the environment) of the EEC Treaty, as amended by the Single European Act.

Taking the environment into account in other policies

489.   The Commission has continued its efforts to take the environment into account in other Community policies, particularly those relating to the co-financing of national or Community development programmes by the structural Funds[4] and other financial instruments.

Likewise, in application of the Council Regulation of 23 July 1985 on the integrated Mediterranean programmes,[5] the Commission ensures that environmental protection is guaranteed particularly in sensitive areas, whenever measures are taken under these programmes.[6]

490.   Similarly, in transport policy, the environmental impact assessment required under Article 4 of the proposal for a Regulation on financial support

---

1   Points 493 and 494 of this Report.
2   OJ C 9, 15.3.1973; Seventh General Report, point 265.
3   OJ L 109, 26.4.1983; Seventeenth General Report, point 151.
4   Point 482 of this Report.
5   OJ L 197, 27.7.1985; Nineteenth General Report, point 465.
6   Point 475 of this Report.

within the framework of a medium-term transport infrastructure programme [1] is one of the criteria for evaluating the applications for Commission support.

491.   In agricultural policy the Council Regulation of 15 June on agricultural structures, the adjustment of agriculture to the new market situation and the preservation of the countryside [2] also stresses the problems of the environment.

Economic aspects and employment

492.   The Council began its examination of a proposal from the Commission [3] for a Decision establishing a five-year Community-wide programme of demonstration projects illustrating how action in the environmental field can also contribute to employment creation.

Public awareness and training

493.   The European Year of the Environment, [4] the first Community-level awareness-raising campaign in this field, was inaugurated on 19 March. [5] Its aims are to make all Community citizens aware of the importance of environmental protection, to promote the inclusion of environmental protection considerations in the Community's economic activities, to emphasize the European dimension of environment policy and to demonstrate the progress made.

Two types of programme have already been implemented — Community measures coordinated by a steering committee and national measures coordinated by national committees. The Community programme includes several subprogrammes covering the four objectives of the Year, namely promoting the use of clean technologies and good environmental practice; [6] encouraging local community activities; [7] providing support for the organization of advanced training courses and competitions in education; [8] and promoting

---

[1]   OJ C 288, 15.11.1986; Twentieth General Report, point 693.
[2]   Point 553 of this Report.
[3]   OJ C 141, 27.5.1987; Bull. EC 2-1987, point 2.1.83.
[4]   OJ C 63, 18.3.1986; Twentieth General Report, point 549.
[5]   Bull. EC 3-1987, point 1.3.1.
[6]   Bull. EC 5-1987, point 2.1.137; Bull. EC 9-1987, points 2.1.101 to 2.1.103; Bull. EC 10-1987, points 2.1.117 and 2.1.118; Bull. EC 11-1987, point 2.1.149.
[7]   Bull. EC 5-1987, point 2.1.136; Bull. EC 6-1987, point 2.1.121; Bull. EC 7/8-1987, point 2.1.161; Bull. EC 9-1987, point 2.1.100; Bull. EC 10-1987, point 2.1.120: Bull. EC 11-1987, point 2.1.150.
[8]   Bull. EC 7/8-1987, points 2.1.162 and 2.1.163; Bull. EC 5-1987, point 2.1.138.

specific measures in conjunction with non-Community countries with a view to increasing the awareness of the general public. [1]

494. The Commission continued[2] to implement its work programme[3] on the experimental project for gathering, coordinating and ensuring consistency of information on the state of the environment and natural resources in the Community (Corine). [4]

International cooperation

495. As it is fully aware of the increased importance of international cooperation in environmental matters, the Community participated in the work being done under international conventions covering such matters as combating air pollution,[5] protecting nature and natural resources[6] and the marine environment and coastal areas.[7] In Montreal in September the Community signed a Protocol to the Vienna Convention on the Protection of the Ozone Layer relating to chlorofluorocarbons.[8] The Community also attended the 14th session of the Governing Council of the United Nations Environment Programme, during which many decisions and resolutions were adopted. [9]

496. On 5 May, at the invitation of the Commission, Mrs Brundtland, who chairs the World Commission on Environment and Development, presented[10] her Commission's report[11] at a meeting in Brussels attended by representatives of the Community and EFTA Member States. In November representatives of the Commission took part in a seminar organized jointly by the OECD and France on strenghtening cooperation with developing countries on the environment.

497. Where bilateral relations are concerned, cooperation was continued with the United States.[12]

---

1 Bull. EC 5-1987, point 2.1.138; Bull. EC 6-1987, point 2.1.122; Bull. EC 7/8-1987, points 2.1.159 and 2.1.160; Bull. EC 9-1987, point 2.1.100; Bull. EC 10--1987, point 2.1.119.
2 Twentieth General Report, point 573.
3 OJ L 176, 3.7.1985; Nineteenth General Report, point 515.
4 Coordination of information on the environment in Europe.
5 Point 505 of this Report.
6 Point 516 of this Report.
7 Point 501 of this Report.
8 Point 484 of this Report.
9 Point 878 of this Report.
10 Bull. EC 5-1987, point 2.1.135.
11 Bull. EC 11-1987, point 2.1.165.
12 Bull. EC 3-1987, point 2.1.137.

498. Pursuant to the Luxembourg Joint Declaration of April 1984,[1] the European Free Trade Association and the Commission also increased their efforts to ensure closer cooperation on environmental matters. On 25 and 26 October the Commission attended a meeting between the Ministers for Environmental Affairs of the Member States of the Community and of EFTA.[2]

Prevention and reduction of pollution and nuisance

Protection of the aquatic environment

499. Under the Council Directive of 4 May 1976 on pollution caused by certain dangerous substances discharged into the aquatic environment of the Community,[3] on 12 October the Commission proposed adding hexachlorobenzene and hexachlorobutadiene,[4] to the Council Directive of 12 June 1986 on pollution.[5]

500. By providing financial support for four pilot projects (in Greece, Yugoslavia, Egypt and Tunisia), the Commission contributed significantly to activities concerned with protecting the marine environment. On 2 April it also proposed[6] that the Council should amend the Decision of 6 March 1986[7] so as to extend the Community information system to inland waterways and should at the same time cooperate closely with the Member States in their efforts to apply the Decision to accidental marine pollution. On 16 September it set up a Community task force to assist the authorities in the Member States responsible for dealing with emergency situations.[8]

501. The Community also participated in the work in progress under various international conventions to protect water, in particular the Paris Convention for the Prevention of Pollution from Land-based Sources,[9] the Barcelona Convention for the Protection of the Mediterranean against Pollution[10] and

---

1   Eighteenth General Report, point 652.
2   Bull. EC 10-1987, point 2.1.133.
3   OJ L 129, 18.5.1976; Tenth General Report, point 277.
4   Bull. EC 10-1987, point 2.1.124.
5   OJ L 181, 4.7.1986; Twentieth General Report, point 551.
6   OJ C 108, 23.4.1987; Bull. EC 4-1987, point 2.1.91.
7   OJ L 77. 22.3.1986; Twentieth General Report, point 554.
8   Bull. EC 9-1987, point 2.1.110.
9   OJ L 194, 25.7.1975; Ninth General Report, point 237.
10 OJ L 240, 19.9.1977; Eleventh General Report, point 293.

the Convention for the Protection of the Rhine against Chemical Pollution,[1] concerning which, following the Sandoz accident on 1 November 1986, work culminated in the decisions of the seventh and eighth Ministerial Conferences held in Rotterdam in December 1986 and Strasbourg on 1 October 1987.[2]

502.   The Commission also attended the second International Conference on the Protection of the North Sea held in London on 24 and 25 November.[3]

Air pollution

503.   The Community actively pursued its policy to combat air pollution and ensure progress on earlier measures. For instance, the Council formally adopted on 19 March the Directive on the prevention of environmental pollution by asbestos[4] and on 30 March an amendment[5] to the Directive of November 1975 on the sulphur content of gas oils.[6] On 21 July it also adopted an amendment[7] to the Directive of 20 March 1985 concerning the lead content of petrol;[8] on 30 October the Commission adopted a Decision on the approximation of the laws of the Member States on this subject in which it welcomed the proposals to prohibit regular unleaded petrol in Luxembourg and the Federal Republic of Germany in the course of 1988.[9]

504.   Parliament having delivered its opinion in second reading (cooperation procedure)[10] on the Council's common position[11] on the proposals for Directives on particulate emissions from private cars[12] and emissions of gaseous pollutants from heavy goods vehicles,[13] the Council adopted these two Directives on 3 December.[14] It also adopted a common position[14] on the proposal to amend[15] the Directive of 20 March 1970 on particulate emissions from diesel engines.[16]

[1]   OJ L 240, 19.9.1977; Eleventh General Report, point 292.
[2]   Bull. EC 10-1987, point 2.1.122.
[3]   Bull. EC 11-1987, point 2.1.152.
[4]   OJ L 85, 28.3.1987; Bull. EC 3-1987, point 2.1.129; Twentieth General Report, point 556.
[5]   OJ L 91, 3.4.1987; Bull. EC 3-1987, point 2.1.130; Twentieth General Report, point 556.
[6]   OJ L 307, 27.11.1975; Ninth General Report, point 237.
[7]   OJ L 225, 13.8.1987; Bull. EC 7/8-1987, point 2.1.170.
[8]   OJ L 96, 3.4.1985; Nineteenth General Report, point 489.
[9]   Bull. EC 10-1987, point 2.1.125.
[10] OJ C 345, 21.12.1987; Bull. EC 11-1987, points 2.1.155 and 2.1.156.
[11] Bull. EC 9-1987, point 2.1.111; Bull. EC 7/8-1987, point 2.1.169.
[12] OJ C 174, 12.7.1986; Twentieth General Report, point 557.
[13] OJ C 193, 31.7.1986; Twentieth General Report, point 557.
[14] Bull. EC 12-1987.
[15] OJ C 175, 15.7.1985; OJ C 245, 26.9.1985; OJ C 257, 28.9.1987.
[16] OJ L 76, 6.4.1970; Fourth General Report, points 64 and 285.

505. On the international front, the Community continued with its initiatives under the 1979 Geneva Convention on Long-range Transboundary Air Pollution,[1] attending the fifth session of the Executive Body set up under the Convention from 16 to 20 November[2] and contributing to the drafting of a Protocol on reducing emissions and transfrontier flows of nitrogen oxides. The Commission also continued to collaborate actively[3] (particularly through the JRC's measurement station at Ispra) in the Convention's EMEP programme (continuous monitoring and evaluation of the long-range transmission of air pollutants in Europe), which receives financial support from the Community.[4]

Noise abatement

506. On 25 June, acting on a Commission proposal,[5] the Council amended[6] the Directive of 17 September 1984 relating to the permissible sound power level of tower cranes.[7]

507. On 30 November the Council adopted[8] common positions on the two proposals[9] to amend the Directive of 17 September 1984 relating to the permissible sound power level of lawnmowers.[7] On 7 April the Commission had adapted the Directive to technical progress.[10]

Controls on chemicals, industrial hazards and biotechnology

508. On 18 December the Council reached a common position[11] on proposed Directives concerning (i) the classification, packaging and labelling of dangerous preparations[12] and (ii) the inspection and verification of the organizational processes and conditions under which laboratory studies are planned, per-

---

[1] OJ L 171, 27.6.1981; Fifteenth General Report, point 335.
[2] Bull. EC 11-1987, point 2.1.157.
[3] Twentieth General Report, point 556.
[4] OJ L 181, 4.7.1986; Twentieth General Report, point 556.
[5] OJ C 267, 23.10.1986; Twentieth General Report, point 560.
[6] OJ L 220, 8.8.1987; Bull. EC 6-1987, point 2.1.131.
[7] OJ L 300, 19.11.1984; Eighteenth General Report, point 371.
[8] Bull. EC 11-1987, point 2.1.158.
[9] OJ C 20, 27.1.1987; Twentieth General Report, point 560.
[10] OJ L 117, 5.5.1987; Bull. EC 4-1987, point 2.1.93.
[11] Bull. EC 12-1987.
[12] Point 203 of this Report.

formed, recorded and reported for the non-clinical testing of chemicals (good laboratory practice). [1]

509. The Commission continued with its work on the classification and labelling of dangerous substances—in particular carcinogens, mutagens and teratogens. On 3 August this culminated in the Council adopting the eighth adaptation to technical progress [2] of the Council Directive of 27 June 1967, [3] which sets out the labelling requirements for 29 carcinogens.

510.   Under its action programme on existing chemicals, the Commission sent the Council a communication on 23 April concerning an action programme to combat environmental pollution by cadmium. [4]

Work on implementing the Council Directive of 18 September 1979 amending for the sixth time [5] the Directive of 27 June 1967 on dangerous substances [6] also proceeded satisfactorily, [7] particularly as regards the notification of new chemicals which are constantly on the increase. In this connection, on 14 September the Commission, acting under its Decision of 11 May 1981, [8] issued the unofficial English-language version of the inventory of existing chemical substances (Einecs). [7] Where these substances are concerned, no notification is required before they are put on the market.

511.   On 18 November the Commission approved [9] the ninth adaptation to technical progress of the Directive of 27 June 1967 on dangerous substances. [6]

512.   In the light of Parliament's opinion, [10] on 1 December the Commission sent to the Council an amendment [11] to its proposal for a Council Regulation concerning trade in certain dangerous chemicals, [12] and its recommendation for a Decision authorizing it to negotiate on behalf of the Community—in the OECD and UNEP—notification and consultation procedures concerning trade in dangerous chemicals.

---

1   Point 211 of this Report.
2   OJ L 239, 21.8.1987; Bull. EC 7/8-1987, point 2.1.172.
3   OJ 196, 16.8.1967; OJ L 247, 1.9.1986; Twentieth General Report, point 561.
4   Bull. EC 4-1987, point 2.1.94.
5   OJ L 259, 15.10.1979; Thirteenth General Report, point 277.
6   OJ 196, 16.8.1967.
7   Twentieth General Report, point 561.
8   OJ L 167, 24.6.1981; Fifteenth General Report, point 346.
9   Bull. EC 11-1987, point 2.1.163.
10 OJ C 281, 19.10.1987; Bull. EC 9-1987, point 2.1.115.
11 Bull. EC 12-1987.
12 OJ C 177, 15.7.1986; Twentieth General Report, point 562.

513. On 19 March, in line with the rules governing the implementation of the Council Directive of 24 June 1982 on the major-accident hazards of certain industrial activities (the 'Seveso' Directive),[1] the Council adopted the first amendment to this Directive.[2] A further amendment is being prepared to extend the Directive's scope to cover the storage of dangerous substances. The Commission has also continued with work on training for the authorities in the Member States responsible for supervising the implementation of the Directive.

514. Similarly, the Commission continued with its work on defining the framework of Community law on biotechnology mapped out in its communication to the Council of November 1986.[3]

Management of environmental resources

515. On 23 July, acting on a proposal from the Commission,[4] the Council extended the validity of, and amended,[5] the Regulation of 28 June 1984 on the funding of certain environmental measures.[6] The new Regulation extends the scope of the measures to recycling and reusing waste, locating and restoring sites contaminated by hazardous wastes and/or substances and the protection or re-establishment of land threatened or damaged by fire, erosion and desertification.

Conservation of the natural heritage

516. On 21 May, acting on a proposal from the Commission,[7] the Council amended[8] its Regulation of 3 December 1982 on the implementation in the Community of the Convention on International Trade in Endangered Species of Wild Fauna and Flora.[9] The Commission further amended this Regulation on 22 May[10] and 19 October[11] to take into account the decisions reached at

---

[1]   OJ L 230, 5.8.1982; Sixteenth General Report, point 364.
[2]   OJ L 85, 28.3.1987; Bull. EC 3-1987, point 2.1.134.
[3]   Twentieth General Report, point 563.
[4]   OJ C 18, 24.1.1987; Twentieth General Report, point 574.
[5]   OJ L 207, 29.7.1987; Bull. EC 7/8-1987, point 2.1.164.
[6]   OJ L 176, 3.7.1984; Eighteenth General Report, point 382.
[7]   OJ C 97, 25.4.1986.
[8]   OJ L 136, 26.5.1987; Bull. EC 5-1987, point 2.1.149.
[9]   OJ L 384, 31.12.1982; Sixteenth General Report, point 374.
[10] OJ L 147, 6.6.1987; Bull. EC 5-1987, point 2.1.150.
[11] OJ L 299, 22.10.1987; Bull. EC 10-1987, point 2.1.131.

the sixth conference of the Contracting Parties to the Convention held in Ottawa from 12 to 25 July, in which the Community participated. [1]

517.   Under the Council Regulation of 28 June 1984 on action by the Community relating to the environment [2] and under the new Regulation adopted on 23 July to replace the 1984 Regulation, [3] the Commission decided this year to grant financial support to nine projects to promote the conservation of biotopes of special interest to the Community as a whole and to eight projects for emergency measures and to promote the conservation of endangered species. [4]

Waste management

518.   On 22 July the Council sent the Commission a proposal [5] for a Decision laying down the conditions for the adoption of the OECD Council Decision concerning those hazardous wastes for which transfrontier movements are to be controlled by the Member States of the Community pursuant to the Council Directive of 6 December 1984. [6]

519.   On 27 October the Commission sent to the Council a proposal for a Decision authorizing the Commission to negotiate on behalf of the Community an international agreement within the OECD framework on the control of transfrontier movements of hazardous waste. [7]

520.   On 18 June the Commission sent the Council and Parliament a report on the transport of dangerous goods and wastes reviewing current national and international control measures and putting forward recommendations regarding harmonization. [8]

---

1   Bull. EC 7/8-1987, point 2.1.176.
2   OJ L 176, 3.7.1984; Eighteenth General Report, point 382.
3   OJ L 207, 29.7.1987; Bull. EC 7/8-1987, point 2.1.164.
4   Bull. EC 5-1987, point 2.1.141; Bull. EC 6-1987, point 2.1.123; Bull. EC 12-1987.
5   Bull. EC 7/8-1987, point 2.1.175.
6   OJ L 326, 13.12.1984; Eighteenth General Report, point 378.
7   Bull. EC 10-1987, point 2.1.130.
8   Bull. EC 5-1987, point 2.1.148.

Section 12

Consumers

Main developments

521.   *In its resolution of 25 June on consumer safety,* [1] *, the Council acknowledged the importance and urgency of adopting a general Directive concerning safe products. It is imperative that completion of the internal market be preceded by the introduction of general legislation ensuring the safety of citizens of the Community as users of products. The Commission's endeavours in setting up a European home and leisure accident surveillance system (Ehlass) and a system for the rapid exchange of information on dangers arising from the use of consumer products are directed towards making the market safe. Futhermore, the proposal for a Directive on toy safety exhibits a new, phased approach to safety in sensitive areas. A general Directive on safety that is designed to protect individuals will make this new approach effective and provide a legal basis giving consumers the assurance that the target of completing the internal market by 1992 is not to be attained at their expense.*

By tackling the question of safety, then, the Community is dealing with a subject which is both important and essential to an informed and sophisticated society. It was in this spirit that on 18 December the Council took note [2] *of the Commission's first report—made in accordance with the Council resolution of 15 December 1986* [3] *— on integration of consumer policy with other common policies and of a communication from the Commission on consumer involvement in standardization.* [4]

Priority activities and objectives

Consumer redress

522.   The Community has accorded great importance to consumer redress, in its broadest sense, i.e. including mechanisms for the out-of-court settlement of disputes, since the implementation of a Community consumer protection and

---

[1]   Bull. EC 6-1986, point 2.1.140.
[2]   Bull. EC 12-1987.
[3]   OJ C 3, 7.1.1987; Twentieth General Report, point 581.
[4]   Point 208 of this Report.

information policy. Its view has been that, so long as consumers did not have the means to either exercise or defend their rights, it would be unrealistic to grant them new ones in a Community legal framework in which the often costly traditional judicial proceedings are not suited to this type of dispute and are so slow and formal that they discourage complainants.

This approach is taken up and developed in the resolution adopted by the Council on 25 June, [1] following the 1984 memorandum [2] and the supplementary communication [3] from the Commission on consumer redress. In it the Council calls on the Commission to pursue its efforts in this area not only by continuing to give its support to pilot projects in the Member States aimed at developing procedures which are better adapted to the needs of consumers, but also by examining and developing mechanisms to reinforce consumers' rights across frontiers in cases where consumers residing in one Member State are involved in disputes in another. The idea of a clearing house for such cases was suggested by Parliament in its resolution [4] relating in particular to the 1984 Commission memorandum.

Physical protection

523.   On 6 October the Commission, responding to Parliament's opinion, [5] transmitted to the Council an amendment [6] to its proposal for a Directive on the approximation of the laws of the Member States on toy safety. [7]

The Council adopted a common position on the proposal on 18 December, [8] and the procedure set out in Article 149(2) of the EEC Treaty is under way.

524.   On 6 March the Commission transmitted to the Council a proposal [9] for a Directive amending for the fourth time the Directive of 27 July 1976 on cosmetic products;[10] on 14 April it presented a proposal[11] to amend Annex III to the 1976 Directive, which contains the list of authorized substances. It also

---

1   OJ C 176, 4.7.1987; Bull. EC 6-1987, point 2.1.144.
2   Eighteenth General Report, point 401; Supplement 2/85 — Bull. EC.
3   Bull. EC 5-1987, point 2.1.154.
4   OJ C 99, 13.4.1987; Bull. EC 3-1987, points 2.1.142 and 2.4.9.
5   OJ C 246, 14.9.1987; Bull. EC 7/8-1987, point 2.1.179.
6   OJ C 343, 21.12.1987; Bull. EC 10-1987, point 2.1.134.
7   OJ C 282, 8.11.1986; Twentieth General Report, point 588.
8   Bull. EC 12-1987.
9   OJ C 86, 1.4.1987; Bull. EC 2-1987, point 2.1.98.
10 OJ L 262, 27.9.1976; Tenth General Report, points 124 and 296; OJ L 149, 3.6.1986; Twentieth General Report, point 585.
11 Bull. EC 4-1987, point 2.1.100.

brought the Directive into line with technical progress, one of the changes made being to ban the use of three substances in cosmetics. [1]

525. On 15 April the Commission adopted a Directive on the indication of alcoholic strength by volume in the labelling of alcoholic beverages for sale to the ultimate consumer. [2]

526. At the same time, a great deal was done to incorporate aspects of the protection of the physical safety and health of consumers in other policies, particularly agricultural policy (definition of milk products and imitations, regulation of biological products, veterinary questions, promotion of quality products and, in general, a food policy), the completion of the internal market (follow-up and operation of the rapid warning system) and health in general (measures against cancer and smoking).

In February the Commission adopted two Directives and two recommendations, supplementing the existing regulations on textile products, designed to remove technical barriers to trade and provide information for consumers. The first Directive[3] —accompanied by a recommendation on methods of checking on the conformity of certain fibres with their mandatory description[4]—amends that of 26 July 1971 on the approximation of the laws of the Member States on textile names.[5] The second Directive[6]—accompanied by a recommendation on methods of checking the accuracy of information supplied to consumers[7]—makes a number of changes and additions to the Directive of 17 July 1972 relating to certain methods for the quantitative analysis of binary textile fibre mixtures.[8]

Consumer safety

527. In its resolution of 25 June[9] the Council welcomed the Commission communication on the safety of consumers in relation to consumer products.[10] The Commission therefore continued its work on a proposal in this area aimed at protecting consumers and at the same time opening up the market.

1   OJ L 56, 26.2.1987; Bull. EC 2-1987, point 2.1.96.
2   OJ L 113, 30.4.1987; Point 201 of this Report.
3   OJ C 56, 26.2.1987; Bull. EC 2-1987, point 2.1.100.
4   OJ L 75, 17.3.1987; Bull. EC 2-1987, point 2.1.100.
5   OJ L 185, 16.8.1971; OJ L 353, 15.12.1983.
6   OJ L 75, 17.3.1987; Bull. EC 2-1987, point 2.1.101.
7   OJ L 57, 27.2.1987; Bull. EC 2-1987, point 2.1.101.
8   OJ L 173, 31.7.1972; OJ L 57, 4.3.1981.
9   OJ C 176, 4.7.1987; Bull. EC 6-1987, point 2.1.140.
10 Bull. EC 5-1987, point 2.1.151.

528.   On 25 June the Council, acting on a proposal from the Commission,[1] adopted a Directive on the approximation of the laws of the Member States concerning products which, appearing to be other than they are, endanger the health or safety of consumers.[2] This Directive prohibits the marketing, importing and either manufacturing or exporting of dangerous imitations of foodstuffs. It provides for the withdrawal of such products from the market and notification of the Commission and the Member States.

529.   The European home and leisure accident surveillance system (Ehlass), set up by Council Decision of 22 April 1986,[3] entered its first year of operation,[4] in the course of which 45 hospitals took part by providing regular information on accidents in the home and during leisure activities. With the aim of reducing the number of such accidents, the Commission will be making proposals for appropriate regulations, standards or accident prevention programmes.

530.   On 18 December the Council took note of the Commission's report on the integration of consumer policy into other Community policies[5] together with a proposal on consumer participation in standardization.[6]

Awareness and prevention campaigns

531.   The Council took note[7] of the communication transmitted by the Commission on 11 May concerning a Community information and awareness campaign on child safety (1988-90).[8] This would focus on certain priority target groups: parents of young children, adolescents who are put in charge of children, teachers, instructors and kindergarten supervisors.

Protection of economic and legal interests

532.   On 25 June the Council adopted a resolution on consumer redress.[9]

533.   On 19 January the Commission presented to the Council a set of technical and organizational measures which, with the cooperation of the banks, should

---

1   OJ C 272, 28.10.1986; Twentieth General Report, point 588.
2   OJ L 192, 11.7.1987; Bull. EC 6-1987, point 2.1.139.
3   OJ L 109, 26.4.1986; Twentieth General Report, point 587.
4   Bull. EC 3-1987, point 2.1.138.
5   Bull. EC 12-1987.
6   Point 198 of this Report.
7   Bull. EC 6-1987, point 2.1.141.
8   Bull. EC 5-1987, point 2.1.152.
9   Point 522 of this Report.

allow all payment cards to be used interchangeably throughout the Community, thus improving matters for cardholders. [1] The Commission therefore welcomed the agreement reached by representatives of the main European banks on 9 October to harmonize electronic payment systems. On 8 December the Commission adopted a recommendation on a European code of conduct relating to electronic payment (relations between financial institutions, traders and service establishments, and consumers). [2]

534.   Over the year the Commission continued its work on a number of issues affecting the economic and legal interests of consumers, such as package tours, electronic fund transfers, calculation of the annual percentage rate of charge (to supplement the Directive on consumer credit [3]) and unfair terms in contracts. It also continued its study on relations between consumers and public services, particularly transport and telephones.

Consumer information

535.   On 18 December the Council adopted a common position [4] on the Commission's amendments [5] to its proposals for Directives on indication of prices for foodstuffs [6] and non-food products. [7] The Commission continued and extended its system of price surveys [8] in cross-frontier regions to improve consumer information on price differences for consumer durables.

536.   On 18 December the Council also adopted a resolution calling on the Commission to pursue its work with a view to transmitting new proposals to extend Community harmonization to new quantity ranges concerning household products. [4]

---

[1]   Point 232 of this Report.
[2]   OJ L 365, 24.12.1987; Bull. EC 12-1987.
[3]   OJ L 42, 12.2.1987; Twentieth General Report, point 589.
[4]   Bull. EC 12-1987.
[5]   OJ C 121, 7.5.1987; Bull. EC 4-1987, point 2.1.102.
[6]   OJ C 53, 25.2.1984; Eighteenth General Report, point 403; OJ C 205, 14.8.1985; Nineteenth General Report, point 531; OJ C 103, 30.4.1986; Twentieth General Report, point 591.
[7]   OJ C 8, 13.1.1984; Seventeenth General Report, point 408; OJ C 205, 14.8.1985; Nineteenth General Report, point 531; OJ C 103, 30.4.1986; Twentieth General Report, point 591.
[8]   Twentieth General Report, point 591.

Consumer education

537.   The Commission continued its pilot training schemes for teachers on consumer education in schools; in implementation of the Council resolution of 9 June 1986, [1] it also endeavoured to gather teaching materials with a view to preparing an exchange of views with Member States in 1988.

Consumer representation

538.   Over the year the Consumers Consultative Committee adopted opinions on consumers and the use of bar codes in the retail trade, [2], toy safety, [3] package tours, [3] the Commission's proposals on agricultural prices and related measures for 1987/88 [1] and the pricing of medicines. [4]

---

[1]   OJ C 184, 23.7.1986; Twentieth General Report, point 592.
[2]   Bull. EC 2-1987, point 2.1.102.
[3]   Bull. EC 5-1987, point 2.1.155.
[4]   Bull. EC 1-1987, point 2.1.82.

Section 13

Agriculture [1]

Main developments

539. Substantial progress in reform of the CAP was made in 1987. Further changes were made in the market organizations with a view to achieving better balance and greater control of spending. These were accompanied by initiatives and decisions designed to facilitate and support the adjustments required, particularly where the weaker farms were concerned. The Council decided to extend, by one year and three years respectively, the transitional periods laid down for Spain and Portugal in the Act of Accession which were due to expire on 31 December 1987. [2]

Priority activities and objectives

Continuing reform of the CAP

540. The principal areas in which progress has been made are reinforcement and extension of producer co-responsibility, flexibility of the intervention arrangements and price restraint.

541. Milk is the most important sector in which producer co-responsibility has been increased. A reduction (combined with a suspension) was made in the overall guaranteed quantities, of 6% in April 1987 to be followed by a further 2.5% in April 1988. In the oils and fats sector the maximum guaranteed quantity arrangements for rape were extended to olive oil and to soya. The penalty for exceeding the maximum quantity was also made more severe. A special elimination levy for sugar was introduced to ensure compliance with the principle that the sector should not be a burden on the Community budget.

---

[1] For further details see *The agricultural situation in the Community — 1987 report,* published in conjunction with this Report (available from the Office for Official Publications).
[2] OJ L 378, 31.12.1987; Bull. EC 12-1987.

Flexibility of intervention differs in form and intensity from one sector to another. Buying-in of beef, which was previously permanent and unconditional, is now more selective and less automatic. In the milk sector buying-in of skimmed-milk powder is now automatically suspended for half the marketing year, with optional suspension for the other half. For butter, suspension throughout the year is possible. Buying-in of cereals, which is already restricted to an eight-month period, will be triggered off only if the average Community market price is below the intervention price. Similar arrangements have been introduced for rape and sunflower, and the intervention period for olive oil has been restricted to the last four months of the marketing year. These changes have been accompanied by a reduction in the number and amount of the monthly increases and even, in the case of olive oil, their elimination. An intervention threshold for tomatoes for processing, markedly reducing the quantities taken into public storage, has also been introduced.

542.   Under the price restraint policy [1] nearly all the institutional prices have been frozen in ECU terms and increased in terms of national currencies by less than the rate of inflation. In a number of sectors price restraint has also been pursued by means of related measures with a direct and often substantial impact on support prices.

543.   A further milestone along the path of CAP reform was reached with the Commission's proposal to introduce expenditure stabilization mechanisms in all market organizations to supplement those already in place or being examined by the Council. [2] For cereals the Commission proposes the introduction of a maximum guaranteed quantity. [3] The consequence of exceeding this would be, during the marketing year in progress and without the need for a Council decision, a reduction in buying-in prices, an increase in the co-responsibility levy and a reduction of the intervention period. The Commission is also proposing reinforcement of the existing stabilization system for oilseeds, its extension to protein crops, the introduction of a similar system for tobacco and, in the fruit and vegetable sector, extension of the existing stabilization mechanisms to other products.

Equally significant are the measures taken to enable farms, in particular those most at risk from the changes, to adjust to the new situation. The suspension of milk quotas has been counterbalanced by a 10 ECU/100 kg allowance; the

---

[1]   Points 545 to 547 of this Report.
[2]   Bull. EC 7/8-1987, points 1.1.11 to 1.1.15; Bull. EC 9-1987, point 1.5.1.
[3]   Bull. EC 9-1987, point 2.1.121.

changes in beef intervention have been accompanied by the introduction of a temporary 25 ECU/head premium for the first 50 cattle on each farm; the aid to small cereal producers has been continued and that to small olive oil producers increased.

544.   In parallel with the adoption of these measures, the range of the Community's structural policy was extended and strengthened. [1] In particular, the schemes for mountain, hill and less-favoured areas were reinforced and subsidies introduced to encourage conversion and extensification of production.

The Commission considered, however, that Community action in this area would gain in effectiveness and coherence if it was possible to provide selective direct support for incomes, and in April it accordingly presented a set of proposals for the introduction of a Community system of agricultural income aids. Support would be given to those farmers who are poorest and most affected by the market adjustments under way, a framework for national income aids would curb the proliferation of national initiatives (or at least increase their transparency) and a voluntary early-retirement scheme for older farmers would be introduced.

Content of the common agricultural policy

Agricultural prices for 1987/88

545.   It was only after holding several meetings [2] that, on 30 June, Parliament having given its opinion, [3] the Council reached agreement on the agricultural prices and related measures for 1987/88. [4] The Commission's original proposals had been presented to the Council in February. [5] The agreement, which was followed on 2 July by formal adoption of the Regulations, [6] marks a further stage in the adjustment of the CAP [7] since the presentation in July 1985 of the Green Paper on perspectives for the common agricultural policy. [8]

---

[1]   Point 553 of this Report.
[2]   Bull. EC 3-1987, point 2.1.143; Bull. EC 4-1987, point 2.1.103; Bull. EC 5-1987, point 2.1.156; Bull. EC 6-1987, point 2.1.147.
[3]   OJ C 156, 15.6.1987; Bull. EC 5-1987, point 2.1.157.
[4]   Bull. EC 6-1987, points 1.3.1 et seq. and 2.1.148 et seq.
[5]   OJ C 89, 3.4.1987; Bull. EC 2-1987, points 1.2.1 et seq. and 2.1.105.
[6]   OJ L 182, 3.7.1987; OJ L 183, 3.7.1987; OJ L 184, 3.7.1987; Bull. EC 6-1987, point 2.1.148 et seq.
[7]   Bull. EC 2-1987, points 1.1.3 to 1.1.7; Bull. EC 7/8-1987, points 1.1.11 to 1.1.15; Bull. EC 9-1987, point 1.5.1.
[8]   Nineteenth General Report, point 538 et seq.

In addition to providing for greater producer co-responsibility and flexibility of intervention [1] it was agreed to continue the policy of price restraint applied over the last few years. Almost all the institutional prices in ECU were kept at their 1986/87 level, but in a number of sectors drastic price reduction was secured either directly or indirectly through related measures. In addition to the 2.7% reduction in the intervention price for durum wheat, the buying-in price for all cereals was set at 94% of the intervention price, effectively reducing the support price by 6% compared with 1986/87. The reduction in the number and amount of the monthly increases in the intervention price brings the overall fall in support prices up to approximately 10%.

546.   To prevent replacement of cereals by other crops and at the same time stabilize production and expenditure, the minimum price for peas, field beans and lupins was reduced by 10%, while in the oilseed sector the combined effect of the direct price reduction for certain seeds, the maximum guaranteed quantity arrangements and other related measures (in particular restriction of the intervention period and smaller monthly increases) should bring about a drop of more than 10% in sunflower and of nearly 14% in rape prices. Substantial price reductions were also decided on for apricots, peaches and mandarins (5%), lemons and oranges (2.5%) and certain varieties of tobacco (4% and 6%). Slight increases were, however, granted for those tobacco varieties in greater demand.

547.   While on average intervention prices in ECU for 1987/88 for the Community of Ten are only 0.2% lower than in 1986/87, the impact of the related measures (including the adjustments for milk and for beef/veal decided on in December 1986 [2]) brings the overall fall in support prices from last year to around 6% in ECUs. It is true that this is partly offset by the rise in national-currency prices resulting from dismantling of the existing negative MCAs, but the net effect overall is downwards both nominally, by 2.8%, and in real terms, by around 7%, thus demonstrating that the policy of price restraint has not been fundamentally impeded by the agrimonetary decisions.

Adjustment of the agricultural market organizations

548.   A number of changes in the market organizations were made along with the 1987/88 price decisions. [3]

549.   The intervention arrangements for cereals were substantially altered in order to spur producers to make a greater effort to find buyers. The Council

---

[1]   Point 541 of this Report.
[2]   Twentieth General Report, points 609, 611, 633 and 634.
[3]   Points 545 to 547 of this Report.

decided that during the intervention period, which would continue to begin on the same date (1 August in the southern Member States and 1 October in the others), buying-in would no longer be automatic but would be triggered off only if the average Community market price was lower than the intervention price. Cereals would be bought in at 94% of the intervention price. Monthly increases were reduced from nine to seven in number and from 2.45 to 2 ECU/tonne.

550.   The maximum guaranteed quantity arrangements for rape and sunflower were strengthened by increasing from 5 to 10% the maximum aid reduction applicable if the threshold is passed. The intervention arrangements and the monthly increases were also changed on the same lines as for cereals. Maximum guaranteed quantities, operating in the same way as for rape and sunflower, were introduced for soya and olive oil, and at the same time the restriction on the olive acreage qualifying for production aid was withdrawn.

551.   In the fruit and vegetable sector the Council reinforced the system of guarantee thresholds now applying to processed tomatoes and set 390 000 tonnes as the maximum quantity that may be bought in. Should this threshold be exceeded, the purchase prices for the following year will be reduced by 1% for every additional fraction of 10 000 tonnes, up to a maximum reduction of 20%.

552.   In the milk sector important decisions on both quotas and intervention were taken in December 1986,[1] and in March.[2] In addition, in order to encourage the restructuring of production, Member States were authorized to resell to certain categories of producer quotas purchased under a production cessation programme. The Commission also presented a report on the application of the milk quota system with proposals for its future.[3] On the same date a report was presented on the common organization of the market in sheepmeat, with proposals for sweeping changes.[4]

---

[1]   Twentieth General Report, points 609 and 633.
[2]   OJ L 78, 20.3.1987; Bull. EC 3-1987, point 2.1.150.
[3]   Bull. EC 9-1987, point 2.1.131.
[4]   Bull. EC 9-1987, point 2.1.133.

Socio-structural measures in agriculture and action on forestry

Agricultural structure

553.   On 15 June the Council adopted amendments [1] (proposed by the Commission in April 1986 [2]) to its Regulation of 12 March 1985 on improving the efficiency of agricultural structures. [3] Essentially, the changes consist of the introduction of financial aid for conversion and extensification of production, withdrawal of the ceilings on purely national aid for investments relating specifically to the protection and improvement of the environment, an increase in the maximum compensatory allowance for farmers in less-favoured areas and extension of the allowance to cover certain crops, the introduction of an annual premium per hectare, repayable by the EAGGF, to farmers using environmentally favourable production methods, and additional aid for vocational training to assist farmers in the reorientation of production, the protection of the environment and woodland management.

554.   On 15 April the Commission referred to the Council a proposal for a Regulation establishing a Community scheme to encourage the cessation of farming. [4] This followed the wish expressed by the Council in March [5] that early retirement be withdrawn from the proposals presented to the Council on 22 April 1986 [2] and resubmitted along with proposals for a Community income aid system and a framework system for national income aids. [6] Parliament adopted an opinion on the three proposals on 28 October. [7]

555.   The Commission examined the proposed integrated Mediterranean programmes presented by France, Greece and Italy in 1986 [8] and approved a number of them, the first being that for Crete. [9]

---

[1]   OJ L 167, 26.6.1987; Bull. EC 6-1987, point 2.1.180.
[2]   OJ C 273, 29.10.1986; Twentieth General Report, points 614 and 615.
[3]   OJ L 93, 30.3.1985; Nineteenth General Report, points 547 and 548.
[4]   OJ C 236, 2.9.1987; Bull. EC 4-1987, point 1.2.1 *et seq.*
[5]   Bull. EC 3-1987, point 2.1.176.
[6]   Point 544 of this Report.
[7]   OJ C 318, 30.11.1987; Bull. EC 10-1987, point 2.1.159.
[8]   Twentieth General Report, point 541.
[9]   Point 475 of this Report.

Forestry

556.   The Commission proposed that the Council reinforce and extend the scope of the measures providing for the afforestation and forest improvement operations begun since 1980 in the Mediterranean regions. [1] These measures, now incorporated in the integrated Mediterranean programmes, [2] have in past years been supplemented by a number of Regulations concerned with regional agricultural development. [3]

557.   The Commission adopted rules [4] for the application of the two Council Regulations on the protection of forests against atmospheric pollution and fire, [5] granting financial assistance of almost 6.5 million ECU towards 68 projects under the 1987 programme. [6]

Management of the common agricultural policy

Market organization

Crop products

558.   The 1986 cereal harvest fell to 153.7 million tonnes from 160.4 million tonnes in 1985 because of drought in the south of the Community. [7] Increased competition on the world market brought about exceptionally large price falls, but despite the unfavourable situation the Community kept its share of the market by exporting approximately 16 million tonnes of common wheat and 9 million tonnes of barley (grain equivalents).

Starting with the 1986/87 marketing year, a co-responsibility levy on cereals was introduced, payable on first processing, exportation or sale to intervention. [8]

---

[1]   OJ L 38, 14.2.1979; OJ L 205, 29.7.1983; OJ L 86, 27.3.1985 (France, Italy); OJ L 214, 22.7.1982; OJ L 68, 10.3.1984 (Greece); OJ L 197, 27.7.1985 (IMPs).
[2]   OJ L 372, 31.12.1985 (Portugal: Pedap); OJ L 194, 17.7.1986 (Spain).
[3]   OJ L 194, 17.7.1986 (Spain).
[4]   OJ L 53, 21.2.1987; Bull. EC 2-1987, point 2.1.147; OJ L 161, 22.6.1987; Bull. EC 6-1987, point 2.1.192.
[5]   OJ L 326, 21.11.1986; Twentieth General Report, point 618.
[6]   Bull. EC 11-1987, points 2.1.213 and 2.1.214.
[7]   For a review of the cereals market in 1986/87, see Bull. EC 2-1987, points 2.1.109 and 2.1.110 and Bull. EC 7/8-1987, point 2.1.188.
[8]   Twentieth General Report, point 608.

The immediate extension of the cereals market organization to Spain led to a serious dispute with the United States.[1] Following an interim agreement concluded on 1 July 1986 the Community and the United States on 29 January concluded a four-year agreement opening an annual Spanish import quota of 2 million tonnes of maize and 300 000 tonnes of sorghum, subject to reduction by the amounts of certain substitute products imported.[2]

Greater stability of cereal substitute imports was achieved by an agreement on the part of China to curb its exports of sweet potatoes and manioc to the Community.[3] The voluntary restraint agreements concluded with the countries that are the major exporters of manioc to the Community were renewed for a further four years.[3]

559.   Rice production in the Community of Eleven in 1986 was 3.3% lower than in 1985. First estimates indicate no change in consumption levels. The downward trend of world market prices during 1985/86 continued during the first eight months of 1987.

In December the Council introduced production aid for certain varieties of Indica rice and adopted a new classification of rice.[4]

Community market prices for the most widely cultivated varieties stayed very close to the intervention price throughout the marketing year.

560.   In 1987 the world sugar market continued to be largely dominated by the existence of surplus stocks resulting from an excess of production over consumption in every year since 1981/82 with the exception of 1985/86.[5] World prices accordingly remain very depressed.

The area sown to beet in the Community of Twelve in spring 1987 was some 3.4% smaller than in spring 1986. Community sugar production in 1987/88 is estimated at 13 million tonnes, 1.1 million tonnes less than in 1986/87, whilst consumption is expected to remain unchanged at around 10.75 million tonnes.

On 30 September the Commission sent the Council a proposal[6] for amendment of the Regulation of 15 March 1986[7] amending the basic Regulation on the

1   Twentieth General Report, point 822.
2   OJ L 98, 10.4.1987; Bull. EC 1-1987, points 1.2.1 and 1.2.2.
3   Bull. EC 2-1987, point 2.1.134.
4   OJ L 365, 24.12.1987; Bull. EC 12-1987.
5   For a review of the sugar market in 1987, see Bull. EC 3-1987, point 2.1.149 and Bull. EC 11-1987, point 2.1.182.
6   Bull. EC 9-1987, point 2.1.123.
7   OJ L 87, 2.4.1986; Twentieth General Report, point 623.

common organization of the market in sugar[1] and also a proposal for a Regulation introducing a special elimination levy for the 1987/88 marketing year. The purpose of these measures is to consolidate the existing legislation and guarantee that the sector will be self-financing every year irrespective of the level of world market prices. The Commission considers it undesirable to adjust the quotas during the course of the current five-year arrangement and believes that if in any year from 1988/89 onwards the ordinary production levies do not entirely cover the losses arising from the export of Community sugar surpluses an additional levy to make good the deficit should be charged to manufacturers.

561.   In contrast to past years, the wine sector was free from serious disturbance in 1987.[2] All the structural and management measures[3] were implemented for the second time, along the lines intended by the Dublin European Council in 1984,[4] in order to curb surplus production and reduce the costs arising from it. A large quantity (some 22 million hectolitres) of table wine went for low-price compulsory distillation, while stricter limits than before were applied to high-price voluntary distillation. The impact of the measures was less marked than in the first year of their application, but they helped to stabilize table-wine prices.

The Commission now has two complementary facilities that it hopes will be of great service in improving the functioning of the market and the surveillance of production: the Community vineyard register,[5] compilation of which has commenced in the Member States, and the possibility of setting up a small corps of Commission inspectors specializing in the wine sector, whose function will be to use all necessary means, including participation in Member States' control work, to secure uniform application of the Community rules.[6]

562.   EAGGF guarantee expenditure on cotton fell because of lower Community production and a higher world price.[7] The operation of the co-responsibility system was also improved.[8]

563.   The Council decided to continue the measures promoting the use of flax.

1   OJ L 177, 1.7.1981; Fifteenth General Report, point 386.
2   For a review of the wine market, see Bull. EC 10-1987, points 2.1.155 and 2.1.156.
3   OJ L 209, 31.7.1987; OJ L 210, 1.8.1987; OJ L 213, 4.8.1987; OJ L 215, 6.8.1987; OJ L 218, 7.8.1987; OJ L 242, 26.8.1987; Bull. EC 7/8-1987, point 2.1.211.
4   Eighteenth General Report, point 420.
5   OJ L 208, 31.7.1986; Twentieth General Report, point 624; OJ L 62, 5.3.1987; Bull. EC 3-1987, point 2.1.171.
6   Bull. EC 6-1987, point 2.1.157.
7   For a review of the cotton, flax and hemp markets, see Bull. EC 11-1987, point 2.1.186.
8   Bull. EC 6-1987, point 2.1.154.

564.   Under the maximum guaranteed quantity arrangements, a reduction in institutional prices and subsidies of 10% of the target price was decided on for rape and sunflower [1] in the Community of Ten and for soya [2] in the Community of Twelve. [3] The Council decided to maintain for 1987/88 the bonus on 'double low' rapeseed.

The Council decided to introduce differential amounts for peas and field beans on the same lines as for oilseeds, [4] and the Commission proposed the introduction of maximum guaranteed quantities. [5]

In the case of olive oil the Council introduced a maximum guaranteed quantity for the production aid, discontinued the monthly increases, restricted intervention to the last four months of the marketing year and adopted new descriptions and definitions of the various oils. [6]

It also decided to introduce monetary compensatory amounts for olive oil, with a maximum neutral margin of 10%, in order to put a stop to certain trade anomalies.

565.   Total production of fresh fruit in the Community rose by 10% in 1986/ 87, but that of vegetables dropped by 6%. [7] Producer prices were satisfactory except for apples, mandarins and lemons. Failure to observe the reference price led to more frequent imposition of countervailing charges than during 1985/ 86. As far as intervention was concerned, the situation worsened for pears, citrus fruit and tomatoes but improved for peaches and apricots.

566.   The Council set the aid amounts for seeds for the 1988/89 and 1989/90 marketing years. [4] The Commission set the indicative ceiling for imports of new potatoes into the Community from Spain in 1987, [8] the indicative ceiling for imports of certain seed potatoes into Spain for 1987/88, [9] new reference prices for hybrid maize and hybrid sorghum for sowing for 1987/88[10] and new countervailing charges on hybrid maize and hybrid sorghum to apply from

---

[1]   OJ L 209, 31.7.1987.
[2]   OJ L 273, 26.9.1987; Bull. EC 9-1987, point 2.1.125.
[3]   For a review of the oils and fats market, see Bull. EC 9-1987, points 2.1.125 and 2.1.126.
[4]   OJ L 184, 3.7.1987.
[5]   Bull. EC 9-1987, point 2.1.129.
[6]   OJ L 183, 3.7.1987.
[7]   For a review of the market in fresh fruit and vegetables in 1986/87, see Bull. EC 3-1987, point 2.1.160 *et seq*. For a review of the market in processed fruit and vegetables, see Bull. EC 9-1987, points 2.1.139 to 2.1.142.
[8]   OJ L 43, 13.2.1987.
[9]   OJ L 166, 25.6.1987.
[10] OJ L 170, 30.6.1987.

1 July 1987.[1] It also adopted a new list of varieties of *Lolium perenne L.*[2] The countervailing charges on hybrid maize were altered five times during 1986/87 and those on hybrid sorghum twice.[3]

567.   The Council adopted increases and reductions in the prices and premiums for raw tobacco from the 1987 harvest on the basis of outlet availability and production trends. They ranged from + 3% to − 6% for prices and from + 5% to − 4% for premiums,[4] depending on the variety. The recognized production areas for each Community variety were also determined. Only tobacco grown in these areas qualifies for the intervention prices and premiums set for the 1987 harvest. The Council also changed the rules so that refunds on raw tobacco could be set by tender.[4] The Commission set refunds for tobacco from the 1986 harvest,[5] extended the period of validity of the refunds set for tobacco from the 1983, 1984 and 1985 harvests[6] and proposed that an overall maximum quantity of 350 000 tonnes be set for 1987/88.[7] This would be divided into maximum guaranteed quantities for each variety or group of varieties in accordance with clearly defined criteria.

568.   The Council set the aid to hop producers for the 1986 harvest and made special provision for certain production areas.[8] Because of the drop in producers' incomes, the average level of the aid is around 12% higher than for 1985.

Livestock products

569.   In 1986 and 1987 the Community substantially boosted its efforts to reduce excess milk production, stop unlimited intervention buying of butter and skimmed-milk powder and dispose of the enormous stocks burdening the market.[9] In December 1986 the Council reduced milk quotas for the period 1988-89 by a further 9.5% (including the 1% reduction to be achieved by

---

[1]   OJ L 174, 1.7.1987.
[2]   OJ L 163, 23.6.1987; Bull. EC 6-1987, point 2.1.179.
[3]   OJ L 30, 31.1.1987; OJ L 63, 5.3.1987; OJ L 92, 4.4.1987; OJ L 117, 5.5.1987; OJ L 142, 2.6.1987; Bull. EC 6-1987, point 2.1.178.
[4]   OJ L 184, 3.7.1987.
[5]   OJ L 327, 22.11.1986.
[6]   OJ L 168, 27.6.1987; Bull. EC 6-1987, point 2.1.177.
[7]   Bull. EC 9-1987, point 2.1.150.
[8]   OJ L 284, 7.10.1987; Bull. EC 9-1987, point 2.1.151.
[9]   For a review of the market in milk and milk products, see Bull. EC 2-1987, points 2.1.114 and 2.1.115; Bull. EC 4-1987, point 2.1.109; Bull. EC 7/8-1987, point 2.1.198; Bull. EC 11-1987, point 2.1.191.

making the system more dissuasive in effect) and increased the aid to farmers who cease milk production. [1]

On 16 March the Council set certain limits on the buying-in of butter and skimmed-milk powder. [2] Once these have been reached, the market in butter may be supported by purchasing under a standing invitation to tender and that in skimmed-milk powder by private storage aid.

The Council agreed on a two-year programme for disposing of one million tonnes of butter from public stocks. [3] In consequence of the policies now being applied there will be 4.5 million fewer dairy cows in the Community in 1988 — 16% down on 1983.

Production of butter and skimmed-milk powder fell spectacularly in 1987, by 15% and 22% respectively, and from June onwards there was virtually no buying-in of either. Consideration is being given to continuing the quota system for at least a limited period. On 30 September the Commission sent the Council a report, with proposals, on the operation of the additional levy designed to control production. [4]

570.   In December 1986, in order to reduce the quality of beef bought in, [5] (which had amounted to some 578 000 tonnes in 1986), the Council made a number of changes in the market rules for beef/veal for the period April 1987 to December 1988. [6] It subsequently decided to lower buying-in prices (by approximately 14% from the beginning of the period of application) and at the same time to continue the premium arrangements with the addition of a special premium of 25 ECU per male animal (18 ECU in Ireland) in all Community countries except the United Kingdom, Italy and Portugal. [7]

On the basis of estimated import requirements, [8] the Community authorized the importation in 1987 of 15 000 tonnes of frozen beef for processing and 168 000 head of young male cattle for fattening. A special autonomous import tariff quota of 8 000 tonnes of high-quality beef was also opened. [9]

The beef/veal market was again very depressed in 1986/87, for two reasons. Production of competing meats was facilitated by a fall in feed prices. Of greater

1   Twentieth General Report, points 609 and 633.
2   OJ L 78, 20.3.1987; Bull. EC 3-1987, point 2.1.150.
3   OJ L 79, 21.3.1987; Bull. EC 3-1987, point 2.1.182.
4   Bull. EC 9-1987, point 2.1.131.
5   For a review of the beef/veal market in 1986, see Bull. EC 2-1987, point 2.1.118.
6   Twentieth General Report, points 611 and 634.
7   OJ L 48, 17.2.1987; Bull. EC 2-1987, point 2.1.116.
8   OJ L 36, 7.2.1987; Bull. EC 1-1987, point 2.1.92.
9   OJ L 133, 22.5.1987; Bull. EC 5-1987, point 2.1.163.

importance, however, was the glut of dairy-cow meat following introduction of the milk quotas. The Community was the leading world beef exporter in 1986 because of the large import requirements of certain non-member countries (Brazil, Egypt and the USSR). Non-EEC import commitments totalled over 450 000 tonnes.

571.   On 30 September the Commission sent the Council a report[1] on the operation of the market organization for sheepmeat and goatmeat,[2] together with proposals for stabilization of expenditure through unification of the market organization by 1992 and certain changes in the foreign trade arrangements.

For 1987 the Council kept the basic price of lamb unchanged from 1986, and it adopted special premium arrangements for Spain and Portugal for 1987 and 1988.[3] Market prices in 1987 were expected to reach 342 ECU/100 kg, 7% less than in 1986, with particularly large falls in Spain, Portugal and France. As a result, the amount paid out in premiums for the 1987 marketing year will probably exceed 1 000 million ECU. The sheep population was forecast to reach 87 million by December 1987, with production at 931 000 tonnes and consumption at 1 154 000 tonnes (6% and 3% higher respectively than in 1986).

Imports, which under the terms of a number of voluntary restraint agreements may go as high as 322 000 tonnes per year, are expected to have totalled approximately 250 000 tonnes in 1987, a level unchanged from 1986.

572.   The pigmeat market remained relatively stable throughout 1987, but increased production meant that the general level of prices was particularly low.[4] However, as in the two previous years, falling feed costs helped lessen the impact of low pigmeat prices on producers' profit margins. The Commission helped towards market stability by granting private storage aid for 25 weeks in the first half of the year.[5] The quantities of pigmeat for which aid was given, at 167 000 tonnes almost 30% greater than the record level reached in 1983, reflected the increase in supply.

573.   The Community egg market recovered from the crisis of summer 1986 to reach a satisfactory position by the beginning of the year, thereafter remaining

[1] Bull. EC 9-1987, point 2.1.133.
[2] For a review of the sheepmeat and goatmeat market, see Bull. EC 3-1987, point 2.1.155 et seq., and Bull. EC 9-1987, points 2.1.134 to 2.1.136.
[3] OJ L 79, 21.3.1987; Bull. EC 3-1987, point 2.1.154.
[4] For a review of the pigmeat market, see Bull. EC 2-1987, point 2.1.119, Bull. EC 7/8-1987, point 2.1.204 and Bull. EC 11-1987, point 2.1.194.
[5] OJ L 14, 16.1.1987.

in balance. [1] The improvement stems from a recovery of prices and a sustained fall in feed costs. The ensuing renewed expansion of flock numbers in certain Member States could, however, give cause for concern. The situation on the poultrymeat market worsened in 1987 and returned to that which had obtained before the past few exceptional years. [1] Prices dropped substantially, and the slight fall in feed costs failed to compensate. This less satisfactory situation necessitated a slowdown in production in some Member States in the second half of the year. Competition on the world market again increased from May onwards after satisfactory Community exports at the beginning of the year.

Approximation of laws [2]

Agrimonetary measures

574.   The main event of 1987 was the introduction of firm arrangements for dismantling existing positive monetary compensatory amounts (MCAs) and future negative ones. [3] On 12 January the 12th currency realignment under the European Monetary System created fairly large new negative MCAs and implied a rise in Community prices of some 2.5%. [4]

575.   In order to mitigate the price-boosting effect of the arrangement whereby the MCAs are calculated on the basis of the strongest currency, the Commission suggested in the 1987/88 price proposals that this method of calculation be retained but with features to limit its effect on Community prices. [5] It also proposed that the impact of MCAs be lessened by means of wider neutral margins, to be determined according to the specific characteristics of each sector, and that the existing negative MCAs be partly dismantled.

576.   On the basis of these proposals the Council decided [6] to retain the 'switch-over' method introduced in 1984 for calculating MCAs, [7] to dismantle the positive MCAs in two stages and to dismantle the negative MCAs created

---

1   For a review of the eggs and poultry market, see Bull. EC 2-1987, point 2.1.120 and Bull. EC 7/8-1987, point 2.1.205.
2   For the approximation of laws on public and animal health, feedingstuffs, plant health products and seeds and seedlings, see points 182 to 195 of this Report.
3   OJ L 13, 15.1.1987; OJ L 25, 28.1.1987; Bull. EC 1-1987, point 2.1.87.
4   Point 132 of this Report.
5   OJ C 89, 3.4.1987; Bull. EC 2-1987, point 1.2.13.
6   OJ L 182, 3.7.1987; Bull. EC 6-1987, points 2.1.162 et seq. and 1.1.6.
7   Under the 'switch-over' arrangement the creation of positive MCAs is avoided by turning any positive monetary gap resulting from a monetary realignment into a negative one.

by the new positive MCA one-point switch-over and also some of the existing negative ones. An automatic mechanism for dismantling newly created negative MCAs was introduced, the maximum neutral margin was raised to five points for the poultry sector and for peas, field beans and sweet lupins, and to 10 points for olive oil, and a method of adjusting the agricultural conversion rates for pigmeat was introduced that will within certain limits prevent the creation of new MCAs.

Competition

577.   The Council authorized Greece, Spain, France and Italy to grant short-term private storage aid for table wine and must,[1] and authorized France to grant aids in the form of an advance on the ewe premium[2] and part payment of the social security contributions of milk producers.[3]

578.   On 16 September the Commission adopted two aid codes that it will in future apply to all existing or projected national aids for the promotion of agricultural and certain allied products and for investment in the production and marketing of certain milk and milk substitute products.[4] Existing national aids must be brought into line with these provisions as from 1 January 1988.

579.   Under Articles 92 to 94 of the EEC Treaty the Commission received 160 notifications of plans to introduce or amend national aid schemes, some of which were specific to farming while others were of a general nature but also applied to agricultural products. The procedure laid down in Article 93(2) was initiated in respect of five German,[5] one Belgian,[6] one French,[7] one Danish,[6] one Dutch[7] and 11 Italian measures,[8] and was terminated in respect of one German,[9] three French,[10] one Greek,[11] one Irish,[12] one Luxembourg[13] and

---

[1]   OJ L 200, 21.7.1987; Bull. EC 7/8-1987, point 2.1.206.
[2]   Bull. EC 7/8-1987, point 2.1.201.
[3]   OJ L 78, 20.3.1987; Bull. EC 3-1987, point 2.1.152.
[4]   OJ C 302, 12.11.1987.
[5]   Bull. EC 4-1987, point 2.1.122; Bull. EC 6-1987, point 2.1.189; Bull. EC 9-1987, point 2.1.158; Bull. EC 10-1987, point 2.1.165.
[6]   Bull. EC 4-1987, point 2.1.122.
[7]   Bull. EC 1-1987, point 2.1.106.
[8]   Bull. EC 4-1987, point 2.1.122; Bull. EC 6-1987, point 2.1.189; Bull. EC 9-1987, point 2.1.158; Bull. EC 10-1987, point 2.1.165; Bull. EC 11-1987, point 2.1.211; Bull. EC 12-1987.
[9]   Bull. EC 6-1987, point 2.1.190.
[10]   Bull. EC 2-1987, point 2.1.144; Bull. EC 6-1987, point 2.1.190; Bull. EC 7/8-1987, point 2.1.227.
[11]   Bull. EC 4-1987, point 2.1.123.
[12]   Bull. EC 6-1987, point 2.1.191.
[13]   Bull. EC 12-1987.

12 Italian [1] measures. Final decisions were issued against one French, [2] one Belgian [3] and two Italian [4] measures.

Other work

Farm accountancy data network (FADN)

580.   The number of commercial holdings selected by the Member States for returning accountancy data to the FADN has now stabilized at around 45 000 for the Community of Ten. This total is to be increased by the 14 100 holdings selected for 1987 in Spain and Portugal. The Commission, in close cooperation with the Member States' liaison agencies, has updated and reinforced the data control and validation programs.

The FADN continued to act as a source of economic information on the situation of holdings and was used in the compilation of the 1987 report on the situation of agriculture in the Community and in numerous analyses of the situation and economic operation of agricultural holdings. The data from individual holdings can be used for the purposes of detailed analyses which take account of the diversity of Community agriculture. The resulting conclusions are valuable in the preparatory work which precedes any Commission proposal and have been particularly useful in the work behind most of the important proposals for CAP reform.

Advisory committees and relations with agricultural and other organizations

581.   Organizations representing farmers and farm workers, processors and workers in the processing industries, traders, agricultural credit establishments and forest owners are regularly consulted, at both Community and national levels, on common agricultural policy matters in which their members have an interest.

582.   Twenty-two advisory committees, four special sections and four joint working parties meet regularly during the year. The European consumers' organizations are also represented on the committees.

---

[1]   Bull. EC 2-1987, point 2.1.143; Bull. EC 4-1987, point 2.1.123; Bull. EC 7/8-1987, point 2.1.227; Bull. EC 11-1987, point 2.1.212; Bull. EC 12-1987.
[2]   Bull. EC 9-1987, point 2.1.159.
[3]   Bull. EC 10-1987, point 2.1.166.
[4]   Bull. EC 2-1987, point 2.1.146; Bull. EC 5-1987, point 2.1.176.

Updated versions of the various Commission decisions relating to the agricultural advisory committees have been published. [1]

TABLE 14

The agricultural management and regulatory committees

	From 1 January to 31 December 1987			
	Meetings[1]	Favourable opinion	No opinion	Unfavourable opinion
Management Committee for Cereals	50	829	49	0
Management Committee for Pigmeat	12	43	1	0
Management Committee for Poultrymeat and Eggs	13	67	4	0
Management Committee for Fruit and Vegetables	14	79	1	0
Management Committee for Wine	32	50	12	0
Management Committee for Milk and Milk Products	33	229	39	0
Management Committee for Beef and Veal	25	137	8	0
Management Committee for Sheep and Goats	9	11	0	0
Management Committee for Oils and Fats	25	136	9	0
Management Committee for Sugar	50	125	11	0
Management Committee for Live Plants	5	5	0	0
Management Committee for Products Processed from Fruit and Vegetables	12	27	8	0
Management Committee for Tobacco	7	16	0	0
Management Committee for Hops	2	4	0	0
Management Committee for Flax and Hemp	3	4	0	0
Management Committee for Seeds	6	10	0	0
Management Committee for Dried Fodder	10	12	2	0
EAGGF Committee	17	14	2	0
Standing Committee on Feedingstuffs	3	6	0	0
Standing Veterinary Committee	26	99	1	0
Standing Committee on Seeds and Propagating Material for Agriculture, Horticulture and Forestry	8	21	0	0
Standing Committee on Agricultural Structures	9	103	0	0
Community Committee on the Farm Accountancy Data Network	2	1	0	0
Standing Committee on Agricultural Research	2	2	0	0
Standing Committee on Plant Health	12	9	1	0
Standing Committee on Zootechnics	2	1	0	0
Committee on Forest Protection	2	5	0	0
Ad hoc Committee on STM	2	3	0	0

[1] Including joint meetings of management committees, except those on trade mechanisms (11 meetings) and on agrimonetary problems (12 meetings).

---

[1]   OJ L 45, 14.2.1987.

Financing the common agricultural policy: the EAGGF

Guarantee Section

583.   EAGGF guarantee appropriations for 1987, including those in the supplementary and amending budget, amounted to 22 988.5 million ECU, a 3.8%
increase on the 1986 figure of 22 153.3 million ECU. [1]

584.   The inadequacy of these appropriations led the European Council, meeting in Brussels on 29 and 30 June, [2] to decide that the overall EAGGF guarantee
budget for 1987 would be respected if a temporary change was made in the
arrangements for advance payments. On 19 October, following a conciliation
meeting with a delegation from Parliament, [3] the Council, acting on a Commission proposal [4] and after Parliament's opinion had been given, [5] accordingly
adopted a Regulation [6] introducing special temporary rules for the financing
of the common agricultural policy so that the problem of the inadequacy of
the 1987 EAGGF guarantee appropriations could be resolved without imposing
an additional burden on 1988 and subsequent financial years. On 23 October
the Commission adopted three Regulations [7] laying down detailed rules and
other measures for implementing the Council Regulation so that the new
arrangements could be applied to expenditure incurred from November 1987
onwards (with repayment to the Member States commencing in January 1988).

Within the framework of the proposals for the future financing of the Community, [8] the Commission suggested [9] that the Council amend the Regulation
of 21 April 1970 on the financing of the common agricultural policy[10] to convert
the arrangement whereby EAGGF guarantee expenditure in support of the
markets is advanced to the Member States into one whereby the Commission
reimburses them for expenditure already incurred.

585.   For 1988 the Commission had proposed to the Council guarantee appropriations of 27 078.5 million ECU, including 33.5 million ECU for fisheries.[11]

---

[1]   Twentieth General Report, point 649.
[2]   Bull. EC 6-1987, point 1.1.7.
[3]   Bull. EC 10-1987, point 2.1.168.
[4]   OJ C 262, 1.10.1987; Bull. EC 7/8-1987, point 2.1.229.
[5]   OJ C 305, 16.11.1987; Bull. EC 10-1987, point 2.1.167.
[6]   OJ L 304, 27.10.1987; Bull. EC 10-1987, point 2.1.169.
[7]   OJ L 304, 27.10.1987; Bull. EC 10-1987, point 2.1.170.
[8]   Points 66 and 68 of this Report.
[9]   OJ C 337, 22.5.1987; Bull. EC 5-1987, point 2.1.177.
[10]   OJ L 94, 2.4.1970.
[11]   Points 74 to 78 of this Report.

This was an increase of almost 18% on 1987, but it must be remembered that the 1987 budget covered only some 10 months of guarantee expenditure.

In its letter of amendment No 1/1988 of 22 December to the preliminary draft budget for 1988 the Commission proposes that the Council allocate 28 273.5 million ECU to cover agricultural spending in 1988. This total would comprise:

(i) for expenditure on the agricultural sectors as such (Titles 1 and 2): 27 033.5 million ECU (including 33.5 million ECU for fisheries);

(ii) for the reimbursement of expenditure on the depreciation of stocks (Title 8): 1 240.0 million ECU.

To cover any further needs arising in 1988 from a significant change in the dollar value of the ECU as compared with the rate used for preparing the preliminary draft, it is proposed that a monetary reserve of 1 000 million ECU be entered in Chapter 100.

TABLE 15

EAGGF guarantee appropriations, by sector

million ECU

	1986 expenditure	1987 appropriations[1]	Proposed 1988 appropriations[2]
Milk and milk products	5 232.9	5 901.0	5 781.0
Cereals and rice	3 393.4	3 630.0	4 569.0
Fruit and vegetables, wine, tobacco	2 399.0	3 073.0	3 598.0
Meat	4 250.4	3 155.0	4 056.0
Olive oil, oilseeds and protein crops[3]	3 091.9	3 739.0	4 408.0
Sugar	1 725.6	1 653.0	2 125.0
Other[4]	737.2	680.7	766.5
Refunds on processed products	502.9	560.0	626.0
Monetary compensatory amounts	481.7	362.0	516.0
Impact of accounts clearance decisions	− 55.3	− 150.2	p.m.
Community compensation, direct aids, other[5]	113.5	—	195.0
Food aid refunds	264.3	385.0	393.0
Total	22 137.4	22 988.5	27 033.5

[1] Budget + supplementary and amending budget No 1.
[2] Preliminary draft budget.
[3] Including for 1988 − 1 270.0 million ECU from the operation of the oils and fats stabilization mechanism.
[4] Including fisheries (18 million ECU in 1986, 27.7 million ECU in 1987 and 33.5 million ECU in 1988).
[5] 1988 preliminary draft budget: direct farm income aids, interest for prefinancing of expenditure, distribution to needy and letter of amendment No 1/1988.

586.   In June,[1] August[2] and October[3] the Commission adopted decisions formally clearing the EAGGF Guarantee Section accounts for 1983, 1984 and 1985. The total expenditure covered by the work was 52 000 million ECU, and the sum of almost 278 million ECU was recovered from the Member States as income for 1987. Work on 1986 is on schedule, and the formal decision should be taken in the second half of 1988.

Financing food aid

587.   The exceptionally cold winter of 1986/87 led the Commission in January to adopt measures to provide needy persons in the Community with certain food products.[4] In sectors such as processed cereals, sugar, beef and butter Regulations were adopted following prior agreement with the Council.[5] The operation, initially scheduled to end on 31 March, was extended by the Council[6] and the Commission[7] up to 30 April for processed cereal products, sugar and olive oil. By 31 March 22 000 tonnes of butter and 25 850 tonnes of milk had been distributed free.[8]

588.   On 10 December the Council, acting on a proposal from the Commission,[9] adopted permanent arrangements for the free supply of foodstuffs from intervention stocks to the needy.[10] Parliament had given its approval in an opinion adopted on 30 October.[11]

589.   The payment appropriations available in 1987 for financing food aid operations outside the Community — excluding refunds, which count as guarantee expenditure — totalled 733.7 million ECU, of which 161.1 million ECU had been carried over from 1986.

---

1   OJ L 195, 16.7.1987; Bull. EC 6-1987, point 2.1.194.
2   OJ L 262, 12.9.1987; Bull. EC 7/8-1987, point 2.1.230.
3   OJ L 324, 14.11.1987; Bull. EC 10-1987, point 2.1.171.
4   OJ L 17, 20.1.1987; Bull. EC 1-1987, point 2.1.85.
5   OJ L 25, 28.1.1987; Bull. EC 1-1987, point 2.1.85.
6   OJ L 91, 3.4.1987; Bull. EC 3-1987, point 2.1.145.
7   OJ L 92, 4.4.1987; Bull. EC 3-1987, point 2.1.146.
8   Bull. EC 2-1987, point 2.1.106; Bull. EC 4-1987, 2.1.108.
9   Bull. EC 10-1987, point 1.2.1 et seq.
10   OJ L 352, 15.12.1987; Bull. EC 12-1987.
11   OJ C 318, 30.11.1987; Bull. EC 10-1987, point 2.1.138.

Guidance Section

590. The sum of 6 350 million ECU was allocated for the financing of guidance schemes over the five-year period 1985-89. [1]

591. The appropriations entered in the 1987 budget totalled 917.7 million ECU for commitments and 847.1 million ECU for payments. This represents a 5% drop in commitments on 1986 (since from 1987 onwards the EAGGF no longer finances expenditure on fisheries) and a 9.5% increase in payment appropriations. These amounts were not, however, enough to meet all reimbursement applications submitted by the Member States, even when boosted by transfers, and the balance of the obligations will be charged to the 1988 budget.

TABLE 16

EAGGF guidance appropriations, by type of measure

	Commitment appropriations							
	1985		1986		1987[1]		1988[2]	
	million ECU	%	million ECU	%	million ECU	%	million ECU	%
1. Projects for the improvement of agricultural structures	313.9	34	371.2	38	226.3	24	240.0	22
2. General socio-structural measures	102.3	11	108.3	11	130.6	14	185.0	17
3. Regionalized measures	356.5	39	298.8	31	463.7	51	543.0	50
4. Market-related measures	80.1	9	75.1	8	96.6	11	117.0	11
5. Structural measures in the fisheries sector	65.9	7	117.1	12	0.5[3]	—	0.4[3]	—
Total	918.7	100	970.8	100	917.7	100	1 085.4	100

[1] Budget, including supplementary and amending budget No 1/87.
[2] Preliminary draft budget.
[3] The new structural programme in the fisheries sector will not be financed by the EAGGF.
NB: 1985: EUR 10; 1986 to 1988: EUR 12.

---

[1] Nineteenth General Report, point 586.

Common provisions

592.   The Member States notified the Commission of 392 cases of irregularities in the period 1 July 1986 to 30 June 1987, involving a total of 48 million ECU, about two thirds of which was accounted for by the wine, fruit and vegetable and milk sectors.

593.   In accordance with Article 10 of the Regulation of 21 April 1970, [1] the Commission sent the Council and Parliament the 16th financial report on the activities of the EAGGF (1986); it was produced in two instalments — in July [2] and in November. [3]

---

[1]   OJ L 94, 28.4.1970.
[2]   Bull. EC 7/8-1987, point 2.1.236.
[3]   Bull. EC 11-1987, point 2.1.215.

Section 14

Fisheries

Main developments

594.   *The new structural policy provided for in the Regulation of 18 December 1986* [1] *having come into force, the Commission approved the multiannual guidance programmes for the fishing fleet and aquaculture, thus setting the structural targets for the period 1987-91. It also stepped up the measures taken to enforce and to monitor application of the Community rules. Adoption of a research programme for the period 1988-92 should enable better use to be made of the results obtained by Community research in the field of marine science and technology.*

The enlargement of the fisheries sector in the Community has also meant increased contacts with other countries, involving the conclusion of numerous wide-ranging fisheries agreements.

Lastly, the adoption of the annual Regulation fixing the total allowable catches and quotas for 1988 and the adoption of several Regulations concerning the conclusion of agreements will enable fishermen to prepare their fishing plans for the coming year.

Resources

Internal measures

Community measures

595.   The Council adopted several amendments [2] to Regulation (EEC) No 4034/86 of 22 December 1986 fixing, for certain fish stocks and groups of fish stocks, the total allowable catches (TACs) for 1987 and certain conditions

---

[1]   OJ L 376, 31.12.1986; Twentieth General Report, point 684.
[2]   OJ L 129, 19.5.1987; Bull. EC 5-1987, point 2.1.179; OJ L 179, 3.7.1987; Bull. EC 6-1987, point 2.1.197; OJ L 285, 8.10.1987; Bull. EC 9-1987, point 2.1.165; OJ L 337, 27.11.1987; Bull. EC 11-1987, point 2.1.217.

under which they may be fished.[1] It also amended[2] Regulation (EEC) No 3094/86 of 7 October 1986 laying down certain technical measures for the conservation of fishery resources.[3] On 15 December it adopted the Regulation fixing, for certain fish stocks and groups of fish stocks, the TACs and quotas for 1988.[4]

596.   On 9 June the Council adopted a Regulation fixing the minimum mesh size for pelagic trawls used in fishing for blue whiting in the area covered by the North-East Atlantic Fisheries Convention[5] and on 23 July Regulations laying down new technical measures for the conservation of fish stocks in the Antarctic[6] and for the conservation of fishery resources in the Baltic Sea, the Belts and the Sound.[7]

597.   On 6 February the Commission adopted a Regulation placing temporary limits on landings of sole from the North Sea.[8]

598.   The Scientific and Technical Committee for Fisheries held its annual meeting from 21 to 25 September and drew up its 13th report.[9]

599.   The Commission exercised its powers to monitor Member States' implementation of the common policy on the conservation of resources and the utilization of fishing quotas by sending out its inspectors to the Member States to be present when checks were made on fishing activities. The Commission initiated or continued infringement procedures against those Member States which exceeded their fishing quotas or failed to apply the requisite control procedures.

600.   On 18 February the Commission adopted a Regulation laying down the rules to govern compensation for fishermen in one Member State who have been unable to fish their quotas because overfishing by another Member State has led to the exhaustion of the TAC and the closure of the fisheries concerned.[10] Certain catch-monitoring arrangements were extended to cover fishing by

---

1   OJ L 376, 31.12.1986; Twentieth General Report, point 659.
2   OJ L 280, 3.10.1987.
3   OJ L 288, 11.10.1986; OJ L 376, 31.12.1986; Twentieth General Report, point 662.
4   OJ L 375, 31.12.1987; Bull. EC 12-1987.
5   OJ L 153, 14.6.1987; Bull. EC 6-1987, point 2.1.198.
6   OJ L 207, 29.7.1987; Bull. EC 7/8-1987, point 2.1.249.
7   OJ L 207, 29.7.1987; Bull. EC 7/8-1987, point 2.1.250.
8   OJ L 36, 7.2.1987; Bull. EC 2-1987, point 2.1.152.
9   Bull. EC 9-1987, point 2.1.167.
10   OJ L 50, 19.2.1987; Bull. EC 2-1987, point 2.1.151.

Member States in the waters of certain developing countries with which the Community has fisheries agreements.

601.   On 19 October[1] the Council adopted and on 15 December amended[2] an autonomous Community system for the inspection of fisheries in the Regulatory Area of the North-West Atlantic Fisheries Organization (NAFO). Under this system, which other NAFO contracting parties may join, Commission inspectors will be able to carry out autonomous control operations in the same way as the inspectors appointed by the Member States.

On 18 May the Council decided to grant Community aid for the modernization of monitoring and supervision facilities,[3] awarding 12 million ECU to Portugal[4] and 10 million ECU to the Member States applying the Community arrangements for the conservation of resources.

National measures

602.   Member States provided notification of 95 national conservation measures (out of a total of 117, no notification being provided in 22 cases); 60 measures have been the subject of comments by the Commission and 57 are still under examination. Pursuant to Regulation (EEC) No 3094/86 of 7 October 1986[5] the Spanish Government provided notification of all the technical measures for the conservation of fishery resources which were applicable on 1 January, the date of the Regulation's entry into force.

Bilateral and multilateral relations

603.   On 28 April the Council adopted a Regulation[6] on the conclusion of an agreement[7] amending for the second time the fisheries agreement with Guinea Bissau.[8] It also adopted Regulations on the conclusion of fisheries agreements with Sao Tome and Principe,[9] Angola[10] and Mauritania[11] on 23 November, 30 November and 14 December respectively.

---

1   OJ L 314, 14.11.1987; Bull. EC 10-1987, point 2.1.193.
2   OJ L 375, 31.12.1987; Bull. EC 12-1987.
3   OJ L 135, 23.5.1987; Bull. EC 5-1987, point 2.1.180.
4   OJ L 135, 23.5.1987; Bull. EC 5-1987, point 2.1.181.
5   OJ L 288, 11.10.1986; Twentieth General Report, point 662.
6   OJ L 113, 30.4.1987; Bull. EC 4-1987, point 2.1.134.
7   Twentieth General Report, point 668.
8   OJ L 84, 30.3.1983; Seventeenth General Report, point 474.
9   OJ L 337, 27.11.1987; Bull. EC 11-1987, point 2.1.231.
10   OJ L 341, 3.12.1987; Bull. EC 11-1987, point 2.1.228.
11   Bull. EC 12-1987.

604. The Community signed fisheries agreements with Equatorial Guinea [1] and Seychelles [2] on 4 November and 28 October respectively.

605. The Community initialled fisheries agreements with Angola on 30 April, [3] with Mauritania and Dominica on 14 May, [4] and with the Comoros on 23 October. [5] Following a break in the fishing activities of Community vessels in Sao Tome and Principe waters since 4 November 1986, [6] a new protocol to the fisheries agreement [7] was initialled on 27 May. [8]

606. The agreement between Spain and Morocco having expired on 31 July, the Communtiy and Morocco exchanged letters [9] on transitional fisheries arrangements for the period 1 August-31 December, pending the conclusion of a longer term agreement.

On 7 December the Council authorized Portugal to extend from 4 January 1988 to 3 January 1989 its bilateral fisheries agreement with Morocco[10]

Bilateral consultations on fishing rights and conditions for 1988 were followed by the conclusion of arrangements with Greenland on 18 and 19 November,[11] with the Faroe Islands on 13 October[12] and with Norway and Sweden on 28 and 30 November.[13] Trilateral consultations with Norway and Sweden led to agreement being reached on 25 November[13] concerning the fishing rights and conditions applicable to all three parties in the Skagerrak and Kattegat in 1988.

The Joint Committees responsible for the management of the fisheries agreements with Guinea-Bissau,[14] Guinea,[15], Madagascar[16] and Mozambique[17] met on 29 and 30 June, 29 and 30 July, 12 November and 7 and 9 December respectively.

---

[1] OJ L 29, 30.1.1987; Bull. EC 1-1987, point 2.1.118; Bull. EC 11-1987, point 2.1.230.
[2] OJ L 160, 20.6.1987; Bull. EC 6-1987, point 2.1.206; Bull. EC 10-1987, point 2.1.186.
[3] Bull. EC 4-1987, point 2.1.135.
[4] Bull. EC 5-1987, points 2.1.192 and 2.1.193.
[5] Bull. EC 10-1987, point 2.1.185.
[6] Twentieth General Report, point 673.
[7] OJ L 284, 14.10.1983; OJ L 54, 25.2.1984; OJ L 114, 27.4.1985.
[8] Bull. EC 5-1987, point 2.1.194.
[9] Bull. EC 7/8-1987, point 2.1.247.
[10] OJ L 346, 10.12.1987; Bull. EC 12-1987.
[11] Bull. EC 11-1987, point 2.1.226.
[12] Bull. EC 10-1987, point 2.1.181.
[13] Bull. EC 11-1987, point 2.1.227.
[14] Bull. EC 6-1987, point 2.1.210.
[15] Bull. EC 7/8-1987, point 2.1.248.
[16] Bull. EC 11-1987, point 2.1.232.
[17] Bull. EC 12-1987.

Negotiations for a fisheries agreement were held with Cape Verde on 24 and 25 March[1] and with Senegal from 3 to 5 November;[2] exploratory talks were held with Somalia on 10 June,[3] with Tanzania from 13 to 15 October[4] and with Kenya from 16 to 19 October.[4]

607. On 15 December the Council agreed on how the 1988 fishing quotas in Norwegian, Faroese, Swedish and Greenland waters should be shared out among the Member States[5] and adopted Regulations laying down for 1988 the conservation measures applicable to vessels flying the flag of Norway, the Faroes or Sweden and fishing in the Community zone.

608. The Community participated, either as a member or as an observer, in the work of a number of international fisheries organizations: the sixth session of the Western-Central Atlantic Fishery Commission (WECAFC), held in Mexico City from 27 to 31 July;[6] the ninth annual session of the North-West Atlantic Fisheries Organization (NAFO), held in Halifax from 14 to 18 September;[7] the 13th annual session of the International Baltic Sea Fishery Commission (IBSFC), held in Warsaw from 21 to 26 September;[7] the fourth session of the North Atlantic Salmon Conservation Organization (Nasco), held in Edinburgh from 8 to 12 June;[8] the 39th meeting of the International Whaling Commission, held in Bournemouth from 22 to 26 June;[9] the 17th session of the Committee on Fisheries of the Food and Agriculture Organization of the United Nations (FAO), held from 18 to 20 May;[10] the sixth meeting of the North-East Atlantic Fisheries Commission (NEAFC), held in London from 25 to 27 November; the sixth meeting of the Commission for the Conservation of Antarctic Marine Living Resources (CCAMLR), held in Hobart from 25 October to 6 November;[11] and the 10th meeting of the Commission for the International Convention on the Conservation of Atlantic Tunas (Iccat), held from 18 to 24 November.[12]

609. On 29 April the Commission approved, on behalf of the Community, a cooperation agreement in the form of an exchange of letters between the

---

1   Bull. EC 3-1987, point 2.1.189.
2   Bull. EC 11-1987, point 2.1.229.
3   Bull. EC 6-1987, point 2.1.211.
4   Bull. EC 10-1987, point 2.1.193.
5   OJ L 375, 31.12.1987; Bull. EC 12-1987.
6   Bull. EC 7/8-1987, point 2.1.252.
7   Bull. EC 9-1987, point 2.1.176.
8   Bull. EC 6-1987, point 2.1.215.
9   Bull. EC 6-1987, point 2.1.216.
10   Bull. EC 5-1987, point 2.1.196.
11   Bull. EC 10-1987, point 2.1.194.
12   Bull. EC 11-1987, point 2.1.233.

Community and the International Council for the Exploration of the Sea
(ICES).Æ It also attended the annual meeting of the ICES, held from
30 September to 7 October. [2]

Market organization

610.   In the light of developments on the Community market for white fish, the
Commission presented to the Council on 15 April a communication concerning
Community fishery product supplies. [3] This report draws attention to the
considerable increase in the Community's supply deficit and recommends
appropriate temporary changes in the customs tariff.

611.   As regards pelagic species, the situation is complex because of the
fluctuations in production from one year to another. [4] Provisional estimates
suggest that production is up overall and that there has been a decline in prices
(except for anchovies) and in the quantities withdrawn (except for Atlantic
sardine and mackerel).

On 12 November the Commission presented to the Council a report on the
herring market [5] and the measures which could be taken to improve the
situation in this sector.

612.   Since sardine production plays an important part in maintaining the
balance of the fisheries sector in certain parts of the enlarged Community and
is now facing serious competition, the Commission sent to the Council on
11 August a report outlining the situation on the market for sardines and the
outlook for the future. [6]

613.   On 7 May the Commission sent to the Council a proposal [7] to amend
Regulation (EEC) No 3796/81 of 28 December 1981 on the common organization of the market in fishery products [8] with a view to establishing an
intervention scheme for certain species which are not yet eligible under the
Community arrangements but which account for a substantial proportion of

1   OJ L 149, 10.6.1987; Bull. EC 4-1987, point 2.1.137.
2   Bull. EC 10-1987, point 2.1.194.
3   Bull. EC 4-1987, point 2.1.138.
4   Twentieth General Report, point 676.
5   Bull. EC 11-1987, point 2.1.235.
6   Bull. EC 7/8-1987, point 2.1.253.
7   OJ C 145, 3.6.1987; Bull. EC 4-1987, point 2.1.139.
8   OJ L 379, 31.12.1981; Fifteenth General Report, point 460.

certain Member States' production, adjusting the private storage aid arrangements for the products listed in Annex II to the basic Regulation in line with the general principles governing other Community intervention schemes, and reforming the Community intervention scheme for tuna.

In the context of the recent enlargement of the Community, the Commission amended several implementing Regulations, including that laying down detailed rules for applying the supplementary trade mechanism [1] and that fixing the annual import quotas for the products subject to quantitative restrictions. [2]

614.   The Commission also adopted measures fixing the reference price for carp for the 1987/88 marketing year, [3] making imports of frozen squid (*Loligo patagonica*) from Poland subject to observance of the reference price, [4] adjusting the standard values [5] and determining the level of compensation for tuna supplied to the canning industry. [6]

Structures

615.   The new structural aspects of the common fisheries policy, adopted by the Council on 18 December 1986, [7] were gradually introduced. On 26 and 27 March and 16 June, as a first step, the Commission adopted three implementing Regulations laying down rules concerning applications for and the granting of Community financial assistance for the construction of fishing vessels, aquaculture and structural works in coastal waters, [8] the modernization of fishing vessels [9] and exploratory fishing voyages, [10] respectively.

The Commission also examined the multiannual guidance programmes for the fishing fleet and aquaculture which had been submitted by the Member States for the period 1987-91. These programmes, approved by the Commission on 11 December, [11] are inteded to reduce the capacity of the Member States' fishing

---

[1]   OJ L 25, 28.1.1987; Bull. EC 1-1987, point 2.1.222; OJ L 386, 31.12.1987; Bull. EC 12-1987.
[2]   OJ L 207, 29.7.1987; Bull. EC 7/8-1987, point 2.1.255a; OJ L 327, 18.11.1987; Bull. EC 11-1987, point 2.1.238.
[3]   OJ L 329, 20.11.1987.
[4]   OJ L 192, 11.7.1987; Bull. EC 7/8-1987, point 2.1.254; OJ L 329, 20.11.1987; Bull. EC 11-1987, point 2.1.239; OJ L 386, 31.12.1987; Bull. EC 12-1987.
[5]   OJ L 210, 1.8.1987; Bull. EC 7/8-1987, point 2.1.155b.
[6]   OJ L 70, 13.3.1987; Bull. EC 3-1987, point 2.1.191; OJ L 313, 4.11.1987; Bull. EC 11-1987, point 2.1.237.
[7]   OJ L 376, 31.12.1986; Twentieth General Report, point 684.
[8]   OJ L 96, 9.4.1987; Bull. EC 3-1987, point 2.1.192.
[9]   OJ L 88, 31.3.1987; Bull. EC 3-1987, point 2.1.192.
[10]   OJ L 180, 3.7.1987; Bull. EC 6-1987, point 2.1.217.
[11]   OJ L 4, 7.1.1988; Bull. EC 12-1987.

fleets and thus bring it into line with the fish stocks available. Both the fleets operating in the waters of Member States and those operating in non-Community waters will be affected by this reduction in capacity.

Acting under the Regulation of 18 December 1986,[1] which laid down the structural policy for the fisheries sector for a 10-year period, the Commission decided to grant, as the single instalment for 1987,[2] aid totalling some 94.1 million ECU towards 271 shipbuilding projects, 272 vessel-modernization projects, 137 aquaculture projects and one project relating to structural works in coastal waters. It also approved five exploratory fishing projects submitted by France and Italy.[2]

616.   Pursuant to the Council Regulation of 15 February 1977 on common measures to improve the conditions under which agricultural and fishery products are processed and marketed,[3] the Commission granted aid totalling some 25.3 million ECU towards 109 investment projects in the fisheries sector. It also approved specific programmes submitted by Spain,[4] Portugal[4] and the Netherlands.[2]

617.   Pursuant to the Council Regulation of 4 October 1983 on measures to encourage exploratory fishing,[5] the Commission approved a project submitted by Italy.

Under the Council Regulation of 20 December 1985 introducing a system of structural aid for the conversion of sardine canning plants,[6] the Commission granted aid totalling some 12.6 million ECU towards four investment projects in France and Italy.

618.   As required by Articles 92 and 93 of the EEC Treaty, the Member States notified the Commission of 22 draft national aid schemes. The Commission raised no objection to 17 schemes notified by Germany,[7] Denmark,[8] Spain,[9] France,[10] Greece,[11] Portugal[12] and the United Kingdom.[13] On the other hand,

---

[1]   OJ L 376, 31.12.1986; Twentieth General Report, point 684.
[2]   Bull. EC 12-1987.
[3]   OJ L 51, 23.2.1977; Eleventh General Report, point 354.
[4]   OJ L 208, 30.7.1987; Bull. EC 7/8-1987, point 2.1.256.
[5]   OJ L 290, 22.10.1983; Seventeenth General Report, point 485.
[6]   OJ L 361, 31.12.1985; Nineteenth General Report, point 609.
[7]   Bull. EC 5-1987, point 2.1.197; Bull. EC 6-1987, point 2.1.219; Bull. EC 10-1987, point 2.1.195.
[8]   Bull. EC 6-1987, point 2.1.219; Bull. EC 9-1987, point 2.1.178.
[9]   Bull. EC 5-1987, point 2.1.197; Bull. EC 9-1987, point 2.1.178; Bull. EC 10-1987, point 2.1.195.
[10]   Bull. EC 1-1987, point 2.1.123; Bull. EC 6-1987, point 2.1.219.
[11]   Bull. EC 9-1987, point 2.1.178.
[12]   Bull. EC 4-1987, point 2.1.140.
[13]   Bull. EC 4-1987, point 2.1.140; Bull. EC 5-1987, point 2.1.197; Bull. EC 9-1987, point 2.1.178.

the Commission decided to initiate the Article 93(2) procedure in respect of three schemes notified by Italy [1] and the Netherlands. [2] The other two schemes are being scrutinized.

619.   The Commission decided to terminate the Article 93(2) procedure in respect of a Sicilian regional law [3] but found that two aid schemes notified by Italy (Sicily) [3] and one type of aid granted in Germany (Lower Saxony) [4] were incompatible with the common market within the meaning of Article 92.

620.   As regards research, the Council adopted on 19 October a Regulation laying down the framework and procedures for a fisheries research policy [5] and a Decision adopting, for the period 1988-92, research programmes in the fields of fisheries management, fishing methods, aquaculture and the upgrading of fishery products. [4] The cost of these programmes is estimated at 30 million ECU.

---

[1]   Bull. EC 1-1987, point 2.1.124; Bull. EC 5-1987, point 2.1.198.
[2]   Bull. EC 1-1987, point 2.1.124.
[3]   Bull. EC 11-1987, point 2.1.241.
[4]   Bull. EC 2-1987, point 2.1.163.
[5]   Point 346 of this Report.

Section 15

Transport [1]

Main developments

621.   *Freedom to provide services and the removal of distortions of competition were the Community's two main common transport policy objectives in 1987.*

Considerable progress was made on civil aviation. In December the Council adopted a package of measures which herald a major change in this sector and should have a real and beneficial effect where European citizens and the civil aviation industry in Europe are concerned. On inland transport limited progress was also achieved, in particular as a result of the increase in the Community quota for 1987, the adoption of a Directive on access to the occupation of inland waterway operator and the opening of negotiations on transport with certain non-Community countries. Lastly, pursuant to the December 1986 Regulations on shipping, [2] the Council adopted two Decisions, one concerning maritime transport with West African and Central African States and the other authorizing Italy to ratify an agreement with Algeria. The latter Decision is the subject of a Commission appeal to the Court of Justice under Article 173 of the EEC Treaty.

The Commission also presented further proposals with a view to completing the single transport market by 1992.

Priority activities and objectives

Common air transport policy

622.   After numerous meetings on civil aviation, in December the Council reached an agreement on a package of measures concerning fares, capacity, market access and competition in this sector. [3] The measures in question which,

---

1   Liberalization measures and simplification of frontier formalities are covered in Section 2 of this chapter, 'Completing the internal market'.
2   OJ L 378, 31.12.1986; Twentieth General Report, point 711.
3   Point 644 of this Report.

it should be emphasized, form a consistent and homogeneous whole, are likely to have a major impact on air transport in Europe. They will enable the airlines to offer more attractive cheaper rates based on commercial criteria. Where services are concerned, the airlines will be able to react more flexibly to traffic trends. The new market-access provisions should promote the establishment of new services and the opening of new lines.

These measures constitute a first step towards a common air transport policy in Europe. The main objectives of this policy are gradual deregulation, very high safety standards and a common approach with regard to non-member countries. The step-by-step pursuit of this policy between now and 1992 will further the balanced development of air transport in Europe.

Infrastructure

623.   On 22 December the Council adopted,[1] on a proposal from the Commission[2] a Regulation on the grant of financial support, amounting to 53 million ECU for transport infrastructure studies and projects under the 1986 and 1987 budgets.

In April Parliament endorsed[3] the proposal for a Council Regulation on financial support within the framework of a medium-term transport infrastructure programme.[4] On 13 October, in the light of Parliament's opinion, the Commission transmitted to the Council an amendment to its original proposal so as to include the obligation that the Commission must give the Council and Parliament a description of the projects likely to receive the financial support provided for in the programme.[5]

Inland transport

Railways

Financial situation

624.   On 8 July the Commission sent the Council its eighth report on the annual accounts of railway undertakings (covering 1984),[6] as required by the Council Regulation of 12 December 1977,[7] and in an own-initiative opinion

[1]   Bull. EC 12-1987.
[2]   Bull. EC 11-1987, point 2.1.242.
[3]   OJ C 125, 11.5.1987; Bull. EC 4-1987, point 2.1.141.
[4]   OJ C 288, 15.11.1986; Twentieth General Report, point 693.
[5]   OJ C 288, 28.10.1987; Bull. EC 10-1987, point 2.1.196.
[6]   Bull. EC 7/8-1987, point 2.1.259.
[7]   OJ L 334, 24.12.1977; Eleventh General Report, point 376.

adopted in February the Economic and Social Committee came out in favour of a common rail policy,[1] while considering that the main responsibility for the success of rail transport lies with the companies themselves.

Road transport

Access to the market

625.   On 30 June the Council decided,[2] on a proposal from the Commission,[3] after receiving the opinion of Parliament,[4] to increase the Community quota by 40% for the rest of the year.[5]

On 6 October the Commission decided[6] to increase the Community quota by 15% in 1988 and allocated the extra 1 742 authorizations. On 26 November the Commission authorized[7] a further increase to take account of the transit difficulties encountered by some Member States.

626.   On 4 March, acting on the Court's judgment of 22 May 1985 on the common transport policy,[8] the Commission sent the Council a proposal for a Regulation laying down the conditions under which non-resident carriers may operate national road passenger transport services within a Member State.[9]

627.   On 15 April the Commission also sent the Council a proposal for a Regulation on common rules for the international carriage of passengers by coach and bus.[10]

628.   Parliament[11] and the Economic and Social Committee[12] delivered opinions on the proposal for a Regulation on access to the market for the carriage of goods by road between Member States.[13]

1   OJ C 105, 21.4.1987; Bull. EC 2-1987, point 2.4.21.
2   OJ L 179, 3.7.1987; Bull. EC 6-1987, point 2.1.222.
3   OJ C 87, 2.4.1987; Bull. EC 3-1987, point 2.1.197.
4   OJ C 190, 20.7.1987; Bull. EC 6-1987, point 2.1.222.
5   Point 234 of this Report.
6   Bull. EC 10-1987, point 2.1.200.
7   Bull. EC 11-1987, point 2.1.243.
8   OJ C 144, 13.6.1985; Nineteenth General Report, points 613 and 1057.
9   OJ C 77, 24.3.1987; Bull. EC 2-1987, point 2.1.169. See also point 235 of this Report.
10   OJ C 120, 6.5.1987; Bull. EC 2-1987, point 2.1.170.
11   OJ C 281, 19.10.1987; Bull. EC 9-1987, point 2.1.186.
12   OJ C 232, 31.8.1987; Bull. EC 7/8-1987, point 2.4.55.
13   OJ C 65, 12.3.1987; Twentieth General Report, point 204.

629.   In July the Economic and Social Committee endorsed [1] the proposal for a Council Decision with regard to the ECE's consolidated resolution on the facilitation of road transport. [2]

Fixing of rates

630.   On 25 November the Commission sent the Council a proposal [3] to amend the Regulation of 1 December 1983 on the fixing of rates for the carriage of goods by road between Member States. [4]

Taxation

631.   On 22 December, acting on the Council resolution of 25 June on the elimination of distortions of competition in the transport of goods by road, [5] the Commission approved, for transmission to the Council, a proposal for a Directive on the charging of transport infrastructure costs to heavy goods vehicles. [6]

632.   On 16 September Parliament adopted a resolution on payment for the use of transport infrastructure in the framework of the common transport policy and eliminations of distortions of competition by vehicle taxes, fuel taxes and road tolls. [7]

633.   In July the Economic and Social Committee endorsed [8] the communication from the Commission on the elimination of distortions of competition of a fiscal nature in the transport of goods by roads: study of vehicle taxes, fuel taxes and road tolls.

Social conditions

634.   On 22 December the Commission adopted a communication, [9] on the Council Regulations of 20 December 1985 [10] relating mainly to questions of interpretation and enforcement.

---

[1]   OJ C 232, 31.8.1987; Bull. EC 9-1987, point 2.4.57.
[2]   Eighteenth General Report, point 504.
[3]   Bull. EC 11-1987, point 2.1.246.
[4]   OJ L 359, 22.12.1983; Seventeenth General Report, point 502.
[5]   Bull. EC 6-1987, point 2.1.221.
[6]   OJ C 3, 7.1.1988; Bull. EC 12-1987.
[7]   OJ C 281, 19.10.1987; Bull. EC 9-1987, point 2.4.13.
[8]   OJ C 232, 31.8.1987; Bull. EC 7/8-1987, point 2.4.56.
[9]   Bull. EC 12-1987.
[10]   OJ L 370, 31.12.1985.

635.   The Governments of Belgium,[1] Denmark,[2] France,[3] Luxembourg[4] and the United Kingdom[5] consulted the Commission about measures to implement the Council Regulations of 20 December 1985 on the harmonization of certain social legislation relating to road transport and on recording equipment (tachographs) in road transport.[6]

Technical aspects

636.   As part of the process of harmonizing certain technical aspects of vehicles used for the carriage of goods, the Commission sent the Council, on 21 May, a proposal[7] to amend—with regard to the width of refrigerated vehicles—the Directive of 19 December 1984 on the weights, dimensions and certain other technical characteristics of certain road vehicles[8] and, on 6 February, a report[9] on the development of the circumstances which justified the derogation accorded to Ireland and the United Kingdom from certain provisions of the Directive.[8]

637.   On 30 June the Commission amended[10] its proposal[11] to amend—in particular with regard to private cars—the Council Directive of 29 December 1976 on roadworthiness tests for motor vehicles and their trailers.[12] On 25 September it sent the Council a proposal for a Directive on the approximation of the laws of the Member States relating to the tread depth of tyres of certain categories of motor vehicle and of their trailers.[13]

638.   On 7 August the Commission sent the Council a proposal for a Regulation on a Community programme in the field of information technology and telecommunications applied to road transport (Drive).[14]

1   Bull. EC 3-1987, point 2.1.195.
2   Bull. EC 3-1987, point 2.1.196.
3   Bull. EC 6-1987, point 2.1.225.
4   Bull. EC 2-1987, point 2.1.168.
5   Bull. EC 4-1987, point 2.1.142; Bull. EC 5-1987, point 2.1.200; Bull. EC 9-1987, point 2.1.185.
6   OJ L 370, 31.12.1985.
7   OJ C 148, 6.6.1987, Bull. EC 5-1987, point 2.1.199.
8   OJ L 2, 3.1.1985; Eighteenth General Report, point 493.
9   Bull. EC 1-1987, point 2.1.125.
10   OJ C 183, 11.7.1987; Bull. EC 6-1987, point 2.1.223.
11   OJ C 133, 31.5.1986; Twentieth General Report, point 706.
12   OJ L 47, 18.2.1977; Tenth General Report, point 448.
13   OJ C 279, 17.10.1987; Bull. EC 9-1987, point 2.1.182.
14   Point 359 of this Report.

639.   The official closing ceremony[1] of European Road Safety Year (1986)[2] took place in Brussels on 16 February, and in June Parliament adopted a resolution entitled 'Road Safety Year: progress and prospects'.[3]

Inland waterways

640.   On 9 November the Council adopted[4] a Directive which it approved[5] in June on access to the occupation of carrier of goods by waterway in national and international transport and on the mutual recognition of diplomas, certificates and other evidence of formal qualifications for this occupation.[6]

Sea transport

641.   On 17 September the Council adopted a Decision authorizing Italy to ratify a maritime transport agreement with Algeria.[7] The Commission took the view that this Decision, which departs from its proposal,[8] provides no guarantee that Community legislation on maritime transport would be correctly applied and therefore decided on 7 October to bring an action against the Council before the Court[9] under Article 173 of the EEC Treaty.

642.   On 20 October the Council adopted,[10] on a proposal from the Commission,[11] a Decision concerning coordinated action to safeguard free access to ocean trades and freedom to provide services in maritime transport with West African and Central African States.

643.   On 5 and 6 May the Commission, in conjunction with the Council, held a symposium to examine possible action at Community level to secure the future of the Member States' fleets.

---

[1]   Bull. EC 2-1987, point 2.1.166.
[2]   OJ C 341, 21.12.1984; Eighteenth General Report, point 495; OJ C 11, 17.1.1986; Nineteenth General Report, point 630.
[3]   OJ C 190, 20.7.1987; Bull. EC 6-1987, point 2.4.19.
[4]   OJ L 322, 12.11.1987; Bull. EC 11-1987, point 2.1.242.
[5]   Bull. EC 6-1987, point 2.1.226.
[6]   OJ C 351, 24.12.1983; Seventeenth General Report, point 500; OJ C 214, 14.8.1984; Eighteenth General Report, point 490.
[7]   OJ L 272, 25.9.1987; Bull. EC 9-1987, point 2.1.187.
[8]   Bull. EC 7/8-1987, point 2.1.264.
[9]   Bull. EC 10-1987, point 2.1.202.
[10]   OJ L 378, 31.12.1986; Bull. EC 10-1987, point 2.1.201.
[11]   Bull. EC 7/8-1987, point 2.1.265.

Air transport

644.   The main features of the agreement on air transport [1] are the possibility for airlines automatically to secure approval for discount or deep discount fares [2] (between 65 and 90% and 45 and 65%, respectively, of the reference fares, provided they meet certain criteria); the possibility of adjusting the capacities offered [3] without reference to the governments concerned as long as the market share of the airline concerned remains within the 45-55% range until 1 October 1989 and the 40-60% range during the following year; and provisions on access to the market, [3] which are intended to enable airlines to start new services and operate new routes (multiple designation, [4] i.e. the option open to a Member State to designate carriers to operate on European routes); starting services between the major airports and regional ones [5] without the need for bilateral negotiations; the fifth freedom, namely, the option open to an airline established in a Member State to carry passengers between two airports located in two other Member States. [4] Lastly, the agreement provides for the application of the competition rules [6] to air transport. [7]

645.   On 26 and 27 November the Commission organized a symposium on air safety; [8] it considers that maintenance and improvement of the level of safety must form an integral part of any overall air transport policy.

Multimodal transport

646.   On 22 December the Council adopted [9] the proposal for a Directive to extend for 1989 the present provisions of the third Directive on summer time in the Community for 1986, 1987 and 1988. [10]

647.   On 4 November the Commission sent the Council a report [11] on the implementation of the Directive [12] of 17 February 1975, as last amended by the

---

[1]   OJ L 374, 31.12.1987; Bull. EC 12-1987.
[2]   OJ C 78, 30.3.1982; Fifteenth General Report, point 490; OJ C 182, 9.7.1984; Eighteenth General Report, point 499.
[3]   OJ C 182, 9.7.1984; Eighteenth General Report, point 499.
[4]   Bull. EC 6-1987, point 2.1.227.
[5]   OJ C 240, 24.9.1986; Twentieth General Report, point 715.
[6]   OJ C 182, 9.7.1984; Eighteenth General Report, point 499; Twentieth General Report, point 714.
[7]   Point 369 of this Report.
[8]   Bull. EC 11-1987, point 2.1.250.
[9]   OJ L 6, 9.1.1988; Bull. EC 12-1987.
[10]   OJ C 325, 4.12.1987; Bull. EC 11-1987, point 2.1.251.
[11]   Bull. EC 10-1987, point 2.1.204.
[12]   OJ L 48, 22.8.1975; Nineteenth General Report, point 368.

Directive [1] of 10 November 1986, on the establishment of common rules for certain types of combined transport of goods between Member States.

International cooperation

648.   The Agreement on the International Road-Rail Combined Carriage of Goods between the Community and certain non-member countries was initialled in Brussels on 24 February. [2] The Agreement aims to promote this form of transport by exempting the initial and terminal road haulage operations from all authorizations and quota restrictions.

649.   On 7 December the Council adopted [3] a recommendation for a Decision on the opening of negotiations on transport matters between the Community and Austria, Switzerland and Yugoslavia. [4] The negotiations will cover a wide range of subjects, and in particular the obstacles encountered in intra-Community transit traffic, namely infrastructure, weights and dimensions, quotas, taxes and tolls, driving restrictions, delays at frontiers and any other factors affecting transit traffic.

650.   On 26 May, after receiving favourable opinions on the Commission proposal [5] from Parliament [6] and the Economic and Social Committee, [7] the Council decided [8] to bring forward to 1 June the entry into force of the provisions set out in Sections II and III of the Agreement on the International Carriage of Passengers by Road by means of Occasional Coach and Bus Services. [9]

[1]   OJ L 320, 15.11.1986; Twentieth General Report, point 7178.
[2]   Bull. EC 2-1987, point 2.1.173.
[3]   Bull. EC 12-1987.
[4]   Bull. EC 9-1987, point 2.1.189.
[5]   OJ C 113, 28.4.1987.1987; Bull. EC 4-1987, point 2.1.143.
[6]   OJ C 156, 15.6.1987; Bull. EC 5-1987, point 2.1.202.
[7]   OJ C 180, 8.7.1987; Bull. EC 5-1987, point 2.4.38.
[8]   OJ L 143, 3.6.1987; Bull. EC 5-1987, point 2.1.202.
[9]   OJ L 230, 5.8.1982; Sixteenth General Report, point 494.

Section 16

Energy

Main developments

651.   *Energy prices were more stable in 1987. In ECU terms the price of imported oil products was 60% below 1985 levels. The effects of this fall on the attainment of the 1995 Community energy objectives have been under examination in the Commission and will be one of the key issues for the forthcoming review of Member States' energy programmes which is expected to be sent to the Council in spring 1988.*

In the Commission's view, this changed market situation necessitates firmer action in the various energy policy sectors to ensure that the Community's long-term energy objectives are attained. This approach was also accepted by the Community's main trading partners at the ministerial-level meeting of the International Energy Agency in May, at which attention focused on energy efficiency, preparedness for emergencies and the development of indigenous energy sources, including new and renewable sources. [1]

Priority activities and objectives

Energy efficiency and progress towards the Community energy objectives for 1995

652.   On 18 May the Commission sent the Council a communication entitled 'Towards a continuing policy for energy efficiency in the European Community', [2] which analyses the energy situation in the Community today and sets out the arguments for continuing energy efficiency programmes despite the fact that they have slowed down as a result of the relaxation of tension on the market. Priority should be given to specific measures in areas such as rational use of energy in industry and third-party financing of energy-sector investment. Following this approach the Commission presented to the Council a communi-

---

[1]   Point 900 of this Report.
[2]   Bull. EC 5-1987, point 2.1.204.

cation on improving the efficiency of electricity use [1] and a proposal for a Directive on information on the energy efficiency of buildings. [2]

653.   In the awareness that low energy prices discourage efforts to find alternative energy sources although continuing research, development and demonstration in this field is vital to meet the Community's long-term energy needs, on 30 September the Commission sent the Council a communication on developing the exploitation of renewable energy sources in the Community [3] which contains a proposal for a recommendation to the Member States to help achieve the objectives set out in the Council resolution of 26 November 1986 on a Community 'orientation' to develop new and renewable energy sources. [4] Priority programmes are defined for all renewable energy sources in the Community.

654.   With a view to helping to complete the internal market by 1992 [5] and to achieve the Community's energy objectives for 1995 [6] the Commission began work on identifying the barriers to a genuine internal energy market. [7]

Community energy strategy

655.   The Commission prepared a report on the progress made by Member States in achieving the 1995 energy objectives, [6] the most urgent of which is security of supply.

656.   Parliament adopted a resolution on 8 April on the 1995 energy objectives. [8]

657.   On another aspect of its energy strategy, the Commission continued its work on energy planning, i.e. on analysing energy demand in regions and/or municipalities and their ability to meet it. [9] In 1987 35 regions in all Member States received funding of 2.7 million ECU (which covers almost half of total costs) from the Commission.

---

[1]   Bull. EC 10-1987, point 2.1.207.
[2]   OJ C 267, 6.10.1987; Bull. EC 9-1987, point 2.1.191.
[3]   OJ C 279, 17.10.1987; Bull. EC 9-1987; point 2.1.192.
[4]   OJ C 316, 9.12.1986; Twentieth General Report, point 746.
[5]   Nineteenth General Report, points 162 to 166.
[6]   OJ C 241, 25.9.1986; Twentieth General Report, point 723.
[7]   Bull. EC 6-1986, point 2.1.229.
[8]   OJ C 125, 11.5.1987; Bull. EC 4-1987, point 2.1.144.
[9]   Twentieth General Report, point 725.

Technological development

658.   Under the 1986-89 Community energy demonstration programme, [1] the Commission, after receiving 438 proposals in response to the invitation to submit proposals published in December 1986, [2] adopted:

(a) one Decision granting 16.9 million ECU to five projects on the liquefaction and gasification of solid fuels; [3]

(b) one Decision granting financial support totalling 15.7 million ECU to 10 projects to replace oil and gas by solid fuels; [3]

(c) one Decision granting financial support totalling 71 million ECU to 187 projects on energy saving, renewable energy sources and replacing oil and gas (use of electricity and heat). [4]

A further invitation to submit proposals (closing date 15 April 1988) was published on 25 November. [5]

659.   Under Regulation No 3639/85 of 20 December 1985 on a programme of support for technological development in the hydrocarbons sector (1986-89), [6] 123 Community firms sent in applications for support relating to 143 projects totalling 337 million ECU in reply to the Commission's invitation to submit proposals. [7] Most were designed to cut costs, improve safety or increase efficiency by means of a variety of advanced technologies. This year there were again more joint proposals from promoters in different countries and more applications from small firms. After receiving the opinion of the relevant Advisory Committee, on 29 July the Commission granted financial support totalling 36 628 584 ECU to 76 of the projects. [8]

A further invitation to submit proposals (closing date 15 January 1988) was published on 7 August. [9]

1   OJ L 350, 27.12.1985; Nineteenth General Report, point 651; Twentieth General Report, point 726.
2   OJ C 311, 5.12.1986; Twentieth General Report, point 726.
3   Bull. EC 7/8-1987, point 2.1.268.
4   Bull. EC 10-1987, point 2.1.208.
5   OJ C 313, 25.11.1987; Bull. EC 11-1987, point 2.1.258.
6   OJ L 350, 27.12.1985; Nineteenth General Report, point 657.
7   OJ C 183, 22.7.1986; Twentieth General Report, point 727.
8   Bull. EC 7/8-1987, point 2.1.270.
9   OJ C 210, 7.8.1987; Bull. EC 7/8-1987, point 2.1.271.

Relations with countries producing or importing energy

660.   The effects of the nuclear accident at Chernobyl[1] and the fall in oil prices were the main items on the agenda at multilateral meetings attended by the Commission. At the annual ministerial-level meeting of the Governing Board of the International Energy Agency in Paris in May nuclear energy's key role in ensuring security of supply and the need for a continuing policy of diversification and energy saving even when there is a fall in oil prices were underlined. [2]

661.   At the 30th General Conference of the International Atomic Energy Agency in Vienna in September the Commission delegation drew attention to the many cooperative ventures being carried out by Euratom and the IAEA and the closer links between these two organizations — the importance of which was demonstrated by the Chernobyl nuclear accident. [3]

662.   The Commission stepped up its cooperation with developing countries in the field of energy planning (budget Article 706). [4] It provided 5.5 million ECU to fund 75 projects, half of the support going to the Community's regular technical assistance to energy planning institutes and half to training for local energy planners and administrators in Asia (including China), Latin America and Africa. Some 3.1 million ECU was spent on studies, 1.6 million ECU on training energy planners, 0.6 million ECU on technical assistance and 0.2 million ECU on seminars.

663.   A seminar on the medium-term and long-term energy outlook, organized jointly by the Commission and the secretariats of the Organization of the Petroleum Exporting Countries (OPEC) and the Organization of Arab Petroleum Exporting Countries (Oapec), was held in Luxembourg in March as part of the regular contacts between the Commission and oil and natural gas producer countries. [5] The discussions enabled the three organizations to get a better idea of how producers and consumers view the future. The participants felt that sound energy policies and broader international cooperation would help to reduce the risks of extreme fluctuations in prices.

---

[1]   Twentieth General Report, points 721, 740 and 759.
[2]   Bull. EC 5-1987, point 2.1.206.
[3]   Bull. EC 9-1987, point 2.1.193.
[4]   Twentieth General Report, point 731.
[5]   Bull. EC 3-1987, point 2.1.203.

664.   Energy matters were also discussed in the regular bilateral talks which are now held between the Community and, for example, Algeria [1] and China. [2]

Sectoral aspects

Oil and gas

665.   On the basis of the Commission's communication of 19 December 1986 [3] the Council adopted conclusions on 2 June on the importance of natural gas to the Community's energy supplies. [4] The use of natural gas should continue to contribute to at least the same extent as at present to the diversification of energy sources, since the supply outlook has improved considerably in recent years, in particular as a result of the gradual integration of the gas network wherever economically justified. This represents an important step towards a Community market for natural gas and necessitates a convergent approach by the Community, the Member States and economic operators. The Commission had organized a seminar on natural gas on 5 May which was attended by representatives of the gas industry in all the Member States. [5]

666.   On 29 July the Commission adopted a Directive [6] supplementing the Council Directive of 5 December 1985 on crude oil savings which can be achieved through the use of substitute fuel components in petrol [7] to allow the provisional use of national methods to determine the proportions of oxygenated compounds in petrol.

667.   On 10 April Parliament adopted a resolution on the consequences of the sharp drop in the price of oil products in the European Community and its Member States. [8]

---

[1]   Bull. EC 3-1987, point 2.1.204.
[2]   Bull. EC 6-1987, point 2.1.233.
[3]   Twentieth General Report, point 736.
[4]   Bull. EC 6-1987, point 2.1.229.
[5]   Bull. EC 5-1987, point 2.1.205.
[6]   OJ L 238, 21.8.1987; Bull. EC 7/8-1987, point 2.1.269.
[7]   OJ L 334, 12.12.1985; Nineteenth General Report, point 659.
[8]   OJ C 125, 11.5.1987; Bull. EC 4-1987, point 2.4.17.

Solid fuels

668.   In July the Commission adopted a report on the market for solid fuels in the Community in 1986 and the outlook for 1987 [1] after receiving the opinion of the ECSC Consultative Committee. [2] On 10 September it drew up a revised version [3] which was sent to the Committee for its opinion. [4]

669.   In April [5] and July, [6] in conformity with its Decision of 30 June 1986 establishing Community rules for State aid to the coal industry, [7] the Commission approved aid in Belgium, France, Germany, Portugal, Spain and the United Kingdom in 1987.

Electricity and nuclear energy

670.   On 28 October the Commission sent a communication to the Council on improving the efficiency of electricity use, [8] noting that the growing share of electricity in total energy consumption and its role in relation to industrial productivity and the standard of living justify stepping up efforts to secure its rational use. It therefore favours a Community action programme in this field, the need for which was confirmed at the Council meeting on energy in November. [9] The action programme would be implemented with the support of the electricity-generating industry.

671.   With a share of 35% of electricity production and 14% of total energy requirements, nuclear energy is steadily increasing its contribution to the attainment of the Community's major energy policy objectives for 1995 in terms of supply security and diversification and the limitation of the role of oil and gas in electricity production. There are now 115 nuclear power reactors operating in the Community, nine of which were commissioned in 1987.

672.   The Commission sent the Council a draft report on the present position and the outlook until 2005 as regards the reprocessing and storage of irradiated nuclear fuels. [10]

---

[1]   OJ C 207, 4.8.1987; Bull. EC 7/8-1987, point 2.1.266.
[2]   Bull. EC 6-1987, point 2.4.28.
[3]   Bull. EC 4-1987, point 2.1.190.
[4]   Bull. EC 9-1987, point 2.4.46.
[5]   OJ L 110, 25.4.1987; Bull. EC 4-1987, point 2.1.145.
[6]   OJ L 241, 25.8.1987; Bull. EC 7/8-1987, point 2.1.267.
[7]   OJ L 177, 1.7.1986; Twentieth General Report, point 737.
[8]   Point 652 of this Report.
[9]   Bull. EC 11-1987, point 2.1.257.
[10]   Bull. EC 7/8-1987, point 2.1.272.

673.   Parliament adopted a resolution on the future of nuclear energy on 8 April. [1]

Energy savings and rational use

674.   On 18 May the Commission sent the Council a communication entitled 'Towards a continuing policy for energy efficiency in the Community'. [2]

675.   The Commission put a proposal to the Council on 14 September for a Directive on information on the energy efficiency of buildings. [3]   On 13 November the Council asked the Commission to consider whether a recommendation might not be more suitable than a Directive. [4]   On the basis of the Commission communication referred to above, [2] the Council also accepted the importance of improving the efficiency of electricity use.

676.   Parliament adopted a resolution on energy saving in buildings in March. [5]

677.   The Commission organized a number of events to promote techniques for saving and making more efficient use of energy and the speedier introduction of such techniques. These included a workshop in Luxembourg on third-party financing of energy-sector investment, [6] a conference in Berlin on energy saving in industry [7] and a number of symposia on demonstration projects receiving Community funding.

New and renewable energy sources

678.   On 13 November the Council established a common position on developing the exploitation of renewable energy sources, [4] on the basis of the communication sent to it by the Commission together with a recommendation to the Member States on 30 September. [8]

---

[1]   OJ C 125, 11.5.1987; Bull. EC 4-1987, point 2.1.147.
[2]   Point 652 of this Report.
[3]   OJ C 267, 6.10.1987; Bull. EC 9-1987, point 2.1.191.
[4]   Bull. EC 11-1987, point 2.1.257.
[5]   OJ C 99, 13.4.1987; Bull. EC 3-1987, point 2.4.9.
[6]   Bull. EC 10-1987, point 2.1.209.
[7]   Bull. EC 12-1987.
[8]   Point 653 of this Report.

Supply Agency

679. As in previous years, the Agency's main task was to ensure the Community's supply of nuclear fuels, concentrating, in its observation of markets, on events which might affect future demand and plans or measures which might have an impact on supply. With the industry's help the Agency kept a close watch on trade in nuclear fuels, making sure that it was not hampered by restrictions which were unacceptable to the Community. There was a decline in authorizations for re-transfer, but this was more than offset by the rise in swaps. The Agency advised the Commission in this connection and with regard to action by the Community *vis-à-vis* certain supplier countries to facilitate this type of transaction.

680. The supply of natural uranium, and the provision of enrichment services for Community users continued satisfactorily. Where natural uranium is concerned, the Agency devoted most of its attention to concluding contracts for spot purchases or swap transactions. The Community continues, however, to obtain most of its supplies on the basis of long-term contracts. Few new long-term contracts for enrichment services were concluded in 1987 as electricity companies' needs had largely been met. There was a continuing trend for spot purchases, swaps and transactions on the secondary market in these two sectors.

681. Supplies of natural uranium seem reasonably assured in the medium term. There are sufficient available resources and production to satisfy long-term demand provided political intervention does not disrupt the operation of normal economic forces and the market develops in an orderly fashion. There is a strong probability that the United States will implement a new system allowing it to limit access to its internal market for uranium of foreign origin, with the exception of Canadian uranium. The Chernobyl accident has made it more difficult to predict the growth of nuclear energy in the Community, but short-term and medium-term demand for uranium will not be significantly affected. The same applies to enrichment services, where capacity should match or even exceed demand by the end of the century.

As regards other fuel-cycle services, demand will probably be outstripped by processing capacity in the short and medium term. Manufacturing and reprocessing services should be sufficient to meet demand.

682. As in previous years, there was little change on the primary market for natural uranium and enrichment services. Consequently, only six medium/long-term procurement contracts for uranium and one long-term enrichment contract were concluded out of a total of 195 contracts signed by the Agency in 1987 (90 for uranium procurement and 105 for the supply of enrichment services and special fissile materials).

683.   The Community depended on imports for about 70% of its supplies of natural uranium. Of the eight external supplier countries, none accounted for more than 30% of total supplies. Since the market was oversupplied, there was a sluggish trend in prices: the average price paid by electricity producers for natural uranium under long-term contracts (accounting for some 90% of supplies) is likely to be the same as in 1986 in current price terms, i.e. 31.50 ECU per pound of U_3O_8. However, spot market prices recovered, rising from USD 17.35 in December 1986 to USD 18.20 in September 1987 per pound of U_3O_8.

Section 17

Safeguards

684.   The tasks of the Euratom Safeguards Directorate are set out in Chapter VII of the Euratom Treaty, which provides that 'the Commission shall satisfy itself that, in the territories of Member States, ores, source materials and special fissile materials are not diverted from their intended uses as declared by the users'. The Commission also makes a major contribution to the world non-proliferation effort through close cooperation with the International Atomic Energy Agency (IAEA).

685.   In 1987 the Safeguards Directorate conducted physical and accounting checks on average stocks of some 123 tonnes of plutonium, 13 tonnes of highly enriched uranium, 25 000 tonnes of low-enrichment uranium and 144 000 tonnes of natural uranium, depleted uranium, thorium and heavy water. These materials were held in 700 nuclear installations in the Community and gave rise to some 335 000 operator entries concerning physical movements and stocks. The checks also covered equipment subject to external commitments under cooperation agreements with non-member countries.

686.   The visits by the Euratom safeguards inspectors accounted for 9 750 man-days this year, including inspections, negotiations and travelling time. The inspections carried out by the Safeguards Directorate accounted for almost 6 700 man-days (6 100 in 1986 [1]).

687.   Discussions on inspection matters of common concern were held with the appropriate authorities in the Community Member States, the United States, Canada and Australia. After discussions with non-member supplier countries concerning exchanges of specific inspection obligation ('flag swaps'), many of the existing cases were dealt with to the satisfaction of the parties concerned.

688.   Relations with the IAEA continued to develop satisfactorily. The liaison committees referred to in Article 25 of the Protocol to the Agreement of 5 April 1973 [2] held several meetings. Negotiations with regard to 'facility attachments' [3] continued.

---

[1]   Twentieth General Report, point 753.
[2]   OJ L 51, 22.2.1978; Eleventh General Report, point 405.
[3]   Nineteenth General Report, point 675.

689.   After the entry into force of the facility attachment concerning a major plant for the fabrication of plutonium fuel elements in 1986,[1] considerable effort was invested in the practical implementation of the agreed safeguards approach and in solving the problems generally encountered in the initial phases of application of modern concepts. After one year of application, the concept can be deemed to have proved its effectiveness, but ways of reducing the cost of safeguards operations still have to be found. Priority continues to be accorded to the implementation of conclusive safeguards in mixed installations, i.e. facilities dealing with both civil and military materials.

690.   The Safeguards Directorate continued to help the IAEA to arrive at an international solution to the problem of checking on unconfirmed movements of materials (transit accounting). It also continued to test and bring into operation instruments and advanced inspection methods and techniques with, where appropriate, the cooperation of the IAEA.

691.   In the course of the year a number of anomalies or irregularities were detected by the Directorate and followed up rigorously by additional inspection; some of these are still being looked into.

Consultations were held with operators and Member States concerning the 'particular safeguard provisions' that lay down the procedures to be followed for fulfilment of thier obligations in respect of safeguards. They enabled such provisions to enter into force in the case of a large-scale enrichment plant of the centrifuge type.

Rapid growth in Europe's nuclear industry, increasing use of mixed oxide fuels in light water reactors and the commissioning of dedicated reprocessing and fabrication facilities have given the Directorate a significantly heavier workload — a development which is likely to persist in the years ahead.

---

[1]   Twentieth General Report, point 755.

Section 18

Nuclear safety

Main developments

692.   *Further steps were taken during the year to give practical effect to the measures initiated after the accident that befell the Chernobyl nuclear power station in April 1986.*[1] *These measures were announced by the Commission in its two outline communications, one on the consequences of the Chernobyl accident and the other on the development of Community measures for the application of Chapter III of Title Two of the Euratom Treaty ('Health and safety').*[2]

693.   *Parliament held two debates, the first on 8 April on the Chernobyl disaster and its consequences*[3] *and the second on 6 July on nuclear energy;*[4] *eight resolutions concerning various aspects of nuclear safety were adopted.*

Radiation protection

694.   On 22 December the Council, acting under Article 31 of the Euratom Treaty and following Commission proposals made on 27 January[5] and 16 June,[6] adopted a Regulation laying down the procedure for determining maximum permitted levels of radioactive contamination of foodstuffs and feedingstuffs in the event of a nuclear accident or any other case of radiological emergency.[7] The Economic and Social Committee had delivered opinions on the two proposals in May[8] and June.[9] Parliament gave its opinion on 16 December.[10]

---

[1]   Twentieth General Report, point 759.
[2]   Twentieth General Report, point 762.
[3]   OJ C 125, 11.5.1987; Bull. EC 4-1987, points 2.4.13 to 2.4.15.
[4]   OJ C 246, 14.9.1987; Bull. EC 7/8-1987, point 2.4.16.
[5]   Bull. EC 1-1987, point 2.1.127.
[6]   OJ C 174, 2.7.1987; Bull. EC 5-1987, point 2.1.208.
[7]   OJ L 371, 30.12.1987; Bull. EC 12-1987.
[8]   OJ C 180, 8.7.1987; Bull. EC 5-1987, point 2.4.39.
[9]   OJ C 232, 31.8.1987; Bull. EC 7/8-1987, point 2.4.58.
[10]   OJ C 13, 18.1.1988; Bull. EC 12-1987.

695.   On a proposal from the Commission,[1] the Council also adopted on
22 December a Regulation[2] extending for a further two years the conditions
governing imports of agricultural products originating in non-member countries
following the accident at the Chernobyl nuclear power station.[3] The original
measures contained in the Regulation of 30 May 1986[4] had been extended on
27 February 1987 until 31 October.[5] The new Regulation also amends the list
of exempted products unfit for human consumption.

696.   On 14 December[2] the Council adopted a Decision, proposed by the
Commission,[6] on Community arrangements for the early exchange of information in the event of a radiological emergency.[2]

696a.   As envisaged in its communication on the application of Chapter III of
the Euratom Treaty,[7] the Commission set up a standing conference on health
and safety, the first meeting of which, from 5 to 7 October, dealt with the
provision of information to the public and the media.[8]

697.   The Commission continued to analyse the after-effects of the Chernobyl
accident, paying particular attention to the preliminary assessment of the
radiological consequences for the population of the Community[9] and updating
its periodical report on radioactivity in the environment so as to take account
of the information needs which arose after the accident.

698.   On 13 May the Commission sent to the Council a report on mutual
medical assistance between Member States in the event of a nuclear accident.[10]

699.   On 21 December the Council, acting on a proposal from the Commission,[11] adopted a Decision[12] revising the multiannual research and training
programme for the European Atomic Energy Community in the field of radi-

---

1   Bull. EC 10-1987, point 2.1.216; Bull. EC 11-1987, point 2.1.259.
2   OJ L 371, 30.12.1987; Bull. EC 12-1987.
3   Twentieth General Report, point 751.
4   OJ L 146, 31.5.1986; OJ L 280, 1.10.1986; Twentieth General Report, point 586.
5   OJ L 58, 28.2.1987; Bull. EC 2-1987, point 2.1.174.
6   OJ C 160, 18.6.1987; Bull. EC 4-1987, point 2.1.148.
7   Twentieth General Report, point 762.
8   Bull. EC 10-1987, point 2.1.95.
9   Bull. EC 3-1987, point 2.1.112.
10 Bull. EC 5-1987, point 2.1.207.
11 OJ C 302, 12.11.1987; Bull. 7/8-1987, point 2.1.61.
12 Bull. EC 12-1987.

ation protection; [1] this relates chiefly to more thoroughgoing treatment of subjects which came to the fore after the Chernobyl accident.

700.   Acting under Article 37 of the Euratom Treaty, the Commission delivered opinions on four plans to discharge radioactive effluents from nuclear installations. [2]

Plant safety

701.   As envisaged in the communications transmitted in 1986, [3] the Commission sent the Council on 14 April a report [4] on the implementation of the Council resolution of 22 July 1975 on the technological problems of nuclear safety. [5]

Radioactive waste

702.   In implementation of its plan of action (1980-92) in this field, [6] the Commission sent to the Council, Parliament and the Economic and Social Committee on 31 July its second communication on the present situation and prospects in the field of radioactive waste management in the Community. [7]

International action

703.   On a proposal from the Commission, [8] the Council approved on 14 December the conclusion by the Community of the Convention of 26 September 1986 on Early Notification of a Nuclear Accident, [9] drawn up under the auspices of the International Atomic Energy Agency (IAEA).[10]

704.   On 15 January the Commission sent the Council a draft Decision approving the conclusion of the IAEA Convention on Assistance in the Case of a Nuclear Accident or Radiological Emergency. [8]

---

[1]   OJ L 83, 25.3.1985; Nineteenth General Report, points 367 and 679.
[2]   OJ L 68, 12.3.1987; OJ L 189, 9.7.1987; Bull. EC 6-1987, point 2.1.234; OJ L 228, 15.8.1986; OJ L 238, 21.8.1987; Bull. EC 7/8-1987, point 2.1.276.
[3]   Twentieth General Report, point 762.
[4]   Bull. EC 4-1987, point 2.1.150.
[5]   OJ C 185, 14.8.1975; Ninth General Report, point 302.
[6]   OJ C 51, 29.2.1980; OJ L 52, 26.2.1980; Fourteenth General Report, point 484.
[7]   Bull. EC 7/8-1987, points 2.1.56 and 2.1.278.
[8]   Bull. EC 1-1987, point 2.1.128.
[9]   Bull. EC 12-1987.
[10]   Twentieth General Report, points 770 and 970.

Section 19

Culture [1]

705.   On 9 November the Council and the Ministers for Cultural Affairs meeting within the Council adopted a resolution on the promotion of translation of important works of European culture, including contemporary works. [2]

706.   On 18 December the Commission sent the Council and Parliament a communication setting out general guidelines for incorporation in a programme covering the period 1988 to 1992 and focusing on five priorities: creation of a European cultural area, promotion of the European audiovisual industry, access to cultural resources, training for the cultural sector and dialogue with the rest of the world. [3]

707.   At the initiative of the Commission, a committee of theatre experts was set up in Brussels in January to identify and implement measures for promoting the European theatre and, in particular, to create a theatre festival to be held concurrently in several European cities, starting in 1988. [4]

708.   At the end of March, to coincide with the events to celebrate the 30th anniversary of the signing of the Treaty of Rome, [5] a Conference was held in Florence entitled 'The changing Community: the cultural challenge — culture, technology and the economy'. [6] One of the main points to emerge was that technology and the economy are in effect simply by-products of culture.

709.   In April the Commission published its fourth notice [7] calling for proposals for projects under its scheme to protect and conserve the Community's architectural heritage. [8] Twenty-two projects have been selected: [9] the city walls of Thessaloniki, Greece (third century BC to fifteenth century AD); the

---

1   For audiovisual activities, see point 48 of this Report.
2   OJ C 309, 19.11.1987; Bull. EC 11-1987, point 2.1.140.
3   Supplement 4/87 —Bull. EC; Bull. EC 12-1987.
4   Bull. EC 1-1987, point 2.1.74.
5   Bull. EC 3-1987, points 1.1.1 to 1.1.5.
6   Bull. EC 3-1987, points 1.1.2 to 1.1.4.
7   OJ C 98, 11.4.1987; Bull. EC 4-1987, point 2.1.85. Third notice: OJ C 97, 25.4.1986; Twentieth General Report, point 777.
8   OJ C 320, 13.12.1986; Twentieth General Report, point 773.
9   Bull. EC 10-1987, point 2.1.98.

frescoes of the Casa Romana, Farnesina, in Rome, Italy (first century BC); Skellig Michael Monastery on Skellig Michael Island, Ireland (seventh to twelfth century); the monastery of Sant Pere de Roda at El Port de la Selva, Spain (tenth to eighteenth century); the Château de Bourglinster, Luxembourg, the Convent of the Knights of Christ at Tomar, Portugal, and a group of farms at Cressing Temple, Witham, Essex, United Kingdom (all dating from the twelfth to the eighteenth century); Drimnagh Castle in Dublin, Ireland (thirteenth to seventeenth century); Saint Peter's Church at Hilvarenbeek, Netherlands (fifteenth to seventeenth century); the Sanctuary of the Virgin of the Mountain in Corfu, Greece (sixteenth century); the Vitelli complex at Città di Castello, Itlay (sixteenth and seventeenth centuries); the park of the Château d'Enghien, Belgium (seventeenth century); the Palacio de Nuevo Baztán, Spain, the Aggersborg half-timbered farm at Løgstør, Denmark, the royal saltworks at Arc-et-Senans, Doubs, France, the sawmill at Leidschendam, Netherlands, the Church of Saint Paulinus in Trier and Schloss Nordkirchen in North-Rhine Westphalia, Germany, and the Whitchurch silk mill in Hampshire, United Kingdom (all dating from the eighteenth century); and the Hôtel Solvay in Brussels built by Horta, the open cereal market at l'Isle-Jourdain, Gers, France, and the museum housed in the frigate *Jylland* at Ebeltoft, Denmark (all dating from the nineteenth century).

710.   The Commission played an active part in the artistic events surrounding the designation of Amsterdam [1] as the third 'European City of Culture'. [2] After Amsterdam, it will be the turn of Berlin in 1988, [3] Paris in 1989 and Glasgow in 1990. [1]

711.   This year the Commission again sponsored a wide variety of cultural activities, including festivals, training awards and events featuring music, ballet, poetry and the theatre.

712.   On 10 July Parliament gave its opinion [4] on the Commission communi-cation on the European dimension with regard to books. [5] Stressing the fact that books have both an economic and a cultural function, Parliament called on the Commission to take various measures for their protection and promotion.

---

[1]   Bull. EC 5-1987, point 2.1.126.
[2]   OJ C 153, 22.6.1985; Nineteenth General Report, point 707.
[3]   Bull. EC 11-1987, point 2.1.141.
[4]   OJ C 246, 14.9.1987; Bull. EC 7/8-1987, point 2.1.145.
[5]   Nineteenth General Report, point 704.

Chapter III

External relations

Section 1

Main developments

713.   *The Community's efforts in the area of multilateral relations were largely devoted to ensuring a satisfactory outcome to the initial phase of the Uruguay Round of multilateral trade negotiations. There were also numerous developments in the Community's bilateral relations with non-member countries.*

714.   *A continuing dialogue and intensive negotiations with the United States made it possible not only to settle the long-running dispute over citrus and pasta products but also to defuse potentially serious trade conflicts in other areas (maize/sorghum, hormones) and make progress on a third contentious issue (Airbus). Nevertheless, the Community was still concerned about the possibility of the United States Congress adopting protectionist trade legislation.*

715.   *Although pleased by the Japanese Government's efforts to stimulate the growth of imports and the first signs of what seems to be a containment of the Community's deficit with Japan, the Community continued to urge the Japanese authorities to take further concrete action to make the Japanese market more open.*

716.   *Real progress, however, was made in normalizing relations with East European countries. Negotiations on either trade or cooperation agreements took place with Hungary, Czechoslovakia and Romania, and exploratory talks were held with other countries. At the same time talks continued on the establishment of formal relations with the Council for Mutual Economic Assistance.*

717.   On the basis of proposals made by the Commission, the Council adopted the broad guidelines for industrial cooperation with certain developing countries in Latin America, Asia, the Gulf and the Mediterranean. It also adopted a number of important conclusions on the strengthening of relations and cooperation links between the Community and Latin America.

718.   Negotiations took place with the Community's Mediterranean partners on ways of maintaining their traditional export flows to the Community following the recent enlargement and on the conclusions of a third generation of financial protocols.

Following numerous informal contracts and preliminary talks, the Community entered into official negotiations with the Gulf countries with a view to concluding a cooperation agreement.

719.   Spain and Portugal became Contracting Parties to the third Lomé Convention. Pending the completion of the ratification formalities, the Protocol of Accession of these two countries to the Convention entered into force in the mean time on 1 July.

In application of the cooperation policy set out in the Lomé Convention between the Community and 66 African, Caribbean and Pacific States, the Commission and the ACP partners went ahead actively with the implementation of the national and regional indicative programmes.

A new special programme allocating 100 million ECU to the poorest and most indebted countries of sub-Saharan Africa was proposed by the Commission, and approved by the Council on 9 November. This aid is additional to Lomé aid and is designed to help these countries to surmount the shortage of foreign exchange and allow them to bring in rapidly the imports needed by their people and by their economies.

720.   The reform of food-aid policy and food-aid management, decided in 1986, became operational this year. The reform consolidates and reinforces the role of food aid as an instrument of development.

The famine that has reappeared in Africa, notably in Ethiopia, is potentially as serious as that of 1984-85 and is threatening the lives of millions. The Commission therefore decided to allocate Ethiopia particularly large quantities of food aid, including over 200 000 tonnes of cereals, and emergency aid of 10 million ECU to deal with the most critical logistical problems.

721.   The number of diplomatic missions accredited to the European Communities stood unchanged at 130 this year.

Section 2

Commercial policy

Implementing the common commercial policy

Commercial policy instruments and import arrangements

722.   On 22 June the Council adopted a Commission proposal[1] for an amendment to the Regulation of 23 July 1984 on protection against dumped or subsidized imports from countries not members of the European Economic Community.[2] The amended Regulation[3] enables an anti-dumping duty to be levied on products which would otherwise have been exempt simply because they were assembled in the Community.

723.   In the course of the year anti-dumping duties were imposed on a number of imported products, including electric motors from Yugoslavia; urea from Czechoslovakia, the German Democratic Republic, Kuwait, Libya, Saudi Arabia, the Soviet Union, Trinidad and Tobago and Yugoslavia; ferro-silico-calcium/calcium silicide from Brazil; iron or steel sheet or plate from Mexico; ferrosilicon from Brazil; and mercury from the Soviet Union.[4] In other cases investigations or proceedings were terminated after the exporters had undertaken to raise their prices. The products concerned included paintbrushes from China; outboard motors from Japan; electric motors from Romania; and copper sulphate from Poland and the Soviet Union.[4]

724.   In April the Commission presented to the Council and to Parliament its fourth annual report on Community anti-dumping and anti-subsidy measures.[5] It deals with the application of the relevant Community rules[6] and GATT codes[7] for the year 1985. European industry is making increasing use of such provisions to defend itself against unfair trading practices.

---

1   OJ C 67, 14.3.1987; Bull. EC 2-1987, point 2.2.2.
2   OJ L 201, 30.7.1984; Eighteenth General Report, point 621.
3   OJ L 167, 26.6.1987; Bull. EC 6-1987, point 2.2.2.
4   For further details see monthly Bulletins for 1987.
5   Bull. EC 4-1987, point 2.2.6; Seventeenth General Report, point 633; Nineteenth General Report, point 748; Twentieth General Report, point 788.
6   OJ L 339, 31.12.1979; OJ L 201, 30.7.1984; OJ L 167, 26.6.1987.
7   OJ L 71, 17.3.1980; Thirteenth General Report, points 494 and 495; Fourteenth General Report, point 556.

725.   The Commission introduced retrospective Community surveillance of imports of urea originating in non-member countries [1] and temporary prior surveillance of certain imports from Japan. [2]

726.   In July the Commission for the first time proposed that Member States' national quotas for State-trading countries should be replaced by a single Community quota; the quotas in question are for nitrogenous chemical fertilizers.

727.   With a view to extending the common commercial policy in preparation for the completion of the single market, the Commission adopted a Decision [3] on 22 July tightening up the procedures whereby Member States may be allowed to take safeguard, surveillance or protective measures under Article 115 of the EEC Treaty.

Trade agreements

728.   The Council authorized the extension or automatic renewal for a further year of a number of trade agreements between Member States and other countries, the agreements in question not constituting an obstacle to the implementation of the common commercial policy. [4]

729.   It also authorized the automatic renewal or continuance in force of certain friendship, trade and navigation treaties and the like between Member States and other countries. [5]

Export credits

Arrangement on Guidelines for Officially Supported Export Credits ('Consensus')

730.   On 9 February the Council approved an OECD agreement [6] between Consensus participants [7] on measures to tighten discipline in the field of tied aid credits. The implementing Decision was adopted on 22 June. [8]

---

[1]   OJ L 42, 12.2.1987; Bull. EC 2-1987, point 2.2.5.
[2]   OJ L 177, 5.5.1987; Bull. EC 5-1987, points 2.2.4 and 2.2.11.
[3]   OJ L 238, 21.8.1987; Bull. EC 7/8-1987, point 2.1.14.
[4]   OJ L 95, 9.4.1987; OJ L 202, 23.7.1987; OJ L 277, 30.9.1987.
[5]   OJ L 111, 28.4.1987; Bull. EC 4-1987, point 2.2.8.
[6]   Bull. EC 2-1987, point 2.2.6.
[7]   Twelfth General Report, point 452; Sixteenth General Report, point 632; Seventeenth General Report, point 637; Eighteenth General Report, point 629; Nineteenth General Report, point 753; Twentieth General Report, point 794.
[8]   Bull. EC 6-1987, point 2.2.4.

731.   Following the Council Decision of 9 February all the other OECD countries also announced their approval of the terms of the agreement on tied aid credits and reached an accord on new rules for mixed credits.[1] At its November meeting the OECD export credits group approved a new text of the Consensus incorporating all the technical amendments needed to take these rules into account.[2]

Export credit insurance

732.   On 29 June the Commission sent the Counccil a proposal for a Regulation setting up a European export credit insurance facility (Eecif) to provide cover for goods or service export contracts performed jointly by firms from two or more Member States, under a single insurance policy subject to unified terms.[3]

Export promotion

733.   Export promotion activities carried out in conjunction with agencies from the Member States were directed chiefly at China, the first designated 'target market', where two sizeable operations were mounted. For the first time 49 exhibitors representing the telecommunications, information technology and office automation industries in eight Member States got together to provide a joint Community presence at an international trade fair: Telecomp China 1987, which took place in Beijing in September.[4] A symposium on European investment in China, chaired by Mr Matutes, was held in December;[5] it provided an opportunity for talks with the Chinese authorities on the problems encountered by European investors and ways of improving the situation. A number of new investment projects presented by the Chinese delegation were also discussed.

734.   The Commission and the Confederation of International Trading Houses Associations (Citha) jointly organized two seminars, one in Athens and one in Brussels, designed to introduce small businesses in Greece and Belgium to the export opportunities provided by the trading houses.

735.   The Commission has continued and stepped up its efforts to promote exports to the Japanese market through the training of young European

---

1   Bull. EC 3-1987, point 2.2.4.
2   Bull. EC 11-1987, point 2.2.3.
3   OJ C 230, 28.8.1987; Bull. EC 5-1987, point 2.2.5.
4   Bull. EC 9-1987, point 2.2.24.
5   Bull. EC 12-1987.

executives in Japan, support for trade missions and participation in specialized fairs, and dissemination of information on the Japanese market.

Individual sectors

Steel [1]

External element of the 1987 steel plan

736.   Since 1978, imports of steel products into the Community have been subject either to special arrangements or to a system of basic prices. [2] Imports into the 12-member Community totalled some 8.5 million tonnes in 1987, about 1 million tonnes down on the 1986 figures. [3]

737.   In accordance with the directives given by the Council in December 1986, [4] arrangements were concluded for 1987 with 12 supplier countries (South Africa, Australia and Japan are no longer on the list), which undertook to restrain their exports to the Community in exchange for price concessions. [5] The 1987 reference figures were the same as for 1986. Monitoring of the arrangements during the year brought to light potential overruns and a tendency on the part of some countries towards undercutting; the sanction of an import ban on certain products was applied for one partner country.

738.   Imports of steel products subject to basic prices — around 35% of the total — increased by 10%. Imports from 'arrangement countries', on the other hand, were down by 10% from 1986 levels. Provisional anti-dumping duties were imposed on imports from one supplier country, an undertaking on quantities was reached with another country, and complaints against four suppliers were investigated.

External element of the 1988 steel plan [6]

739.   On 8 December, on the basis of a Commission communication, [7] the Council confirmed [8] the 1987 provisions in full, retaining the reference tonnages in the existing arrangements. Negotiations will be held with the same countries

---

[1]   Points 276 and 280 of this Report.
[2]   Twelfth General Report, point 953.
[3]   Twentieth General Report, point 798.
[4]   Twentieth General Report, point 801.
[5]   Bull. EC 3-1987, point 2.1.35.
[6]   Point 280 of this Report.
[7]   Bull. EC 11-1987, point 2.1.47.
[8]   Bull. EC 12-1987.

as this year. The introduction on 1 January 1988 of the common Harmonized System nomenclature will affect the subdivision of products into categories.

Autonomous arrangements

740.   The five Member States which have retained autonomous quotas for State-trading countries renewed them unchanged in June, by decision of the Representatives of the Governments of the Member States of the ECSC.[1] As before,[2] the Commission authorized a number of temporary safeguard quotas.[3] In April Spain adopted a general ECSC safeguard clause (i.e. not applicable to 'arrangement countries'),[4] as a result of which bilateral negotiations were held to fix ceilings on imports from most of the supplier countries concerned.

Textiles

Bilateral agreements with non-member countries

741.   The 26 bilateral textile trade agreements renegotiated in 1986[5] within the framework of the Multifibre Arrangement[6] were applied de facto from 1 January 1987. These agreements generally functioned satisfactorily throughout the year.

742.   The Textile Committee set up in 1978[7] assisted the Commission in the management of the agreements and helped with the preparation of consultations held during the year with various supplier countries.[8] As a result of the consultations a number of new quantitative limits were introduced and other management problems were also resolved.

743.   In the course of the year the GATT textiles surveillance body, meeting in Geneva at regular intervals, reviewed most of the Community's bilateral agreements. The GATT Textiles Committee also met in December.

---

1   Bull. EC 6-1987, point 2.1.29.
2   Twentieth General Report, point 802.
3   Bull. EC 3-1987, point 2.1.38.
4   Bull. EC 4-1987, point 2.1.32.
5   Twentieth General Report, point 804.
6   OJ L 341, 4.12.1986; Twentieth General Report, points 815 to 817.
7   OJ L 365, 27.12.1978; Twelfth General Report, point 454.
8   Bull. EC 2-1987, points 2.2.7 and 2.2.8; Bull. EC 3-1987, point 2.2.6; Bull. EC 4-1987, points 2.2.9 and 2.2.10; Bull. EC 5-1987, points 2.2.7 and 2.2.8; Bull. EC 6-1987, points 2.2.5 and 2.2.6; Bull. EC 7/8-1987, points 2.2.9 to 2.2.14; Bull. EC 9-1987, points 2.2.7 and 2.2.8; Bull. EC 10-1987, point 2.2.12; Bull. EC 11-1987, point 2.2.4.

Arrangements with preferential countries

744.   The Commission held consultations with several of the countries with which it has concluded administrative cooperation arrangements, [1] to examine issues arising from their management.

In the latter half of the year the Commission renewed the arrangement with Malta for the period 1988-90. The negotiations with Egypt led to the renewal of the arrangement on cotton yarns for 1987-89. Several consultations were held with the Turkish Association of Exporters of Textile Products, with a view to the renewal of the textiles arrangement, and an agreed text was initialled on 3 December. [2] The Commission will communicate the results of the negotiations with Egypt and Turkey to the Council for final approval.

Non-ferrous metals

745.   The export arrangements in force in 1987 [3] for waste and scrap of certain non-ferrous metals were renewed for 1988. [4] The arrangements, introduced by the Council Regulation of 20 December 1969, [5] impose quotas on exports of copper ash and waste and provide for the surveillance of exports of aluminium and lead waste. There is also provision for Community safeguard measures to prevent exports of aluminium and lead products leading to shortages on the Community market.

---

[1]   Bull. EC 3-1987, point 2.2.7; Bull. EC 4-1987, point 2.2.11; Bull. EC 5-1987, point 2.2.9; Bull. EC 7/8-1987, point 2.2.15; Bull. EC 9-1987, point 2.2.9; Bull. EC 10-1987, point 2.2.13; Bull. EC 11-1987, points 2.2.5 and 2.2.6.
[2]   Bull. EC 12-1987.
[3]   OJ L 377, 31.12.1986; Twentieth General Report, point 809.
[4]   OJ L 371, 30.12.1987; Bull. EC 12-1987.
[5]   OJ L 324, 27.12.1969.

Section 3

Multilateral relations

New round of multilateral trade negotiations in GATT

746.   The initial phase of the new round of multilateral trade negotiations, the Uruguay Round, [1] was virtually completed by the end of the year. Overall, sustained progress has been made in the 14 negotiating groups set up by the Group of Negotiations on Goods [2] and also in the Group of Negotiations on Services, [3] owing ot the interest shown by numerous Contracting Parties and the resulting submission of many ideas and proposals.

On the basis of the general principles established at the outset and the guidelines that have emerged from the Council, the Community has contributed substantially to the search for overall and sector-based solutions by providing suggestions, information or comments. [4] In line with the priority set in Punta del Este, it accordingly made an offer in Geneva that was intended to benefit the developing countries, concerning the liberalization of trade in tropical products. [5]

In other areas the Community has made its position known. On tariffs, it stressed the need to reduce tariff 'peaks' (customs duties well above the average) [6] and achieve a better balance in the obligations of the Contracting Parties.

747.   On agriculture, the Community took part in the work of the negotiating group, which completed its allotted task for the initial phase. [7] It submitted, as did other countries, a proposal which outlines the negotiating approach it advocates.

748.   With regard to the 'new issues' (trade in services, trade-related aspects of intellectual property rights and trade-related investment measures), the Community played an active part in defining the scope of the negotiations. It

---

1   Twentieth General Report, point 810.
2   Bull. EC 1-1987, point 2.2.3.
3   Bull. EC 1-1987, point 2.2.4.
4   Bull. EC 5-1987, point 2.2.1.
5   Bull. EC 6-1987, point 2.2.1.; Bull. EC 10-1987, point 2.2.8.
6   Bull. EC 10-1987, point 2.2.3.
7   Bull. EC 10-1987, point 2.2.1.

also stressed the need to adhere to the standstill and rollback commitments in order to ensure the success of the negotiations [1] and notified the surveillance body of certain measures taken by other participants which it considered to be in violation of the standstill commitments. [2]

Economic relations between developing and industrialized countries

749.   Development and economic relations between developing and industrialized countries were issues which formed the subject of a number of major meetings and conferences in international forums. In GATT, [3] the Committee on Trade and Development devoted some time to discussing the implications of the Uruguay Round [4] for the developing countries. North-South issues generally also figured prominently on the agendas of the ministerial meeting of the OECD Council in May [5] and the Western Economic Summit held in Venice in June. [6]

750.   The debt issue dominated the seventh session of the United Nations Conference on Trade and Development, [7] which in July and August made an important contribution to the improvement of North-South relations and achieved significant results in this area. Particularly important was the consensus view of the world economic situation that emerged for the first time at such a conference, based on the concept of co-responsibility established in Seoul in 1985 at the annual meetings of the IMF and of the World Bank. [8] At its 42nd annual session, the UN General Assembly also discussed the issues dealt with by Unctad, in particular the debt question. [9] Far-reaching discussions on the indebtedness of the developing countries and its effect on their growth also took place at meetings of the UN Economic and Social Council, [10] at which the Community spoke in favour of efforts to be deployed in the framework of Unctad VII and stressed the importance of the Uruguay Round [4] in the search for a solution to this problem.

---

[1]   Bull. EC 1-1987, point 2.2.2.
[2]   Bull. EC 10-1987, point 2.2.4.
[3]   Point 888 of this Report.
[4]   Points 746 to 748 of this Report.
[5]   Point 895 of this Report.
[6]   Point 752 of this Report.
[7]   Points 821 to 824 of this Report.
[8]   Nineteenth General Report, points 152 and 154.
[9]   Point 872 of this Report.
[10]   Point 873 of this Report.

The International Conference on the relationship between disarmament and development, [1] which took place at UN headquarters in August and September, ended with an agreement reflecting the Community position in recognizing that disarmament and development are two distinct processes and that development progress cannot be left to await the mobilization of additional resources through disarmament.

The second session of the Unido General Conference, held in Bangkok from 9 to 13 November, [2] reaffirmed this organization's key role in connection with the industrial development policy of the Third World countries and cooperation with the more developed countries and also in the implementation of cooperation programmes centred on markets and enterprises and the mobilization of financial resources to resolve the debt problem.

751.   On the initiative of the UN Economic Commission for Africa, a Conference on economic recovery and accelerated development in Africa was held in Abuja, Nigeria, in June, [3] one year after the UN General Assembly's special session on Africa. [4] In the course of the Conference, which took stock of the economic situation in Africa, the recovery efforts undertaken by the African countries themselves and the support received from the international community, the Commission representative explained how Lomé III [5] was particularly suited to Africa's current critical needs and urged that the parties involved seek realistic means of tackling the debt problem.

Western Economic Summit

752.   The Western Economic Summit was held in Venice from 8 to 10 June. [6] The eight participants adopted statements on East-West relations, [7] terrorism, [8] the Iraq-Iran war and freedom of navigation in the Gulf, [9] a declaration on economic and monetary cooperation, [10] and statements on AIDS [11] and drugs. [12]

---

1   Point 871 of this Report.
2   Point 825 of this Report.
3   Bull. EC 6-1987, point 2.2.31.
4   Twentieth General Report, point 902.
5   Nineteenth General Report, point 714.
6   Bull. EC 6-1987, points 1.2.1. to 1.2.10 and 3.7.1. to 3.7.39.
7   Bull. EC 6-1987, points 1.2.3 and 3.7.37.
8   Bull. EC 6-1987, points 1.2.4. and 3.7.38.
9   Bull. EC 6-1987, points 1.2.5. and 3.7.39.
10   Bull. EC 6-1987, points 1.2.6. and 3.7.36.
11   Bull. EC 6-1987, points 1.2.7 and 3.7.1. to 3.7.28.
12   Bull. EC 6-1987, point 1.2.8.

The discussions were concentrated primarily on non-economic issues. However, the Summit's principal outcome concerned economic matters, in particular the coordination of economic policies (the Group of Seven and the governors of the central banks were asked to improve the effectiveness of the coordination process), the strengthening of the multilateral trading system in order to combat protectionism, and consideration for the problems of the most heavily indebted countries. This approach covers the areas on which the Community had put the main emphasis and had spoken with one voice.

Euro-Arab Dialogue

753.   The Euro-Arab Dialogue remained in a state of impasse all year owing to political factors. As last year,[1] the *ad hoc* 'troika' group responsible for preparing for the sixth meeting of the General Committee, the highest body of the Dialogue at ambassador level, did not meet. The 'troika' meeting at ministerial level, which should have restarted discussions halted nearly two years ago,[2] could not take place. Owing to political problems, the seven working committees—none of which met—and numerous specialist working parties dealing with the economic and technical elements of the Dialogue made no further progress. Only one specialist working party, set up by the Committee on Industrialization to discuss refining and petrochemicals, met in February. By the middle of the year it had concluded its work, with the help of two consultancy firms, on the establishment of an econometric model for the petrochemicals and refining industry.[3]

---

[1]   Twentieth General Report, point 818.
[2]   Nineteenth General Report, point 795.
[3]   Nineteenth General Report, point 796.

Section 4

Relations with industrialized countries

United States

754.   Despite the bilateral agreement reached on 29 January[1] on the effects of the Community's enlargement,[2] relations with the United States continued to be affected by the protectionist attitude of Congress, deriving from the persistence of the US trade deficit (Some USD 165 billion this year following the USD 156 billion in 1986 and USD 148 billion in 1985).[3] The Community expressed concern on a number of occasions both to the US Government and to Congress regarding the potential damage — to the multilateral trading system in general and Community exports to the United States in particular[3] — from the bills before the Senate and the House of Representatives to amend US trade legislation. It also renewed its protests and its warning of retaliatory action in response to the adoption in the United States of unilateral restrictive measures: the Council recalled the multilateral commitments entered into by the United States,[4] while the Commission — in statements, letters to the US authorities and meetings between Mr De Clercq and the US Trade Representative, Mr Clayton Yeutter — expressed its concern over the possible adoption by Congress of bills introducing restrictions in trade in textiles and footwear[5] and in general trade arrangements.[6]

For information purposes and to act as a deterrent, the Commission published in April[7] and again in December[8] an inventory of numerous US trade measures of different kinds which constitute barriers to or restrict Community exports.

755.   Despit the continuing threat of adoption of new protectionist measures by the United States, bilateral negotiations were undertaken or continued to resolve specific difficulties in a number of areas. Negotiators from the two sides reached agreement on 7 August[9] on an arrangement in the dispute

[1]   OJ L 98, 10.4.1987; Bull. EC 1-1987, points 1.2.1 and 1.2.2.
[2]   Twentieth General Report, points 819 and 822.
[3]   Twentieth General Report, point 819.
[4]   Bull. EC 3-1987, point 2.2.10.
[5]   Bull. EC 3-1987, point 2.2.9; Bull. EC 7/8-1987, point 2.2.16; Bull. EC 9-1987, point 2.2.11.
[6]   Bull. EC 7/8-1987, point 2.2.16; Bull. EC 9-1987, point 2.2.12.
[7]   Bull. EC 4-1987, point 2.2.14.
[8]   Bull. EC 12-1987.
[9]   OJ L 275, 29.9.1987; Bull. EC 7/8-1987, point 2.2.17.

concerning Community refunds on exports of pasta products.[1] The compromise arrangement forms an integral part of the Agreement of 10 August 1986[2] on Mediterranean preferences, citrus fruit and pasta[3] and entered into force on 1 October; it provides for an initial 27.5% cut in the refund on exports of Community pasta to the United States and the reintroduction of inward processing arrangements[4] — with equivalent compensation — permitting 50% of the exports concerned to be covered by IPT arrangements, plus a mechanism for reviewing and adjusting the refund.

756.   At the request of the United States, which feels that its commercial supremacy in the industry is threatened by the success of the Airbus-Industrie consortium, the GATT Committee on Trade in Civil Aircraft held a number of formal and informal meetings[5] to seek a common interpretation of certain provisions of the Agreement on Trade in Civil Aircraft. The Community and the United States also conducted bilateral negotiations on this issue.[5]

757.   In July the delegations narrowed the gap between their views on the incentives that are prohibited in connection with the sale or purchase of civil aircraft but could not agree on production subsidies.[6] Following a meeting on 27 October between Mr De Clercq, the Trade Ministers of the four Member States concerned and Mr Yeutter, the two sides agreed on a programme of negotiations that have been pursued vigorously since then.[7]

758.   Other bilateral issues remain to be dealt with. The United States reacted sharply against the projected implementation of the Council Directive of 31 December 1985[8] banning the use in the Community of hormones for fattening purposes and hence, by extension, imports of animals or meat of animals on which hormones had been used. The Directive comes into force on 1 January 1988 but will not affect meat exports from non-member countries to the Community market for a year. Efforts to find a lasting solution to the problem will continue next year, notably through an examination of the Directive's provisions in relation to the General Agreement on Tariffs and Trade. The United States is also opposed to the Council Directive of

---

[1]   OJ L 235, 21.8.1986; Twentieth General Report, point 819.
[2]   Twentieth General Report, point 819; Bull. EC 2-1987, point 2.2.9.
[3]   OJ L 62, 5.3.1987; Bull. EC 2-1987, point 2.2.9.
[4]   OJ L 188, 20.7.1985; Nineteenth General Report, point 179.
[5]   Bull. EC 3-1987, point 2.2.46; Bull. EC 7/8-1987, point 2.2.66; Bull. EC 10-1987, point 2.2.16.
[6]   Bull. EC 7/8-1987, point 2.2.66.
[7]   Bull. EC 10-1987, point 2.2.16.
[8]   OJ L 382, 31.12.1985; Nineteenth General Report, point 203; Twentieth General Report, point 195.

12 December 1972 on meat imports,[1] which was aimed at ensuring that slaughterhouse health standards for imported fresh meat are in line with Community legislation, and has asked for a panel to be set up under Article XXIII of the General Agreement. On the other hand, the United States was told that it must repeal a discriminatory tax on imports of petroleum products which was intended to help finance the cleaning up of hazardous waste, after the GATT panel set up to examine the matter found in July that the tax was incompatible with the United States' international undertakings.

The *ad valorem* nature of the customs user fee on merchandise imports introduced by the United States was judged incompatible with GATT provisions by a special working party set up at the request of the Community and Canada.[2] A GATT panel is still examining the United States-Japan agreement on the prices of Japanese semiconductor exports.[3]

759.   The talks which Mr George Bush had with Mr Delors and Mr De Clercq, during the US Vice-President's official visit to the Commission on 2 October,[4] concerned salient international issues (the importance of growth, particularly for the indebted countries, in improving the world trade situation) and also bilateral problems, notably in agriculture; the Commission stressed the arduous efforts being made to reform the CAP and called for comparable efforts on the part of the United States. The Commission also confirmed the Community position with regard to the protectionist attitude of Congress and urged the US authorities to continue to resist it.

The annual ministerial meeting was held in Brussels on 12 December between a Commission delegation headed by Mr Delors and a US ministerial team led by Secretary of State Mr George Shultz.[5] This provided an opportunity to set economic relations in the broader context of common interests and to look for ways and means, on this wider political front, of expanding or reinforcing cooperation between the US Administration and the Commission, both bilaterally and multilaterally.

Japan

760.   Structural change in the Japanese economy, aimed at gearing economic growth more to domestic demand and improving access for imports, seemed to gather pace during the year. The first signs appeared of a correction of

---

[1]   OJ L 302, 31.12.1972.
[2]   Point 890 of this Report.
[3]   Twentieth General Report, point 825.
[4]   Bull. EC 10-1987, point 2.2.14.
[5]   Bull. EC 12-1987.

Japan's trade imbalances both overall and with the Community. [1] Japan's trade surplus with the Community measured in yen stabilized, but at a high level, while its surplus with the rest of the world shrank markedly. These two trends point to some degree of deflection of Japanese exports to the Community following the changes in the yen/dollar/ECU exchange rates.

This trend partly satisfies the wishes of the Community, which in discussions with the Japanese authorities has constantly stressed the need to improve the working of the free trade system and hence Japan's duty — as one of the main beneficiaries of that system — to open up its market properly to products from other countries and cease to rely on an export-based growth policy.

761.   On the basis of Commission communications, the Council discussed in March [2] and again in July [3] the trend of relations between the Community and Japan. It confirmed the strategy adopted in March 1986 [4] of restoring balanced relations through the opening-up of the Japanese market and by means of increased cooperation. It agreed that Japan should introduce the structural reforms that are essential for integrating its economy more closely into the world economy, and at the same time should base its economic growth more on domestic demand, increase imports of manufactures and liberalize its financial markets. The Commission continued to step up its efforts to promote Community exports to the Japanese market. [5]

762.   In April Japan announced a package of measures to stimulate its economy, costing over USD 41 billion and intended to boost domestic demand and growth. [6] After being eroded by the yen's appreciation against the dollar, economic growth picked up and could exceed the official forecast of 3.5% in the current financial year.

763.   The bulk of the measures adopted under the 1985 three-year action programme for trade [7] have now been implemented, although the effects fall well short of what was expected. As this leaves a number of major problems still unresolved, the Community decided that its future action would be on a sector-by-sector basis. The Japanese Government also announced an exceptional government procurement programme worth USD 1 billion, in connection

---

[1]   Bull. EC 7/8-1987, point 2.2.21.
[2]   Bull. EC 3-1987, point 2.2.11.
[3]   Bull. EC 7/8-1987, point 2.2.22.
[4]   Twentieth General Report, point 830.
[5]   Point 735 of this Report.
[6]   Bull. EC 4-1987, point 2.2.17.
[7]   Nineteenth General Report, point 811.

with which the Commission approached the Japanese authorities at various times to ensure that there was no discrimination against interested European firms. [1].

764.   The conclusions of the negotiations that the Commission conducted with Japan under Article XXIV.6 of the General Agreement following the Community's enlargement, and the resulting tariff measures (rebinding), were approved by the Council on 23 November. [2]

765.   On 13 October the GATT panel set up at the Community's request to look into taxes on alcoholic beverages [3] published its report, [4] in which it condemned discriminatory practices by Japan (grading of whisky and brandy, *ad valorem* taxes and differential taxation of Japanese and imported spirits). The GATT Council, meeting on 10 and 11 November, adopted the report and its recommendations. [5]

Participation by Community firms in major public works projects in Japan — the building of the new Kansai airport in particular — represents a test of whether the Japanese authorities are really willing to open their markets to European products, services and techniques. The Commission was active both in informing European firms concerned by such projects and in insisting that Japan pursue a policy of genuine openness.

766.   Discussions were begun with Japan on opening up its market in the motor manufacturing, medical equipment and cosmetics industries [6] with promising but as yet inadequate results. Japan needs to implement the concessions agreed and to come forward with others. At the same time the Commission took the first steps towards negotiations on other industries. [7] A number of rounds of consultations were also held with the Japanese authorities to achieve more satisfactory implementation of the 1986 agreement on imports into Japan of leather footwear and other leather products. [8]

767.   Industrial cooperation between the Community and Japan was marked by a sharp rise in bilateral investment and the organization in Tokyo in

1   Bull. EC 7/8-1987, point 2.2.19.
2   Bull. EC 11-1987, point 2.2.9.
3   Twentieth General Report, point 832.
4   Bull. EC 10-1987, point 2.2.17.
5   Bull. EC 11-1987, point 2.2.10.
6   Bull. EC 2-1987, point 2.2.11; Bull. EC 7/8-1987, point 2.2.22.
7   Bull. EC 7/8-1987, point 2.2.22.
8   Twentieth General Report, point 832.

December of the sixth industrial cooperation symposium, co-chaired by Mr Narjes.[1] The establishment in Tokyo of the EEC-Japan industrial cooperation centre, with the two sides sharing the cost of providing further training for European engineers and managers, was the most concrete achievement in this area of cooperation.

768.   The annual round of financial consultations between the Commission and the Japanese authorities was concerned mainly with the liberalization of Japanese financial and capital markets and likely developments on this front in the Community in preparation for 1992.[2] The Commission called for improved arrangements for financing imports of Community products into Japan. Mr De Clercq, who was in Tokyo for the first EEC-Japan conference of journalists in September,[3] urged upon the Japanese authorities the need for the financing system to be improved in collaboration with the Bank of Japan. Mr De Clercq made another trip to Japan in December to meet the new Prime Minister and leading members of his government.[1] In talks with them he insisted that Japan should continue to open its market and make its trade more balanced. He announced that the Community wanted to extend the trade talks to cover other areas in 1988 in order to ensure that the GATT rulings on alcoholic beverages were speedily incorporated into Japan's tax legislation[4] and that European firms did not suffer discrimination in tendering for major works in Japan.

Countries of the European Free Trade Association

769.   Relations between the Community and the EFTA countries[5] centred on the continuing implementation of the guidelines laid down in the Luxembourg Joint Declaration of 9 April 1984.[6] Diplomatic relations were consolidated by the official opening on 9 November of the Commission Delegation in Norway[7] and by the signing on 15 October of the headquarters agreement for a Commission Delegation in Austria.[8]

Strengthened cooperation and legislative moves in EFTA in parallel with those being carried out by the Community to bring about a single internal market

[1]   Bull. EC 12-1987.
[2]   Bull. EC 7/8-1987, point 2.2.20.
[3]   Bull. EC 9-1987, point 2.2.14.
[4]   Point 890 of this Report.
[5]   Austria, Finland, Iceland, Norway, Sweden and Switzerland.
[6]   Eighteenth General Report, point 652.
[7]   Bull. EC 7/8-1987, point 2.2.27; Bull. EC 11-1987, point 2.2.16.
[8]   Bull. EC 10-1987, point 2.2.22.

resulted in further significant progress towards establishing a dynamic, wider European economic area. At the annual ministerial-level meeting, which was held in Interlaken on 20 May, [1] Mr De Clercq (for the Community) and the EFTA ministers reviewed work in the various sectors before signing two multilateral conventions (one on the single administrative document and the other on common arrangements for goods in transit) [2] which will promote transfrontier trade.

770.   EEC-EFTA cooperation also formed the subject of discussion at numerous meetings between Commission and EFTA officials and during the visits to the Commission by Mrs Gro Brundtland, Norway's Prime Minister, on 5 May, [3]   Mr Matthias Matthiesen, Iceland's Foreign Minister, on 26 February, [4] Mr Alois Mock, the Austrian Vice-Chancellor, on 17 and 18 March, [5]   Mr Robert Graf, Austria's Minister for Economic Affairs, on 23 July, [6] Mr Pertti Salolainen, Finland's Minister for Foreign Trade, on 27 July, [7] Mr Franz Blankart, Swiss State Secretary for External Economic Affairs, on 25 June, [8] Mr Jean-Pascal Delamuraz, Swiss Federal Councillor, on 12 and 13 November [9] and Dr Franz Vranitzky, the Austrian Chancellor, on 20 November. [10] Progress in cooperation was also discussed during the official visits paid by Mr De Clercq to Norway on 1 June, [11] Sweden on 2 July [12] and Austria on 15 and 16 October, [13] and in the annual ministerial-level consultations. The joint committees set up under the free trade agreements met in June (Austria, Finland, Iceland and Switzerland) [14] and December (Finland, Norway, Sweden and Switzerland). [15]

---

[1]   Bull. EC 5-1987, point 2.2.14.
[2]   Point 177 of this Report.
[3]   Bull. EC 5-1987, point 2.2.15.
[4]   Bull. EC 2-1987, point 2.2.12.
[5]   Bull. EC 3-1987, point 2.2.12.
[6]   Bull. EC 7/8-1987, point 2.2.25.
[7]   Bull. EC 7/8-1987, point 2.2.26.
[8]   Bull. EC 6-1987, point 2.2.13.
[9]   Bull. EC 11-1987, point 2.2.17.
[10] Bull. EC 11-1987, point 2.2.14.
[11] Bull. EC 6-1987, point 2.2.12.
[12] Bull. EC 7/8-1987, point 2.2.28.
[13] Bull. EC 10-1987, point 2.2.22.
[14] Bull. EC 6-1987, point 2.2.10.
[15] Bull. EC 12-1987.

State-trading countries

Council for Mutual Economic Assistance

771.   The continuing normalization and improvement of relations between the Community and the CMEA member countries paved the way for progress in bilateral negotiations and in the liberalization of trade under the existing unilateral arrangements. [1] The Commission and the CMEA Secretariat had further talks in Geneva in March on establishing official relations between the Community and the CMEA. [2] A number of seminars and symposia on subjects connected with the Community's relations with the CMEA and its member countries were arranged during the year. The Commission continued exploratory talks with Poland [3] and Bulgaria and, on the basis of directives given by the Council, [4] entered into negotiations with Romania, Hungary and Czechoslovakia with a view to concluding trade and cooperation agreements with the first two countries and a trade agreement with the latter. [5] In addition, an agreement on sheep and goat meat was signed with the German Democratic Republic and a Soviet delegation had talks with the Commission to discuss arrangements for establishing diplomatic relations between the Soviet Union and the Community. [6]

Poland

772.   The 2 million ECU in aid earmarked for the private farm sector in Poland under the 1986 Community budget was allocated by the Commission to two projects — the improvement and expansion of a vocational training school in Oswiecim (1.9 million ECU) and a study and training programme geared to small and medium-sized farm holdings (0.1 million ECU). On 26 October the Commission decided to grant 2 million ECU in emergency medical aid for the purchase of medicines and small items of medical equipment, to be transported by non-governmental organizations and distributed by the charity boards of the Polish Church and by non-State pharmacists. [7]

---

[1]   OJ L 346, 8.12.1983; Seventeenth General Report, point 631; OJ L 31, 2.2.1987; Twentieth General Report, point 722.
[2]   Bull. EC 3-1987, point 2.2.23.
[3]   Bull. EC 9-1987, point 2.2.25.
[4]   Twentieth General Report, points 845 to 847.
[5]   Points 773, 774 and 775 of this Report.
[6]   Bull. EC 1-1987, point 2.2.22; Bull. EC 10-1987, point 2.2.38.
[7]   Bull. EC 10-1987, point 2.2.37.

Romania

773. On the basis of the negotiating directives adopted by the Council on 15 December 1986,[1] the Commission held three negotiating sessions with the Romanian authorities on establishing a trade and commercial and economic cooperation agreement to replace the two existing agreements signed in 1980.[2] The new agreement would apply to both industrial and agricultural products.

Czechoslovakia

774. Following the Council's adoption in November 1986 of directives for the negotiation of an agreement on trade in industrial products between the Community and Czechoslovakia,[3] an initial negotiating meeting took place in July and a second one was held in December.[4]

Hungary

775. The visit to the Commission on 11 February by the Deputy Prime Minister of Hungary, Mr Jozsef Marjai, was the first official visit by a member of the Hungarian Government to a Community institution.[5] Talks were concerned mainly with the normalization of relations between the Community and Hungary and the prospects for negotiating a trade and commercial and economic cooperation agreement. These topics were also broached at meetings held by Mr Delors and Mr De Clercq with Mr János Kádár, General Secretary of the Socialist Workers' Party, and Mr Péter Várkonyi, Hungary's Foreign Minister, when they came on an official visit to Belgium.[6]

On 27 April the Council adopted, on the basis of the recommendation presented by the Commission in November 1986,[7] negotiating directives for a cooperation agreement, on which three negotiating sessions have already been held.[8]

---

1 Twentieth General Report, point 845.
2 OJ L 352, 29.12.1980; Fourteenth General Report, point 705.
3 Twentieth General Report, point 846.
4 Bull. EC 12-1987.
5 Bull. EC 2-1987, point 2.2.20.
6 Bull. EC 11-1987, point 2.2.34.
7 Twentieth General Report, point 847.
8 Bull. EC 4-1987, point 2.2.28.

Canada

776.   Despite a flurry of bilateral difficulties at the beginning of the year resulting, among other things, from Canada's application of countervailing duties on imports of beef and pasta products from the Community [1] and high tariffs on other products (tea bags, asphaltum oil and books), relations between the Community and Canada improved over the first half of the year. Before the end of January, following a tribunal decision that the measures concerned were invalid, the countervailing duties on pasta were removed, [2] while the high tariffs were removed in February.

777.   However, a number of trade disagreements over (notably) beef, a Canadian decision taken in May changing the customs classification of pasta products, [3] and the provincial liquor boards [1] could not be settled during the official visit in May to the Commission by Ms Patricia Carney, Canada's Trade Minister, [4] nor in the half-yearly high-level consultations. [5] The Community therefore initiated the disputes settlement procedure under GATT, which in September pronounced in favour of the Community on the beef dispute. [6] In addition there is still disagreement between the Community and Canada over fisheries.

778.   Two cooperation agreements between the Community and Canada, in the fields of research on the health and environmental effects of radiation and the processing of complex sulphide minerals, were signed on 28 July. [7] The cooperation agreement between Euratom and Canada continued to operate satisfactorily. [8]

Australia and New Zealand

Australia

779.   The sixth round of ministerial consultations between the Community and Austrialia took place in Brussels from 8 to 12 October. [9] The Community was represented by Mr Andriessen and Mr De Clercq, who had wide-ranging

1   Twentieth General Report, point 894.
2   Bull. EC 1-1987, point 2.2.9.
3   Bull. EC 6-1987, point 2.2.9.
4   Bull. EC 5-1987, point 2.2.10.
5   Bull. EC 6-1987, point 2.2.9; Bull. EC 11-1987, point 2.2.8.
6   Point 891 of this Report.
7   Bull. EC 7/8-1987, point 2.2.18.
8   Twentieth General Report, point 383.
9   Bull. EC 10-1987, point 2.2.19; Twentieth General Report, point 898.

discussions with Mr John Kerin, Australia's Minister for Primary Industry and Energy, and Mr Michael Duffy, Minister for Trade Negotiations. The discussions were concerned mainly with the general economic situation, progress and prospects in the new round of multilateral trade negotiations (notably in the agricultural sector), restructuring in industry and agriculture, and also bilateral relations. Both sides expressed satisfaction with the contacts established under the arrangement concluded in November 1986 on cooperation in science and technology [1] and were in favour of extending this cooperation to other sectors. In agriculture, a number of technical matters were raised with regard to beef, sheepmeat, wine and dairy products.

New Zealand

780.   Mr Andriessen and Mr De Clercq met Mr Michael Moore, New Zealand's Overseas Trade Minister, in Strasbourg on 13 October [2] for talks on the multilateral trade negotiations, with particular reference to agriculture, the functioning of GATT and the United States trade bill, [3] and also on a number of specifically agricultural topics (butter, sheepmeat, the Community 'hormones' Directive, and so on). On 23 November they had talks with the New Zealand Agriculture Minister, Mr Colin Moyle, on the future of New Zealand's exports of milk products and sheepmeat in the light, notably, of the reforms undertaken or planned for those sectors by the two parties and in the context of the multilateral negotiations. [4]

---

[1]   Twentieth General Report, point 898.
[2]   Bull. EC 10-1987, point 2.2.22.
[3]   Point 754 of this Report.
[4]   Bull. EC 11-1987, point 2.2.11.

Section 5

Relations with Mediterranean, Asian and Latin American countries

781. On 22 June the Council approved [1] the principal guidelines put forward by the Commission in its communication on industrial cooperation with certain developing countries in Latin America, Asia, the Gulf and the Mediterranean [2] aimed at extending the Community's development policies by means of an approach specifically geared to the needs of these countries, combining financial engineering, joint ventures and on-the-job training. It was decided to set up a joint programme on industrial cooperation with India, with particular reference to cooperation on industrial standards, telecommunications and electronics, and to have European and Brazilian consultants carry out joint studies to identify opportunities for joint ventures between medium-sized companies in Europe and Brazil.

Mediterranean countries

The impact of enlargement

782. Protocols making economic and technical adjustments to the trade arrangements under the cooperation and association agreements following enlargement [3] were signed with Algeria, Tunisia, Egypt, Jordan, Lebanon, Israel, Cyprus, Turkey and Yugoslavia. [4] Their main aim is to ensure the continuation of traditional agricultural exports from the countries concerned to the Community in accordance with the Council statement of 30 March 1985. [3] These protocols, which also contain the technical provisions required for their implementation by Spain and Portugal, have already entered into force or, in the case of some countries, are due to enter into force at the beginning of 1988. It was with regard to these protocols that the new procedure involving Parliament's assent was implemented for the first time, [5] in accordance with

---

[1] Bull. EC 6-1987, points 2.2.14 and 3.6.1.
[2] Twentieth General Report, point 936.
[3] Nineteenth General Report, point 831.
[4] Twentieth General Report, point 848.
[5] OJ C 281, 19.10.1987; Bull. EC 9-1987, point 2.2.15.

Article 9 of the Single European Act, concerning external relations.[1] The protocols to be concluded with Syria should be signed in the early part of the new year. Negotiations on protocols with Malta and Morocco had not resulted in agreement by the end of the year.

Turkey

783.   In 1987 normalization of relations between the Community and Turkey continued. On 14 April Turkey made formal application for membership of the Community.[2]

Normalization found expression in the successful negotiation of a protocol[3] to the EEC-Turkey Association Agreement[4] consequent on the accession of Spain and Portugal to the Community[5] and also in the conclusion of an economic protocol.[6] Moreover, as part of the special measures agreed on in 1980,[7] a contribution of 10 million ECU was made towards the financing of a geothermal project in Anatolia,[8] an anti-malaria campaign and the organization of a business week in Turkey.[9]

Cyprus

784.   Two protocols were adopted by Council Decision on 21 December.[8] The first, which covers the implementation of the second stage of the 1973 Association Agreement,[10] provides for the establishment of a customs union between the Community and Cyprus to be completed in two phases. The second protocol concerns the adaptation of the Association Agreement consequent on the accession of Spain and Portugal to the Community.[5]

Malta

785.   Negotiations continued on trade relations between the Community and Malta and the adaptation of the Agreement.[11]

---

[1]   Twentieth General Report, points 1 to 4; Supplement 2/86 — Bull. EC.
[2]   Bull. EC 4-1987, points 1.3.1 and 1.3.2.
[3]   OJ L 297, 21.10.1987; Bull. EC 9-1987, point 2.2.16.
[4]   OJ C 182, 12.12.1986; Seventh General Report, point 279.
[5]   Point 782 of this Report.
[6]   Bull. EC 5-1987, point 2.2.16.
[7]   Fourteenth General Report, point 649.
[8]   Bull. EC 12-1987.
[9]   Bull. EC 11-1987, point 2.2.20.
[10]   OJ L 133, 21.5.1973; OJ L 174, 30.6.1981.
[11]   Twentieth General Report, point 856.

Yugoslavia

786.   This year saw the negotiation of protocols amending the 1980 EEC-Yugoslavia Cooperation Agreement. [1] The protocol establishing new trade arrangements and those adjusting the Agreement to take account of the accession of Spain and Portugal to the Community were initialled on 10 July [2] and approved on behalf of the Community by Council Decision on 21 December. [3] As a result of these protocols, the concessions granted to Yugoslavia by the Community were improved.

787.   The second financial protocol, which was initialled on 17 June [4] and approved on behalf of the Community by Council Decision on 21 December, [3] provides for a substantial increase in the amount of EIB loans to 550 million ECU, compared with 200 million ECU under the first protocol. [5]

788.   The official visit paid by Mr Delors to Belgrade from 23 to 25 July provided an opportunity to reaffirm the importance which the Community attaches to its relations with Yugoslavia. [6] Wide-ranging discussions were held on the prospects for strengthening economic and technical cooperation in science and technology, statistics and agricultural research, as well as the possibility of extending cooperation to new areas such as environment, tourism and energy.

The Cooperation Council met at ministerial level in Brussels on 14 December. [3] It indicated its approval of the above approach in a resolution on the future of relations between the Community and Yugoslavia.

Maghreb (Algeria, Morocco, Tunisia), Mashreq (Egypt, Jordan, Lebanon, Syria) and Israel

789.   The year was marked by the establishment of protocols to take account of the consequences of enlargement [7] and by the renewal of the financial protocols with Algeria, Tunisia, Egypt, Jordan, Lebanon and Israel, which had expired on 31 October 1986. The financial protocols should enter into force at

---

[1]   OJ L 130, 27.5.1980; Fourteenth General Report, point 656.
[2]   Bull. EC 7/8-1987, point 2.2.33.
[3]   Bull. EC 12-1987.
[4]   Bull. EC 6-1987, point 2.2.18.
[5]   Fourteenth General Report, point 656.
[6]   Bull. EC 7/8-1987, point 2.2.34.
[7]   Point 782 of this Report.

the beginning of 1988, Parliament having endorsed them under the assent procedure. [1] The negotiations on financial protocols with Morocco and Syria had not been completed by the end of the year.

The third financial protocols reflect the Council statement of 30 March 1985 [2] in providing for cooperation to be concentrated on priority sectors for development — in particular agriculture and industry — and on Mediterranean regional cooperation. To this end the Council adopted an overall package of 1 618 million ECU [3] — a 59% increase over the budget set for the previous protocols (second generation) [4] — to be divided between grants from budget funds 615 million ECU) and European Investment Bank loans (1 003 million ECU).

Table 17

Third financial protocols

million ECU

Recipient country	Budget funds		EIB loans		Total	
	Amounts	% increase	Amounts	% increase	Amounts	% increase
Algeria	56	27	183	71	238	58
Morocco	173	58.7	151	67.77	324	62.81
Tunisia	93	52.45	131	67.9	224	61.15
Egypt	200	56.7	249	66	449	62.68
Jordan	38	42.3	63	70.27	100	58.73
Lebanon	20	25	53	55.8	74	46
Israel	—	—	63	57.5	63	57.5
(Balance)	36	9	110	71.8	147	50.5
Total	615	48	1 003	67	1 618	59

790. At 31 December financing decisions had been taken for nearly all the aid granted under the second financial protocols, [4] accounting for 960 million ECU, or 94.6% of the 1 015 million ECU available. In the case of Israel, which under its protocol is eligible only for EIB loans, funds were again found in the Community budget, as in previous years, for a few cooperation schemes.

[1]   OJ C 13, 18.1.1988; Bull. EC 12-1987.
[2]   Nineteenth General Report, point 831.
[3]   Bull. EC 3-1987, point 2.2.14.
[4]   OJ L 337, 29.11.1982; OJ L 356, 17.12.1982; Sixteenth General Report, point 689.

791.   The fifth meeting of the EEC-Israel Cooperation Council and the third meeting of the EEC-Tunisia Cooperation Council were held in Brussels on 27 January [1] and 26 May [2] respectively. The EEC-Algeria Cooperation Council meeting in Brussels on 27 April [3] was the first since the Agreement was signed in 1976. [4]

792.   A meeting between a European Parliament delegation and a parliamentary delegation from Algeria took place during the year.

793.   Visitors to the Commission during 1987 included Mr Amin Gemayel, President of Lebanon, [5] and Mr Abdellatif Filali, Morocco's Foreign Minister. [6] In return, Mr Delors paid an official visit to Morocco from 7 to 11 October. [7] Mr Cheysson, Member of the Commission with special responsibility for Mediterranean policy, paid official visits to Lebanon, Tunisia, [3] Syria, [8] Israel [9] and Jordan. [10]

794.   On 8 July King Hassan II presented an application for Morocco's accession to the Community. [6] The President of the Council replied on 1 October, pointing out that the Community wished to continue strengthening and extending its cooperation with Morocco, in view of the special nature of existing relations and joint interests. [11]

795.   The fisheries sector has become of considerable importance in relations between the Community and Morocco because of the agreements concluded with Morocco by Spain and Portugal before their accession. Negotiations on a fisheries agreement with the Community to replace the agreements with Spain and Portugal had not proved successful by the end of the year.

---

[1]   Bull. EC 1-1987, point 2.2.14.
[2]   Bull. EC 5-1987, point 2.2.21.
[3]   Bull. EC 4-1987, point 2.2.25.
[4]   OJ L 175, 1.7.1976; Tenth General Report, point 509.
[5]   Bull. EC 2-1987, point 2.2.14.
[6]   Bull. EC 7/8-1987, point 2.2.35.
[7]   Bull. EC 10-1987, point 2.2.30.
[8]   Bull. EC 9-1987, point 2.2.21.
[9]   Bull. EC 10-1987, point 2.2.31.
[10]   Bull. EC 12-1987.
[11]   Bull. EC 9-1987, point 2.2.19.

Countries of the Gulf and the Arabian Peninsula

796.   Contacts between the Community and the countries of the Gulf Cooperation Council (GCC) were stepped up this year. At the second joint meeting between the Community and the GCC at ministerial level,[1] which was held in Brussels on 23 June,[2] the two sides reaffirmed their desire to conclude a cooperation agreement and to improve trade. The Ministers of the Twelve and the GCC countries met in New York in September while attending the new session of the UN General Assembly and confirmed this position.

As a result of the exploratory talks begun in 1986,[3] on 23 November the Council adopted directives for the Commission to negotiate a cooperation agreement with the GCC countries.[4] The negotiations began on 7 December.

Yemen Arab Republic

797.   The programme of economic and development cooperation which was started up following the first meeting of the EEC-Yemen Joint Cooperation Committee[5] was continued and extended.[6]

Asia

South Asia

798.   Under the cooperation agreements with several South Asian countries (Bangladesh, India, Pakistan and Sri Lanka), the Commission continued to implement cooperation schemes in various fields: rural development, food aid, trade promotion and scientific and industrial cooperation. The Commission also applied the new compensation system for loss of export earnings for the least-developed countries in the region (Bangladesh and Nepal).

799.   Meetings of the Joint Commissions, whose purpose is to examine all aspects of relations between the Community and the partner countries, were

---

[1]   Nineteenth General Report, point 854.
[2]   Bull. EC 6-1987, point 2.2.20.
[3]   Twentieth General Report, point 865.
[4]   Bull. EC 11-1987, point 2.2.26.
[5]   Nineteenth General Report, point 856.
[6]   Twentieth General Report, point 869.

held with India in January[1] and Sri Lanka in November.[2] On the latter occasion the Commission undertook to support the national reconstruction programme.

800.   At the first meeting of the EEC-India Industrial Cooperation Working Party, which took place in New Delhi in March,[3] a programme aimed at promoting cooperation in specific economic areas was drawn up; it was confirmed in June, when Mr Vengala Rao, the Indian Minister for Industry, paid an official visit to the Commission.[4]

801.   In January Mr Sirajul Hossain Khan, the Bangladesh Minister for Fisheries and Livestock, held discussions with Mr Cheysson concerning the new pattern of bilateral cooperation between the Community and Bangladesh as regards rural development and inland fisheries.[5]

802.   The Prime Minister of Pakistan, Mr Muhammad Khan Junejo, accompanied by several members of his government, was received by Mr Delors and Mr Cheysson on 13 April.[6] This first-ever visit to the Commission by a Prime Minister of Pakistan highlighted the importance Pakistan attaches to its relations with the Community.

Association of South East Asian Nations

803.   The year was spent implementing the policy decisions taken at the sixth ministerial meeting between the EEC and Asean, held in Jakarta in October 1986.[7] With a view to promoting European investment in South-East Asia the Commission appointed a high-level investment adviser and prompted the setting-up of joint investment committees in all the Asean capitals.

In this connection, at the fifth EEC-Asean industrial conference, which was held in Bangkok from 30 November to 2 December,[8] 250 European and Asean businessmen from the agricultural processing industry established useful contacts with a view to setting up trade and industrial cooperation links.

---

[1]   Bull. EC 1-1987, point 2.2.17.
[2]   Bull. EC 11-1987, point 2.2.29.
[3]   Bull. EC 3-1987, point 2.2.21.
[4]   Bull. EC 6-1987, point 2.2.22.
[5]   Bull. EC 1-1987, point 2.2.16.
[6]   Bull. EC 4-1987, point 2.2.26.
[7]   Twentieth General Report, point 877.
[8]   Bull. EC 11-1987, point 2.2.28.

804.   The annual meeting of Asean Foreign Ministers with their most important partners [1] was held in Singapore from 18 to 20 June [2] The Community
was represented by Mr Leo Tindemans, President of the Council, and
Mr Cheysson.

805.   The seventh meeting of the EEC-Asean Joint Cooperation Committee [3]
was held in Jakarta from 30 April to 2 May. [4] Both sides agreed to implement
new initiatives concerning joint research programmes and to instruct a working
party of trade experts to examine a number of bilateral trade questions. The
Joint Committee agreed on the need for fresh efforts to promote industrial
cooperation.

806.   At the third plenary session of the EEC-Asean Business Council, held in
Brussels on 20 and 21 October, Community and Asean representatives from
the private sector looked at the possibilities of promoting trade and setting up
joint ventures. [5]

China

807.   The excellent relations between the Community and the People's Republic of China were confirmed at a number of meetings. The Joint Committee
met in Brussels in January [6] and in Beijing in November. [7] The Community is
now China's second-largest trading partner and its main supplier of technology; [8] its trade surplus with China, which had already fallen in 1986,
dropped very sharply this year. [6] The Community continued to apply measures
in favour of China through the generalized preferences scheme, more flexible
import arrangements and trade promotion. [6]

808.   Cooperation activities between the Community and China were increased
and diversified. The main schemes concern assistance in developing China's
rural sector, science and technology, energy and various aspects of training. [6]
Mr Song Jian, the Chairman of the State Scientific and Technological Commission, visited Brussels in March. An agreement was signed on the establish-

[1]   Australia, Canada, the Community, Japan, New Zealand and the United States.
[2]   Bull. EC 6-1987, point 2.2.21.
[3]   Twentieth General Report, point 879.
[4]   Bull. EC 5-1987, point 2.2.22.
[5]   Bull. EC 10-1987, point 2.2.23.
[6]   Bull. EC 1-1987, point 2.2.24.
[7]   Bull. EC 11-1987, point 2.2.32.
[8]   Bull. EC 3-1987, point 2.2.24.

ment of a joint biotechnology research centre in Beijing. [1] On 30 June Mr De Clercq presented diplomas [2] to the first group of Chinese students who had completed their training at the EEC-China Business Management Centre. [3] The programme will continue to receive Community support.

809.   Relations between the two sides were enhanced by meetings at ministerial level. Mr De Clercq met the Chinese Deputy Minister for International Economic Relations and Foreign Trade in Brussels in June, [4] Mr Mosar paid an official visit to China, [5] and in September a 'troika' meeting was held in New York with the Chinese Foreign Minister.

Mr De Clercq was accompanied by European businessmen from the chemical and pharmaceutical industries during his official visit to China from 26 March to 3 April, when he signed the headquarters agreement for the opening of a Commission Delegation in Beijing. [6] In September, for the first time in China, there was a Community pavilion at a telecommunications and data-processing exhibition in Beijing. [7] In November senior Commission officials took part in an information seminar on the Community organized by the Chinese authorities, [8] and in December there was a symposium in Beijing on investment conditions in China, at which concrete projects were examined. [9] The Community delegation on that occasion was led by Mr Matutes, the Member of the Commission with special responsibility for credit, investments and financial instruments, and small business policy.

Korea

810.   The fourth round of high-level talks between the Commission and the Republic of Korea took place in Brussels in April.[10]

811.   The Community had four main points of concern: continuing tariff and non-tariff barriers making access to the Korean market difficult; the rapid growth in exports of Korean footwear articles to the Community; problems

---

[1]   Bull. EC 3-1987, point 2.1.44.
[2]   Bull. EC 6-1987, point 2.2.26.
[3]   Eighteenth General Report, point 709.
[4]   Bull. EC 6-1987, point 2.2.25.
[5]   Point 664 of this Report.
[6]   Bull. EC 3-1987, point 2.2.24.
[7]   Point 733 of this Report.
[8]   Bull. EC 11-1987, point 2.2.33.
[9]   Bull. EC 12-1987.
[10] Bull. EC 4-1987, point 2.2.27.

relating to shipbuilding; and, above all, the adoption by Korea of measures in the intellectual property sphere that favour the United States but discriminate against the Community. A meeting was held in Seoul in November between the Commission and the Korean authorities [1] with the aim of finding a solution to the problems created by this discrimination. As it proved impossible to arrive at a satisfactory solution, the Council decided in December, [2] on the basis of a Commission proposal, [3] to suspend the tariff preferences accorded to Korea under the generalized preferences system.

812.   There is also still serious concern on the Community side about shipbuilding, because the Korean Government is holding back from participation in the international effort to restructure this industry.

Latin America

813.   This was a particularly important year for the development of relations between the Community and Latin America. As a follow-up to the Commission's communication in November 1986, [4] on 22 June the Council and the Representatives of the Governments of the Member States adopted a number of conclusions on the implementation of an overall strategy aimed at strengthening relations and cooperation between the Community and Latin America in both political and economic fields. [5] This was a clear statement of the Community's desire to reorganize its efforts and harmonize its activities with those of the Member States in the areas of official development assistance, support for regional integration, trade promotion, scientific and technical cooperation and, in particular, industrial cooperation.

814.   There were several meetings at bilateral level. Mr Cheysson paid official visits to Peru on 6 and 7 February, [6] Uruguay on 26 and 27 October [7] and Argentina on 28 and 29 October. [8] The EEC-Mexico Joint Committee met in Mexico City on 12 and 13 February. [9] The EEC-Uruguay Joint Committee met

---

[1] Bull. EC 11-1987, point 2.2.30.
[2] OJ C 369, 29.12.1987; Bull. EC 12-1987.
[3] OJ C 334, 12.12.1987; Bull. EC 12-1987.
[4] Twentieth General Report, point 887.
[5] Bull. EC 6-1987, points 2.2.23 and 3.5.1.
[6] Bull. EC 2-1987, point 2.2.19.
[7] Bull. EC 10-1987, point 2.2.35.
[8] Bull. EC 10-1987, point 2.2.34.
[9] Bull. EC 2-1987, point 2.2.18.

in Montevideo on 19 and 20 March [1] and the EEC-Brazil Joint Committee met in Brasilia from 3 to 5 November. [2] High-level consultations were held between the Commission and Argentina in Buenos Aires on 28 and 29 October. [3]

815.   Latin America received various kinds of Community aid, mainly technical and financial assistance and food aid, and also cooperation in industrial, energy, scientific and trade matters.

Central America

816.   The third ministerial conference between the Community and the countries of Central America and the Contadora Group [4] was held in Guatemala City on 9 and 10 February. [5] A joint political declaration and a joint economic communiqué were issued at the end of the conference.

817.   The Cooperation Agreement between the Community and the five countries of the Central American Common Market and Panama [6] came into force on 1 March. [7] The first meeting of the joint committee set up by this Agreement was held in Brussels on 17 and 18 June. [8] It resulted in priorities being laid down for economic and trade cooperation and development.

818.   During his official visit to the Commission on 21 May the President of Costa Rica, Mr Oscar Arias Sánchez, devoted most of his discussions to his peace plan for Central America and to an examination of the general situation and the prospects for cooperation between the Community and Central America. [9]

Andean Group

819.   The Cooperation Agreement signed in 1983 between the Community and the countries of the Andean Group[10] entered into force on 1 February.[11] An Andean Group delegation paid its first official visit to the Commission on 6 and 7 July to discuss the new pattern for the Andean integration process and the prospects for cooperation between the Community and the Group.[12]

1   Bull. EC 3-1987, point 2.2.22.
2   Bull. EC 11-1987, point 2.2.31.
3   Bull. EC 10-1987, point 2.2.34.
4   Nineteenth General Report, point 869.
5   Bull. EC 2-1987, points 1.3.1 to 1.3.3.
6   OJ L 172, 30.6.1986; Twentieth General Report, point 889.
7   OJ L 58, 28.2.1987; Bull. EC 2-1987, point 2.2.17.
8   Bull. EC 6-1987, point 2.2.24.
9   Bull. EC 5-1987, point 2.2.23.
10   OJ L 153, 8.6.1984; Seventeenth General Report, point 708.
11   Bull. EC 1-1987, point 2.2.19.
12   Bull. EC 7/8-1987, point 2.2.37.

Section 6

Development cooperation

Cooperation through the United Nations

Abuja Conference on economic recovery and accelerated development in Africa

820.   The Conference at Abuja in Nigeria, [1] convened on the initiative of the UN Economic Commission for Africa in order to take stock of the current economic situation in Africa one year after the General Assembly's special session on Africa, [2] endorsed the general guidelines adopted by the special session, in particular the key role of the African countries in the search for solutions to their own predicament and the implementation of structural reforms. The Conference ended with the adoption of the 'Abuja Statement', which mentioned a number of controversial proposals made but was not binding on the governments and institutions represented, which included the Commission.

United Nations Conference on Trade and Development

821.   The seventh session of the United Nations Conference on Trade and Development, in which the Community played an active part following lengthy and detailed preparations, took place in Geneva from 9 July to 3 August. [3]

822.   The Commission was active in the preparations for the Conference, [4] in respect of which the Council laid down guidelines for a Community position in June. [5]

823.   The Conference may be considered a success: it adopted, by consensus, a final document [3] containing an assessment of economic trends as well as

---

1   Bull. EC 6-1987, point 2.2.31.
2   Twentieth General Report, point 902.
3   Bull. EC 7/8-1987, point 2.2.38.
4   Bull. EC 1-1987, point 2.2.25; Bull. EC 2-1987, point 2.2.23.
5   Bull. EC 6-1987, point 2.2.32.

proposals for policies in four areas (resources for development, commodities, trade and the least-developed countries) and guidelines for the future.

The final document was welcomed by representatives of the various negotiating groups. It marked the first time for a number of years that a major North-South meeting had ended in a general consensus on such a wide range of issues. [1] One of the key features of the Conference was the common assessment of the world economic situation, which noted and defined many of the difficulties, while at the same time assessing the possibilities for appropriate policy responses and setting up broad guidelines for action. This part of the document represents an overall approach on the issue of interdependence, recognizing on the one hand the essential role of the developing countries' own domestic policies in ensuring development and, on the other, the particular responsibility of the industrialized countries with regard to the world economic environment. The developing countries stressed the importance of market forces and the need to improve the functioning of their public sector, while the industrialized countries undertook to keep up their concerted efforts to eliminate major structural imbalances. The final document of the Conference thus echoes in many ways the Community's own objectives; [2] it is also a significant point of reference in the efforts to revitalize growth, development and international trade through intensified multilateral cooperation.

824.   During these negotiations, the Trade and Development Board carried on with its usual work. The 34th session of the Board, held from 5 to 16 October, was dominated by discussions on how to give practical effect to the content of the Unctad VII concluding document and by an examination of the draft report containing Unctad's recommendations on interaction with other bodies. [3] The Board also reached agreement on the date, duration and terms of reference of the conference —to be held in Paris in 1990— to examine the new programme of special action to help the least-developed countries. An extra session, held on 20 November, provided an opportunity to discuss the operational report on Unctad before it was transmitted to the Economic and Social Council. [4]

[1]   This was not the case at Unctad VI, held in Belgrade from 6 June to 3 July 1983: Seventeenth General Report, point 756.
[2]   Bull. EC 6-1987, point 2.2.32.
[3]   Bull. EC 10-1987, point 2.2.39.
[4]   Points 873 to 876 of this Report.

United Nations Industrial Development Organization

825.   The second session of the Unido General Conference was held in Bangkok from 9 to 13 November.[1] This provided a first opportunity for the Member States to comment on the policy approaches and achievements of Unido since it became a specialized agency.[2] It reconfirmed Unido's double role as a forum for exchanges on the Third World countries' industrial development policies and cooperation with the more developed countries, and as an agency for identifying and implementing cooperation programmes related to markets and industry. Three resolutions —on Namibia, South Africa and the Palestinians— were adopted. The developed countries and the Group of 77 reached agreement on the more political aspects of the mobilization of financial resources and the external debt. The Community played an active role at the conference, in particular contributing declarations on its bilateral industrial cooperation and its relations with Unido and on the organization's own role.

826.   Consultations —the role and importance of which had been reaffirmed in 1985[3]— also took place on specific industries this year. A third round of consultations on the pharmaceuticals industry, organized in close cooperation with the World Health Organization in Madrid in October,[4] centred on the industrial use of medicinal plants in developing countries and international cooperation to develop the pharmaceuticals industry.

World Food Programme

827.   The Community, the third largest contributor to the WFP, provided food products in 1987, plus funds to cover transport costs, amounting in all to 93.8 million ECU, in the form of contributions to regular programmes, the International Emergency Food Reserve and a food programme for refugees.

It also took part in the two meetings of the Committee on Food Aid Policies and Programmes, which were held in Rome.[5] At its autumn meeting, the Committee discussed the Community's food programme and noted that following its reform the Community's food-aid policy[6] would henceforth function

1   Bull. EC 11-1987, point 2.2.38.
2   Nineteenth General Report, point 898; Twentieth General Report, point 906.
3   Nineteenth General Report, point 900.
4   Bull. EC 10-1987, point 2.2.41.
5   Bull. EC 6-1987, point 2.2.35; Bull. EC 11-1987, point 2.2.40.
6   OJ L 370, 30.12.1986; Twentieth General Report, point 934.

as a fully fledged development instrument wholly independent of the common agricultural policy.

World Food Council

828. The Bureau of the World Food Council met in Brussels on 5 and 6 January.[1] There were detailed discussions with various Members of the Commission on the problems affecting the agricultural economies of the developing countries and, in particular, the world food imbalances (agricultural surpluses in certain countries, hunger and malnutrition in others) which are the underlying cause.

829. At its 13th ministerial session, held in Beijing,[2] the WFC elected new officers to serve for a period of two years; during this period the Western countries will be represented by the Swedish Minister for Agriculture. The principal world agricultural problems were discussed, with particular emphasis on those affecting the Third World, international trade in agricultural food products and South-South relations.

Food and Agriculture Organization of the United Nations

830. In June the Community participated in the 91st meeting of the FAO Council and in the work of the specialized committees which met in Rome to examine the world situation regarding agriculture and food with a view to tackling the Third World's serious food problems and improving their agricultural economies and international trade in agricultural and food products.[3]

831. The Community also took part in the FAO's biennial conference, held in November, at which its Director-General was elected for a third term.[4] The conference asked a working party to draw up proposals on internal organization and working methods in view of the precarious financial situation following the non-payment of the United States' financial contribution, which accounted for 25% of the budget.

---

[1]   Bull. EC 1-1987, point 2.2.26.
[2]   Bull. EC 6-1987, point 2.2.36.
[3]   Bull. EC 6-1987, point 2.2.34.
[4]   Bull. EC 11-1987, point 2.2.39.

Generalized tariff preferences

832. On 17 November and 3 December the Council adopted the various regulations and the decision concerning the opening of the Community's generalized preferences for 1988 concerning agricultural, industrial and iron and steel products, and also textiles, [1] proposals for which had been transmitted in June [2] and November. [3] The Economic and Social Committee and Parliament gave their opinions on 23 September [4] and 16 October [5] respectively.

833. Because of the difficulties encountered in the transposition of the existing Customs Cooperation Council nomenclature into the Harmonized Commodity Description and Coding System, [6] the Community had to confine itself to making adjustments in the industrial sector only where economic reasons or the application of more incisive differentiation criteria in respect of sensitive products made them necessary. [7] In the context of the plan for completion of the Community internal market by 1992, four preferential ceilings for countries that have recently become highly competitive were converted into zero-duty fixed amounts rather than allocated quotas.

The reference basis for non-sensitive products was updated and, except in some cases, set at 5% of imports from outside the Community in 1986, thus including for the first time import statistics for Spain and Portugal.

834. In the agricultural sector adjustments of the preferential offer were cut down to the minimum, again because of the difficulties in transposing nomenclature. Following the agreed reduction in the Community customs duty arising from the negotiations conducted under Article XXIV.6 of the General Agreement on Tariffs and Trade, the Community reduced the GSP rate in respect of four products (avocados, roasted nuts, grapefruit juice and cigars) in order to restore, at least partially, their preferential margin. As a result of GATT's unbinding of the rate of duty on sweet potatoes for animal consumption and the introduction of zero-duty quotas, the GSP preference is now limited to sweet potatoes for human consumption. Lastly, an additional product was included in the special list for the least-developed countries.

---

1   OJ L 350, 12.12.1987; OJ L 367, 28.12.1987; Bull. EC 11-1987, point 2.2.42.
2   Bull. EC 6-1987, point 2.2.38.
3   Bull. EC 11-1987, point 2.2.41.
4   Bull. EC 9-1987, point 2.4.43.
5   OJ C 305, 16.11.1987; Bull. EC 10-1987, point 2.2.43.
6   Points 156 and 157 of this Report.
7   OJ L 373, 31.12.1986; Twentieth General Report, points 913 and 915.

835.   In the case of textiles, the structure of the scheme for products covered by the Multifibre Arrangement has been drastically revised. Preferential amounts are no longer to be calculated on the GSP beneficiary's performance, but on the volume of Community imports of a given category. Differentiation in respect of highly competitive suppliers having reached a certain level of development has been stepped up. The introduction of these changes, however, will be staggered over two years. A new non-ACP beneficiary, Burma, has been added to the list of least-developed countries. Because of South Korea's discriminatory practices towards the Community,[1] application of the 1988 GSP to that country was suspended.[2]

Commodities and world agreements

836.   Portugal is currently completing the necessary formalities for its accession to the International Agreement on Jute and Jute Products, which was concluded in 1982[3] and has been in force since 9 January 1984.[4].

The International Jute Council and the Committee on Projects each held two meetings.[5] The International Jute Organization is currently engaged in promoting sales of jute products in Japan and is carrying out an industrial research project and two agricultural research and development projects. In addition, the Organization has approved four further projects, concerning the long-term supply of jute, improvements in fibre quality and sales promotion. Project financing comes chiefly from voluntary contributions by member countries. Project implementation has been considerably slowed down by a shortage of funds. The International Agreement on Jute and Jute Products was formally approved by the Community on 23 November.[6]

837.   The international Cocoa Agreement concluded in 1986[7] entered into force provisionally on 20 January.[8] The Community took all the necessary steps for applying the Agreement.[9]

At its 32nd regular session, held in London in March, the International Cocoa Council adopted rules concerning the functioning of the buffer stock.[10] Its entry

---

1 Point 811 of this Report.
2 Bull. EC 12-1987.
3 OJ L 185, 8.5.1983; Sixteenth General Report, point 746.
4 Eighteenth General Report, point 724.
5 Bull. EC 4-1987, point 2.2.31.
6 OJ L 337, 27.11.1987; Bull. EC 11-1987, point 2.2.24.
7 Twentieth General Report, point 919.
8 Bull. EC 1-1987, point 2.2.28.
9 OJ L 69, 12.3.1987; Bull. EC 1-1987, point 2.2.27.
10 Bull. EC 4-1987, point 2.2.29.

into operation had been delayed owing to differing interpretations of the provisions introduced in 1986. The Community position provided the basis for the compromise reached.

The low level of prices justified massive intervention by the buffer stock, which rapidly reached its operational limit. Despite three meetings of the Council,[1] no agreement proved possible on a revision of the intervention price range.

838.   The second meeting[2] of the International Tropical Timber Council, which took place in March at the Organization's new headquarters in Yokohama, Japan, concluded with the adoption of an indicative work programme for 1987-88.[3] This concerned the start-up of three 'pre-projects' or studies concerning market information, the forestry industry, and reafforestation and forestry management, which were approved at the Council's third meeting in November.[4] They will be part-financed by voluntary contributions from various countries signatory to the Agreement.

839.   The fourth negotiating session for a second International Natural Rubber Agreement[5] ended with agreement on a text approved by all the participants. The new Agreement provides in particular for automatic readjustment of price ranges on the basis of market trends.[6] Pending the completion of the signing and ratification procedures, the Council set up under the first Agreement[7] authorized the buffer stock manager to sell off stocks as required in order to finance administrative expenditure during the interim period.

840.   The sixth International Tin Agreement,[8] which was due to expire on 30 June, was extended for two years so as not to impede the legal proceedings brought by bankers and brokers following the international crisis into which the tin market was plunged in 1985[9] and which has led to the cessation of payements under the Agreement. As a result, the setting-up of an international study group on tin has been adjourned.[10]

---

1   Bull. EC 7/8-1987, point 2.2.42; Bull. EC 9-1987, point 2.2.29; Bull. EC 12-1987.
2   Twentieth General Report, point 920.
3   Bull. EC 4-1987, point 2.2.30.
4   Bull. EC 11-1987, point 2.2.43.
5   Twentieth General Report, point 921.
6   Bull. EC 9-1987, point 2.2.31.
7   Thirteenth General Report, point 513.
8   Fifteenth General Report, point 669; OJ L 342, 3.12.1982; Sixteenth General Report, point 745.
9   Nineteenth General Report, point 923.
10   Twentieth General Report, point 922.

841. At the meeting of the Inernational Coffee Council held in London from 21 September to 5 October[1] it was agreed to reintroduce the system of export quotas (suspended since 18 February 1986) from 6 October.[2]

On 30 September the Community lodged with the United Nations the instruments of conclusion of the 1983 Agreement.[3] The Council had adopted, on a proposal from the Commission,[4] a Decision on the conclusion of the Agreement on behalf of the Community and a Regulation on the application of the system of certificates of origin.[5] On 6 October the Commission adopted a Regulation establishing the date of implementation in the Community of this system.[6]

842. The United Nations conference on sugar, which took place on 10 and 11 September,[7] concluded negotiations on a new International Sugar Agreement;[8] the new Agreement is essentially administrative but will permit the International Sugar Organization to extend the scope of its statistical activities and studies to cover all types of sweeteners. The Commission therefore transmitted to the Council a proposal for a Decision on the signing and conclusion of this Agreement on 25 November.[9]

Campaign to combat AIDS

843. In July the Commission, following the conclusions adopted earlier by the Council,[10] approved the financing of a programme to combat AIDS in the ACP countries.[11] The programme, which will last for three years and have a budget of 35 million ECU, will help to strengthen the public health services of the recipient countries and provide technical, financial and scientific assistance to those countries which are implementing national AIDS control programmes; it will also promote coordination, at Community level, of bilateral aid operations. The programme is intended to provide an identifiable Community contribution to international AIDS control efforts directed and coordinated by the WHO special programme on AIDS.

---

[1]   Bull. EC 10-1987, point 2.2.44.
[2]   Bull. EC 6-1987, point 2.2.40; Bull. EC 10-1987, point 2.2.44.
[3]   Seventeenth General Report, point 732.
[4]   Bull. EC 6-1987, point 2.2.41.
[5]   OJ L 276, 29.9.1987; Bull. EC 9-1987, point 2.2.28.
[6]   OJ L 284, 7.10.1987; Bull. EC 10-1987, point 2.2.45.
[7]   Bull. EC 9-1987, point 2.2.30.
[8]   OJ L 22, 25.1.1985; Eighteenth General Report, point 721.
[9]   Bull. EC 11-1087, point 2.2.45.
[10] Bull. EC 5-1987, point 2.2.26.
[11] Bull. EC 7/8-1987, point 2.2.51.

Food aid

844.   Under the new framework Regulation of 22 December 1986 [1] the Commission was given powers to determine — on the basis of the funds approved by the budgetary authority — the overall quantities of food aid and the list of products concerned. Accordingly, the Commission decided on 10 March to grant the following aid: [2] cereals — an initial instalment of 927 700 tonnes and a second instalment of up to 232 300 tonnes; milk powder — a maximum of 94 100 tonnes; butteroil — a maximum of 27 300 tonnes; sugar — a maximum of 11 000 tonnes; vegetable oil (seed oil and olive oil) — a maximum of 34 000 tonnes; and, for other products, quantities corresponding to not more than 279 600 tonnes of cereal equivalent. In addition, a special food-aid reserve corresponding to not more than 160 600 tonnes of cereal equivalent was set up to cater for exceptional needs.

845.   The new framework Regulation also makes the Commission responsible for the execution of food-aid purchasing and transport operations. The Commission therefore adopted on 8 July a Regulation laying down general rules for the mobilization in the Community of products to be supplied as Community food aid. [3] In contrast to the situation existing under the previous arrangements, [4] the new rules give the Commission responsibility for supervising all food-aid mobilization and delivery operations up to and including the handing-over stage in the recipient country. In addition, the successful tenderer will in future have to assume responsibility up to the place of delivery specified in the agreement with the recipient country. Lastly, the Regulation provides for monitoring of food-aid operations from start to finish by undertakings duly authorized by the Commission.

On 26 November the Commission sent to the Council a revised version [5] of its original proposal to amend the Regulation of 22 December 1986. [6] The proposal incorporates some amendments suggested by Parliament [7] and is designed to alter the provisions of the Regulation to take account of the new procedures laid down by the Council on 13 July concerning the different types of committee that may assist the Commission in the exercise of its powers. [8]

---

1   OJ L 370, 30.12.1986; Twentieth General Report, point 934.
2   OJ L 80, 24.3.1987; Bull. EC 3-1987, point 2.2.28.
3   OJ L 204, 25.7.1987; Bull. EC 7/8-1987, point 2.2.45.
4   OJ L 352, 14.12.1982; Sixteenth General Report, point 728.
5   Bull. EC 11-1987, point 2.2.47.
6   OJ C 309, 19.11.1987; Bull. EC 10-1987, point 2.2.46.
7   OJ C 345, 21.12.1987; Bull. EC 11-1987, point 2.2.46.
8   Point 4 of this Report.

846.   By integrating food aid into the development policies of the countries concerned, the 1986 Regulation creates greater scope for triangular operations. It also authorizes operations where products are purchased and allocated within the same country, as long as they are used to assist specific population groups (e.g. refugees).

Standard food-aid programme

847.   A sizeable proportion of the aid decided upon by the Commission [1] under the Regulation of 22 December 1986 is allocated to individual countries (direct aid) or to international and non-governmental organizations (indirect aid), the remainder being set aside for emergency operations. The breakdown of food-aid allocations in 1987 at 31 December is given in the table below.

848.   Good harvests in Africa enabled the Commission to approve alternative operations in place of food-aid deliveries, notably for Chad, Mali and Senegal. These countries were given the financial counterpart of the aid that they would normally have received. Details of this financial aid, totalling 5.128 million ECU (equivalent to 45 000 tonnes of cereals) are given in the table; the aid is intended to develop the agricultural and food production potential of the countries concerned, contribute to their food security and so enable them to improve their food self-sufficiency. Further aid to the value of 3 070 million ECU (equivalent to 20 000 tonnes of cereals) was granted under the 1986 programme.

	Cereals	Milk powder	Butteroil	Vegetable oil	Sugar	Other products	Alternative operations
	(tonnes)					(million ECU)	
Africa	382 100	5 980	1 296	6 150	2 200	5 500	5 128
Indian and Pacific Oceans	27 000	600	180	100	100	—	—
Caribbean	1 480	950	200	—	—	—	—
Mediterranean	200 000	6 600	2 700	—	—	—	—
Latin America	29 220	6 100	800	3 150	—	2 900	—
Asia	215 000	21 070	10 800	11 000	—	—	—
Total direct aid	854 800	41 300	15 976	20 500	2 300	8 400	5 128
Total indirect aid	360 800	50 890	8 625	11 080	8 700	19 500	—
Grand total	1 215 600	92 190	24 601	31 580	11 000	27 900	5 128

---

[1]   Point 844 of this Report.

In spite of the good harvests, the Commission nevertheless had to draw from the special reserve set aside for exceptional shortages a total quantity of 160 000 tonnes of cereal equivalent, to top up the aid already given to Ethiopia, Mozambique, Angola and Bangladesh.

Emergency food aid

849.   The definition of emergency food aid and the rules for its implementation were laid down in the framework Council Regulation of 1986;[1] its allocation at 31 December was as follows:

Ethiopia (via RRC[2] and NGOs)	60 000 tonnes cereals equivalent
Bangladesh	25 000 tonnes cereals equivalent
Laos	20 000 tonnes cereals equivalent
Malawi	13 000 tonnes cereals equivalent
Niger	5 000 tonnes cereals equivalent
Uganda	5 000 tonnes cereals equivalent
Kampuchea (WFP/Trocaire)	14 000 tonnes cereals equivalent
ICRC (Ethiopia)	1 500 tonnes vegetable oil
	1.2 million ECU to buy legumes

Emergency aid

850.   During the year the Commission decided on emergency aid operations totalling 44 058 300 ECU for disaster victims in the developing countries and other non-Community countries. This sum consists of 22 573 000 ECU from the European Development Fund for 30 ACP States and 21 485 300 ECU from the 1987 Community budget which was used to finance emergency aid operations in 18 non-associated countries and one ACP State (Ethiopia).

Substantial emergency aid was allocated from the European Development Fund for victims of drought and the civil war in Mozambique (5 650 000 ECU) and in Ethiopia (5 000 000 ECU) — the latter also received 5 million ECU under Article 950 of the budget — the conflicts in Angola (1 200 000 ECU), Sudan (650 000 ECU), Suriname (340 000 ECU) and Uganda (200 000 ECU), the

---

[1]   Point 844 of this Report.
[2]   Relief and Rehabilitation Commission.

cyclones in Vanuatu (460 000 ECU) and Fiji (300 000 ECU) and torrential rains and flooding in Benin (250 000 ECU) and Jamaica (180 000 ECU). Emergency medical programmes were also financed in Uganda (350 000 ECU) and Burundi (180 000 ECU) in order to stem the spread of AIDS and halt epidemics such as yellow fever in Mali (165 000 ECU), Mauritania (100 000 ECU) and Guinea (85 000 ECU).

During the year the Commission continued [1] its support for the international campaign against locusts and grasshoppers in Africa by providing pesticides, spraying equipment and financing technical assistance and supplying small planes for spraying. [2] It adopted a number of emergency aid decisions covering a total of 3 970 000 ECU for this campaign, this sum being in addition to the residue of 1 301 200 ECU from the rehabilitation and recovery plan and the 603 300 ECU committed in 1986 but allocated this year, so making a total of 5 874 500 ECU.

851.   Decisions covering a total of 21 485 300 ECU were also taken to assist people stricken by disaster in other developing countries including Ethiopia, for example the victims of drought (India: 5 000 000 ECU) and civil conflict (Lebanon: 5 060 300 ECU). Emergency operations were also decided on following torrential rainfall and flooding in Bangladesh (500 000 ECU), Chile (250 000 ECU), Vietnam (200 000 ECU), South Africa (200 000 ECU) and Peru (150 000 ECU), an earthquake in Ecuador [3] (500 000 ECU) and a massive fire in China [4] (500 000 ECU), a shortage of medicines in Poland (2 000 000 ECU), a typhoon in the Philippines (500 000 ECU) and an invasion of locusts in Morocco (670 000 ECU). Ethiopia, hard hit by drought, was given further aid of 5 million ECU. [5]

Emergency aid funds were used to provide food, medical equipment and assistance, clothing, shelter, seeds and transport. The funds were administered by the governments concerned, specialized international and non-governmental organizations and the Commission.

---

1   Twentieth General Report, point 935.
2   Bull. EC 2-1987, point 2.2.29; Bull. EC 7/8-1987, point 2.2.47.
3   Bull. EC 3-1987, point 2.2.32.
4   Bull. EC 5-1987, point 2.2.33.
5   Bull. EC 11-1987, point 2.2.50.

Industrial cooperation with non-associated developing countries

852. On 22 June the Council adopted conclusions, based on a communication from the Commission, aimed at strengthening industrial cooperation between the Community and the countries of Latin America, Asia, the Gulf and the Mediterranean. [1]

Financial and technical cooperation with non-associated developing countries in Latin America and Asia

853. Of the funds available under the 1987 programme of aid to non-associated developing countries in Latin America and Asia (a budget of 174.8 million ECU less overheads), 75% was allocated for Asia and 25% for Latin America. Including the carryover from the previous budget, [2] total funds available for the 1987 programme amount to 361.5 million ECU. In all, the programme should cover about 30 projects of direct benefit to 16 developing countries and three regional organizations. The funds may be committed in 1987 and 1988.

As in previous years, [2] agricultural production in the broad sense or projects connected with agriculture (research, protection and conservation of crops) have been the main beneficiaries.

On 11 November the Commission transmitted to the Council and Parliament the guidelines for 1988 [3] and on 3 December presented the report on the implementation of the 1986 programme. [4]

Cooperation through non-governmental organizations

854. The funds earmarked for development cooperation through NGOs amounted to 52 million ECU for the year. The whole amount had been committed by September, and an additional appropriation of 10 million ECU was requested and granted. At 31 December 56.6 million ECU had been committed for the co-financing of 423 development projects in 99 countries in Africa, Asia and Latin America.

---

[1]   Point 781 of this Report.
[2]   Twentieth General Report, point 937.
[3]   OJ C 323, 3.12.1987; Bull. EC 11-1987, point 2.2.56.
[4]   Bull. EC 11-1987, point 2.2.57.

Furthermore, at the end of the year a total of 5.7 million ECU had been set aside for operations aimed at making European public opinion more aware of development issues. The funds available under budget Article 992, created in 1986, [1] for the people of Chile (2 million ECU) were also fully committed during the year.

This year block grants reached their highest level since operations began. Fifty-nine such grants were made, for a total of 6.8 million ECU, enabling 822 mini-operations to be carried out.

---

1   Twentieth General Report, point 938.

Section 7

Relations with the African, Caribbean and Pacific countries and the overseas countries and territories

Implementation of the ACP-EEC Convention

855. As the third Lomé Convention[1] entered its second year,[2] the ACP-EEC Council of Ministers, meeting in Brussels on 14 and 15 May,[3] reached agreement on a protocol concerning the accession to the Convention of Spain and Portugal.[4] The protocol allows them a seven-year transitional period during which they will accord industrial and agricultural goods, including tropical products, from the ACP States the same treatment as those from the Ten. The Council also decided to apply the protocol from 1 July, pending its ratification.[4]

856. Financial and technical cooperation activities continued throughout the year.[5] Following the successful drafting of indicative programmes and simultaneous completion of the regional programming exercise,[6] the commitment rate picked up. Individual projects are gradually being replaced by major sectoral or broad-based 'thematic' operations.

857. The Lomé Convention is one channel for the Community's concern for the countries of sub-Saharan Africa, reflected in a Commission communication to the Council, plus a proposal for a decision, calling for a special programme to help a number of highly indebted low-income countries in the region which are engaged in serious attempts to restructure their economies.[7] This initiative is a follow-up to the Western Economic Summit at Venice in June,[8] whose conclusions on development reflected the views of the Community's representatives. The communication calls on Member States to take coordinated action to relieve these countries' debt burden and make available new, quick-disbursing resources. On 9 November the Council approved a Commission proposal that

---

[1]   Nineteenth General Report, point 942.
[2]   Twentieth General Report, point 939.
[3]   Bull. EC 5-1987, point 2.2.38.
[4]   OJ L 172, 30.6.1987; Bull. EC 6-1987, point 2.2.37.
[5]   Twentieth General Report, points 940 and 955.
[6]   Twentieth General Report, point 941.
[7]   Bull. EC 9-1987, points 1.4.1 and 1.4.4.
[8]   Point 752 of this Report.

the Community itself should put in hand a 100 million ECU quick-disbursing programme to supplement Lomé III, using the 40 million ECU left over from the earlier Conventions, plus repayments by ACP States of special loans and risk capital obtained from the EDF. [1]

Trade cooperation

858.   The Spanish/Portuguese accession protocol [2] allows access for certain ACP fruit and vegetables on terms more generous than those specified in the Convention itself. [3]

859.   The Commission continued [4] to provide ACP States and OCTs with financial assistance for trade promotion, including 2 030 000 ECU from the sixth EDF for measures to enable them to participate effectively in international trade fairs and follow up earlier successful promotional activities. The Commission also provided technical and financial support for a trade conference in Harare, Zimbabwe, the first event of this type ever held in an ACP State.

Stabex

860.   The Commission received 70 applications for transfers under Stabex, the export earnings stabilization scheme which continues under Lomé III, in respect of the trading year 1986. Under the Stabex rules laid down in the Convention, 28 of the applications were held inadmissible; the remaining 42 were processed and gave rise to transfers totalling 278 451 554 ECU.

The breakdown of the transfers by recipient country is shown in Table 18.

861.   On 9 February the Council adopted two Regulations, one establishing a system of compensation for loss of export earnings for least-developed countries not signatory to the Lomé Convention and the other laying down implementing rules for the system. [5] Three of the intended beneficiaries submitted a total of eight transfer applications for the first year.

---

1   Bull. EC 11-1987, point 2.2.36.
2   Nineteenth General Report, points 728, 729 and 737.
3   Point 855 of this Report.
4   Twentieth General Report, point 945.
5   OJ L 43, 13.2.1987; Bull. EC 2-1987, point 2.2.32.

TABLE 18

	Product	Amount of transfer (ECU)
Benin	Oilcake	1 395 535
	Palm-kernel oil	3 589 471
Burkina Faso	Shea nuts	2 690 995
	Cotton	1 782 613
	Sesame seeds	364 879
Central African Republic	Cotton	1 681 896
Chad	Cotton	12 776 377
Comoros	Cloves	2 977 156
Côte d'Ivoire	Wood	44 954 653
Equatorial Guinea	Cocoa beans	1 079 795
Ethiopia	Beans	6 344 738
Gambia	Groundnuts	3 330 728
	Groundnut oil	1 328 737
Grenada	Cocoa beans	371 379
Guinea Bissau	Groundnuts	2 069 162
	Shrimps	388 231
Kiribati	Copra	1 639 090
Malawi	Tea	2 370 156
Mali	Cotton	14 180 528
Mauritius	Tea	2 950 299
Mozambique	Cashew nuts and kernels	1 065 009
	Copra	299 093
	Cotton	6 216 147
	Tea	3 627 855
Papua New Guinea	Copra	7 569 597
	Coconut oil	17 067 636
	Palm products	21 764 451
Rwanda	Tea	3 398 714
Samoa	Wood in the rough	122 513
	Copra	259 211
	Coconut oil	4 299 597
Senegal	Groundnut products	54 567 358
Solomon Islands	Copra	12 328 129
	Palm products	6 657 167
Sudan	Groundnuts	3 272 524
	Groundnut oil	8 114 018
	Sesame seeds	590 168
	Oilcake	5 519 522
Togo	Shea nuts	651 838
Tonga	Coconut oil	1 254 017
Tuvalu	Copra	102 407
Vanuatu	Copra	11 438 165
Total		278 451 554

Four of the applications were ruled inadmissible after appraisal; transfers payable [1] on the remaining four totalled 6 228 876 ECU, broken down as shown in the following table.

	Product	Amount of transfer (ECU)
Bangladesh	Jute	4 389 100
Nepal	Tea	1 228 004
	Hides and skins	232 759
Yemen Arab Republic	Coffee	379 013
	Total	6 228 876

Sysmin

862.   Two Sysmin applications were ruled admissible in 1987 — one submitted by Jamaica under Lomé II, in respect of bauxite/alumina, and the other by Mauritania under Lomé III, in respect of iron ore. [2]

In connection with the Liberian application accepted at the end of 1986, [3] approval was granted for a 49.3 million ECU scheme to rehabilitate an iron ore production unit. [4]

Prospecting and technical assistance operations for the mining sector financed out of programmable aid totalled 268 000 ECU.

Sugar Protocol

863.   On 19 January the Council adopted a Regulation concluding two Agreements, one with certain ACP States and one with India, in the form of exchanges of letters on the guaranteed prices for cane sugar for the 1986/87 delivery period. [5] The prices were set at 44.92 ECU/100 kg for unrefined sugar and 55.39 ECU/100 kg for white sugar.

On the administrative side the Commission, after consulting the ACP States, applied a Decision of 23 December 1985 reallocating an additional 5 000 tonnes

1   Bull. EC 7/8-1987, point 2.2.54.
2   Bull. EC 7/8-1987, point 2.2.55.
3   Twentieth General Report, point 950.
4   Bull. EC 11-1987, point 2.2.54.
5   OJ L 185, 4.7.1987; Bull. EC 1-1987, point 2.2.34.

of sugar, Kenya's agreed quantity having been reduced by that amount in accordance with Article 7(3) of the Protocol. [1]

Financial and technical cooperation

864. This year saw the completion of the programming exercise put in hand in 1986. [2] The first stage of the dialogue, involving the formulation of reciprocal undertakings proved most satisfactory. Stage two, the implementation of these undertakings, will be more demanding in terms of administrative costs and the need for skilful handling of coordination with other donors and improved awareness on the part of all those involved in cooperation activities. Financing operations are now increasingly concerned with large-scale structured programmes, [3] which include the provision of quick-disbursing aid for sectoral import programmes. As these bring an inflow of foreign exchange, they are particularly helpful for a number of ACP States in getting the development process under way again. [4]

The results to date are encouraging. Less that two years after the entry into force of Lomé III, 40% of the money available under the indicative programmes has already been committed, a significant improvement on the figure of 32% for the same stage of Lomé II. The bulk of this is Lomé III money, with 1 500 million ECU committed from the sixth EDF since the Convention's entry into force on 1 May 1986; commitments from the fifth EDF (Lomé II) are now tailing off.

Regional cooperation

865. Most of the year was taken up with the programming of regional cooperation appropriations. Negotiations were conducted with each ACP 'sub-region', either through a regional organization or with representatives of each of the countries concerned.

---

[1] OJ L 86, 31.3.1986; Nineteenth General Report, point 955.
[2] Twentieth General Report, point 940.
[3] Bull. EC 7/8-1987, point 2.2.58.
[4] For details of the special measures to help certain highly indebted low-income countries of sub-Saharan Africa, see point 857 of this Report.

TABLE 19

Lomé I, II and III financing decisions (EDF and EIB[1]) for ACP States, by sector, at 31 December

	Commitments								
	1981	1982	1983	1984	1985	1986	1987[2]	Total	
	million ECU							million ECU	%
Development of production	312.2	690.6	383.7	416.0	427.6	499.4	1 141.9	3 871.4	53.1
Industrialization	237.6	329.9	219.3	225.0	259.9	260.6	434.3	1 966.6	26.9
of which: energy	(86.7)	(84.7)	(116.1)	(76.2)	(72.4)	(78.6)	(30.6)	(545.3)	(7.5)
Sysmin		(95.0)		(3.0)	(30.8)	(91.0)	(49.3)	(269.1)	(3.7)
Tourism	0.2	5.6	11.6	0.8	3.5	0.2	2.4	23.9	0.3
Rural production	74.4	355.1	152.8	190.2	164.2	239.0	705.2	1 880.9	25.9
Economic infrastructure, transport and communications	84.8	112.1	251.1	151.4	129.4	131.7	425.7	1 286.2	17.6
Social development	117.5	117.4	127.0	101.7	100.1	94.9	159.9	818.5	11.3
Education and training	22.2	65.3	77.3	55.1	39.3	33.7	64.5	357.4	4.9
Health	7.5	11.0	17.0	18.0	22.5	20.8	53.7	150.5	2.1
Water engineering, urban infrastructure, housing	87.8	41.1	32.7	28.6	38.3	40.4	41.7	310.6	4.3
Trade promotion	8.4	9.4	7.1	15.9	7.1	9.5	21.5	78.9	1.1
Emergency aid	24.5	19.1	12.7	32.8	12.2	33.1	22.3	156.7	2.1
Stabex[2]	138.0	142.8	103.2	50.4	38.5	251.4	278.5	1 002.8	13.7
Other	10.7	3.3	7.6	6.1	10.6	25.5	19.3	83.1	1.1
Total	696.1	1 094.7	892.4	774.3	725.5	1 045.5	2 069.1	7 297.6	100.0

[1] For EIB operations, see the Bank's annual report.
[2] Estimates.

866.　As a result of the negotiations, it was agreed that in West Africa the Commission's main contribution would be in the fields of desertification control and transport. In central Africa the emphasis will be on transport and communications, rural development, and the exploitation of forestry and fishery resources. Operations in East Africa, a less homogeneous region, will be carried out on a pragmatic basis in the light of the priorities or of practical opportunities for joint action. Important areas of activity identified by the Commission through individual bilateral contacts are the transport corridor and control of desertification. Almost a third of the available finance was committed in 1987. In the case of southern Africa, approximately 48% of the allocation has been committed for transport and other projects under the Memorandum of Understanding signed by the Commission and the Southern Africa Development Coordination Conference in January 1986. [1] A similar memorandum concluded between the Commission and Caribbean regional organizations places the emphasis on tourism and trade (which together account for 35% of the allocation), transport and communications (30%) and agriculture and fisheries (20%). The large sums outstanding from the Lomé II regional cooperation budget covered commitments. The Commission has likewise reached agreement with the Indian Ocean Commission on a programme broadly centred on inter-island cooperation and the sea. With the aid of technical assistance supplied under Lomé II, preparations for the planned operations continued. As regards the ACP States of the Pacific subregion, the Commission and the South Pacific Bureau for Economic Cooperation (SPEC), in accordance with a protocol signed in March 1986, will be concentrating on natural resources and on transport and communications. [2] Agreement was reached on technical assistance for the SPEC to speed up the preparation of programmes.

Institutional relations

867.   Following a preparatory meeting of the ACP-EEC Committee of Ambassadors, the ACP-EEC Council of Ministers held its annual meeting in Brussels on 14 and 15 May, [3] when agreement was reached on the terms on which Spain and Portugal would accede to Lomé III. [4] Ministers discussed the situation in southern Africa, with the ACP side pressing the Community to isolate South Africa completely, notably by means of tougher sanctions, and calling for a ministerial meeting later in the year. The ACP States also called on the Community to play an active, positive role in international negotiations on commodities, particularly in connection with the coffee [5] and cocoa [6] agreements. The Community's assurances on this score were reflected in its position at the coffee negotiations in October. Also on the agenda in May were the Uruguay Round [7] and other trade issues, including the Commission's proposal for a tax on oils and fats, [8] and matters relating to the implementation of Lomé III.

---

1   Twentieth General Report, point 957.
2   Twentieth General Report, point 941.
3   Bull. EC 5-1987, point 2.2.38.
4   Point 855 of this Report.
5   Point 841 of this Report.
6   Point 837 of this Report.
7   Point 746 of this Report.
8   Points 546, 550 and 564 of this Report.

868.   The ACP-EEC Joint Assembly held two sessions, the first at Arusha, Tanzania, in February[1] and the second in Lisbon in September/October.[2] Proceedings were dominated by the finalization and adoption of the Assembly's annual general report, which this year dealt with regional cooperation between ACP States under the Lomé Convention. The Assembly adopted by a large majority a resolution on southern Africa calling for increased pressure on South Africa and an ACP-EEC ministerial conference on the subject. Resolutions were also adopted on ACP debt and commodities, two issues of importance to the ACP countries.

The working parties on rural development, women and population in the development process and the debt problems of ACP countries passed resolutions recommending guidelines for policies in those fields.[1] New working parties were set up to deal with commodities, refugees, technology and training, and health. The Joint Assembly also discussed the outcome of a fact-finding mission to the Netherlands and Suriname, and human rights issues.[2]

Overseas countries and territories

869.   Under the Council Decision of 30 June 1986 on the association of the overseas countries and territories (OCTs) with the Community,[3] work continued on the programming of EDF resources for the period 1986-90.

Allocations of 6.625 million ECU and 19.875 million ECU respectively from the sixth EDF went to Aruba and the Netherlands Antilles under indicative programmes, plus a further 4.1 million ECU to finance regional projects.

In the case of the British and French OCTs allocated a total of 10.5 million ECU and 26.5 million ECU respectively, programming took the form of apportionment of these sums between the numerous OCTs concerned in London and Paris; the results of this exercise were sent to the Commission, which could then proceed to discuss project identification jointly with the authorities of each individual OCT. In addition, 1.475 million ECU is available for British OCTs and 4.1 million ECU for French OCTs for regional projects.

Implementation of projects financed under earlier EDFs continued.

---

[1]   Bull. EC 2-1987, point 2.2.36.
[2]   Bull. EC 9-1987, point 2.2.41.
[3]   OJ L 175, 1.7.1986; Twentieth General Report, point 943.

870. Two OCTs submitted transfer applications under the export earnings stabilization scheme established by the Decision on the association of OCTs with the Community. Both were admissible, but the amounts involved were well in excess of the allocation for the 1986 application year, and the applications are therefore pending.

Section 8

International organizations and conferences

United Nations

Conference on Disarmament and Development

871.   The Community had observer status at the International Conference on the Relationship between Disarmament and Development held at UN headquarters in New York from 22 August to 11 September, in which all the Member States took part. [1] In the absence of the United States, the Community Member States acted as chief spokesmen for the developed world and contributed substantially to the establishment of the final consensus.

During the proceedings, the Community urged the importance of regional political and economic integration in the search for peace. The final document recognizes that disarmament and development are distinct processes and that the pursuit of development cannot wait for the release of resources from disarmament.

General Assembly

Forty-second session

872.   The 42nd session of the General Assembly, which opened on 22 September, [2] dealt with a wide range of topics. [3] The main political issues debated were East-West relations, the talks in Geneva on eliminating intermediate-range nuclear missiles, the Iran-Iraq war, the Central American peace plan [4] and the summoning of an international conference on peace in the Middle East. Other topics discussed were the problems of apartheid and Namibia, disarmament,

---

[1]   Bull. EC 9-1987, point 2.2.45.
[2]   Bull. EC 9-1987, point 2.2.44.
[3]   Bul. EC 11-1987, point 2.2.67.
[4]   Point 818 of this Report.

the convening of an international conference on terrorism, condemnation of the invasion of Afghanistan and the Western Sahara question.

In the economic sphere, resolutions were adopted [1] on the matters dealt with at Unctad VII,[2] notably debt and the preparation of the second conference on the least-developed countries, due to be held in 1990. The Assembly also considered the Secretary-General's report on the implementation of the United Nations programme of action for African economic recovery and development;[3] it adopted a resolution on the continuation of the programme and on the preparation of an interim report for the next session. A major debate was held on environmental issues: resolutions were adopted on a number of subjects, including the prospects for the year 2000 and beyond and also the Brundtland Commission report on development and the environment.[4] In contrast to last year,[5] the questions of the United Nations' financial crisis and its reorganization seemed to have been pushed into the background. Speaking on behalf of the Community, Mr Uffe Ellemann-Jensen, President of the Council, stressed the theme of inderdependence both in his references to the solutions needed for international political difficulties and in his remarks on economic matters.[6]

Economic and Social Council

873.   The Economic and Social Council held the first of the year's regular sessions in New York from 4 to 29 May.[7] The agenda included economic issues and a review of the organization's structure and activities. On economic matters, Ecosoc adopted reports from its Statistical Commission, Committee on Natural Resources, and Commission on Transnational Corporations. For the Community, the main subjects of interest among those discussed were racism, drugs, women's status (on all of which resolutions were adopted without a vote) and human rights.

874.   The second regular session was held in Geneva from 23 June to 9 July.[8] The UN Secretary-General addressed the session to appeal for greater coordination between the work of Ecosoc and the General Assembly. He also

1   Bull. EC 11-1987, point 2.2.67.
2   Point 823 of this Report.
3   Twentieth General Report, point 902.
4   Point 878 of this Report.
5   Twentieth General Report, point 963.
6   Bull. EC 9-1987, point 3.4.1.
7   Bull. EC 5-1987, point 2.2.41.
8   Bull. EC 6-1987, point 2.2.55.

called for an attempt to be made to strike a better balance between the requirements of monitoring the full range of social and economic activities and the urgent need to look more closely at priority issues. The main subject of the general debate was the world economic situation, with particular reference to its repercussions on Third World indebtedness. Both the Council Presidency and the Commission emphasized the importance of the matters dealt with at Unctad VII [1] and the new round of multilateral trade negotiations. [2]

Resolutions were adopted on the reverse transfer of resources from developing to developed countries, measures adopted by the United Nations and the operational activities of the UN system, the industrial development decade in Africa and agricultural and food questions, including the target for the World Food Programme, set at USD 1 400 million for 1989-90.

875.   At the final session, which was held on 1 October, [3] the Secretary-General of Unctad reported on Unctad VII and its results, which were regarded as encouraging for development, growth and international trade.

876.   At its 42nd annual session, held in Geneva from 31 March to 10 April, [4] the Economic Commission for Europe took a substantial number of decisions on environmental matters, transport, trade and energy. The decisions in these and other matters, relating more specifically to East-West cooperation, were taken in a working atmosphere that was much improved compared with previous years. It was also decided to set up an *ad hoc* committee to review the organization's structure and activities; the report presented by this committee was approved at the special session held on 9 and 10 November [5] before being submitted to the Special Commission of Ecosoc.

Convention on the Law of the Sea

877.   On 23 November the Commission sent the Council a communication [6] on deposit by the Member States of instruments of ratification of the Convention on the Law of the Sea. [7]

---

[1]   Point 823 of this Report.
[2]   Points 746 to 748 of this Report.
[3]   Bull. EC 10-1987, point 2.2.63.
[4]   Bull. EC 4-1987, point 2.2.44.
[5]   Bull. EC 11-1987, point 2.2.68.
[6]   Bull. EC 11-1987, point 2.2.69.
[7]   Eighteenth General Report, point 756.

United Nations Environment Programme

878.   The Community took part as an observer in the 14th session of the Governing Council of the United Nations Environment Programme in Nairobi, Kenya, from 8 to 10 June, [1] which adopted the report of the World Commission on Environment and Development [2] —regarded as a frame of reference for future action—and also the document on the prospects for the environment up to the year 2000 and beyond. The World Commission's report highlights the need to reorient policies towards sustainable development which meets the legitimate requirements of the world's present population without imperilling the environment for future generations.

Other decisions and resolutions were adopted in areas of vital interest to the Community: protection of the ozone layer, [3] international monitoring of chemicals and dangerous waste [4] and climatic change and the conservation of biological diversity. [5]

United Nations Educational, Scientific and Cultural Organization

879.   The two meetings of the Executive Board were devoted to continuation of the reform of Unesco [6] and the stabilization of its budget.

880.   The year was marked by the election of a new Director-General. After much debate, the 24th General Conference voted by a substantial majority for Mr Federico Mayor Zaragoza (Spain).

881.   The Commission was represented regularly at the numerous meetings of the 12 Member States' permanent representatives to Unesco and the meetings of the Western countries group, at which strategies for joint action on all specifically political matters were worked out.

---

[1]   Bull. EC 6-1987, point 2.1.137.
[2]   Bull. EC 5-1987, point 2.1.135.
[3]   Point 484 of this Report.
[4]   Points 512, 518 and 519 of this Report.
[5]   Point 516 of this Report.
[6]   Twentieth General Report, point 966.

International Monetary Fund and World Bank

882. The IMF and the World Bank held their annual meetings in Washington in October. Commission representatives took part in the proceedings and also attended the meetings of the Interim Committee of the IMF's Board of Governors in April and September.[1]

International Atomic Energy Agency

883. The negotiation of a trilateral safeguards agreement between Spain, Euratom and the IAEA,[2] undertaken in accordance with directives approved by the Council on 25 June 1986, lapsed following Spain's decision to sign the Non-Proliferation Treaty. By signing the Treaty, Spain will become a full party to the verification agreement of 5 April 1973.[3]

884. The Commission took part in the General Conference of the IAEA in Vienna from 21 to 25 September,[4] which marked the Agency's 30th anniversary. In discussions with the IAEA Director-General and representatives of a number of non-Community countries, the Commission delegation laid particular stress on the development of relations between Euratom and the IAEA.

885. The Commission took part in two meetings held under the auspices of the IAEA, in March and October, with delegations from the United States, Japan and the Soviet Union, to examine prospects for quadripartite collaboration in research on fusion for peaceful purposes, notably in connection with the preparation in 1990 of a pre-design for an international nuclear fusion reactor (ITER — International Thermonuclear Experimental Reactor).[5]

General Agreement on Tariffs and Trade

886. The pace of work on the initial phase of the new Uruguay Round of multilateral negotiations[6] was stepped up during the year.[7]

887. The 43rd session of the GATT Contracting Parties was held in Geneva from 1 to 3 December.[8] The Contracting Parties noted the real progress made

---

[1] Points 138 and 139 of this Report.
[2] Twentieth General Report, point 972.
[3] OJ L 51, 22.2.1978; Eleventh General Report, point 515.
[4] Bull. EC 9-1987, point 2.1.193.
[5] Point 336 of this Report.
[6] Twentieth General Report, point 974.
[7] Points 746 to 748 of this Report.
[8] Bull. EC 12-1987.

in the first year of the Uruguay Round and also called for greater collaboration in the face of the worsening economic climate.

888.   The Committee on Trade and Development continued its examination of the application of Part IV of the General Agreement. [1] It also devoted part of its time to considering the latest Uruguay Round developments and their implications for the developing countries.

889.   In February the Committee on Government Procurement adopted a Protocol [2] embodying a string of improvements to the Agreement on Government Procurement. [3] The changes are the result of over three years of negotiations between the signatories on the basis of Article IX.6 of the Agreement and should enter into force at the start of 1988. On 16 November the Council, acting on a Commission proposal, [4] adopted a Decision concerning the conclusion of the Protocol amending the GATT Agreement on Government Procurement. [5]

890.   The disputes settlement procedures under Article XXIII.2 were brought into action on a number of occasions. The GATT Council adopted the report of the panel which looked into the Community's complaint that the tax imposed on oil imports by the United States [6] was incompatible with the General Agreement. It also received from the panel set up to examine the Community's complaint against Japan's taxation of alcoholic beverages [7] a report accepting the Community's line of argument and confirming the discriminatory nature of the arrangements and their incompatibility with the General Agreement. [8] In addition, the Council set up at the Community's request two more panels to examine complaints against the United States concerning the customs user fee [9] and the application of Section 337 of the US Tariff Act.

891.   The Committee on Subsidies and Countervailing Duties[10] continued with its normal work programme (examination of national legislation and other measures adopted by signatories, notification of subsidies, and so on). A panel

---

1   Twentieth General Report, point 976.
2   Bull. EC 2-1987, point 2.2.41.
3   OJ L 185, 16.8.1971; OJ L 13, 15.1.1977; Fourteenth General Report, point 557.
4   Bull. EC 7/8-1987, point 2.2.65.
5   OJ L 345, 9.12.1987; Bull. EC 11-1987, point 2.2.71.
6   Bull. EC 2-1987, point 2.2.40.
7   Bull. EC 2-1987, point 2.2.65.
8   Point 765 of this Report.
9   Bull. EC 3-1987, point 2.2.45.
10   Twentieth General Report, point 979.

settled the dispute arising out of a complaint by the Community concerning Canada's imposition of countervailing duties on beef and veal, concluding that Canada had failed in its obligations under the Agreement on Subsidies and Countervailing Duties.

892.   The work on Morocco's accession [1] ended on 17 June when Morocco became a Contracting Party to the General Agreement. [2] The Community also participated in three working parties concerned with the accession of China, Costa Rica and Tunisia.

893.   The work begun last year [3] under Article XXIV.5 to examine the overall effects of the Community's latest enlargement continued. A four-year agreement concluded on 30 January put an end to a dispute that had been dragging on with the United States. [4] The other negotiations initiated under Article XXIV.6 of the General Agreement reached a new stage and resulted in agreement with Argentina. The negotiations with Canada were suspended pending arbitration on a point of fact.

Organization for Economic Cooperation and Development

894.   The position adopted by the Community in the OECD was one of firm support for a policy of cooperation aimed at improving conditions for economic growth, resisting protectionist trends and reducing the imbalances which are at present the dominant feature of agricultural markets.

895.   The annual ministerial meeting of the OECD Council took place on 12 and 13 May. [5] It reviewed the economic and social situation in the member countries and also problems related to agriculture. On the first point, ministers agreed to make full use of opportunities for international cooperation as regards both macroeconomic and structural adjustment policies.

On the second, the meeting reached unprecedented agreement on joint action. Ministers recognized that excessive support policies had to bear most of the responsibility for the structural imbalance existing on most agricultural markets; they were agreed that it was essential to effect a concerted reform of

---

[1]   Twentieth General Report, point 982.
[2]   OJ L 10, 14.1.1988; Bull. EC 4-1987, point 2.2.45.
[3]   Twentieth General Report, point 983.
[4]   Point 754 of this Report.
[5]   Bull. 5-1987, point 2.2.42.

agricultural policies through a progressive and coordinated reduction of support and protection.

Ministers also approved the publication of an OECD report on national policies and agricultural trade.

896. On trade, the member countries expressed their determination to resist protectionist pressures and work for progress in the Uruguay Round. [1]

897. Work relating to the developing countries was aimed at increasing cooperation in dealing with the debt problem and exploring new approaches to providing finance for the poorest countries.

In March the participants in the OECD 'Consensus' reached agreement on tied-aid credits. [2]

898. The third high-level meeting of the Working Party on Chemical Products was held on 17 and 18 March. [3] It was decided that international cooperation should be stepped up to prevent industrial accidents.

899. A ministerial meeting of the Committee for Scientific and Technological Policy was held on 28 and 29 October to consider how science and technology could contribute more to economic growth and social development. Mr Narjes, Vice-President of the Commission, laid particular emphasis on the importance of support for fundamental research, the need to strengthen the scientific and technological basis of industry and the key role of free dissemination worldwide of knowledge resulting from fundamental research.

International Energy Agency

900. At a ministerial-level meeting of the Governing Board of the International Energy Agency held in Paris on 11 May, [4] at which the Commission was represented, the general conclusion was that security of supply remained a concern for the IEA countries.

---

[1] Points 746 to 748 of this Report.
[2] Point 731 of this Report.
[3] Bull. EC 3-1987, point 2.1.136.
[4] Bull. EC 5-1987, point 2.1.206.

Conference on Security and Cooperation in Europe

901. The second negotiating phase[1] of the third follow-up meeting of the Conference on Security and Cooperation in Europe opened in Vienna on 27 January.[2] A total of 151 new proposals[3] were presented with a view to developing cooperation and security in Europe on the basis of the provisions of the Helsinki Final Act[4] and the Madrid concluding document.[5] The proposals concern security and human rights (Basket I), economic cooperation (Basket II) and the Mediterranean and cooperation in human contacts (Basket III).[6] The tone of the proposals was more constructive than at the preceding Madrid meeting.

The participating States examined the proposals carefully at the third negotiating phase from 9 May to 31 July.[7] The Soviet Union and the Eastern European countries emphasized the security aspects and showed a preference for contacts at expert level after the Vienna meeting. The Community and the Member States insisted on the importance of the human dimension and sought to have specific commitments written into the Vienna concluding document.

The agreed deadline for ending the Vienna meeting — 31 July — having been missed, a fourth phase began on 22 September and ended on 18 December.[8] However, it did not result in agreement. During this phase the Community argued in favour of speedy action on the environment, greater transparency of general economic data and a reduction in the role of countertrade.

Council of Europe

902. On 16 June the President of the Commission and the Secretary-General of the Council of Europe exchanged letters with the aim of fostering closer cooperation between the two organizations.[9] The purpose of the arrangements agreed is to encourage the participation of the Community, represented by the Commission, in the Council of Europe's work.

---

1 Twentieth General Report, point 988.
2 Bull. EC 1-1987, point 2.2.42.
3 Bull. EC 4-1987, point 2.2.46.
4 Ninth General Report, points 510 to 512.
5 Seventeenth General Report, point 778.
6 Bull. EC 2-1987, point 2.2.44.
7 Bull. EC 5-1987, point 2.2.46; Bull. EC 7/8-1987, point 2.2.67.
8 Bull. EC 9-1987, point 2.2.47; Bull. EC 11-1987, point 2.2.72.
9 OJ L 273, 26.9.1987; Bull. EC 6-1987, point 2.2.56.

903. The activities of the Council of Europe, which comprises the 21 democratic countries of Europe — including all the Community Member States — relate mainly to projects for European cooperation between now and the end of the century and involve both the Parliamentary Assembly [1] and the Committee of Ministers.

904. On 10 February the Community signed the European Convention for the Protection of Vertebrate Animals used for Experimental and Other Scientific Purposes, [2] and on 30 March it became a contracting party to three Agreements in the public health field. [3]

Discussions on the Community's accession to other conventions continued. [4] Cooperation between the two organizations also took the form of joint projects such as the organization of a campaign for rural areas in connection with the European Year of the Environment (1987), European Cinema and Television Year (1988) and a public campaign on North-South interdependence.

905. The Commission was invited to attend the first ministerial meeting on the open partial Agreement on the prevention of, protection against, and organization of relief in major natural and technological disasters, which was held in Athens on 22 and 23 September on the initiative of the Council of Europe. [5] This Agreement opens the possibility of cooperation in the sphere of civil protection with European countries which are not members of the Community. [6]

906. At its autumn session from 1 to 8 October, [7] the Parliamentary Assembly discussed nuclear accidents, scientific and technological cooperation in Europe and political cooperation between Europe and Africa. It also heard statements from Mr Jean-Claude Paye, Secretary-General of the OECD, on the latter's activities, and from Mrs Anita Gradin, the Swedish Minister for External Trade and Chairman of the EFTA Council, on the development of cooperation between the EFTA countries and the Community. In the light of this and in view of the projected completion of the single internal market by 1992, the Assembly called for rationalization of the institutional framework for the construction of Europe in the coming years in order to avoid the weakening

---

[1] Bull. EC 2-1987, point 2.2.43; Bull. EC 5-1987, point 2.2.44.
[2] Bull. EC 2-1987, point 2.1.94.
[3] Bull. EC 3-1987, point 2.1.63.
[4] Twentieth General Report, point 989.
[5] Bull. EC 9-1987, point 2.2.46.
[6] Point 154 of this Report.
[7] Bull. EC 10-1987, point 2.2.64.

of economic ties between the Community Member States and the other countries of the Council of Europe.

907.   Progress made in cooperation between the Council of Europe and the Commission was examined at the annual talks [1] between the Secretary-General of the Commission, Mr Emile Noël, and the Council of Europe ministers' deputies in Strasbourg on 22 June. [2]

---

[1]   Twentieth General Report, point 991.
[2]   Bull. EC 6-1987, point 2.2.57.

Section 9

European political cooperation

908.   The entry into force of the Single European Act on 1 July provided a legal framework for European political cooperation, which is now governed by the provisions of Title III of the Act in addition to the previously existing texts and practices. [1]

909.   Political cooperation activities during the year were centred on four major issues in the field of international relations: the Middle East, East-West relations, Central America and southern Africa.

910.   The Iran-Iraq conflict loomed increasingly large in discussions on the Middle East. On several occasions the Twelve expressed great disquiet about developments in the fighting. On 26 January they called on both parties to cease hostilities. [2] On 27 May Ministers strongly condemned the use of chemical weapons in Iran and Iraq. [3] In July [4] and again in September [5] the Twelve expressed whole-hearted support for the efforts of the United Nations to bring about a cease-fire and reiterated their firm support for the fundamental principle of freedom of navigation. The European Council, at its December meeting, deplored the continuing failure to find solutions to the problems of the Middle East. [6]

The lack of progress in finding a solution to the Arab-Israeli conflict was of continuing concern to the Twelve. In February they came out in favour of an international peace conference to be held under United Nations auspices. [7] In July they reiterated their commitment to respect for human rights in the occupied territories and agreed to continue supporting the economic and social development of those territories. [4] On 14 September the Foreign Ministers condemned Israel's settlement policy in the occupied territories. [8] In December the Twelve reaffirmed their position on the Arab-Israeli conflict. [6]

[1]   Supplement 2/86 — Bull. EC.
[2]   Bull. EC 1-1987, point 2.4.1.
[3]   Bull. EC 5-1987, point 2.4.1.
[4]   Bull. EC 7/8-1987, point 2.4.1.
[5]   Bull. EC 9-1987, point 2.4.1.
[6]   Bull. EC 12-1987.
[7]   Bull. EC 2-1987, point 2.4.3.
[8]   Bull. EC 9-1987, point 2.4.3.

911.   The Twelve discussed East-West relations on a number of occasions. On 13 July they welcomed the stepping-up of the dialogue between the United States and the Soviet Union on arms control. [1] They reaffirmed their commitment to the total elimination of chemical weapons and stressed the need for a stable and verifiable conventional balance with a lower level of forces in the whole of Europe. The Twelve expressed a strong desire to see the CSCE follow-up meeting in Vienna achieve concrete results. They also expressed interest in the new possibilities opened up by the recent developments in the Soviet Union. The December European Council noted with satisfaction the improved outlook for better East-West relations. [2] The Twelve hoped for a speedy implementation of the INF agreement. They reiterated their support for the CSCE and desire for a satisfactory outcome to the Vienna meeting.

The Twelve reaffirmed their position that a rapid withdrawal of Soviet troops from Afghanistan according to an irrevocable timetable remained an essential precondition for bringing the long conflict to an end. They called for a political solution guaranteeing the Afghan people's right to self-determination and condemned attacks on civilian targets in Pakistan. [3] The Twelve repeated this call to the Soviet Union in December and also stated that the participation of the Afghan resistance was indispensable for any overall political settlement. [2]

912.   The Twelve continued to follow developments in Central America closely. The third ministerial conference of the Community and its Member States, the Central American countries and the Contadora group was held on 9 and 10 February in Guatemala City. [4] On 13 August the Twelve warmly welcomed the agreement on a peace plan reached at the Guatemala Summit on 7 and 8 August between the five Central American Presidents in response to the President of Costa Rica's peace initiative. [1] On 23 November the Twelve called on the Central American countries to continue their efforts to advance the peace process. [5]

913.   The situation in southern Africa continued to cause concern. On 28 April the Twelve condemned South Africa's military action on Zambian territory on 25 April as a serious threat to peace and stability in the region. [6] On 25 May the Foreign Ministers expressed their concern over the serious risk of a further

---

[1]   Bull. EC 7/8-1987, point 2.4.1.
[2]   Bull. EC 12-1987.
[3]   Bull. EC 3-1987, point 2.4.1; Bull. EC 7/8-1987, point 2.4.1.
[4]   Point 816 of this Report.
[5]   Bull. EC 11-1987, point 2.4.2.
[6]   Bull. EC 4-1987, point 2.4.4.

polarization of attitudes following the elections in South Africa on 6 May.[1] Ministers reaffirmed the need for the total dismantling of apartheid and its replacement by a genuinely democratic, non-racial system of government. The Twelve urged President Botha to take the steps necessary to allow a national dialogue to begin and underlined their intention of supporting those within South Africa in favour of peaceful change and assisting neighbouring countries. On 3 June the Twelve strongly condemned the military action in Maputo, Mozambique, on 28 May,[2] and on 23 November they strongly condemned South African military activity in Angola.[3]

914.   On 13 November the Twelve condemned the attack on a United Nations convoy in Ethiopia.[4]

915.   The Twelve discussed the situation in Sri Lanka a number of times.[5]

916.   On 4 February they welcomed the outcome of the recent referendum in the Philippines and expressed complete confidence in President Corazon Aquino.[6] On 28 August they reiterated their support for the President and condemned the recent attempt by the military to overthrow her.[7]

917.   On 9 October[8] and 23 November[3] the Twelve appealed for free elections in Chile and Haiti respectively.

918.   The Ministers for Justice of the Member States met in conference on 25 May.[9] Three international instruments were opened for signature: an Agreement on the application of the Council of Europe Convention on the Transfer of Sentenced Persons, a Convention on Double Jeopardy and a Convention abolishing the Legalization of Documents.

Other intergovernmental cooperation

919.   The Ministers for Justice and for the Interior met in Brussels on 28 April[10] and in Copenhagen on 9 December,[11] first as Ministers with responsibility for immigration, drugs and counter-terrorism and then as the Trevi Group.

---

[1]   Bull. EC 5-1987, point 2.4.1.
[2]   Bull. EC 6-1987, point 2.4.1.
[3]   Bull. EC 11-1987, point 2.4.2.
[4]   Bull. EC 11-1987, point 2.4.1.
[5]   Bull. EC 4-1987, point 2.4.3; Bull. EC 6-1987, point 2.4.2.
[6]   Bull. EC 2-1987, point 2.4.1.
[7]   Bull. EC 7/8-1987, point 2.4.4.
[8]   Bull. EC 10-1987, point 2.4.1.
[9]   Bull. EC 5-1987, point 2.4.3 and points 3.4.1 to 3.4.3.
[10] Bull. EC 4-1987, point 2.4.6.
[11] Bull. EC 12-1987.

Chapter IV

Community law

Section 1

General matters

Powers

920. The Court's judgment in *Foto-Frost v HZA Lübeck-Ost* [1] has important implications for the system of judicial remedies established by the EEC Treaty. The Court interpreted Article 177 of the Treaty extensively, to mean that any court, whether or not there is a domestic judicial remedy against its decision, must refer a question to the Court of Justice if it considers that an act of a Community institution is invalid. The Court did, however, expressly confirm its previous finding that Article 177 does not require the courts of Member States to refer questions to it in the course of urgent proceedings for interim measures. That rule holds good where in the course of such proceedings a national court finds it has to decide on the validity of a Community act. In that very limited context, therefore, national courts have jurisdiction provisionally to declare a Community act invalid.

In reaching this conclusion the Court was drawing the logical consequences from its judgment in *Union Deutsche Lebensmittelwerke and Others v Commission,* [2] where it accepted a strict interpretation of Article 173 of the Treaty, which regulates the admissibility of actions brought by individuals. That approach would also act as a bar to applications for interim measures in certain situations; in the interests of proper judicial redress, therefore, the Court had to accept that national courts had power even to declare Community acts

---

[1] Case 314/85: OJ C 307, 17.11.1987.
[2] Case 97/85: OJ C 169, 26.6.1987; point 968 of this Report.

invalid where necessary, though only on a provisional basis. Clarification of the precise way in which this power is to be exercised will have to await further decisions by the Court.

921.   In *Deutsche Babcock Handel v HZA Lübeck-Ost*[1] the Court was asked whether Council Regulation No 1430/79 on the repayment or remission of import or export duties[2] applied directly to ECSC products even though it cited only Article 235 of the EEC Treaty as its legal basis.

The Court considered the fields of application of the EEC and ECSC Treaties, and concluded that the Regulation did apply directly. The EEC Treaty applied to all goods without qualification; the Court interpreted Article 232 of the EEC Treaty to mean that where a question was not covered by any provision of the ECSC Treaty or the secondary legislation adopted pursuant to it, the EEC Treaty and secondary EEC legislation applied to products within the scope of the ECSC Treaty, no specific legal act or interpretative statement being needed.

Human rights and fundamental rights

Human rights

922.   In 1987, as in previous years, respect for human rights and fundamental freedoms continued to be one of the bases of Community action.[3] In the exercise of their powers and in the pursuit of the Community's objectives, the institutions have taken steps contributing to the promotion of human rights both within the Community and in non-member countries.

Within the Community

923.   An important contribution to the promotion of fundamental economic and social rights is exemplified by the attention the Community has given to social questions. The reduction of inequalities and suffering are among the Community's major preoccupations, and with this objective in view it has given particular attention to those sections of the population most at risk. In the

---

[1]   Case 328/85.
[2]   OJ L 175, 12.7.1979; Thirteenth General Report, point 149.
[3]   Twentieth General Report, points 1003 and 1004.

context of Community action against poverty, [1] for instance, the Commission has given assistance towards projects for combating poverty in urban areas and impoverished rural areas and improving the situation of those in greatest need.

924.   The efforts undertaken to bring about a 'people's Europe' may be viewed in the same light, particularly those concerned with the elimination of physical frontiers within the Community, [2] the free movement of persons [3] and the general right of nationals of Member States to remain in the territory of another Member State. The Council continued its examination of the proposals for directives easing frontier checks and formalities. In application of Community law, the Commission took steps against certain Member States, initiated or continued proceedings for infringement of certain directives and examined complaints addressed to it.

925.   The Community has also studied the most serious health problems, particularly by contributing to medical research and to the prevention of cancer [4] and AIDS. [4] On the latter, it is collaborating with the WHO in promoting research and in action in developing countries. [5] As regards those suffering from this disease, the Community is seeking to preserve their freedom of movement and equality of treatment.

Conscious of the positive link between improvement in the quality of life and the promotion of fundamental rights, the Community has taken numerous steps which can be seen against the background of the European Year of the Environment [6] and which were aimed at encouraging an improvement in the background and conditions of life for European citizens, who are particularly threatened by the development of new technology and by industrial effluents, the sources of much pollution; in order to limit these effects the Commission reinforced the provisions of the Directive concerning the major-accident hazards of certain industrial activities. Moreover, the Commission has undertaken an information programme designed to show that the application of a high level of environmental standards can also have favourable effects on employment.

---

[1]   Point 426 of this Report.
[2]   Point 260 of this Report.
[3]   Point 262 of this Report.
[4]   Point 440 of this Report.
[5]   Point 843 of this Report.
[6]   Points 483 and 493 of this Report.

Relations with non-member countries

926.   In relations with non-member countries, particularly in the context of the Community's development policy, the Commission's approach has been essentially positive since it is concerned with people, who are at once the targets and the agents of the development process, and calls attention to the link between development and the promotion of human dignity in all its aspects. Real progress in developing countries cannot take place unless the value of the human person is fully respected.

The Commission continued its work for the development and economic and social welfare of people in the poorest countries. This policy is carried out by means of programmes of structural aid for development (particularly as regards the guarantee of food supplies),[1] humanitarian action to deal with immediate problems (particularly by means of food aid,[2] emergency disaster aid,[3] aid to refugees to enable them to survive and to re-establish a normal economic and social life[3]) and increasing support to European non-governmental organizations in developing countries.[4] Among the numerous humanitarian actions for refugees are major efforts to assist refugees from Mozambique and Afghanistan, support for the work of UNRWA for Palestinian refugees and positive measures of aid to the victims of apartheid in South Africa.

927.   As regards non-member countries the practice of the Community as a member of the international community is:

(i)   publicly to express its condemnation of violations of human rights;

(ii) to approach the countries concerned in flagrant cases;

(iii) to take steps in accordance with its international obligations to encourage respect for human rights in these countries.

In this context, European political cooperation plays a major role, on the basis in particular of the statement on human rights adopted on 21 July 1986 by the Foreign Ministers meeting in the framework of political cooperation and in the Council. The many steps taken most often remain confidential in order to preserve their effectiveness.

928.   Parliament played a very active role in the defence of human rights. The provisions of the Treaties concerning its powers of discussion and supervision

---

[1]   Points 844 to 846 of this Report.
[2]   Points 847 and 848 of this Report.
[3]   Point 850 of this Report.
[4]   Point 854 of this Report.

form the basis of its activities. These take several forms, such as the formulation of opinions on the Commission's proposals, reports on its own initiative on specific topics, and emergency resolutions. As regards human rights in non-member countries, Parliament's powers are shared between the Political Affairs Committee — more precisely the Subcommittee on Human Rights — and the Committee on Development and Cooperation; for internal matters, powers are delegated to the Committee on Legal Affairs and Citizens' Rights. There is also a Committee, set up in 1987, which devotes itself exclusively to examining petitions.

At its March part-session Parliament adopted its fourth annual report on human rights, [1] in which, having noted the persistence of numerous violations, it requests the Community institutions to intervene in the spheres appropriate to their powers. The topics that aroused its interest during the year include the situation of children and the right of asylum.

Judicial review and fulfilment by the Member States of their obligations

929.   The number of cases in which the infringement procedure laid down in Article 169 of the EEC Treaty was initiated rose once again in 1987, as it has done regularly for many years, apart from 1983, when there were fewer cases concerning transposition of directives. This year 572 letters of formal notice were sent to Member States, compared with 516 in 1986 and 503 in 1985.

There was a similar increase at the second stage of the procedure, where the Commission sent 197 reasoned opinions, as compared with 164 in 1985; but the number of infringements followed through to the third stage fell, with only 61 Court actions brought, as compared with 71.

This uneven movement is also seen in the removal from the Court register of 41 Cases, the Member States involved having complied with the Community legislation during the Court proceedings.

Of the 61 cases brought before the Court, 35 concerned the non-implementation or incorrect implementation of directives, and 11 concerned infringements of Articles 9, 30 or 95 of the EEC Treaty, the basic provisions relating to free movement of goods, an essential element in the functioning of the common market.

---

[1]   OJ C 99, 13.4.1987; Bull. EC 3-1987, point 2.4.10.

To take each country separately, the Commission brought proceedings before the Court against Italy on 21 occasions (14 concerning directives), against Greece on 11 (three concerning directives), against France on eight (five concerning directives), against Belgium on seven (five concerning directives), against the Netherlands on four (two concerning directives) against Ireland on three (one concerning a directive) and against Germany on two; against Luxembourg on two occasions, against the United Kingdom on two and against Spain on one (for these last three Member States all cases concerned directives).

The Court delivered 41 judgments in cases brought under Article 169, censuring Member States for failure to fulfil their obligations under Community law in 36 cases.

Fuller information on the application of the rules of the Treaty by Member States will be given in the fifth annual report to Parliament on Commission monitoring of the application of Community law.

930. Case 70/86 *Commission v Greece* [1] was concerned with Greece's compliance with Article 11 of Regulation No 2891/77. [2]

The Commission sought a declaration that Greece, by failing to pay over to the Commission financial contributions for the month of June 1983 on the proper date and subsequently refusing to pay the interest provided for by Article 11 of Regulation No 2891/77, had failed to fulfil its obligations under the EEC Treaty. Greece pleaded that the strike by employees of the Bank of Greece on 1 and 2 June amounted to *force majeure*.

The Commission, in its argument before the Court, accepted that *force majeure* could apply in such a case but maintained that the facts relied on did not amount to a case of *force majeure* since they were not outside the control of the Greek Government and were foreseeable.

The Advocate General in his Opinion took the view that a Member State cannot rely on *force majeure* in order to avoid its obligation to pay default interest under the provision in question. In the view of the Advocate General, these financial provisions form part of the basic rules of the Community's legal system, which must be strictly observed in order to ensure the effective functioning of the Community. He went on to conclude that the facts relied upon did not amount to a case of *force majeure*.

---

[1]   OJ C 274, 13.10.1987.
[2]   OJ L 336, 27.12.1977; Eleventh General Report, point 64.

The Court, upholding the Commission's argument, held that Greece had indeed failed to fulfil its obligations as alleged and that the strike relied on by the Greek Government could not be considered a case of *force majeure*. The Court did not examine whether, if there was a case of *force majeure,* Member States would be required to pay the interest in question.

Section 2

Interpretation and application
of the substantive rules of Community law

Free movement of goods and customs union

931.   A Belgian court asked the Court of Justice (under Article 177 of the EEC Treaty) whether the obligation imposed by a Belgian law, solely on Belgian butter manufacturers, to indicate their name on the packaging was compatible with Article 30 of the EEC Treaty.

932.   In the *Mathot* and *Rousseau* cases[1] the Court confirmed its earlier decisions to the effect that unfavourable treatment on the part of a Member State of goods produced within the country in comparison with imported goods (reverse discrimination) in a sector not subject to Community rules or to a harmonization of national legislation did not fall within the scope of Community law.

933.   The judgments given by the Court in Cases 176 and 178/84 *Commission v Greece* and *Commission v Germany*[2] are of great interest from the point of view of completing the single internal market. First, the Court emphasized that the common market is intended to offer consumers a wider choice of products; any national provision which has the effect of 'crystallizing' consumer habits around the national manufacturing tradition, so as to confer a competitive advantage on domestic products, is incompatible with the Treaty. Second, the Court for the first time applied the *Cassis de Dijon* rule to the full in the sphere of public health; it concluded that an absolute ban on the use of additives in beer constituted disguised discrimination. The Court made it clear to Member States that the desirability of proper protection of public health could not be allowed to serve as a pretext for measures which were out of proportion to their objective. Lastly, the Court held once again that Member States bore the burden of proving that national measures of this kind were justified.

934.   The judgment in Case 154/85 *Commission v Italy*[3] is a sequel to the order made on 7 June 1985 in the same case,[4] by which the President of the

---

[1]   Case 98/86: OJ C 69, 17.3.1987; Case 168/86: OJ C 77, 24.3.1987.
[2]   OJ C 95, 8.4.1987.
[3]   OJ C 183, 11.7.1987.
[4]   OJ C 178, 16.7.1985; Nineteenth General Report, points 254 and 1022.

Court enjoined Italy to suspend the application of circulars which from 1 July 1984 imposed administrative formalities having the effect of blocking parallel imports of vehicles from other Member States.

In view of the role of parallel imports in the development of trade, the judgment makes a definite contribution to the achievement of the large internal market. For the first time, the Court had occasion to censure the requirement that certificates accompanying goods must be authenticated and/or legalized by consular authorities (Italian in this case) in the Member State of exportation. The Court also stressed that the other formalities introduced by Italian legislation, such as production of the certificate of origin issued by the vehicle manufacturer or the length of time required for its issue and for the technical inspection of the vehicle, also amount to measures having an equivalent effect to quantitative restrictions prohibited by Article 30 of the Treaty.

935.   The Commission sought an interim order against Ireland on the grounds that the Irish authorities were seeking to prevent the use of imported pipes in the construction of a water main in Dundalk, by requiring that they meet Irish safety standards for pipes of this kind. The only company manufacturing pipes to those standards was located in Ireland.

936.   The President of the Court initially granted the application, without having been able to hear the Irish Government, and forbade the award of the contract for the time being; but he subsequently overturned his first order. In his second order he accepted that the damage suffered by the Community in the event of an infringement of Community law might indeed be irreparable, but took the view that this damage had to be balanced against the fire hazards and danger to public health which were cited by the Irish Government. He concluded that in this case these dangers tilted the balance of interests in favour of the defendant. [1]

937.   In its preliminary ruling in *Gofette and Gilliard* [2] the Court went further than the position hitherto adopted by the Commission. It held that at the present stage of the development of Community law Articles 30 and 36 of the EEC Treaty were to be interpreted as meaning that where vehicles were imported from another Member State and already approved for use in that State a fresh approval procedure could not be required in the Member State of importation unless the testing procedure did not entail any unreasonable costs

---

[1]   Orders of 16.2.1987 and 13.3.1987 in Case 45/87R *Commission v Ireland*.
[2]   Case 406/85: OJ C 172, 30.6.1987.

or delays, and the public authorities ensured that those conditions were fully met where the manufacturer or his authorized agent had the task of carrying out the necessary tests, and unless the importer could, as an alternative to the testing procedure, produce documents issued in the exporting Member State where those documents provided the necessary information based on tests already carried out.

Competition

938.   In *Verband der Sachversicherer v Commission*[1] the Court dismissed an application by an association of insurers for the annulment of a Commission Decision finding that there had been an infringement of Article 85(1) of the EEC Treaty and refusing to grant it negative clearance or exemption. This Decision concerned a recommendation by the association aimed at stabilizing premium levels. The judgment is of particular importance in that it confirms that the Community competition rules apply in their entirety to the insurance industry and that a requirement that an insurance company with its head-quarters in another Member State which proposed to do business in Germany must establish a branch office there did not mean that there could be no trade in insurance services between Member States, however independent the branch office might be in legal terms.

939.   In *Deufil v Commission*[2] the Court upheld a Decision in which the Commission found that assistance granted to the Deufil company was incompatible with Article 92 of the EEC Treaty, and had to be repaid by the recipient. Deufil argued that the Commission's order requiring Germany to recover the subsidy was incompatible with the principle that legitimate expectations should be protected. But the Court held that the aid should have been notified to the Commission in advance, and should not have been granted until the advance notification procedure was complete.

940.   For the first time a firm (Hoechst) refused to submit to an investigation ordered by Commission Decision, and asked the Court to suspend the application of the Decision. The President of the Court dismissed the application.[3]

---

[1]   Case 45/85: OJ C 40, 18.2.1987.
[2]   Case 310/85: OJ C 78, 25.3.1987.
[3]   Case 48/87R *Hoechst v Commission:* OJ C 114, 29.4.1987.

941. In five cases,[1] dealt with together, the Court dismissed applications for declarations that Council Regulation (EEC) No 2089/84 imposing a definitive anti-dumping duty on imports of certain ball-bearings originating in Japan is void. The Court upheld the arguments put forward by the Commission (intervener) concerning the method used to calculate the dumping margin in the event of variations in the prices of goods exported to the Community and the use of different methods for calculating the export price and the 'normal value' (i.e., in this case, the price in Japan). A more important aspect is that the Court agreed that the Commission can use the prices paid to sales subsidiaries in Japan as the basis for the normal value and that it reaffirmed that the institutions are not compelled to accept price undertakings which are offered and that they enjoy a margin of discretion as regards such undertakings.

942. In Case 5/86 *Commission v Belgium*[2] the Court censured Belgium for failing to implement, within the prescribed period, a Commission Decision on aid granted by the Belgian Government to a manufacturer of polypropylene fibre and yarn.

943. In Case 142/87R *Belgium v Commission*[3] the President of the Court dismissed an application for an order that application of the Commission Decision of 4 February 1987[4] requiring the recovery of aid unlawfully granted to the firm Tubemeuse be suspended.

This ruling not only reaffirms the Court's severity in regard to unlawful aid but,in addition, introduces very restrictive interpretative criteria, some of which are new.These criteria are likely to strengthen significantly the Commission's position in relation to Member States which in the first place fail to comply with the procedural requirements laid down in Article 93(3) of the EEC Treaty (*inter alia* the requirement concerning prior notification of planned aid) and then claim that it is impossible to recover aid by citing considerations based on the survival of the recipient firm or the confidence of creditors. The two grounds on which the Belgian application was dismissed are centred on the finding that:

(a) the detriment to which the Belgian Government alludes in this case concerns
    the possible detriment which Tubemeuse and its creditors would suffer if

---

[1]   Case 240/84 *NTN Toyo v Council;* Case 255.84 *Nachi Fujikoshi v Council;* Case 256/84 *Koyo Seiko v Council;* Case 258/84 *Nippon Seiko v Council;* Case 260/84 *Minebea v Council;* OJ C 152, 10.6.1987.
[2]   OJ C 123, 9.5.1987.
[3]   OJ C 183, 11.7.1987.
[4]   Bull. EC 2-1987, point 2.1.61.

the application for an order suspending application of the Decision were refused and not the detriment which it would necessarily suffer itself in that situation;

(b) even if Tubemeuse itself were to claim that the recovery procedure initiated by the Belgian Government pursuant to the Commission's Decision of 4 February 1987 could cause it serious and irreparable harm, it would still have to plead circumstances or put forward arguments showing that the national remedies available to it under Belgian law for the purpose of opposing the procedure did not enable it to avoid sustaining such harm.

944.   Case 248/84 *Germany v Commission*[1] raised important questions of principale as regards the law governing state aid. The Commission and the Federal Republic of Germany disagreed on the question whether and to what extent regional aid was caught by Article 92(1) of the EEC Treaty, and whether the admissibility of regional aid had to be assessed in the light of national or Community averages. In Germany regional aid is granted and financed both by the Länder acting in their own right and by the Federal Government and the Länder together through a joint scheme. The Land of North Rhine-Westphalia has its own regional programmes operating alongside those of the joint scheme. The dispute concerned one of these programmes.

The Court annulled the Commission Decision of 23 July 1984[2] which found that the aid granted by the Land was incompatible with the common market within the meaning of Article 92(1). The Court accepted that the Decision did not satisfy the obligation to state reasons laid down in Article 190. In annulling the Decision on the ground that it infringed essential procedural requirements the Court was holding to its existing case law on the subject.[3]

The Court confirmed that Article 92(1) would apply to the regional aid programmes of the Länder if they affected trade between Member States and distorted competition. The judgment provides valuable guidance on two points here: in assessing 'aid to promote the economic development of areas where the standard of living is abnormally low or where there is serious underemployment' (Article 92(3)(a)), the situation of the region must be looked at in relation to the Community as a whole; in the case of 'aid to facilitate the development of ... certain economic areas, where such aid does not adversely affect trading conditions to an extent contrary to the common interest' (Article 92(3)(c)), the situation of the region must be looked at in relation to the national average.

---

1   OJ C 294, 5.11.1987.
2   OJ L 7, 9.1.1985; Eighteenth General Report, point 230.
3   Joined Cases 296 and 318/82 *Netherlands and Leeuwarder Papierwarenfabriek v Commission* [1985] ECR 817.

945. The judgment in Case 118/85 *Commission v Italy*[1] makes a definite contribution to resolving the problem of the financial relations between Member States and their public undertakings. By giving a functional definition of the term public undertaking in accordance with the Commission's wishes, it puts an end to any ambiguity which might still exist in this field.

The case arose from action by the Italian Government, which in connection with the Commission Directive of 25 June 1980 on the transparency of financial relations between Member States and public undertakings[2] had refused to supply the Commission with the balance sheet of the Amministrazione Autonoma dei Monopoli di Stato (AAMS) on the ground that it could not be regarded as a public undertaking since it lacked legal personality distinct from that of the State but was simply a branch of administration of the Italian Government. The latter accordingly contended that AAMS ought to have been regarded as a 'public authority' within the meaning of the Directive.

The Court reaffirms the principle that the State may either act as a public authority or participate in economic activities of an industrial or commercial nature. In the latter situation, the Court emphasizes that it is of no consequence that the State pursues its economic activities through an organ which forms an integral part of the administration. The fact that AAMS is an integral part of the administration of the Italian State does not, accordingly, prevent its being regarded as a public undertaking.

946. In *Vereniging van Vlaamse Reisbureaus*[3] the Court delivered an important preliminary ruling, holding that legislative provisions or regulations requiring travel agents to observe the price and tariffs for travel set by tour operators, and prohibiting them from sharing the commission paid in respect of the sale of such travel with their customers or granting rebates to their customers, were incompatible with the obligations of the Member States pursuant to Article 5 of the EEC Treaty, in conjunction with Articles 3(f) and 85, where the object or effect of such national provisions was to reinforce the effects of restrictive practices which were contrary to Article 85. The ruling goes a considerable way towards clarifying the question whether Member States' business legislation must conform to the principles laid down by the Treaty regarding competition. It thus takes the findings in *Nouvelles Frontières*[4] a stage further.

---

[1]   OJ C 181, 9.7.1987.
[2]   OJ L 195, 29.7.1980; Fourteenth General Report, point 195.
[3]   Case 311/85 *Vereniging van Vlaamse Reisbureaus v Sociale Dienst van de Plaatselijke en Gewestelijke Overheidsdiensten:* OJ C 290, 30.10.1987.
[4]   Joined Cases 209 to 213/84 *Ministère Public v Asjes and Others:* Twentieth General Report, point 1023.

On the question of the protection of travel agents' independence in relation to
tour operators, the Court took the view that the travel agent was an independent
intermediary supplying separate services. The travel agent could not be
described as an auxiliary organ forming an integral part of a tour operator's
business.

947.   In *RSV v Commission* [1] the Court annulled Commission Decision
85/351/EEC concerning aid granted by the Netherlands Government to an
engineering company. [2] The Commission had initiated the procedure laid down
in Article 93(2) of the EEC Treaty following notification of the aid measure;
the procedure culminated in the adoption of the contested Decision, in which
the Commission found that aid was incompatible with the common market
and had to be withdrawn, requiring the Government to recover the assistance
paid to the recipient.

The Court found that the Commission's delay in adopting the contested
Decision (26 months) could in the present case engender in the applicant a
legitimate expectation such as to prevent the Commission from requiring the
Dutch authorities to withdraw the aid. Clearly the Commission will have to
take practical account of the implications of this judgment.

948.   In *BNIC v Aubert* [3] the Court for the first time held that a State measure
whereby an agreement which was contrary to Article 85 of the EEC Treaty
was made binding on third parties was incompatible with Article 5 in conjunction with Articles 3(f) and 85.

The French National Cognac Industry Board *(Bureau National Interprofession-
nel du Cognac)* brought procedings against a wine-grower accusing him of
exceeding a marketing quota, and seeking payment of a penalty provided for
in an agreement laying down quotas and penalties which had been concluded
between cognac growers and shippers and which a ministerial order had made
generally binding.

Answering questions put by the national court hearing the case, the Court of
Justice found first of all that the agreement itself was contrary to Article 85(1)
of the EEC Treaty.

The Court then considered the second question put. The Treaty prohibited
State measures likely to deprive Articles 85 and 86 of their effectiveness. The

---

[1]   Case 223/85 *Rijn-Schelde-Verolme Machinefabrieken en Scheepswerven v Commission.*
[2]   OJ L 188, 20.7.1985.
[3]   Case 136/86.

Court held that there was such a measure where a Member State reinforced the effects of agreements contrary to Article 85 by means of an order making those agreements generally binding.

This finding is in line with the principle already stated in *Nouvelles Frontières* [1] and *Vereniging Vlaamse Reisbureaus* [2] to the effect that Member States compromise the effectiveness of Article 85 not only where they require or encourage firms to engage in restrictive practives but also where they reinforce the effects of such practices.

949.   In its judgment in *BAT and Reynolds v Commission* [3] which concerned the acquisition by one company of a shareholding in a competitor, the Court upheld the position taken by the Commission. It accepted that in certain circumstances such a transaction would be caught by Article 85 of the EEC Treaty, and set out a number of principles for determining when this was so. These principles had to be applied taking account of the circumstances in the particular case, particularly the economic context and the situation on the relevant market. The Court rejected the applicants' contention that the acquisition of a stake in the capital of a competing company, even a minority stake, would necessarily influence the conduct of the two companies, and would therefore by itself have the effect of restricting competition. But it might do so, and the influence which the share acquisition would have on the companies' conduct on the market on which they operated was the key test for determining whether the transaction was caught by Article 85.

The judgment did not settle the question whether Article 85 would apply to the acquisition of a majority stake or a straight buy-out of a competing company. Issues of that kind will not be cleared up until the Commission's proposal for a merger control Regulation has been adopted by the Council.

Free movement of persons, social provisions and capital movements

950.   In Case 221/85 *Commission v Belgium* the Court delivered a major judgment concerning freedom of establishment. [4]

The Court rejected the Commission's view that the ban on restrictions on the right of establishment laid down in the EEC Treaty was not confined to

---

1   Joined Cases 209 to 213/84 *Ministère Public v Asjes and Others;* Twentieth General Report, point 1023.
2   Point 946 of this Report.
3   Joined Cases 142 and 156/84 *British-American Tobacco Company and R.J. Reynolds Industries v Commission:* OJ C 329, 8.12.1987.
4   OJ C 58, 6.3.1987.

discriminatory measures, but also caught measures which applied to nationals and to non-nationals alike if they constituted an unjustified obstacle to non-nationals. The Court took the view that only discrimination on grounds of nationality was prohibited by Article 52 of the Treaty.

This fresh judgment is indicative of a restrictive approach to freedom of establishment on the part of the Court.

951.   The judgment in Case 225/85 *Commission v Italy* [1] represents the latest stage in the development of the Court's case law on the application of Article 48(4) of the EEC Treaty, the exception to the principle of freedom of movement for workers which is permitted by the Treaty in the case of employment in the public service.

The Commission brought an action against Italy on account of its refusal to establish researchers who were nationals of other Member States and who had been working for some considerable time for the Consiglio Nazionale delle Ricerche (National Research Council — 'CNR') under two-yearly renewable contracts. Researchers of Italian nationality who satisfied the same conditions and possessed the same qualifications had been established.

The Court found in favour of the Commission and made a number of very interesting points regarding the definition of employment in the public service.

It held that only management duties or duties involving advising the Government on scientific and technical matters could be classed as employment in the public service within the meaning of Article 48(4) but that it had not been established that such duties were carried out by the CNR researchers.

This is the first time that the Court has accepted that duties which involve simply advising a Government may be reserved by that Government for its own nationals.

Hitherto the only posts to which, according to the case law of the Court, the Member States were not by law required to apply the principle of the prohibition of discrimination based on nationality were those which involved 'the exercise of powers conferred by public law and safeguarding the general interests of the State'. Henceforth, employment which involves simply assisting or advising those empowered to exercise public authority may also be classed as 'reserved' employment for the purposes of Article 48(4). There is an obvious danger that

---

[1]   OJ C 181, 9.7.1987.

the Member States will interpret such 'advisory' duties broadly (and improperly) in order to deny them to nationals of the other Member States.

In addition, in two very important passages in the judgment, the Court no longer applies in a cumulative manner (as it did most recently in *Lawrie-Blum*[1]) the two criteria that enable the employment covered by Article 48(4) to be identified (exercise of powers conferred by public law *and* safeguarding the general interests of the State) but refers to them individually (exercise ... *or* safeguarding ...), which would appear to be a substantial restriction of the possibility of applying the general rule prohibiting discrimination based on nationality to employment in respect of which the fulfilment of one requirement (say, involvement in the exercise of powers conferred by public law) is obviously beyond question, whereas fulfilment of the second requirement (say, safeguarding the general interests of the State) can be easily challenged. It will accordingly have to be seen whether the Commission is faced with a genuine change of attitude on the part of the Court in this regard or whether this is simply an *obiter dictum*.

952.   In a series of actions brought by Member States against the Commission, the Court rejected the argument that migration policy in relation to non-member countries fell entirely outside the social field within the meaning of Article 118 of the EEC Treaty.[2] The Court accepted the Commission's argument that employment and working conditions in the Community could be affected by the policy which Member States followed with regard to workers from non-Community countries. But promotion of cultural integration fell outside the scope of the first paragraph of Article 118.

The Court applied the 'effectiveness doctrine' to conclude that 'the second paragraph of Article 118 must be interpreted as conferring on the Commission all the powers which are necessary in order to arrange the consultations' it called for; in particular, 'the Commission must necessarily be able to require the Member States to notify essential information ... likewise it must be able to require them to take part in consultations'.

The judgment represents a victory for the Commission's view of migration policy in relation to non-member countries, and sets a precedent which will be relevant both as regards the Commission's general powers and as regards the other fields listed in the first paragraph of Article 118.

---

[1]   Case 66/85 *Lawrie-Blum v Land Baden-Württemberg*: Twentieth General Report, point 1033.
[2]   Joined Cases 281, 283, 284, 285 and 287/85 *Germany, France, Netherlands, Denmark and United Kingdom v Commission*: OJ C 205, 1.8.1987.

953.   In *Demirel v Stadt Schwäbisch Gmünd* the Court delivered a judgment containing important findings on two points — Community powers and the effect of an association agreement. [1]

The scope of Community powers under Article 238 of the EEC Treaty, the legal basis of the EEC-Turkey Agreement, had long been in dispute. The Court clearly espoused the broad interpretation supported by the Commission, holding that in the case of an association agreement which created specific and preferential links with a non-member country that was intended, at least in part, to join the system established by the Community, Article 238 necessarily empowered the Community to give undertakings to non-member countries in all the areas covered by the Treaty. Pursuant to Article 48 *et seq.* of the Treaty the free movement of workers was a field covered by the Treaty, and undertakings given in that sphere consequently fell within the competence of the Community under Article 238.

This finding was necessary if the Court was to have jurisdiction to interpret the Association Agreement. On the restrictive interpretation the subject-matter fell within the competence of the Member States, the agreement being a mixed one to which the Member States were also party; if the Court had accepted that view it would probably have had to hold that it had no jurisdiction to hear the case. It follows that the other fields which are covered by the Treaty and are within the terms of the Association Agreement, notably freedom of establishment, freedom to provide services, and free movement of capital, also fall within the competence of the Community. The importance of this finding goes beyond the narrow context of the EEC-Turkey Agreement itself, and raises the question whether the participation of the Member States in such agreements is still justified.

On the substance, the Court rejected the argument that the provisions of the Agreement on the free movement of workers combined with Article 7 of the Agreement constituted rules of Community law which had direct effect in the Member States. Thus individuals could not rely on them to claim rights before the national courts.

From the grounds of the judgment it would appear that this finding holds not only for the transitional period — which ended on 31 October 1986 — but thereafter too, when the freedom of movement of workers between the Community and Turkey ought already to have been secured, a process which was to have been 'guided by' Articles 48, 49 and 50 of the EEC Treaty.

---

[1]   Case 12/86: OJ C 282, 20.10.1987.

954.   The judgment in *Unectef v Heylens and Others*[1] concerned mutual recognition of qualifications and its implications for the free movement of workers. Mr Heylens, a Belgian national who held a Belgian football trainer's diploma was engaged by the Lille Olympic Sporting Club as trainer of their professional football team, beginning in the 1984/85 season; he had to stop training the team, however, when the French board adjudicating on the equivalence of qualifications refused to recognize his diploma as equivalent to a French football trainer's diploma. The Court of Justice ruled that the decision of the French authorities was contrary to Article 48 of the EEC Treaty. The principle of freedom of movement for workers laid down in Article 48 allowed a national authority to refuse to recognize a diploma conferred in another Member State only if it stated its reasons for doing so and if its decision was open to judicial review.

The Court said that where the qualifications necessary for the pursuit of a particular occupation had not been harmonized, Member States were entitled to define such qualifications and to require production of a diploma certifying that the holder possessed them; the procedure for recognition of equivalence had to allow the national authorities to satisfy themselves objectively that the foreign diploma certified that its holder had if not identical at least equivalent knowledge and qualifications to those which the national diploma certified. The existence of a legal remedy against any decision by a national authority refusing to recognize such a right was essential in order to guarantee the individual effective protection of that right. This requirement represented a general principle of Community law, deriving from the constitutional traditions common to the Member States and embodied in Articles 6 and 13 of the European Convention on Human Rights.

Taxation

955.   In Case 235/85 *Commission v Netherlands*[2] the Court held that by not subjecting to the VAT system the public services performed by notaries and sheriffs' officers the Netherlands had failed to fulfil its obligations under Article 2 and Article 4(1), (2) and (4) of the sixth VAT Directive.[3]

The judgment provides a clear delimitation of the exemption from VAT for the activities of public-law bodies acting in their capacity as public authorities.

---

[1]   Case 222/86: OJ C 300, 10.11.1987.
[2]   Case 235/85: OJ C 108, 23.4.1987.
[3]   OJ L 145, 13.6.1977; Eleventh General Report, point 219.

In accordance with established precedent the Court held that any exemption from the general rule of liability to VAT whenever goods or services were supplied for consideration had to be express and precise. The exemption therefore could not apply to activities performed in an independent capacity and against payment by persons who did not form part of a public administration and did not act on the instructions of a public authority.

956.   In Case 196/85 *Commission v France*[1] the Court dismissed an action brought by the Commission against France concerning alleged tax discrimination arising from the more favourable tax treatment granted in France to certain wines called 'natural sweet wines'.

The Commission had raised three objections dealing respectively with the concept of 'traditional and customary production' as a criterion enabling a wine to benefit from the more favourable treatment, the system of controls for imported wines affording guarantees equivalent to those required of natural sweet wines coming from French vineyards and the requirement of special accompanying documents for imported sweet wines.

The Court dismissed the first objection on the ground that the criterion of 'traditional and customary production' required to enable a wine to enjoy favourable tax treatment applied without distinction both to national and to imported products. It also dismissed the second objection. The Court noted, however, in its grounds of judgment that a system of control, in order to be compatible with the principle of proportionality, must leave to the Member State of origin the choice of the methods and of the authority responsible for applying the controls and must not make the recognition of equivalence depend on a prior agreement negotiated between the national administrations concerned. The Commission had withdrawn its third objection during the proceedings since France had amended its legislation to meet this point.

957.   The judgments given by the Court in Case 184/85 *Commission v Italy* and in *Cooperativa Co-frutta* were both concerned with the conformity with Community law of the excise duty charged in Italy on bananas.[2] The Commission in an action brought under Article 169 had based its arguments solely on Article 95 of the Treaty and the discrimination suffered by bananas produced in other Member States (especially in the French overseas departments) in relation to table fruit produced in Italy. The District Court [*Tribunale*], Milan

---

[1]   OJ C 123, 9.5.1987.
[2]   Case 184/85 *Commission v Italy* and Case 193/85 *Cooperativa Co-Frutta v Amministrazione delle Finanze dello Stato*: OJ C 152, 10.6.1987.

extended the analysis of the question to Articles 9 and 12 of the Treaty and to bananas originating in non-member countries which are in free circulation in the other Member States.

The Court of Justice held first that the consumer tax on bananas formed part of a general system of internal taxation (excise duties) governed by common rules and applied to categories of products in accordance with objective criteria irrespective of the origin of the products. The question of its compatibility with Community law had therefore to be examined under Article 95 and not under Articles 9 and 12 (charges having equivalent effect). The Court went on to hold that table fruit of typically Italian production and bananas are in a situation of partial competition since bananas offer an alternative choice to consumers of fruit. Consequently, a tax charged exclusively on bananas was contrary to the second paragraph of Article 95 of the Treaty since it was of such a nature as to protect domestic fruit production. Finally, Article 95 supplemented the provisions of the Treaty concerning the elimination of customs duties and charges having equivalent effect, since its aim was to ensure free movement of goods between the Member States by the elimination of all forms of protection that might result from the application of discriminatory internal taxation. It followed that an interpretation of Article 95 which excluded its application to products in free circulation would attain a result contrary both to the spirit of the Treaty as expressed in Articles 9 and 10 (free movement of goods) and to its system (the Court expressly mentioned the exclusive competence of the Community for commercial policy in relation to non-member countries).

Consequently, Article 95 of the Treaty concerned all products coming from Member States, including products from non-member countries which are in free circulation in the Member States.

This last statement, which is contrary to the restrictive interpretation of Article 95 proposed both by the Commission and by Mr Advocate General Lenz, makes the judgment in *Cooperativa Co-frutta* a landmark in the application of the fundamental principle of prohibition of tax discrimination.

958.   In Case 356/85 *Commission v Belgium*[1] the Court dismissed an action brought by the Commission against Belgium, which applies a higher rate of VAT on wine of fresh grapes, an imported product, than on beer, a domestic product. The Commission argued that this infringed Article 95 of the EEC Treaty.

---

[1]   OJ C 205, 1.8.1987.

The Court said that only the cheaper wines could compete as a genuine alternative to beer for purposes of the second paragraph of Article 95, and that the Commission had not shown that the difference in the rates of tax charged on the two products could have the effect of protecting domestic products, a point which had to be established if that Article was to apply.

959.   The Court decided against France in *Feldain v Directeur Général des Impôts*,[1] concerning the French system of taxation on imported motor cars with a taxable horsepower rating of over 16, which corresponded to the largest cylinder capacity manufactured in France.

The Court said that a system of road tax of that kind, in which one tax band comprised more taxable power ratings than the others, with the result that the normal progression of the tax was restricted in such a way as to afford an advantage to top-of-the-range cars of domestic manufacture, and in which the taxable power rating was calculated in a manner which placed vehicles imported from other Member States at a disadvantage, had a discriminatory or protective effect within the meaning of Article 95 of the Treaty.

The grounds of the judgment are similar to those in the Court's 1985 judgment in *Humblot v Directeur des Services Fiscaux*,[2] where it condemned the French special *'supervignette'* tax which applied only to imported top-of-the-range cars. Following the judgment France introduced a new system of road tax, which appeared to be based on neutral criteria but in fact allowed the discriminatory taxation of imported cars to continue.

Equal treatment for women and men

960.   In *Bonino v Commission*[3] the Court observed that Article 25 of the Staff Regulations of Officials of the European Communities did not require the appointing authority to give its reasons for a decision assigning an official to a new post, either to the successful official, who was in no way adversely affected by the decision, or to unsuccessful applicants for the post, who might be adversely affected by the arguments put forward in a statement of reasons. The presence of women among the applicants for the post, and the principle of equal treatment for men and women, were of no relevance here.

---

[1]   Case 433/85: OJ C 274, 13.10.1987.
[2]   Case 112/84: OJ C 133, 1.6.1985.
[3]   Case 233/85: OJ C 57, 5.3.1987.

The Court said that the appointing authority could, without casting any doubt on the ability of one applicant to perform the duties of group head in a translation department, nevertheless take the view, in the light of trial periods spent performing the relevant duties, that another candidate was better suited to the particular post.

Nor could it be maintained that such an approach reflected a general prejudice against women, and was therefore contrary to the principle of equal treatment for men and women.

It was not necessary to consider the argument put forward only by the intervener, the European Public Service Union, to the effect that a preference should always be given to applications by women, as the intervener itself had maintained only that such a preference should apply where the appointing authority was faced with a choice between a woman and a man whom it considered equally suitable and qualified for the post, and this was not the case here, as the Court had already concluded.

The Commission had argued that the application to intervene made by the European Public Service Union was inadmissible, as a trade union should be allowed to intervene only in order to defend the general interests of the staff and not in support of the particular interests of an individual official. But the Court allowed the intervention, on the ground that respect for the principle of equality between men and women did fall under the heading of the general interests of the staff which the intervener proposed to defend. The Court added that a new and important question of principle was raised by the applicant's argument that where there was clear under-representation of women the principle of equality would require a particularly detailed statement of reasons for the rejection of an application by a female officer; the answer to that question would have direct implications for female officials at the Commission.

961.   In *Delauche v Commission*[1] Mrs Delauche, a Commission official who had applied for a vacant post of head of division, sought the annulment of a decision by which the Commission appointed another applicant to the post.

Mrs Delauche argued that where several applicants were equally qualified for a post and one sex was seriously under-represented at the level in question preference should be given to an applicant of the under-represented sex. The Court rejected this contention in this case, citing the Commission's answer to her original complaint, from which it emerged that the Commission did not

---

[1]   Case 111/86.

consider her as well qualified as the other applicant to occupy the post; thus the Court did not have to consider whether an applicant of the under-represented sex would indeed have been entitled to preference in the situation described.

The Court also held that the principle of equal treatment for men and women did not impose any obligation to state reasons to promote officials, even where certain applicants were women, a finding it had already made in the *Bonino* case. [1]

Common agricultural policy and fisheries

962. In two judgments [2] the Court upheld the legality of a Commission Regulation taking transitional measures in anticipation of a change in the green rates for the German mark for cereals and sugar, which had been decided by the Council and was to take effect from 1 January 1985. [3] The Commission's objective was to avoid massive sales of cereals and sugar into intervention, for purely speculative reasons, towards the end of 1984. There were two main questions at issue: whether the Commission had complied with the rules governing the management committee procedure, and whether it had stayed within the terms of the powers which the Council had delegated to it to take transitional measures which might be necessary for 'avoiding disturbances following the revaluation of the representative rates of the German mark ... as at 1 January 1985'.

On the procedural point the Court confirmed that the Commission was entitled itself to determine whether a particular case was a matter of urgency or indeed of the 'greatest urgency'.

On the second question the Court rejected the German Government's argument that despite the broad wording used the powers conferred on the Commission were delegated for the sole purpose of fixing compensation for the fall in prices for marketing and processing undertakings in Germany towards the end of 1984. The Court held that the powers delegated were sufficiently broad to allow the Commission to take transitional measures bringing forward by three months the changes in the green rates for Germany which under the Council Regulation were to take place on 1 January 1985.

---

[1]   Point 960 of this Report.
[2]   Case 278/84 *Germany v Commission* and Case 281/84 *Zuckerfabrik Bedburg and Others v EEC*: OJ C 26, 4.2.1987.
[3]   OJ L 253, 21.9.1984; Eighteenth General Report, point 445.

963. Several margarine manufacturers brought actions against the Commission in respect of losses suffered as a result of the 'Christmas butter' scheme at the end of 1984. The operation consisted in the sale to consumers of large quantities of stored butter at a price close to or below that of margarine; the applicants argued that this was unlawful, because it was outside the Commission's powers and because it was contrary to the objectives of the common agricultural policy, the principle forbidding discrimination between Community producers, and the principle of proportionality.

In three judgments delivered on the same day, the Court rejected all of these objections, against the advice of the Advocate General.[1] It confirmed in particular that the powers delegated by the Council to the Commission in the agricultural sphere were to be interpreted very broadly. The Court also confirmed once again that the prohibition of discrimination did not mean that goods which were competing or which were partial substitutes (butter and margarine) had to be treated in an identical fashion, but rather that producers had to be treated equally. Where there were two common organizations of the market (in milk products and fats) with very different characteristics, and with markets in different situations (with particular reference to the crisis in milk), producers found themselves in different situations. There was therefore no discrimination if they were treated differently.

The Court held that the principle of proportionality had not been infringed, even though the operation was of limited effectiveness, because the measure did help to reduce surpluses.

964. The Court dismissed an application for damages brought against the Council and the Commission by a cooperative organization, GAEC de la Segaude, supported by the fédération nationale des syndicats d'exploitants agricoles (FNSEA).[2]

In order to compensate German farmers for the loss of revenue they would suffer as a result of the adoption of Council Regulation No 855/84,[3] which sought to dismantle positive MCAs, the Council authorized Germany to grant its farmers special aid from 1 January 1985 onwards, consisting of VAT relief of up to 3%. In May 1984 the German Government asked the Commission for authorization to bring forward this aid to 1 July 1984, and to increase the rate

---

[1] Joined Cases 279, 280, 285 and 286/84 *Walter Rau Lebensmittelwerke and Others v EEC;* Case 27/85 *Vandemoortele v Commission;* and Case 265/85 *Van den Bergh en Jurgens and Others v Commission:* OJ C 95, 8.4.1987, and OJ C 96, 9.4.1987.
[2] Case 253/84 *GAEC de la Segaude v Council and Commission:* OJ C 34, 12.2.1987.
[3] OJ L 90, 1.4.1984; Eighteenth General Report, point 445.

of relief to 5%. The Commission refused authorization, but the Council then granted it, in a Decision adopted on 30 June and based on the third subparagraph of Article 93(2) of the EEC Treaty. [1]

GAEC brought an action for damages pursuant to Articles 2 and 5 of the Treaty; the Court dismissed the action, confining itself to the finding that the applicant had not shown that damage had actually occurred or that there was a causal link between the measure complained of and the alleged damage. It was therefore unnecessary to decide on the lawfulness of the Council Decision of 30 June 1984.

965.   The two *Romkes* judgments [2] were important landmarks in fisheries law.

In *Romkes v Officier van Justitie* the Court held that Council Regulation No 1/85, [3] which divided the total allowable catch for plaice in the North Sea into national quotas according to the same formula already used for 1982, was valid although the quota of one Member State was exhausted while those of certain other Member States remained partially unused each year. This judgment made it possible to resolve numerous criminal cases in the Netherlands involving fishermen who had exceeded the quotas, which had been suspended by the courts pending the decision of the Court of Justice.

In *Officier van Justitie v Romkes and Others* the Court ruled that a national measure imposing only on the fishermen of the Member State concerned a stricter minimum size of fish caught than the Community norm was covered by Article 20(1) of Council Regulation No 171/83 of 25 January 1983, [4] which authorizes the Member States to adopt stricter measures provided they are limited to their national fishermen. The Court expressly declined to rule on Mr Romkes's contention that this provision was incompatible with the basic Regulation (171/83) [4] and with Community law as being discriminatory, a point referred to by the Court at the oral hearing but left undecided because the court referring the questions had not raised this particular matter.

966.   In *Coopérative Agricole des Avirons* [5] the plaintiffs in the main action — maize importers on the island of Réunion — had challenged the levy which

---

[1]   OJ L 185, 12.7.1984; Eighteenth General Report, point 446.
[2]   Cases 46/86 and 53/86: OJ C 183, 11.7.1987.
[3]   OJ L 1, 1.1.1985; Eighteenth General Report, point 461.
[4]   OJ L 24, 27.1.1983; Seventeenth General Report, point 466.
[5]   Case 58/86 *Coopérative Agricole d'Approvisionnement des Avirons (Île de la Réunion) v Receveur des Douanes de Saint-Denis and Directeur Régional des Douanes de la Réunion*: OJ C 116, 2.5.1987.

had been imposed on them. They based their case on two arguments: (a) by definition, the levy, whose purpose was to protect the Community market from imports from a non-member country where the product was sold at a price lower than the Community price, could not be imposed where the purchase price was higher than the Community price; and (b) the application of the same levy to the rest of the Community and to the island of Réunion constituted an infringement of the principle of non-discrimination in that different situations were ultimately treated in the same way. In delivering its judgment, the Court defined very clearly the purpose of the agricultural levies, which was to ensure that the principle of Community preference was respected and the objectives of the common agricultural policy secured. The abstruse nature of the methods of calculation was the logical consequence of this. As to the argument that the principle of non-discrimination had been violated, the Court drew attention to the Treaty provision which required that the common agricultural policy should as a rule apply to the French overseas departments. It was for the Community legislature to decide whether the economic, geographical and social circumstances of Réunion required derogating provisions. In this particular case the Court did not find that the legislature had exceeded its discretion.

Lastly, the national court asked the Court of Justice whether the circumstances in which maize was imported into Réunion constituted 'special circumstances' within the meaning of the first paragraph of Article 13 of Council Regulation No 1430/79 [1] such as to justify repayment of the levies. The plaintiffs explained that they were bound, by a kind of *force majeure,* to buy the maize on the world market at a higher price than that obtaining in the Community.

The court ruled that the general principle of equity embodied in Article 13 of the Regulation could not apply in this instance since the geographical and economic situation of Réunion was of an objective nature and affected an indefinite number of traders. The 'special circumstances' referred to in the provision in question could not therefore apply in this case.

967.   In Case 363/85 *Commission v Italy* [2] the Court dismissed the Commission's action based on failure to incorporate into national law the definitions of 'animals' contained in Council Directive 80/502/EEC on undesirable substances in feedingstuffs. [3] This judgment confirms that the Court adopts a certain flexibility as regards the incorporation of directives. The Court held

---

[1]   OJ L 175, 12.7.1979; Thirteenth General Report, point 149.
[2]   OJ C 136, 21.5.1987.
[3]   OJ L 124, 20.5.1980.

that the incorporation of a directive into national law does not necessarily require a formal and verbatim reproduction of its provisions in an express and specific legal provision but may, depending on its content, arise from a general legal context, provided the latter effectively ensures the full application of the directive in a sufficiently clear and precise manner so that, where the directive seeks to confer rights on individuals, those entitled are enabled to know the full extent of their rights and to enforce them where necessary before the national courts.

968.   In order to see how consumers would react to a cut in the price of butter, the Commission on 25 February 1985 ordered, by a Decision that was not published and was notified only to one Member State (the Federal Republic of Germany), organization of a sale of 900 tonnes of intervention butter in West Berlin. Since the butter was to be offered to consumers in a package containing two packets of 250 grams (one containing fresh open-market butter and the other containing butter from stock which was to be labelled 'free EEC butter'), several rules of German law concerning unfair competition were infringed.

As soon as the Commission's Decision became known, several margarine manufacturers, relying *inter alia* on German legislation on unfair competition, sought an injunction from the civil and administrative courts of Frankfurt/ Main restraining the intervention organization (BALM) from carrying out the Decision. The civil courts, while holding that there had been several infringements of German legislation, dismissed these actions. The Frankfurt Administrative Court, on the other hand, granted an injunction as a matter of urgency, restraining BALM from making butter from public stocks available free of charge to commercial firms, whereupon the Commission intervened to support BALM in appealing against the Decision.

When the Decision was quashed by the Appeal Court, the courts of first instance referred to the Court of Justice a series of preliminary questions concerning the legality of the action (Cases 133 to 136/85) and the question whether a decision such as the Commission had made in February 1985 precluded the national courts from applying their national law on unfair competition.

By its judgments in *Rau v BALM* and *Albako v BALM*[1] the court not only rejected all the doubts expressed by the Frankfurt Administrative Court but

---

1   Cases 133 to 136/85 *Walter Rau Lebensmittelwerke and Others v Bundesanstalt für Landwirtschaftliche Marktordnung* and 249/85 *Albako v Bundesanstalt für Landwirtschaftliche Marktordnung:* OJ C 169, 26.6.1987.

also ruled that an operation like the one ordered by the Commission for West Berlin could not be made subject to national law on unfair competition. The Court explained, however, that the validity of a Community instrument could be affected by its incompatibility with the principles of Community competition law, particularly the requirement that transactions be fair. While the Court did not criticize the Berlin operation from this point of view, this was apparently due to the fact that the requirements arising from the competition rules have to be reconciled with the objectives of Article 39 of the Treaty.

An action for annulment brought by the margarine manufacturers was at the same time dismissed as inadmissible. By an order of 3 May 1985 [1] the President of the Court had already dismissed an application for interim measures seeking to have the execution of the Commission's Decision suspended.

969.   In *Noord-Nederland*, [2] in reply to preliminary questions raised by the College van Beroep voor het Bedrijfsleven (Dutch administrative court of last instance in matters of trade and industry), the Court confirmed the validity of the system of different interest rates in different Member States for determining the financing costs in connection with the private storage of butter. This system had been introduced by the Commission by Regulation No 1746/84, [3] which amended Article 24 of Regulation No 685/69, [4] replacing the uniform rate applied until then (11%) by different rates depending on the Member States where the butter is stored: 7% in the Federal Republic of Germany and the Netherlands, 9.5% in the United Kingdom and 10.5% in the other Member States. (On 17 May 1986 these rates were changed to 6.5% in Germany and the Netherlands and 9.5% in the other Member States.)

The amount of aid for the private storage of butter has to be determined by the Commission taking into account not only the costs of storage but also foreseeable developments in the prices of fresh butter and of butter from stock. The aid must provide those holding butter with a sufficient incentive to store themselves the butter which cannot be disposed of on the market instead of selling it to the intervention agency.

Before 1984 the Commission had set flat-rate amounts applicable to the whole of the Community for all components of storage costs, including the financing costs. By the Regulation in question, however, it had set differential interest

---

[1]   Case 97/85R *Union Deutsche Lebensmittelwerke and Others v Commission*: OJ C 147, 15.6.1985.
[2]   Cases 424 and 425/85 *Coöperatieve Melkproducentenbedrijven Noord-Nederland and Others v Voedsel-voorzienings In- en Verkoopbureau*: OJ C 184, 14.7.1987.
[3]   OJ L 164, 22.6.1984; Eighteenth General Report, point 432.
[4]   OJ L 90, 15.4.1969.

rates for calculating the financing costs. This was designed to avoid an unjustified enrichment of traders at the expense of the Community and to prevent a disturbance of the functioning of the common organization of the market by artificial and speculative movements of butter towards the Member States where interest rates are low in order to put it into private storage with Community aid when it could have been disposed of normally on the market.

The Court ruled that this system of different interest rates did not constitute a discrimination prohibited by Article 40(3) of the Treaty and was not incompatible with the rule of uniformity of prices and with the unity of the butter market, nor with the principle of free movement of capital.

970.   In *Grand Moulins de Paris v Council and Commission* [1] the Court held that the Commission's refusal to include a new cereal product manufactured by the applicant, *'granidon'*, among the starch products eligible for production refunds did not render the Community liable for compensation to the applicant.

The judgment sums up previous findings on the non-contractual liability of the Community; in the case before it the Court found that there was no infringement of the principle of equal treatment of producers, as the applicant had failed to satisfy the Court that *granidon* was a full substitute for the products qualifying for a Community subsidy, nor had the Commission manifestly and seriously disregarded the limits on the exercise of its powers.

The Court thus confirmed that the Community institutions' liability for loss suffered as a result of regulations adopted by them was subject to strict limits, and stressed the breadth of the discretion left to them to deal with new situations; this contrasts with the Court's previous findings regarding the ending of advantangs already enjoyed.

971.   Six Member States brought actions seeking annulment of a total of eight Commission Decisions on the clearance of the accounts presented by them in respect of the EAGGF Guarantee Section expenditure for 1981 and 1982, in so far as the Commission refused to allow as EAGGF expenditure sums spent by the Member States on intervention measures or export refunds for fish which according to the Commission had been caught in excess of the authorized quotas.

In July 1981, the Council having failed to set catch quotas, the Commission asked the Member States nevertheless to operate in line with the proposals which it had presented.

---

[1]   Case 50/86.

In its judgments [1] the Court annulled the Commission Decisions on the ground that there were no Community rules within the meaning of Articles 2 and 3 of Council Regulation No 729/70 [2] which would justify a refusal to allow the export refunds and intervention measures at issue as EAGGF expenditure, in the absence in particular of the necessary cooperation between the Member States concerned and the Commission. While it accepted that the Council had failed to discharge its obligations with regard to catch quotas, therefore, the Court held that the Commission proposals could not have any binding force.

Nevertheless, in the judgments concerning Germany and the Netherlands, the Court did acknowledge that measures for the conservation of fish stocks formed part of the common organization of the fisheries market within the meaning of Articles 2 and 3 of Council Regulation No 729/70, [2] and that export refunds and intervention measures which infringed such measures could not be financed by the EAGGF. Where there is a binding rule laying down quotas, then, the Commission is entitled to disallow expenditure incurred as a result of overfishing.

Commercial policy

972.   In Case 45/86 *Commission v Council* [3] the Court annulled two Council Regulations applying generalized tariff preferences for 1986 to textile products and certain industrial products originating in developing countries. [4] The Court accepted the Commission's view that the lack of any precise indication of the legal basis meant that the Council had failed to state the reasons on which the Regulations were based; the Regulations were wholly within the scope of the common commercial policy called for by Article 113 of the EEC Treaty.

External policy

973.   For the first time, the Court considered the Regulations implementing the arrangement reached with the United States in January 1985 on steel tubes and pipes. [5] A Dutch dealer had brought an action for compensation on the

---

1   Case 325/85 *Ireland*, Case 326/85 *Netherlands*, Case 332/85 *Germany*, Case 336/85 *France*, Case 346/85 *United Kingdom*, Case 348/85 *Denmark*, Case 237/86 *Netherlands* and Case 239/86 *Ireland v Commission*.
2   OJ L 94, 28.4.1970.
3   OJ C 116, 2.5.1987.
4   OJ L 352, 30.12.1985; Nineteenth General Report, point 908 and 911.
5   OJ L 9, 10.1.1985; Nineteenth General Report, point 806.

ground that it could not obtain export licences that would enable it to export tubes and pipes to the United States. The arrangements introduced by the Regulations in question allocate export licences to steelmakers only, leaving them free to transfer such licences to dealers if desired.

In *De Boer Buizen* [1] the Court assessed the legality of the Regulations from the viewpoint of discrimination against dealers *vis-à-vis* steelmakers. The Court emphasized that in introducing a system of licences for exporting tubes and pipes to one of the largest markets, the Community institutions had a duty to consider the particular situation of firms specializing in the distribution of those products. Such firms should not bear more than their fair share of the burden resulting from the restriction of export markets. The Court concluded, however, that this was not the situation in this instance.

Staff

974.   In *Ainsworth,* [2] after proceedings which had lasted more than three-and a-half years, the full Court found against all the applicants, who had argued that certain provisions of the Statutes of the Joint European Torus (JET) joint undertaking constituted a discrimination on grounds of nationality.

The Court upheld the Statutes, however, only because of the very special circumstances of the case (the role of the JET staff and the proximity of the Culham site to that of the Ukaea).

975.   In Case 186/85 *Commission v Belgium* and Case 189/85 *Commission v Germany* [3] the Court addressed the question whether, and to what extent, officials entitled to family benefits under the Staff Regulations of Officials and the Conditions of Employment of Other Servants of the Communities were still eligible for corresponding national benefits. Were the provisions in the Staff Regulations simply rules which prohibited the drawing of concurrent benefits, leaving the Member States sovereign in the matter of family benefits? Or did they establish that Community benefits were supplementary to national ones, which were payable *per se*?

The Court held first that Community family allowances supplemented those payable by a Member State and pointed out that such allowances were part of

---

[1]   Case 81/86 *De Boer Buizen v Council and Commission:* OJ C 282, 20.10.1987.
[2]   Cases 271/83, 15, 36, 113, 158, 203/84 and 13/85 *Ainsworth and Others v Commission and Council:* OJ C 40, 18.2.1987.
[3]   OJ C 152, 10.6.1987.

the salary payable by the Communities; it went on to find that an allowance was in principle payable by the Member State, but that this obligation should be interpreted in a restrictive fashion. In no circumstances could the obligation in question lead to the Communities being relieved of having to pay something that was part of an official's salary. The Court rejected the main argument put forward by the Commission in its action against Germany (application of the consequences of *Forcheri*[1] to family allowances) on the ground that it was too general.

The Court drew a distinction between the two types of allowance by linking the Community family allowance to an official's employment. Where a family allowance was linked to the exercise of salaried activity in a Member State, it must be paid in that State and the Community allowance must be regarded as supplementary. The Court applied this solution to Germany, where the system of family allowances was financed by the State. The German allowance was payable in respect of a child of a salaried official's spouse, but not of a child of a spouse who was not working or was self-employed.

In the case of Belgium, the national allowance was not payable where the spouse of an official or the official, whether active or retired, worked in a self-employed capacity, even though such activity was subject to contributions and conferred a right to allowances; this contrasted with the position as regards salaried activity, which would give rise to the payment of national allowances.

---

[1]   Case 152/82 *Forcheri and Marino v Belgium* (1983) ECR 2323.

Section 3

Computerization of Community law

976.   At the end of 1987 nearly 92 000 documents could be interrogated via Celex, the computerized documentation system for Community law, which is now available to the public in five language versions (French, German, English, Dutch and Italian). Danish, Greek, Spanish and Portuguese versions are in preparation.

977.   During the year, Celex as transferred from the Euris private centre to the Commission's Computer Centre in Luxembourg. Development work was consequently interrupted but will resume as soon as the move has been completed. It will lead, in particular, to the modernization of the system during 1988-90. The preliminary analysis for this project was carried out at the end of 1987.

978.   Celex continues to be accessed in one of three ways: direct on-line access via the Commission's Computer Centre; indirect on-line access by means of a gateway; and the distribution of Celex data on magnetic tapes to commercial hosts. The number of subscriptions went up by 60% in 1987.

979.   Celex is linked to the national telecommunications networks through the Belgian DCS network; its subscribers, in most European countries, include government departments, semi-public bodies, parliaments, law firms, industrial and commercial concerns and university research and teaching establishments.

980.   The eighth edition of the *Directory of Community Legislation,* listing Community legislation in force at 1 December 1986, was published in the nine Community languages. From now on the Directory will be published twice a year, showing the legislation in force at 1 December and 1 June. The ninth edition (situation at 1 June 1987) came out at the beginning of September.

The Year in Brief [1]

January

20 January

Sir Henry (now Lord) Plumb elected new President of Parliament; Vice-Presidents also elected.

Point 5
of this Report

22 January

New Council President, Mr Tindemans, presents Parliament with programme for Belgium's six-month term in Council chair.

Bull. EC 1-1987,
point 3.4.1

25 January

General election in Federal Republic of Germany.

February

9 and 10 February

Third ministerial conference, held in Guatemala City, between the Community and its Member States, the Central American States and the Contadora States.

Point 816
of this Report

17 February

General election in Ireland.

---

[1] This chronological summary does not claim to be exhaustive. For further details, see the passages of this Report and the Bulletin cited in the margin.

18 February

Mr Delors presents Commission's programme for 1987 to Parliament, accompanied by the communication 'The Single Act: A new frontier for Europe', setting out the conditions for achieving the aims of the Single Act and proposals for completing the reform of the common agricultural policy, the structural instruments and the Community's financial arrangements.

Point 2
of this Report
Supplement 1/87 —
Bull. EC

March

19 March

Inauguration in Brussels of European Year of the Environment.

Point 493
of this Report

25 March

Official celebration in Rome of 30th anniversary of signing of Treaties of Rome.

Point 708
of this Report
Supplement 2/87 —
Bull. EC

April

10 April

Mr Delors writes to Heads of State or Government of the Member States, emphasizing the critical situation of the Community budget and rejecting the expedients of the past to balance the budget.

Bull. EC 4-1987,
point 2.3.1.

14 April

Turkish Government presents its application to join Communities.

Point 783
of this Report

May

13 May

Bank of Spain signs Agreement of 13 March 1979 between Member States' central banks laying down the operating procedures for the European Monetary System.

Point 134
of this Report

26 May

Referendum in Ireland approves constitutional amendment clearing way for the Government to deposit instruments of ratification of the Single European Act.

Point 1
of this Report

June

8 to June

Western Economic Summit in Venice.

Point 752
of this Report

10 June

European elections in Spain.

11 June

General election in United Kingdom.

14 June

General election in Italy.

15 June

Council adopts action scheme for the mobility of university students (Erasmus). Commission to grant first instalment of financial aid for 1987/88 academic year in October to first 240 inter-university cooperation programmes.

Point 396
of this Report

29 to 30 June

European Council in Brussels studies various aspects of Commission communication 'The Single Act: A new frontier for Europe'. Eleven delegations accept Presidency's conclusions on the guidelines and work programme for acting on the communication.

Points 2, 13 and 129 of this Report

July

1 July

Single European Act enters into force.

Point 1 of this Report

8 July

New Council President, Mr Ellemann-Jensen, presents Parliament with programme for Denmark's six-month term in Council chair.

Bull. EC 7/8-1987 point 3.4.1

13 July

Council adopts Decision laying down the procedures for the exercise of implementing powers conferred on the Commission.

Point 4 of this Report

19 July

General election and European elections in Portugal.

20 July

Council adopts amendments to its rules of procedure as regards putting matters to the vote in Council: as well as calling votes on his own initiative, the President of the Council must call a vote at the request of a member of the Council or the Commission if the majority of Council members are in favour.

Point 3 of this Report

August

4 August

In line with work programme adopted by European Council in June, Commission sends Council a communication on budgetary discipline, a proposal for a Decision on own resources, a second amendment to the proposal amending the Financial Regulation of 21 December 1977, a review of action taken to control the agricultural markets and outlook for the common agricultural policy and a proposal on reform of the structural Funds.

Bull. EC 7/8-1987, points 1.1.3 to 1.1.10

September

8 September

General election in Denmark.

12 September

At informal meeting in Nyborg, Ministers for Economic and Financial Affairs adopt measures to strengthen EMS.

Points 119 to 121 of this Report

18 September

To mark the retirement of Mr Emile Noël, Secretary-General of the Commission, Commission holds special symposium on the subject 'Crises and progress: the bricks and mortar of Europe'.

Bull. EC 9-1987 point 1.2.1 *et seq.*

22 September

The Representatives of the Governments of the Member States appoint Mr Peter Schmidhuber Member of the Commission to replace Mr Alois Pfeiffer, who died on 1 August.

Point 16 of this Report

28 September

Council adopts 1987-91 research and technological development framework programme.

Point 307 of this Report

30 September

Further to its communication entitled 'Review of action taken to control the agricultural markets and outlook for the common agricultural policy', Commission presents communication to Council on agricultural stabilizers.

Point 543
of this Report

October

5 October

Council adopts Decision setting out guidelines to Commission for conduct of negotiations on cooperation between Euratom, Japan, Soviet Union and United States on predesign work for international thermonuclear experimental reactor.

Point 336
of this Report

7 October

Following Council's failure to adopt a draft budget by 5 October as required by EEC Treaty, Parliament and Commission announce their intention to refer the matter to Court of Justice should Council fail to act within the two months laid down in Article 175. These two institutions brought actions before the Court of Justice in December.

Point 65
of this Report

22 October

Council adopts broad lines of Community position for negotiations on agriculture at Uruguay Round.

Point 747
of this Report

November

10 November

Bank of Portugal signs Agreement of 13 March 1979 between Member States' central banks laying down the operating procedures for the European Monetary System.

Point 134
of this Report

16 November

European Finance Ministers issue statement on recent developments on financial and foreign-exchange markets.

Point 128
of this Report

18 and 19 November

Parliament and Economic and Social Committee deliver opinions on Commission's package of communications and proposals 'The Single Act: A new frontier for Europe'.

Points 6 and 28
of this Report

December

4 and 5 December

European Council in Copenhagen decides to continue examination in February 1988 of the different aspects of plan for giving effect to the Single Act.

Points 2, 13 and 129
of this Report

7 December

Council adopts first set of measures for liberalizing civil aviation in Community. They come into force on 1 January 1988.

Points 622 and 644
of this Report

13 December

General election in Belgium.

Annexes

Annex to Chapter II, Section 2

Directives and proposals concerning the removal of technical barriers to trade in industrial products

I — *Directives adopted by the Council*

Reference	Subject	Date adopted	OJ No and page ref.	OJ date
87/354/EEC	Distinctive numbers and letters indicating the Member States on industrial products (amendment of several Directives)	25.6.1987	L 192/43	11.7.1987
87/355/EEC	Measuring instruments and methods of metrological control (amendment of Directive 71/316/EEC)	25.6.1987	L 192/46	11.7.1987
87/356/EEC	Ranges of nominal quantities and nominal capacities permitted for certain prepackaged products (amendment of Directive 80/232/EEC)	25.6.1987	L 192/48	11.7.1987
87/358/EEC	Type-approval of motor vehicles and their trailers (amendment of Directive 70/156/EEC)	25.6.1987	L 192/51	11.7.1987
87/402/EEC	Roll-over protection structures mounted in front of the driver's seat on narrow-track wheeled agricultural and forestry tractors	25.6.1987	L 220/1	8.8.1987
87/403/EEC	Type-approval of motor vehicles and their trailers (amendment of Directive 70/156/EEC)	25.6.1987	L 192/51	11.7.1987
87/404/EEC	Simple pressure vessels	25.6.1987	L 220/48	8.8.1987
87/405/EEC	Permissible sound power level of tower cranes (amendment to Directive 84/534/EEC)	25.6.1987	L 220/60	8.8.1987
—	Measures to be taken against air pollution by gases from positive-ignition engines of motor vehicles (amendment of Directive 70/220/EEC)	3.12.1987	—	—
—	Measures to be taken against the emission of polluting gases from diesel engines for use in vehicles	3.12.1987	—	—
—	Making-up by volume of certain prepackaged liquids (amendment of Directive 75/106/EEC)	18.12.1987	—	—

II — Directives adopted by the Commission

Reference	Subject	Date adopted	OJ No and page ref.	OJ date
87/137/EEC	Cosmetic products (adaptation to technical progress of Annexes II, III, IV, V and VI to Council Directive 76/768/EEC)	2.2.1987	L 56/20	26.2.1987
87/140/EEC	Textile names (amendment of Annex II to Council Directive 71/307/EEC)	6.2.1987	L 56/24	26.2.1987
87/143/EEC	Methods of analysis necessary for checking the composition of cosmetic products (amendment of Directive 80/1335/EEC)	10.2.1987	L 57/56	27.2.1987
87/184/EEC	Certain methods for the quantitative analysis of binary textile fibre mixtures (amendment of Annex II to Council Directive 72/276/EEC)	6.2.1987	L 75/21	17.3.1987
87/250/EEC	Indication of alcoholic strength by volume in the labelling of alcoholic beverages for sale to the ultimate consumer	15.4.1987	L 113/57	30.4.1987
87/308/EEC	Radio interference caused by electrical household appliances, portable tools and similar equipment (adaptation to technical progress of Council Directive 76/889/EEC)	2.6.1987	L 155/24	16.6.1987
87/310/EEC	Suppression of radio interference with regard to fluorescent lighting luminaires fitted with starters (adaptation to technical progress of Council Directive 76/890/EEC)	3.6.1987	L 155/27	16.6.1987
87/477/EEC	Prohibition of the placing on the market and use of plant protection products containing certain active substances (third amendment of the Annex to Council Directive 79/117/EEC)	9.9.1987	L 273/40	26.9.1987
87/524/EEC	Community methods of sampling for chemical analysis for the monitoring of preserved milk products	6.10.1987	L 306/24	28.10.1987
87/566/EEC	Methods of sampling and analysis for fertilizers (amendment of Directive 77/535/EEC)	24.11.1987	L 342/32	4.12.1987
—	Classification, packaging and labelling of dangerous substances (ninth adaptation to technical progress of Council Directive 67/548/EEC)	18.11.1987	—	—
—	Control of characteristics of, limits for and resistance to detonation of straight ammonium nitrate fertilizers of high nitrogen content (amendment of Directive 87/94/EEC)	22.12.1987	—	—

III — Proposals sent to the Council but not yet adopted

Reference	Subject	Date sent	OJ No and page ref.	OJ date
COM(86) 613 final	Fruit jams, jellies and marmalades and chestnut puree (amendment of Directive 79/693/EEC)	14.1.1987	C 25/8	3.2.1987
COM(86) 756 final/3	Construction products	15.1.1987	C 93/1	6.4.1987
COM(86) 777 final	Type-approval of wheeled agricultural or forestry tractors (amendment of Directive 74/150/EEC)	19.1.1987	C 88/10	3.4.1987
COM(87) 26 final	Type-approval of motor vehicles and their trailers (amendment of Directive 70/156/EEC)	6.2.1987	C 48/4	25.2.1987
COM(87) 44 final	Publication of attestations and certificates (amendment of several Directives)	12.2.1987	—	—
COM(87) 109 final	Type-approval of motor vehicles and their trailers (adaptation to technical progress of Directive 70/156/EEC)	3.4.1987	C 108/9	23.4.1987
COM(87) 132 final	Spray-suppression devices of certain categories of motor vehicle and their trailers	12.8.1987	C 265/1	5.10.1987
COM(87) 132 final	Lateral protection (side guards) of certain motor vehicles and their trailers	12.8.1987	C 265/21	5.10.1987
COM(87) 194 final	Components and characteristics of wheeled agricultural or forestry tractors	19.5.1987	C 218/1	17.8.1987
COM(87) 527 final	Electromagnetic compatibility	12.11.1987	C 322/4	2.12.1987
COM(87) 564 final	Machinery	8.12.1987	—	—
COM(87) 581 final	Cocoa and chocolate products intended for human consumption (ninth amendment of Directive 73/241/EEC)	8.12.1987	—	—
COM(87) 646 final	Calcium, magnesium, sodium and sulphur content of fertilizers (supplement to and amendment of Directive 76/116/EEC)	21.12.1987	—	—

Annex to Chapter IV

Activities of the Court in figures

TABLE 1

Cases since 1953 analysed by subject-matter[1]

Situation at 31 December 1987

	ECSC				EEC									Euratom	Privileges and immunities	Proceedings by staff of institutions	Total
	Scrap compensation	Transport	Competition	Other[2]	Free movement of goods and customs union	Right of establishment and freedom to supply services	Taxation	Competition	Social security and free movement of workers	Agriculture	Transport	Article 220 Conventions	Other[3]				
Actions brought	167	35	66	252 (24)	603 (45)	107 (12)	210 (35)	377 (34)	382 (35)	1 004 (81)	46 (5)	62 (4)	269 (40)	14 (3)	12	2 289 (77)	5 895 (395)
Cases not resulting in a judgment	25	6	24	107 (16)	124 (19)	26 (3)	39 (1)	40 (9)	31 (4)	87 (10)	9 (3)	4 (1)	75 (24)	1 (—)	2 (1)	1 340 (10)	1 940 (101)
Cases decided	142	29	41	119 (14)	394 (19)	63 (11)	107 (9)	275 (13)	304 (30)	793 (66)	31 (6)	54 (3)	135 (33)	10 (7)	9 (—)	846 (106)	3 352 (317)
Cases pending	—	—	1	26	85	18	64	62	47	124	6	4	59	3	1	103	603

The figures in brackets represent the cases dealt with by the Court in 1987.

1 Cases concerning more than one subject are classified under the most important heading.

2 Levies, investment declarations, tax charges, miners' bonuses, production quotas.

3 Contentious proceedings, Staff Regulations, Community terminology, Lomé Convention, short-term economic policy, commercial policy, relations between Community law and national law and environment.

TABLE 2

Cases analysed by type (EEC Treaty)[1]
Situation at 31 December 1987

			Proceedings brought under											
	Arts 169, 93 and 171	Art. 170	Art. 173 By governments	By individuals	By Community institutions	Total	Art. 175	Art. 177 Validity	Interpretation	Total	Art. 181	Art. 215	Protocols to Art. 220 Conventions	Grand total[2]
Actions brought	561	2	119	21	464	604	34	219	1 390	1 609	9	218	62	3 099
Cases not resulting in a judgment	199	1	11	4	68	83	5	8	99	107	3	43	4	445
Cases decided	243	1	67	7	295	369	25	197	1 120	1 317	6	167	54	2 182
In favour of applicant[3]	218	1	33	4	77	114	3				5	12	—	353
Dismissed on the merits[4]	24	—	32	3	143	178	3				1	137	—	343
Rejected as inadmissible	1	—	2	—	75	77	19				—	18	—	115
Cases pending	119	—	41	10	101	152	4	14	171	185	—	8	4	472

1 Excluding proceedings by staff and cases concerning the interpretation of the Protocol on Privileges and Immunities and of the Staff Regulations (see Table 1).
2 Totals may be smaller than the sum of individual items because some cases are based on more than one Treaty article.
3 In respect of at least one of the applicant's main claims.
4 This also covers proceedings rejected partly as inadmissible and partly on the merits.

TABLE 3

Cases analysed by type (ECSC and Euratom Treaties)[1]

Situation at 31 December 1987

	Number of proceedings instituted						Art. 41 ECSC Questions of validity	Art. 150 Euratom Questions of interpretation	Art. 153 Euratom	Total	
	By governments		By Community institutions		By natural or legal persons						
	ECSC	Euratom	ECSC	Euratom	ECSC	Euratom				ECSC	Euratom
Actions brought	31	—	—	1	488	10	4	4	2	523	17
Cases not resulting in a judgment	14	—	—	—	148	—	—	—	1	162	1
Cases decided	15	—	—	1	315	8	4	3	1	334	13
In favour of applicant[2]	6	—	—	1	70	1	—		—	76	2
Dismissed on the merits[3]	9	—	—	—	183	7	—		1	192	8
Rejected as inadmissible	—	—	—	—	62	—	—		—	62	—
Cases pending	2	—	—	—	25	2	—	1	—	27	3

[1] Excluding proceedings by staff and cases concerning the interpretation of the Protocol on Privileges and Immunities and of the Staff Regulations (see Table 1).
[2] In respect of at least one of the applicant's main claims.
[3] This also covers proceedings rejected partly as inadmissible and partly on the merits.

Institutions and other bodies

European Parliament

Secretariat
Centre européen, Plateau du Kirchberg
L-2929 Luxembourg
Tel.: 43001

Council of the European Communities

General Secretariat
Rue de la Loi 170
B-1048 Brussels
Tel.: 234 6111

Commission of the European Communities

Rue de la Loi 200
B-1049 Brussels
Tel.: 235 1111

Court of Justice

Plateau du Kirchberg
L-2925 Luxembourg
Tel.: 43031

Court of Auditors

29 rue Aldringen
L-1118 Luxembourg
Tel.: 47731

Economic and Social Committee

Rue Ravenstein 2
B-1000 Brussels
Tel.: 512 3920

List of abbreviations

ACP	African, Caribbean and Pacific countries party to the Lomé Convention
AIM	Advanced informatics in medicine in Europe
Asean	Association of South-East Asian Nations
Brite	Basic research in industrial technologies for Europe
Caddia	Cooperation in automation of data and documentation for imports/exports and agriculture
CCT	Common Customs Tariff
CGC	Management and Coordination Advisory Committee (Comité consultatif en matière de gestion et de coordination)
CMEA	Council for Mutual Economic Assistance
Codest	Committee for the European Development of Science and Technology
Comett	Community programme in education and training for technology
COST	European cooperation on scientific and technical research
Crest	Scientific and Technical Research Committee
CSCE	Conference on Security and Cooperation in Europe
DAC	Development Assistance Committee (OECD)
Delta	Developing European learning through technological advance
Drive	Dedicated road infrastructure for vehicle safety in Europe
EAGGF	European Agricultural Guidance and Guarantee Fund
ECE	Economic Commission for Europe (UN)
Eclair	European collaborative linkage of agriculture and industry through research
EDF	European Development Fund
EFTA	European Free Trade Association
EIB	European Investment Bank
EMS	European Monetary System
Erasmus	European Community action scheme for the mobility of university students

ERDF	European Regional Development Fund
Esprit	European strategic programme for research and development in information technology
Euronet-Diane	Direct information access network for Europe
EVCA	European Venture Capital Association
FADN	EEC farm accountancy data network
FAO	Food and Agriculture Organization of the United Nations
FAST	Forecasting and assessment in the field of science and technology
GATT	General Agreement on Tariffs and Trade (UN)
GCC	Gulf Cooperation Council
GSP	Generalized system of preferences
IAEA	International Atomic Energy Agency (UN)
IBRD	International Bank for Reconstruction and Development (World Bank) (UN)
IDA	International Development Association (UN)
IDB	Inter-American Development Bank
IEA	International Energy Agency (OECD)
IMF	International Monetary Fund (UN)
IMP	Integrated Mediterranean programme
Irdac	Industrial Research and Development Advisory Committee
JET	Joint European Torus
JRC	Joint Research Centre
MCA	Monetary compensatory amount
MFA	Multifibre Arrangement (Arrangement regarding International Trade in Textiles)
NCI	New Community Instrument
NET	Next European Torus
NGO	Non-governmental organization
OCTs	Overseas countries and territories
OECD	Organization for Economic Cooperation and Development
RACE	Research and development in advanced communication technologies for Europe
Science	Plan to stimulate the international cooperation and interchange necessary for European researchers (Stimulation des coopérations internationales nécessaires aux chercheurs européens)
Sprint	Strategic programme for innovation and technology transfer
Stabex	System for the stabilization of ACP and OCT export earnings

STAR	Community programme for the development of certain less-favoured regions of the Community by improving access to advanced telecommunications services
Sysmin	Special financing facility for ACP and OCT mining products
TAC	Total allowable catch
Tedis	Trade electronic data interchange systems
UN	United Nations
Unctad	United Nations Conference on Trade and Development
Unesco	United Nations Educational, Scientific and Cultural Organization
UNHCR	United Nations High Commissioner for Refugees
Unido	United Nations Industrial Development Organization
UNRWA	United Nations Relief and Works Agency for Palestine Refugees in the Near East
Valoren	Community programme for the development of certain less-favoured regions of the Community by exploiting indigenous energy potential
WFC	World Food Council (UN)
WFP	World Food Programme (UN)
YES	Youth exchange scheme for Europe

Publications cited in this Report

General Report on the Activities of the European Communities
(abbr.: General Report), published annually by the Commission

— *the Agricultural Situation in the Community*
(Published in conjunction with the General Report)
(abbr.: Agricultural Report), published annually

— *Report on Social Developments*
(Published in conjunction with the General Report)
(abbr.: Social Report), published annually

— *Report on Competition Policy*
(Published in conjunction with the General Report)
(abbr.: Competition Report), published annually

Bulletin of the European Communities
(abbr.: Bull. EC), published monthly by the Commission

Supplement of the Bulletin of the European Communities
(abbr.: Supplement...—Bull. EC), published at irregular intervals by the Commission

    2/85   Consumer redress

    8/85   A general system for the recognition of higher education diplomas

    2/86   Single European Act

    3/86   Equal opportunities for women—Medium-term Community programme 1986-90

    4/86   Community action in the field of tourism

    5/86   The Community's broadcasting policy—Proposal for a Council Directive concerning broadcasting activities

    6/86   A new impetus for consumer protection policy

    7/86   Voting rights in local elections for Community nationals

    1/87   The Single Act: A new frontier for Europe
The Commission's programme for 1987

    4/87   A fresh boost for culture in the European Community

Official Journal of the European Communities
Legislation series (abbr.: OJ L)
Information and notices series (abbr.: OJ C)
Supplement on public works and supply contracts (abbr.: OJ S)

Reports of Cases before the Court
    (abbr.: ECR), published by the Court of Justice in annual series, parts appearing at irregular intervals throughout the year

**All the above publications are printed and distributed through
the Office for Official Publications of the European Communities,
L-2985 Luxembourg**

Annual Report of the European Investment Bank
    published and distributed by the EIB,
    100, boulevard Konrad Adenauer
    L-2950 Luxembourg

European Communities—Commission

Twenty-first General Report on the Activities of the European Communities—1987

Luxembourg: Office for Official Publications of the European Communities

1987 — 424 pp. — 16.2 × 22.9 cm

ES, DA, DE, GR, EN, FR, IT, NL, PT

ISBN 92-825-7782-1

Catalogue number: CB-50-87-352-EN-C

Price (excluding VAT) in Luxembourg:

ECU 9.50   BFR 400   IRL 7.10   UKL 6.50   USD 11

The General Report on the Activities of the European Communities is published annually by the Commission as required by Article 18 of the Treaty of 8 April 1965 establishing a Single Council and a Single Commission of the European Communities.

The Report is presented to the European Parliament and provides a general picture of Community activities over the past year.